The Ways of Paradox

and Other Essays

W. V. Quine is Edgar Pierce Professor of Philosophy at Harvard University.

The Ways of Paradox

and Other Essays

REVISED AND ENLARGED EDITION

W. V. Quine

Harvard University Press
Cambridge, Massachusetts
and London, England
1976

Copyright © 1966, 1976 by the President and Fellows of Harvard College
All rights reserved

Printed in the United States of America

Library of Congress Catalog Card Number 76-4200

ISBN 0-674-94835-1 (cloth)
ISBN 0-674-94837-8 (paper)

To my daughter

Margaret

Preface

This book first appeared in 1966, embracing twenty-one essays. Three of them dated from the thirties, nine from 1951–1955, and nine from 1960–1964. Eight more are now added, all of later vintage.

The twenty-nine essays are arranged according not to date but to character and content. The first ten or eleven are meant for a wider public than philosophers. They begin with four semipopular pieces on logic and the foundations of mathematics. Next comes a reminiscence of Carnap, who dominates several of the essays. There follow three logicophilosophical pieces aimed at linguists. After these, two radio talks treat lightly of knowledge and necessary truth; and so I move onward to more professional concerns having to do with controversial issues of analyticity, modal logic, and propositional attitudes. With the eighteenth essay I take an abrupt turn into ontology, for the space of eight essays. After these the focus moves to variables. The last two essays, more austerely logical, deal with algebraic logic and Tarski's theory of truth.

I gratefully acknowledge a grant of the National Science Foundation, which supported the writing of some of the added essays in this edition. I remain grateful also for the support and assistance rendered by the Center for Advanced Study at Wesleyan University when I was assembling and editing the first edition.

I thank Basil Blackwell, the D. Reidel Publishing Co., the American Mathematical Society, the New York Academy of Sciences, the New, York University Press, the Journal of Philosophy, the American Academy of Arts and Sciences, the Trustees of Columbia University, the University of Massachusetts Press, the Plenum Publishing Co., and Bobbs-Merrill for permission to reprint Essays 2, 5–8, 12–16, 19, 21, 22, 24–26, 28, and 29.

W. V. Q.

October 1975

Contents

The Ways of Paradox

and Other Essays

1

❧ *The Ways of Paradox*

Frederic, protagonist of *The Pirates of Penzance*, has reached the age of 21 after passing only five birthdays. Several circumstances conspire to make this possible. Age is reckoned in elapsed time, whereas a birthday has to match the date of birth; and February 29 comes less frequently than once a year.

Granted that Frederic's situation is possible, wherein is it paradoxical? Merely in its initial air of absurdity. The likelihood that a man will be more than n years old on his nth birthday is as little as 1 to 1,460, or slightly better if we allow for seasonal trends; and this likelihood is so slight that we easily forget its existence.

May we say in general, then, that a paradox is just any conclusion that at first sounds absurd but that has an argument to sustain it? In the end I think this account stands up pretty well. But it leaves much unsaid. The argument that sustains a paradox may expose the absurdity of a buried premise or of some preconception previously reckoned as central to physical theory, to mathematics, or to the thinking process. Catastrophe may lurk, therefore, in the most innocent-seeming paradox. More than once in history the discovery of paradox has been the occasion for major reconstruction at the foundations of thought. For some decades, indeed, studies of the foundation of mathematics have been confounded and greatly stimulated by confrontation with

---

I presented this as a lecture at the University of Akron, November 1961, and again at a Shop Club at Harvard. It was published under the title "Paradox" in *Scientific American* (Volume 206, 1962).

two paradoxes, one propounded by Bertrand Russell in 1901 and
the other by Kurt Gödel in 1931.

As a first step onto this dangerous ground, let us consider
another paradox: that of the village barber. This is not Russell's
great paradox of 1901, to which we shall come, but a lesser one
that Russell attributed to an unnamed source in 1918. In a
certain village there is a man, so the paradox runs, who is a
barber; this barber shaves all and only those men in the village
who do not shave themselves. Query: Does the barber shave
himself?

Any man in this village is shaved by the barber if and only if
he is not shaved by himself. Therefore in particular the barber
shaves himself if and only if he does not. We are in trouble if we
say the barber shaves himself and we are in trouble if we say he
does not.

Now compare the two paradoxes. Frederic's situation seemed
absurd at first, but a simple argument sufficed to make us
acquiesce in it for good. In the case of the barber, on the other
hand, the conclusion is too absurd to acquiesce in at any time.

What are we to say to the argument that goes to prove this
unacceptable conclusion? Happily it rests on assumptions. We
are asked to swallow a story about a village and a man in it who
shaves all and only those men in the village who do not shave
themselves. This is the source of our trouble; grant this and we
end up saying, absurdly, that the barber shaves himself if and
only if he does not. The proper conclusion to draw is just that
there is no such barber. We are confronted with nothing more
mysterious than what logicians have been referring to for a couple
of thousand years as a *reductio ad absurdum*. We disprove the
barber by assuming him and deducing the absurdity that he
shaves himself if and only if he does not. The paradox is simply a
proof that no village can contain a man who shaves all and only
those men in it who do not shave themselves. This sweeping
denial at first sounds absurd; why should there not be such a man
in a village? But the argument shows why not, and so we
acquiesce in the sweeping denial just as we acquiesced in the
possibility, absurd on first exposure, of Frederic's being so much
more than five years old on his fifth birthday.

Both paradoxes are alike, after all, in sustaining prima facie
absurdities by conclusive argument. What is strange but true in

the one paradox is that one can be $4n$ years old on one's nth birthday; what is strange but true in the other paradox is that no village can contain a man who shaves all and only those men in the village who do not shave themselves.

Still, I would not limit the word 'paradox' to cases where what is purportedly established is true. I shall call these, more particularly, veridical, or truth-telling, paradoxes. For the name of paradox is suited equally to falsidical ones. (This word is not so barbarous as it sounds; *falsidicus* occurs twice in Plautus and twice in earlier writers.)

The Frederic paradox is a veridical one if we take its proposition not as something about Frederic but as the abstract truth that a man can be $4n$ years old on his nth birthday. Similarly, the barber paradox is a veridical one if we take its proposition as being that no village contains such a barber. A falsidical paradox, on the other hand, is one whose proposition not only seems at first absurd but also is false, there being a fallacy in the purported proof. Typical falsidical paradoxes are the comic misproofs that $2 = 1$. Most of us have heard one or another such. Here is the version offered by Augustus De Morgan: Let $x = 1$. Then $x^2 = x$. So $x^2 - 1 = x - 1$. Dividing both sides by $x - 1$, we conclude that $x + 1 = 1$; that is, since $x = 1$, $2 = 1$. The fallacy comes in the division by $x - 1$, which is 0.

Instead of 'falsidical paradox' could I say simply 'fallacy'? Not quite. Fallacies can lead to true conclusions as well as false ones, and to unsurprising conclusions as well as surprising ones. In a falsidical paradox there is always a fallacy in the argument, but the proposition purportedly established has furthermore to seem absurd and to be indeed false.

Some of the ancient paradoxes of Zeno belong under the head of falsidical paradoxes. Take the one about Achilles and the tortoise. Generalized beyond these two fictitious characters, what the paradox purports to establish is the absurd proposition that so long as a runner keeps running, however slowly, another runner can never overtake him. The argument is that each time the pursuer reaches a spot where the pursued has been, the pursued has moved a bit beyond. When we try to make this argument more explicit, the fallacy that emerges is the mistaken notion that any infinite succession of intervals of time has to add up to all eternity. Actually when an infinite succession of intervals of time is so chosen that the succeeding intervals become shorter and shorter, the whole succession may take either a finite or an infinite time. It is a question of a convergent series.

GRELLING'S PARADOX

The realm of paradox is not clearly exhausted even by the veridical and falsidical paradoxes together. The most startling of all paradoxes are not clearly assignable to either of these domains. Consider the paradox, devised by Kurt Grelling in 1908, concerning the heterological, or non-self-descriptive, adjectives.

To explain this paradox requires first a definition of the autological, or self-descriptive, adjective. The adjective 'short' is short; the adjective 'English' is English; the adjective 'adjectival' is adjectival; the adjective 'polysyllabic' is polysyllabic. Each of these adjectives is, in Grelling's terminology, autological: each is true of itself. Other adjectives are heterological; thus 'long', which is not a long adjective; 'German', which is not a German adjective; 'monosyllabic', which is not a monosyllabic one.

Grelling's paradox arises from the query: Is the adjective 'heterological' an autological or a heterological one? We are as badly off here as we were with the barber. If we decide that 'heterological' is autological, then the adjective is true of itself. But that makes it heterological rather than autological, since whatever the adjective 'heterological' is true of is heterological. If we therefore decide that the adjective 'heterological' is heterological, then it is true of itself, and that makes it autological.

Our recourse in a comparable quandary over the village barber was to declare a *reductio ad absurdum* and conclude that there was no such barber. Here, however, there is no interim premise to disavow. We merely defined the adjective 'heterological' and asked if it was heterological. In fact, we can get the paradox just as well without the adjective and its definition. 'Heterological' was defined as meaning 'not true of self'; we can therefore ask if the adjectival phrase 'not true of self' is true of itself. We find that it is if and only if it is not, hence that it is and it is not; and so we have our paradox.

Thus viewed, Grelling's paradox seems unequivocally falsidical. Its proposition is a self-contradictory compound proposition to the effect that our adjective is and is not true of itself. But this paradox contrasts strangely with the falsidical paradoxes of Zeno, or of '$2 = 1$', in that we are at a loss to spot the fallacy in the argument. It may for this reason be best seen as representing a third class of paradoxes, separate from the veridical and falsidical ones.

ANTINOMIES

The paradoxes of this class are called antinomies, and it is they that bring on the crises in thought. An antinomy produces a self-contradiction by accepted ways of reasoning. It establishes that some tacit and trusted pattern of reasoning must be made explicit and henceforward be avoided or revised.

Take Grelling's paradox, in the form in which it shows the adjective phrase 'not true of self' to be both true and false of itself. What tacit principles of reasoning does the argument depend on? Notably this one: the adjective 'red' is true of a thing if and only if the thing is red; the adjective 'big' is true of a thing if and only if the thing is big; the adjective 'not true of self' is true of a thing if and only if the thing is not true of itself; and so on. This last case of the principle is the case that issues directly in the paradox.

There is no denying that this principle is constantly used, tacitly, when we speak of adjectives as true of things: the adjective 'red' is true of a thing if and only if the thing is red, and correspondingly for all adjectives. This principle simply reflects what we mean in saying that adjectives are true of things. It is a hard principle to distrust, and yet it is obviously the principle that is to blame for our antinomy. The antinomy is directly a case of this principle. Take the adjective in the principle as the adjectival phrase 'not true of self' instead of the adjective 'red', and take the 'thing' in the principle, of which the adjective is to be true, as that adjective over again; thereupon the principle says outright that 'not true of self' is true of itself if and only if it is not true of itself. So the principle must be abandoned or at least somehow restricted.

Yet so faithfully does the principle reflect what we mean in calling adjectives true of things that we cannot abandon it without abjuring the very expression 'true of' as pernicious nonsense. We could still go on using the adjectives themselves that had been said to be true of things; we could go on attributing them to things as usual; what we would be cutting out in 'true of' is merely a special locution for talking about the attribution of the adjectives to the things.

This special locution, however, has its conveniences, and it would be missed. In fact, we do not have to do without it altogether. Speaking of adjectives as true or not true of things has made trouble in one special case, involving one special adjective, namely the phrase 'not true of self', in attribution to one special thing, namely that same phrase over again. If we forswear the use of the locution 'true of' in connection with this particular phrase in relation to itself as object, we thereby silence our antinomy and may go on blithely using the locution 'true of' in other cases as always, pending the discovery of further antinomies.

Actually related antinomies are still forthcoming. To inactivate the lot we have to cut a little deeper than our one case; we have to forswear the use of 'true of' not only in connection with 'not true of self' but also in connection with various other phrases relating to truth; and in such connections we have to forswear the use not only of 'true of' but also of various other truth locutions. First let us look at some of the antinomies that would otherwise threaten.

THE PARADOX OF EPIMENIDES

There is the ancient paradox of Epimenides the Cretan, who said that all Cretans were liars. If he spoke the truth, he was a liar. It seems that this paradox may have reached the ears of St. Paul and that he missed the point of it. He warned, in his epistle to Titus: "One of themselves, even a prophet of their own, said, The Cretans are always liars."

Actually the paradox of Epimenides is untidy; there are loopholes. Perhaps some Cretans were liars, notably Epimenides, and others were not; perhaps Epimenides was a liar who occasionally told the truth; either way it turns out that the contradiction vanishes. Something of paradox can be salvaged with a little tinkering; but we do better to switch to a different and simpler rendering, also ancient, of the same idea. This is the *pseudomenon*, which runs simply: 'I am lying'. We can even drop the indirectness of a personal reference and speak directly of the sentence: 'This sentence is false'. Here we seem to have the irreducible essence of antinomy: a sentence that is true if and only if it is false.

In an effort to clear up this antinomy it has been protested that the phrase 'This sentence', so used, refers to nothing. This is claimed on the ground that you cannot get rid of the phrase by supplying a sentence that is referred to. For what sentence does the phrase refer to? The sentence 'This sentence is false'. If, accordingly, we supplant the phrase 'This sentence' by a quotation of the sentence referred to, we get: ' "This sentence is false' is false'. But the whole outside sentence here attributes falsity no longer to itself but merely to something other than itself, thereby engendering no paradox.

If, however, in our perversity we are still bent on constructing a sentence that does attribute falsity unequivocally to itself, we can do so thus: ' 'Yields a falsehood when appended to its own quotation' yields a falsehood when appended to its own quotation'. This sentence specifies a string of nine words and says of this string that if you put it down twice, with quotation marks around the first of the two occurrences, the result is false. But that result is the very sentence that is doing the telling. The sentence is true if and only if it is false, and we have our antinomy.

This is a genuine antinomy, on a par with the one about 'heterological', or 'false of self', or 'not true of self', being true of itself. But whereas that earlier one turned on 'true of', through the construct 'not true of self', this new one turns merely on 'true', through the construct 'falsehood', or 'statement not true'. We can avoid both antinomies, and others related to them, by ceasing to use 'true of' and 'true' and their equivalents and derivatives, or at any rate ceasing to apply such truth locutions to adjectives or sentences that themselves contain such truth locutions.

This restriction can be relaxed somewhat by admitting a hierarchy of truth locutions, as suggested by the work of Bertrand Russell and Alfred Tarski. The expressions 'true', 'true of', 'false', and related ones can be used with numerical subscripts '0', '1', '2', and so on always attached or imagined; thus 'true$_0$', 'true$_1$', 'true$_2$', 'false$_0$', and so on. Then we can avoid the antimonies by taking care, when a truth locution T is applied to a sentence or other expression S, that the subscript on T is higher than any subscript inside S. Violations of this restriction would be treated as meaningless, or ungrammatical, rather than as true or false sentences. For instance, we could meaningfully ask whether the adjectives 'long' and 'short' are true$_0$ of themselves; the answers are respectively no and yes. But we could not meaningfully speak of the phrase 'not true$_0$ of self' as true$_0$ or false$_0$ of itself; we would have to ask whether it is true$_1$ or false$_1$ of itself, and this is a question that leads to no antinomy. Either way the question can be answered with a simple and unpenalized negative.

This point deserves to be restated: Whereas 'long' and 'short' are adjectives that can meaningfully be applied to themselves, falsely in the one case and truly in the other, on the other hand 'true$_0$ of self' and 'not true$_0$ of self' are adjectival phrases that cannot be applied to themselves meaningfully at all, truly or falsely. Therefore to the question 'Is 'true$_0$ of self' true$_1$ of itself?' the answer is no; the adjectival phrase 'true$_0$ of itself' is meaningless of itself rather than true$_1$ of itself.

Next let us consider, in terms of subscripts, the most perverse version of the *pseudomenon*. We have now, for meaningfulness, to insert subscripts on the two occurrences of the word 'falsehood', and in ascending order, thus: ' 'Yields a falsehood$_0$ when appended to its own quotation' yields a falsehood$_1$ when appended to its own quotation.' Thereupon paradox vanishes. This sentence is unequivocally false. What it tells us is that a certain described form of words is false$_1$, namely the form of words ' 'Yields a falsehood$_0$ when appended to its own quotation' yields a falsehood$_0$ when appended to its own quotation.' But in fact this form of words is not false$_1$; it is meaningless. So the preceding sentence, which said that this form of words was false$_1$, is false. It is false$_2$.

This may seem an extravagant way of eliminating antinomies. But it would be much more costly to drop the word 'true', and related locutions, once and for all. At an intermediate cost one could merely leave off applying such locutions to expressions containing such locutions. Either method is less economical than this method of subscripts. The subscripts do enable us to apply truth locutions to expressions containing such locutions, although in a manner disconcertingly at variance with custom. Each resort is desperate; each is an artificial departure from natural and established usage. Such is the way of antinomies.

A veridical paradox packs a surprise, but the surprise quickly dissipates itself as we ponder the proof. A falsidical paradox packs a surprise, but it is seen as a false alarm when we solve the underlying fallacy. An antinomy, however, packs a surprise that can be accommodated by nothing less than a repudiation of part of our conceptual heritage.

Revision of a conceptual scheme is not unprecedented. It happens in a small way with each advance in science, and it happens in a big way with the big advances, such as the Copernican revolution and the shift from Newtonian mechanics to Einstein's theory of relativity. We can hope in time even to get used to the biggest such changes and to find the new schemes natural. There was a time when the doctrine that the earth revolves around the sun was called the Copernican paradox, even by the men who accepted it. And perhaps a time will come when truth locutions without implicit subscripts, or like safeguards, will really sound as nonsensical as the antinomies show them to be.

Conversely, the falsidical paradoxes of Zeno must have been, in his day, genuine antinomies. We in our latter-day smugness point to a fallacy: the notion that an infinite succession of intervals must add up to an infinite interval. But surely this was part and parcel of the conceptual scheme of Zeno's day. Our recognition of convergent series, in which an infinite number of segments add up to a finite segment, is from Zeno's vantage point an artificiality comparable to our new subscripts on truth locutions. Perhaps these subscripts will seem as natural to our descendants of A.D. 4000, granted the tenuous hypothesis of there being any, as the convergent series does to us. One man's antinomy is another man's falsidical paradox, give or take a couple of thousand years.

I have not, by the way, exhausted the store of latter-day antinomies. Another good one is attributed by Russell to a librarian named G. G. Berry. Here the theme is numbers and syllables. Ten has a one-syllable name. Seventy-seven has a five-syllable name. The seventh power of seven hundred seventy-seven has a name that, if we were to work it out, might run to 100 syllables or so; but this number can also be specified more briefly in other terms. I have just specified it in 15 syllables. We can be sure, however, that there are no end of numbers that resist all specification, by name or description, under 19 syllables. There is only a finite stock of syllables altogether, and hence only a finite number of names or phrases of less than 19 syllables, whereas there are an infinite number of positive integers. Very well, then; of those numbers not specifiable in less than 19 syllables, there must be a least. And here is our antinomy: the least number not specifiable in less than nineteen syllables is specifiable in 18 syllables. I have just so specified it.

This antinomy belongs to the same family as the antinomies that have gone before. For the key word of this antinomy, 'specifiable', is interdefinable with 'true of'. It is one more of the truth locutions that would take on subscripts under the Russell–Tarski plan. The least number not specifiable$_0$ in less than nineteen syllables is indeed specifiable$_1$ in 18 syllables, but it is not specifiable$_0$ in less than 19 syllables; for all I know it is not specifiable$_0$ in less than 23. This resolution of Berry's antinomy is the one that would come through automatically if we paraphrase 'specifiable' in terms of 'true of' and then subject 'true of' to the subscript treatment.

RUSSELL'S ANTINOMY

Not all antinomies belong to this family. The most celebrated of all antinomies, discovered by Russell in 1901, belongs outside this family. It has to do with self-membership of classes. Some classes are members of themselves; some are not. For example, the class of all classes that have more than five members clearly has more than five classes as members; therefore the class is a member of itself. On the other hand, the class of all men is not a member of itself, not being a man. What of the class of all classes that are not members of themselves? Since its members are the non-self-members, it qualifies as a member of itself if and only if it is not. It is and it is not: antinomy's by now familiar face.

Russell's antinomy bears a conspicuous analogy to Grelling's antinomy of 'not true of self', which in ,fact it antedates. But Russell's antinomy does not belong to the same family as the Epimenides antinomy and those of Berry and Grelling. By this I mean that Russell's antinomy cannot be blamed on any of the truth locutions, nor is it resolved by subjecting those locutions to subscripts. The crucial words in Russell's antinomy are 'class' and 'member', and neither of these is definable in terms of 'true', 'true of', or the like.

I said earlier that an antinomy establishes that some tacit and trusted pattern of reasoning must be made explicit and be henceforward avoided or revised. In the case of Russell's antinomy, the tacit and trusted pattern of reasoning that is found wanting is this: for any condition you can formulate, there is a class whose members are the things meeting the condition.

This principle is not easily given up. The almost invariable way of specifying a class is by stating a necessary and sufficient condition for belonging to it. When we have stated such a condition, we feel that we have "given" the class and can scarcely make sense of there not being such a class. The class may be empty, yes; but how could there not be such a class at all? What substance can be asked for it that the membership condition does not provide? Yet such exhortations avail us nothing in the face of the antinomy, which simply proves the principle untenable. It is a simple point of logic, once we look at it, that there is no class, empty or otherwise, that has as members precisely the classes that are not members of themselves. It would have to have itself as member if and only if it did not.

Russell's antinomy came as a shock to Gottlob Frege, founder of mathematical logic. In his *Grundgesetze der Arithmetik* Frege thought that he had secured the foundations of mathematics in the self-consistent laws of logic. He received a letter from Russell as the second volume of this work was on its way to press. "Arithmetic totters," Frege is said to have written in answer. An appendix that he added to the volume opens with the words: "A scientist can hardly encounter anything more undesirable than to have the foundation collapse just as the work is finished. I was put in this position by a letter from Bertrand Russell . . ."

In Russell's antinomy there is more than a hint of the paradox of the barber. The parallel is, in truth, exact. It was a simple point of logic that there was in no village a man who shaved all and only those men in the village who did not shave themselves; he would shave himself if and only if he did not. The barber paradox was a veridical paradox showing that there is no such barber. Why is Russell's antinomy then not a veridical paradox showing that there is no class whose members are all and only the non-self-members? Why does it count as an antinomy and the barber paradox not? The reason is that there has been in our habits of thought an overwhelming presumption of there being such a class but no presumption of there being such a barber. The barber paradox barely qualifies as paradox in that we are mildly surprised at being able to exclude the barber on purely logical grounds by reducing him to absurdity. Even this surprise ebbs as we review the argument; and anyway we had never positively believed in such a barber. Russell's paradox is a genuine antinomy because the principle of class existence that it compels us to give up is so fundamental. When in a future century the absurdity of that principle has become a commonplace, and some substitute principle has enjoyed long enough tenure to take on somewhat the air of common sense, perhaps we can begin to see Russell's paradox as no more than a veridical paradox, showing that there is no such class as that of the non-self-members. One man's antinomy can be another man's veridical paradox, and one man's veridical paradox can be another man's platitude.

Russell's antinomy made for a more serious crisis still than did Grelling's and Berry's and the one about Epimenides. For these strike at the semantics of truth and denotation, but Russell's strikes at the mathematics of classes. Classes are appealed to in an auxiliary way in most branches of mathematics, and increasingly so as passages of mathematical reasoning are made more explicit. The basic principle of classes that is tacitly used, at virtually every turn where classes are involved at all, is precisely the class-existence principle that is discredited by Russell's antinomy.

I spoke of Grelling's antinomy and Berry's and the Epimenides as all in a family, to which Russell's antinomy does not belong. For its part, Russell's antinomy has family connections of its own. In fact, it is the first of an infinite series of antinomies, as follows. Russell's antinomy shows that there is no class whose members are precisely the classes that are not members of themselves. Now there is a parallel antinomy that shows there is no class whose members are precisely the classes that are not members of members of themselves. Further, there is an antinomy that shows there is no class whose members are precisely the classes that are not members of members of members of themselves. And so on ad infinitum.

All these antinomies, and other related ones, can be inactivated by limiting the guilty principle of class existence in a very simple way. The principle is that for any membership condition you can formulate there is a class whose members are solely the things meeting the condition. We get Russell's antinomy and all the others of its series by taking the condition as non-membership in self, or non-membership in members of self, or the like. Each time the trouble comes of taking a membership condition that itself talks in turn of membership and non-membership. If we withhold our principle of class existence from cases where the membership condition mentions membership, Russell's antinomy and related ones are no longer forthcoming. This restriction on class existence is parallel to a restriction on the truth locutions that we contemplated for a while, before bringing in the subscripts; namely, not to apply the truth locutions to expressions containing any of the truth locutions.

Happily we can indeed withhold the principle of class existence from cases where the membership condition mentions membership, without unsettling those branches of mathematics that make only incidental use of classes. This is why it has been possible for most branches of mathematics to go on blithely using classes as auxiliary apparatus in spite of Russell's and related antinomies.

THE MATHEMATICS OF CLASSES

There is a particular branch of mathematics in which the central concern is with classes: general set theory. In this domain one deals expressly with classes of classes, classes of classes of classes, and so on, in ways that would be paralyzed by the restriction just now contemplated: withholding the principle of class existence from cases where the membership condition mentions membership. So one tries in general set theory to manage with milder restrictions.

General set theory is rich in paradox. Even the endless series of antinomies that I mentioned above, of which Russell's was the first, by no means exhausts this vein of paradox. General set theory is primarily occupied with infinity—infinite classes, infinite numbers—and so is involved in paradoxes of the infinite. A rather tame old paradox under this head is that you can exhaust the members of a whole class by correlating them with the members of a mere part of the class. For instance, you can correlate all the positive integers with the multiples of 10, thus: 1 with 10, 2 with 20, 3 with 30, and so on. Every positive integer gets disposed of; there are as many multiples of 10 as integers altogether. This is no antinomy but a veridical paradox. Among adepts in the field it even loses the air of paradox altogether, as is indeed the way of veridical paradox.

Georg Cantor, the nineteenth-century pioneer in general set theory and infinite arithmetic, proved that there are always more classes of things of a given kind than there are things of that kind; more classes of cows than cows. A distinct air of paradox suffuses his proof of this.

First note the definition of 'more'. What it means when one says there are more things of one kind than another is that every correlation of things of the one kind to things of the other fails to exhaust the things of the one kind. So what Cantor is proving is that no correlation of cow classes to cows accommodates all the cow classes. The proof is as follows. Suppose a correlation of cow classes to cows. It can be any arbitrary correlation; a cow may or may not belong to the class correlated with her. Now consider the cows, if any, that do not belong to the classes correlated with them. These cows themselves form a cow class, empty or not. And it is a cow class that is not correlated with any cow. If the class were so correlated, that cow would have to belong to the class if and only if she did not.

This argument is typical of the arguments in general set theory that would be sacrificed if we were to withhold the principle of class existence from cases where the membership condition mentions membership. The recalcitrant cow class that clinched the proof was specified by a membership condition that mentioned membership. The condition was non-membership in the correlated cow class.

But what I am more concerned to bring out, regarding the cow-class argument, is its air of paradox. The argument makes its negative point in much the same way that the veridical barber paradox showed there to be no such barber, and in much the same way that Russell's antinomy showed there to be no class of all and only the non-self-members. So in Cantor's theorem—a theorem not only about cows and their classes but also about things of any sort and their classes—we see paradox, or something like it, seriously at work in the advancement of theory. His theorem establishes that for every class, even every infinite class, there is a larger class: the class of its subclasses.

So far, no antinomy. But now it is a short step to one. If for every class there is a larger class, what of the class of everything? Such is Cantor's antinomy. If you review the proof of Cantor's theorem in application directly to this disastrous example—speaking therefore not of cows but of everything—you will quickly see that Cantor's antinomy boils down, after all, to Russell's.

So the central problem in laying the foundations of general set theory is to inactivate Russell's antinomy and its suite. If such theorems as Cantor's are to be kept, the antinomies must be inactivated by milder restrictions than the total withholding of the principle of class existence from cases where the membership condition mentions membership. One tempting line is a scheme of subscripts analogous to the scheme used in avoiding the antinomies of truth and denotation. Something like this line was taken by Russell himself in 1908, under the name of the theory of logical types. A very different line was proposed in the same year by Ernst Zermelo, and further variations have been advanced in subsequent years.

All such foundations for general set theory have as their point of departure the counsel of the antinomies; namely, that a given condition, advanced as a necessary and sufficient condition of membership in some class, may or may not really have a class corresponding to it. So the various alternative foundations for general set theory differ from one another with respect to the membership conditions to which they do and do not guarantee corresponding classes. Non-self-membership is of course a condition to which none of the theories accord corresponding classes. The same holds true for the condition of not being a member of any own member; and for the conditions that give all the further antinomies of the series that began with Russell's; and for any membership condition that would give rise to any other antinomy, if we can spot it.

But we cannot simply withhold each antinomy-producing membership condition and assume classes corresponding to the rest. The trouble is that there are membership conditions corresponding to each of which, by itself, we can innocuously assume a class, and yet these classes together can yield a contradiction. We are driven to seeking optimum consistent combinations of existence assumptions, and consequently there is a great variety of proposals for the foundations of general set theory. Each proposed scheme is unnatural, because the natural scheme is the unrestricted one that the antinomies discredit; and each has advantages, in power or simplicity or in attractive consequences in special directions, that each of its rivals lacks.

I remarked earlier that the discovery of antinomy is a crisis in the evolution of thought. In general set theory the crisis began sixty years ago and is not yet over.

GÖDEL'S PROOF

Up to now the heroes or villains of this piece have been the antinomies. Other paradoxes have paled in comparison. Other paradoxes have been less startling to us, anyway, and more readily adjusted to. Other paradoxes have not precipitated sixty-year crises, at least not in our time. When any of them did in the past precipitate crises that durable (and surely the falsidical paradoxes of Zeno did), they themselves qualified as antinomies.

Let me, in closing, touch on a latter-day paradox that is by no means an antinomy but is strictly a veridical paradox, and yet is comparable to the antinomies in the pattern of its proof, in the surprisingness of the result and even in its capacity to precipitate a crisis. This is Gödel's proof of the incompletability of number theory.

What Kurt Gödel proved, in that great paper of 1931, was that no deductive system, with axioms however arbitrary, is capable of embracing among its theorems all the truths of the elementary arithmetic of positive integers unless it discredits itself by letting slip some of the falsehoods too. Gödel showed how, for any given deductive system, he could construct a sentence of elementary number theory that would be true if and only if not provable in that system. Every such system is therefore either incomplete, in that it misses a relevant truth, or else bankrupt, in that it proves a falsehood.

Gödel's proof may conveniently be related to the Epimenides paradox or the *pseudomenon* in the 'yields a falsehood' version. For 'falsehood' read 'non-theorem', thus: ' 'Yields a non-theorem when appended to its own quotation' yields a non-theorem when appended to its own quotation'.

This statement no longer presents an antinomy, because it no longer says of itself that it is false. What it does say of itself is that it is not a theorem (of some deductive theory that I have not yet specified). If it is true, here is one truth that that deductive theory, whatever it is, fails to include as a theorem. If the statement is false, it is a theorem, in which event that deductive theory has a false theorem and so is discredited.

What Gödel proceeds to do, in getting his proof of the incompletability of number theory, is the following. He shows how the sort of talk that occurs in the above statement—talk of non-theoremhood and of appending things to quotations—can be mirrored systematically in arithmetical talk of integers. In this way, with much ingenuity, he gets a sentence purely in the arithmetical vocabulary of number theory that inherits that crucial property of being true if and only if not a theorem of number theory. And Gödel's trick works for any deductive system we may choose as defining 'theorem of number theory'.

Gödel's discovery is not an antinomy but a veridical paradox. That there can be no sound and complete deductive systematization of elementary number theory, much less of pure mathematics generally, is true. It is decidedly paradoxical, in the sense that it upsets crucial preconceptions. We used to think that mathematical truth consisted in provability.

Like any veridical paradox, this is one we can get used to, thereby gradually sapping its quality of paradox. But this one takes some sapping. And mathematical logicians are at it, most assiduously. Gödel's result started a trend of research that has grown in thirty years to the proportions of a big and busy branch of mathematics sometimes called proof theory, having to do with recursive functions and related matters, and embracing indeed a general abstract theory of machine computation. Of all the ways of paradoxes, perhaps the quaintest is their capacity on occasion to turn out to be so very much less frivolous than they look.

2

✤ *On a Supposed Antinomy*

A puzzle that has had some currency from 1943 onward is concerned with a man who was sentenced on Sunday to be hanged on one of the following seven noons, and to be kept in ignorance, until the morning of the fatal day, as to just which noon it would be. By a faulty argument the man persuaded himself that the sentence could not be executed, only to discover his error upon the arrival of the hangman at 11:55 the following Thursday morning. What his faulty argument was is almost too familiar now to bear recounting (though I shall recount it); for the puzzle has kept recurring in the oral tradition and it has broken into *Mind*[1] in two variant versions, one relating to a surprise air-raid drill and the other to a surprise hour examination. The puzzle in each case is to find the fallacy. What is remarkable is that the solution, a solution which at any rate has contented me for nine years, seems seldom to have been clearly apprehended. There is a false notion abroad that actual antinomy is involved. This notion has even brought Professor Weiss[1] to the desperate extremity of entertaining Aristotle's fantasy that 'It is true that *p* or *q*' is an insufficient condition for 'It is true that *p* or it is true that *q*.'

I circulated the gist of this in typescript in 1943 and on subsequent occasions as the question arose, but did not sense until 1952 that it should be published. The paper appeared in *Mind* (Volume 62, January 1953), under the title "On a so-called paradox," and is reprinted by permission of the editor of *Mind*. I have now changed "paradox" to "antinomy," in the title and at one point in the text, in observance of distinctions drawn above in "The ways of paradox."

[1] D. J. O'Connor, 1948, 358; L. J. Cohen, 1950, 86; Peter Alexander, 538; Michael Scriven, 1951, 403ff.; Paul Weiss, 1952, 265ff.

The plot, in each of its embodiments, is as follows: K knows at time t and thereafter that it is decreed that an event of a given kind will occur uniquely and within K's ken at time $t + i$ for some integer i less than or equal to a specified number n, and that it is decreed further that K will not know the value of 'i' until after (say) time $t + i - \frac{1}{2}$. Then K argues that $i \leqq n - 1$; for, if i were n, K would know promptly after $t + n - 1$ that i was n. Then, by the same reasoning with '$n - 1$' for 'n' he argues that $i \leqq n - 2$; and so on, finally concluding after n steps that $i \leqq 0$ and hence that the event will not occur at all.

It is notable that K acquiesces in the conclusion (wrong, according to the fable of the Thursday hanging) that the decree will not be fulfilled. If this is a conclusion which he is prepared to accept (though wrongly) in the end as a certainty, it is an alternative which he should have been prepared to take into consideration from the beginning as a possibility.

Thus K erred in his argument that $i \leqq n - 1$. Looking ahead at time t to the possible states of affairs at time $t + n - 1$, K discerned just two alternatives as follows: (a) the event will have occurred at or before that time; (b) the event will (in keeping with the decree) occur at time $t + n$, and K will (in violation of the decree) be aware promptly after $t + n - 1$ that the event will occur at time $t + n$. Rejecting (b) because of its violation of the decree, he elected (a). Actually K should have discerned not two alternatives but four, viz., (a) and (b) and two more as follows: (c) the event will (in violation of the decree) fail to occur at time $t + n$; (d) the event will (in keeping with the decree) occur at time $t + n$, and K will (in keeping with the decree) remain ignorant meanwhile of that eventuality (not knowing whether the decree will be fulfilled or not). He erred in not recognizing that either (a) or (d) could be true even compatibly with the decree. The same fault recurred in each of his succeeding $n - 1$ steps.

The tendency to be deceived by the puzzle is perhaps traceable to a wrong association of K's argument with *reductio ad absurdum*. It is perhaps supposed that K is quite properly assuming fulfillment of the decree, for the space of his argument, in order to prove that the decree will not be fulfilled. This, if it were all, would be good *reductio ad absurdum;* and it would entitle K to eliminate (b) and (c), but not (d). To suppose that the assumption of fulfillment of the decree eliminates (d) is to confuse two things: (i) a hypothesis, by K at t, that the decree will be fulfilled, and (ii) a hypothesis, by K at t, that K will know at $t + n - 1$ that the decree will be fulfilled. Actually hypothesis (i), even as a hypothesis made by K, admits of two subcases: K's hypothetical ignorance and K's hypothetical awareness of the hypothetical fact.

Thus suppose that a mathematician at work on the Fermat problem assumes temporarily, for the sake of exploring the consequences, that Fermat's proposition is true. He is not thereby assuming, even as a hypothesis for the sake of argument, that he knows Fermat's proposition to be true. The difference can be sensed by reflecting that the latter would actually be a contrary-to-fact hypothesis, whereas the former may or may not be.

K's fallacy may be brought into sharper relief by taking n as 1 and restoring the hanging motif. The judge tells K on Sunday afternoon that he, K, will be hanged the following noon and will remain ignorant of the fact till the intervening morning. It would be like K to protest at this point that the judge was contradicting himself. And it would be like the hangman to intrude upon K's complacency at 11:55 next morning, thus showing that the judge had said nothing more self-contradictory than the simple truth. If K had reasoned correctly, Sunday afternoon, he would have reasoned as follows: "We must distinguish four cases: first, that I shall be hanged tomorrow noon and I know it now (but I do not); second, that I shall be unhanged tomorrow noon and know it now (but I do not); third, that I shall be unhanged tomorrow noon and do not know it now; and fourth, that I shall be hanged tomorrow noon and do not know it now. The latter two alternatives are the open possibilities, and the last of all would fulfill the decree. Rather than charging the judge with self-contradiction, therefore, let me suspend judgment and hope for the best."

3

⚔ *Foundations of Mathematics*

Irrefragability, thy name is mathematics. Mathematics is where the proofs are. Scientific standards have turned austere indeed, it would seem, if anyone is to fuss about foundations for mathematics. Where might he find foundations half so firm as what he wants to found?

Yet concern for the foundations of mathematics is nothing new. It has been indulged for centuries, and with reason. For there have been shaky ideas in mathematics. One was the idea of the infinitesimal, which figured centrally in the differential calculus in the days of its founders Newton and Leibniz. It was the idea of a fractional quantity infinitely close to zero, yet different from zero. It seemed to be needed in the study of rates, which was the business of the differential calculus.

Thus consider an accelerating car. At some instant it is going a mile a minute, at earlier instants less, at later ones more. The instantaneous speed of a mile a minute does not consist in going a mile in a minute, for it is not maintained for a minute. Nor does it consist in going 88 feet in a second, for it is not maintained for a second. The speed of a mile a minute is maintained by the accelerating car for no time at all, and the distance so covered is

---

This is the original version of an article that was commissioned by the *Scientific American,* who published an edited version of it (Volume 208, 1964). Terminal portions are dropped which dealt with points covered in "The ways of paradox."

zero. In this characterization, however—no miles an instant—no distinction remains between one speed and another. So the founding fathers of the calculus assumed infinitesimal numbers, just barely distinct from zero and from one another. Going a mile a minute then meant going one of those infinitesimal distances in some infinitesimal time. Going half a mile a minute meant going half that infinitesimal distance in that infinitesimal time.

We are used to there being no end of smaller and smaller numbers, $\frac{1}{8}$ and $\frac{1}{16}$ and so on, nearer and nearer zero. But these are not infinitesimals. An infinitesimal is supposed to go into 1 not just sixteen times, or a thousand times, but infinitely many times.

The idea was seen as absurd. 1 divided by infinity is simply 0 and not infinitesimally more. Still the resulting calculus proved indispensable in reasoning mathematically about rates. So a problem arose that is characteristic of problems in the foundations of mathematics: how to get rid of the infinitesimal and make do with clearer ideas while still saving the useful superstructure.

Cauchy and his followers in the nineteenth century solved the problem. Consider shorter and shorter intervals of time, each of them straddling our given instant. Over each interval, write the distance the car went during it. Each such distance-to-time ratio will multiply out to about a mile a minute, if the time interval is short. In fact, whatever degree of accuracy of approximation to a mile a minute we care to stipulate, there is a time interval such that, if we confine our attention to the intervals inside it, all our distance-to-time ratios will approximate to a mile a minute with the stipulated accuracy. This complicated fact about short but not infinitesimal times and distances can be used as a definition of what it means to be going a mile a minute at a given instant. The differential calculus can be reconstructed on this basis, and the objectionable foundation dispensed with.

The idea of the infinitesimal is not the only mathematical idea that has needed to be legitimized or eliminated. Thus take the sixteenth-century idea, still very much with us, of imaginary numbers: square roots of negative numbers. Square any real number, negative or positive, and the result is positive; what then are the imaginary numbers? Whatever they are, they are not to be summarily dismissed. So central are they to applied mathematics that if you so much as divide a time by a distance you end up, according to Einstein's relativity physics, with an imaginary number. The maxim here is as in the differential calculus: rebuild the foundation if you must, but save the superstructure.

The square root of -1 is the imaginary unit, called i. The rest of the imaginary numbers are the multiples of i by real numbers. Thus corresponding to the real number 3 there is the imaginary $3i$; corresponding to the real number ½ there is the imaginary $i/2$; corresponding to the real number π there is the imaginary πi. The imaginary numbers, thus constituted, then combine with the reals all over again by addition; we get $3 + \pi i$, $\pi + i/2$, and the like, known as complex numbers. It is through the complex numbers that the imaginary numbers find their real utility.

The utility of the complex numbers proves to be due mainly to this simple circumstance: any complex number $x + yi$ is a convenient coding or packaging of two real numbers x and y, each of which can be uniquely recovered on demand. In principle the mystification about square roots of negative numbers could have been omitted. The purposes of complex numbers and therewith of the imaginaries, in applied mathematics, could have been met by speaking merely of "ordered pairs" of real numbers.

The idea of ordered pair is useful at many other junctures in mathematics besides those where complex numbers are talked of. Its utility is always the same: it is a way of handling two things as one, while losing track of neither. Commonly the ordered pair of x and y, whether these be numbers or other things, is called $\langle x, y \rangle$. I have not said what things such pairs are, and traditionally the question is skipped; what is important is what they do. Their one property that matters is that if $\langle x, y \rangle$ is $\langle z, w \rangle$ then x is z and y is w.

I said that in principle the myth of imaginary roots could be skipped. Still it has value. It greatly simplifies the laws of algebra. Now by what has come to be a familiar kind of maneuver in foundational studies we can retain that advantage and still explain the imaginary and complex numbers away. The maneuver is this: *Define* the complex numbers as mere ordered pairs of real numbers, and then extend the usual algebraic operations of plus, times, and power, by definition, so as to make sense of these operations when they are applied to these ordered pairs. The definitions can be so devised as to provide us in the end with an algebra of ordered pairs of real numbers that is formally indistinguishable from the classical algebra of complex numbers. One tends to say not that the complex numbers have been eliminated in favor of ordered pairs, but that they have been explained as ordered pairs. One may say either; the difference is only verbal.

We have noted two occasions for activity in the foundations of mathematics. Both were emergencies: there was nonsense to make sense of. The next example is more sedate.

Consider again the ordered pair. Instead of skipping the question what things these pairs are, one might choose to adopt some version. Any version, however artificial, will serve so long as the law of pairs holds: if $\langle x, y \rangle$ is $\langle z, w \rangle$ then x is z and y is w. The usual version adopted nowadays is due to Norbert Wiener and Casimir Kuratowski, and has to do with classes of one and two members. It does not identify the ordered pair $\langle x, y \rangle$ simply with the class whose members are x and y, for that would confuse $\langle x, y \rangle$ with $\langle y, x \rangle$; but it identifies $\langle x, y \rangle$ with the class whose two members are (1) the class whose sole member is x and (2) the class whose members are x and y. By elementary argument this artificial version of $\langle x, y \rangle$ can be shown to fulfill the law of pairs.

Here again, as in the case of complex numbers, there are two ways to describe what we have done. We can say that we have eliminated ordered pairs in favor of certain two-member classes of classes, or we can say that we have explained ordered pairs as these two-member classes of classes. The difference is verbal. Philosophically the first description is better, for it avoids suggesting that other ways of fulfilling the law of pairs give less correct explanations of the ordered pair. Practically the second is better, for it preserves the notation '$\langle x, y \rangle$' and the word 'pair'.

Questions come in grades. At the top there are the indignant questions of offended common sense: "What is an infinitesimal? What is the square root of a negative number?" At the bottom there are the compulsive questions of a bored child on a rainy Saturday. Between are the philosophical questions. The inquiry into ordered pairs is at about the top of these. Farther down there is the question, "What is number?" Let us train this question first on just the natural numbers, that is, the positive integers and 0.

Numerals name numbers. '12' names 12. What the numerals

name, that is the question. What is 12? It is how many Apostles there are, how many months in a year, how many eggs in a box. 12 is a property, not indeed of the several eggs and months and Apostles, but of the classes. It is the property of being a dozen.

One of the sources of clarity in mathematics is the tendency to talk of classes rather than properties. Whatever is accomplished by referring to a property can generally be accomplished at least as well by referring to the class of all the things that have the property. Clarity is gained in that for classes we have a clear idea of sameness and difference: it is a question simply of their having the same or different members. Not so for properties.

In particular then we do best to explain 12 not as the property of being a dozen, but as the class of all dozens, the class of all 12-member classes. Each natural number n becomes the class of all n-member classes. There is a vicious circle in using n thus to define n, but we can avoid it by defining each number in terms rather of its predecessor. Once we have got to 5, for instance, we can explain 6 as the class of those classes which, when deprived of a member, come to belong to 5. Starting at the beginning, we can explain 0 as the class whose sole member is the empty class; then 1 as the class of those classes which, when deprived of a member, come to belong to 0; then 2 as the class of those classes which, when deprived of a member, come to belong to 1; and so on up.

The question about numbers resembles the one about ordered pairs. One knew what ordered pairs were for, what law they had to fulfill. One could construe pairs in any arbitrary way, just so the law was fulfilled. Similarly one is readier to say what the numbers are for than what they are. It is possible in the case of the numbers, no less than in the case of the pairs, to set down a law and assure ourselves that any version fulfilling it will serve the purpose of the numbers. The law is just that there is a first number and a successor operator that yields something new every time. Any version of number will suffice that causes the numbers to consist of a first together with the total yield of such an operator. The version of number set forth above, due essentially to Gottlob Frege (1884), seemed very natural, but others would serve too. An alternative version due to John von Neumann identifies each number rather with the class of all the preceding numbers. Thus 0 for him is itself the empty class; 1 is the class whose sole member is 0; 2 is the class of 0 and 1.

Frege's version made it easy to say that a class had n members: just say it belongs to n. But von Neumann's serves too. Here you just say instead that the members of the class can be paired off with the members of n; for each number n is itself, on von Neumann's version, a class of n numbers.

Whether we take numbers in either of these ways or in some other, a next step is to define the arithmetical operations. The idea behind addition is evident: $m + n$ is how many members a class has if part of it has m members and the rest has n. As for the product, $m \cdot n$, this is how many members a class has if it falls into m parts having n members each.

There are the negative numbers still to account for, and the fractional ones, and all the irrational numbers such as $\sqrt{2}$ and π, in short all the real numbers except the natural numbers. Here again any version will serve that meets certain requirements. I shall pass over the requirements and merely describe an acceptable overall version which has more unity than most. It construes each real number as a certain relation between natural numbers; in fact a certain relation of comparative size. Take in particular the real number ½. It is identified with the relation "less than half as big as": the relation that 1 bears to each integer from 3 on, and that 2 bears to each from 5 on, and so on. Similarly in general: each positive real number x is identified with the relation "less than x times as big as." The real number π, thus, comes out as a relation that 1 bears to each integer from 4 on, and 2 bears to each from 7 on, and 3 to each from 10 on, and so on. As for the negative real numbers, these are taken as the converse relations; thus, ½ being the relation "less than half as big as," −½ comes out as the relation "more than twice as big as."

My description of the positive real number x as the relation "less than x times as big as" falls into the same circularity that we noticed in describing n as the class of all n-membered classes. Still, here as on that earlier occasion, the description seems despite its circularity to make us see what objects the numbers are to be. The reason it serves is that the circular re-use of 'n' or 'x' inside the description has a common-sense context: 'n-membered classes', 'x times as big'. Actually the circularity can be eliminated, in the one case as in the other, by careful and complex definition; but I shall not pause over this.

We had to have the natural numbers before construing the real numbers in general; for we took these as relations of natural numbers. There results an unnatural but manageable distinction between those antecedent natural numbers and the corresponding whole real numbers that come out. For instance the real number 5 comes out as the relation "less than 5 times as big as," and this is a relation between natural numbers in the prior sense; it is not the old 5 itself.

Once we have the real numbers we can go on, as noted, and define the complex numbers as ordered pairs of the reals. Again there are alternative ways. By complicating the construction a little we can even cause the complex number $x + 0 \cdot i$ to coincide, as one wants it to, with the real number x;[1] this does not happen if we explain $x + yi$ in general as $\langle x, y \rangle$.

What else can we ask about? Functions. But these are easy if you allow relations, as we have lately been doing. A function can be identified with the relation of its values to its arguments. The function "square of" can be explained as the relation of square to root: the relation that 0 bears to 0, that 1 bears to 1, that 4 bears to 2, that $\frac{4}{9}$ bears to $\frac{2}{3}$, and so on.

At the risk of sounding increasingly like the child on the rainy Saturday, we may next ask: What is a relation? Again the answer is easy, thanks to ordered pairs. A relation can be identified with the class of all the ordered pairs $\langle x, y \rangle$ such that x bears the relation to y. The father relation becomes the class of all father-offspring pairs. The square function, above, becomes the class of all the pairs $\langle 0, 0 \rangle$, $\langle 1, 1 \rangle$, $\langle 4, 2 \rangle$, $\langle \frac{4}{9}, \frac{2}{3} \rangle$, in general $\langle x^2, x \rangle$.

Our sample studies in the foundations of mathematics started with trouble-shooting, and have leveled out into a general tidying up. It is a process, we see, of reducing some notions to others, and so diminishing the inventory of basic mathematical concepts.

If we are to keep track, we must render our successive reductive definitions in explicit detail and take note of all the logical and mathematical devices that are used in them. Each definition explains how to eliminate some locution by paraphrasing it, or its containing sentences, into terms of a residual vocabulary; and the residual vocabulary shrinks progressively as

---

[1] On this point and previous ones see my *Set Theory and Its Logic*.

we continue. Thus consider how we would define 'prime number', or '*n* is a prime number'. It means:

n is a natural number and, for all natural numbers h and k, if n is h·k then h or k is 1.

The residual vocabulary contains the multiplicative notation '*h·k*' among other things, but we saw how to eliminate that. We expand the clause '*n = h·k*' to read:

A class of n members falls into h parts having k members each.

More fully analyzed, this clause means that

For every class x with n members there is a class y of h members such that each member of y has k members and no members of y share members and all and only the members of the members of y are members of x.

Cumbersomeness is increasing apace, but the vocabulary is diminishing. Now an element of the surviving vocabulary that we are in a position to eliminate in turn is seen in '*x* has *n* members' and kindred clauses. This simply becomes '*x* is a member of *n*', we saw, if we choose Frege's version of the natural numbers. So our original phrase '*n* is a prime number' has now been analyzed to this:

n is a natural number and, for all natural numbers h and k, if for every member x of n there is a member y of h such that all members of y are members of k and no members of y share members and all and only the members of the members of y are members of x, then h or k is 1.

The dwindling of perspicuity here is less noteworthy than the dwindling of vocabulary. Where perspicuity is to our purpose the eliminated locutions can be restored, after all, as defined abbreviations.

In the dwindling vocabulary, the element that calls next for elimination is 'is a natural number' (said of *n*, *h*, and *k*). To say that *n* is a natural number is to say that *n* is 0 or successor of 0 or successor of that or so on. Frege showed how to dodge the "so on" idea. The class of the natural numbers is simply, he observed, the smallest class *z* such that 0 is a member of *z* and all successors of members of *z* are members of *z*. So he defined '*n* is a natural number' thus:

n is a member of every *class z such that* 0 *is a member of z and all successors of members of z are members of z.*

As for '0' and 'successor', we saw what they were on Frege's version: 0 is the class whose sole member is the class without members, and the successor of any *m* is the class of all the classes which, when deprived of a member, come to belong to *m*.

If we rewrite the above version of 'is a natural number' accordingly, eliminating '0' and 'successor', and then use the result in rewriting the preceding version of '*n* is a prime number' so as to eliminate 'natural number', we end up with a long story in a short vocabulary. The '1' at the end of it gets resolved too, of course, for 1 is successor of 0. The vocabulary that remains talks of class membership and little else. There is an assortment of elementary logical particles: 'is', 'and', 'or', 'if–then', 'every', 'all', and the like.

By some further steps of regimentation which we need not pause over, all this can be got down to the following four basic locutions. One is 'and', as a connective of sentences. One is 'not', as applied to sentences. One is the idiom of universal quantification, 'everything is such that . . . it . . .'. For flexibility this needs to be rendered rather 'everything x is such that . . . x . . .', with changeable letters 'x', 'y', etc., to keep cross-references straight in complex cases. The prefix 'everything x is such that', called a universal quantifier, is compactly symbolized as '(x)'. Fourth and last there is the transitive verb 'ϵ', meaning 'is a member of'. Perhaps I should count also the use of parentheses for the grouping of clauses. The following, then, is a typical sentence in our frugal notation:

$$(x) \text{ not } (y) \text{ not } (x \in y \text{ and not } y \in x).$$

It amounts in effect to the words 'Everything is a member of something not a member of it'.

Every sentence expressible in the notation of pure classical mathematics, whether in arithmetic or the calculus or elsewhere, can be paraphrased into this thumbnail vocabulary. The illustrative reductions set forth above are not enough to enable the reader to carry the job through in full, but they are perhaps enough to lend plausibility to this otherwise implausible claim.

What '*n* is a prime number' was seen to come to is as nothing compared to what it or another sentence of arithmetic would come to if fully paraphrased into our four basic idioms. The four are not to be recommended as a *lingua franca* of mathematics, nor as a practical medium of computation. It is matter rather of theoretical interest that so much in the way of mathematical ideas can be generated from so meager a basis, and from this basis in particular.

Three of our four basic locutions belong to logic. The fourth belongs to set theory, or the mathematics of classes. Or we could say that all four belong to set theory; for the purely logical locutions are best looked upon as in the common domain and reckoned automatically to the apparatus of any and every theory.

Since all mathematics can be so paraphrased, all mathematical truth can be seen as truth of set theory. Every mathematical problem can be transformed into a problem of set theory. Either this augurs well for the outstanding problems of mathematics, or else set theory is itself as deep in problems as any part of mathematics.

The latter is the case. And the worst of set theory is not just that sentences can be written whose truth or falsity is hard to prove. Sentences can be written whose simultaneous truth and falsity seem all too easy to prove. One such is the sentence:

not (y) not (x) (not $(x \in y$ and $x \in x)$ and not (not $x \in y$ and not $x \in x))$.

Partially transcribed with an eye to mortal communication, what it says is this:

There is something y such that $(x)(x \in y$ if and only if not $x \in x)$.

And this is recognizable as Russell's paradox.

As a foundation for mathematics, then, set theory is far less firm than what is founded upon it; for common sense in set theory is discredited by the paradoxes. Clearly we must not look to the set-theoretic foundation of mathematics as a way of allaying misgivings regarding the soundness of classical mathematics. Such misgivings are scarce anyway, once such offenses against reason as the infinitesimal have been set right. Conceptual unification, merely, is what the set-theoretic foundation is notable for. Foundation ceases to be the apt metaphor; it is as if a frail foundation were supported by suspension from a sturdy superstructure. For the one thing we insist on, as we sort through the various possible plans for passable set theories, is that our set theory be such as to reproduce, in the eventual superstructure, the accepted laws of classical mathematics. This requirement is even useful as a partial guide when in devising a set theory we have to choose among intuitively undecidable alternatives. We may look upon set theory, or its notation, as just a conveniently restricted vocabulary in which to formulate a general axiom system for classical mathematics—let the sets fall where they may.

4

৵ On the Application of Modern Logic

Up to now the importance of modern logic may be said, in a somewhat paradoxical phrase, to have lain in theoretical applications. Modern logic has been most useful as a tool in the most theoretical inquiries into the foundations and mechanisms of pure mathematics, and it is this rather lofty utility that has mainly stimulated modern developments in logic.

Thus consider Gödel's celebrated theorem of 1931.[1] That it is true is surprising, and that it could be proved is more surprising still. It is a strictly mathematical theorem about what can or cannot be done in the way of deducing some sentences of number theory logically from others; and in order to prove it Gödel had to be mathematically precise and explicit, as mathematicians traditionally were not, about what counts as logical deduction. Thus it was that the modern mathematical formalization of logic served Gödel as an indispensable practical instrument toward establishing his highly theoretical result, the impossibility of a complete number theory. This is one of many cases, but justly the most celebrated, where modern logic has served as a practical tool in advancing our theoretical understanding of what goes on in mathematics.

This was broadcast in German translation over the radio in the American Sector, Berlin, in 1960. An early segment has been eliminated by dint of the following footnote.

[1] See above, end of "The ways of paradox."

It can be argued, in another vein, that most problems throughout mathematics are problems in applied logic. Thus consider the
famous conjecture of Goldbach, still unsettled, that every even
number is the sum of two primes. We are able right now, without
knowing whether Goldbach's conjecture is true or false, to write
down a certain complex true sentence T of number theory and
show that *if* Goldbach's conjecture is false then its negation is
logically deducible from T. If on the other hand Goldbach's
conjecture is true, of course its negation is not deducible from T.
Therefore the Goldbach problem is *equivalent* to the purely
logical question whether a certain already specified sentence—the
negation of Goldbach's conjecture—is deducible by logic alone
from the already specifiable sentence T.

So in general, for any mathematical conjecture S: if we
produce a known truth T and then show, perhaps of S or perhaps
of its negation, that it must follow from T if true, we have
thereby reduced the problem of S to a problem of logic. The
Goldbach problem is not unusual in being thus reducible to logic;
the same is true of many others, including the celebrated Fermat
problem which has been exercising some of the best minds for
three centuries past.

The Goldbach and Fermat problems are impressive examples,
but what I have said of them is evidence of no great problem-
solving facility on the part of modern logical techniques. It is
evidence only of how rich in problems logic is. For I say only that
the Goldbach and Fermat problems and others like them can be
transformed into problems of logical deducibility, and not that
the problems are likelier to be solved under this transformation
than otherwise. It is a consideration calculated rather to motivate the improvement of techniques in mathematical logic than
to extol existing ones.

Existing ones are, however, impressive. Like techniques in
other parts of mathematics, they fall into two phases: paraphrasing and solving. This is the distinction that comes out so vividly
in the exercises of high-school algebra: first we get the verbally
expressed problem into an equation, and then we solve the
equation. Similarly, in modern logic, first we paraphrase a
problem into a canonical notation best adapted to known
techniques of deduction or evaluation, and then we bring those
techniques to bear.

Now in algebra, as most of us remember, the preparatory

operation of paraphrase was of no interest except as a means of getting an equation to solve. In logic, on the other hand, the preparatory operation proves to be of consuming interest on its own account. For it provides a sharp analysis of concepts, a revelation of fundamental structures which go undetected as long as our sentences are couched in ordinary language. The deepened understanding afforded by paraphrasing ordinary discourse into the specially devised idiom of modern logic has conspicuously influenced the course of philosophy. Among twentieth-century philosophers of scientific temper, indeed, "logical analysis" is a watchword. And in particular the enterprise of paraphrasing into logical notation has brought unprecedented progress in the philosophy of mathematics—progress which has been at once a result and a main motivation of modern logic.

In modern logic there are also, after the paraphrasing is done, powerful techniques corresponding to the algebraic business of solving formulated equations: techniques, this time, for testing or exploring the connections of logical implication among logical formulas. But it must be said that up to now the practical application of these new techniques has been less important and less widespread than the vast generality of the subject might tempt one to expect. The techniques have served certainly to expedite steps that previously involved more labor and frequent fumbling, but they have played no role comparable to that played by various branches of mathematics in application to physics.

In the future, however, they well may. In the era of Roman numerals, problems having to do with exponents or with differential equations were not merely difficult of solution; they did not arise, for lack of appropriate concepts and notation. The conceptual apparatus of modern logic is rich likewise in problems that simply would not occur to us in the primitive framework of ordinary language. Some such problems may, as natural science goes on evolving in full cognizance of modern logic, prove germane to natural science just as problems of exponents and differentials have done; and then the existing problem-solving techniques of modern logic will prove their worth to natural science. Further logical techniques will then be developed, also, to suit special needs of natural science, if we may predict by analogy to events elsewhere in mathematics.

There is indeed one bit of modern logical technique that is

already being intensively applied in engineering. Ironically, it is the most elementary part of logic: the theory of truth functions. The truth functions are essentially the 'not', 'and', and 'or' of ordinary language, used in compounding sentences to form composite sentences whose truth or falsity depends in obviously specifiable ways on the truth or falsity of the component sentences. Claude Shannon discovered a valuable application of truth-function logic to the designing of electric circuits. The relevance of 'and' and 'or' to electric circuits is this: if terminals are separated by switches A and B in series, the circuit is closed just in case A *and* B are closed; if they are separated rather by A and B in parallel, the circuit is closed just in case A *or* B is closed. 'Not' also comes into the picture, simply in opening a switch. A consequence of this correspondence is that the very practical problem of simplifying a complex electric circuit, the problem of devising a simplest possible circuit for a given job, reduces to the logical problem of simplifying a truth-functional formula.

An added irony is that though the logic of truth functions, unlike most of modern logic, is easy and simple to the point of triviality, the general problem of simplifying truth-functional formulas proves difficult. If you compound a few sentences into a composite sentence by means of 'not', 'and', and 'or', the result is indeed as transparent in its meaning and as simple in its logical behavior as you could wish. But the curious point is that such a compound cannot always be transformed into a simplest equivalent by obvious steps of progressive simplification. Twelve years ago I, for one, supposed the contrary as a matter of course, and confidently expected to turn up the appropriate little set of easy steps in short order. But no such set of steps has been found. Unimaginative methods of exhausting possibilities are indeed available, obvious, and unfailing as means of finding simplest equivalents; but when the composite sentence concerned is built of many components, such methods run to astronomical lengths and become impracticable.

Straightforward methods of progressive simplification are out of the question in the general case. Indirect methods are still to be hoped for, however, which involve less than prohibitive processes of exhaustion. Progress in this direction has been made, and much effort is being expended toward furthering it. Quite a body of theory to the purpose is developing, under pressure of the needs of electrical engineering. For the boom in computing machines has put an enormous premium on finding simplest circuits for given purposes. In America there are many establishments, some commercial and some governmental, where research goes forward in the design of computing machines and other automata; and it seems nowadays to be the usual thing, at such centers, for some of the research staff to be occupied with trying to devise increasingly powerful techniques for simplifying truthfunctional formulas. I know the same to be true to some degree in Russia and Australia, and it is doubtless true in other countries as well. Publications on the problem of simplifying truth-functional formulas are appearing with increasing frequency, in mathematics journals and in manuals and journals of computer engineering. The problem has reached the point where part of the concern is to so frame the simplification techniques as to be able to enlist the aid of computing machines in carrying them through. Computers thus figure increasingly as instruments to simplify the design of computers.

There is a remarkably definite sense in which the logic of truth functions may be said nevertheless to be a simple, even a trivial, subject. It is this: Every specific question of logical implication or equivalence in this part of logic can be settled by a routine computation. This is what is meant, in technical language, by saying that the logic of truth functions is *effective*. The next more serious portion of modern logic, known as the logic of quantifiers or of predicates, is not effective. In this domain there is indeed still a general routine of computation whereby every specific question of implication or equivalence can be settled affirmatively if the right answer happens to be affirmative; but negative answers are not in general obtainable, as Alonzo Church proved in 1936, by any dependable routine whatever. This halfway effectiveness is sometimes expressed nowadays by saying that the logic of quantifiers is *constructive*. As for number theory, it is not even constructive; this is a way of putting the theorem of Gödel touched on earlier.

There is cause for surprise in that the logic of truth functions, trivial as it is to the point of effectiveness, should have proved so central to computer engineering; and there is much more cause for surprise in that the relevant problems should prove so stubborn.

But higher parts of modern logic bear on computer engineering also, less surprisingly, and in deeper ways. As mechanical brains come to be adapted to purposes farther and farther beyond mere arithmetical calculation, ever-increasing importance attaches to the business of *programming:* the business, that is, of so analyzing and paraphrasing a problem as to cause its solution to organize itself into steps which a machine can be made to take. Programming is analogous, again, to that old affair in school algebra of transmuting verbally phrased problems into equations amenable to the mechanics of algebraic manipulation. It is analogous also, therefore, to the business in modern logic of translating ordinary language into logical symbols. One may argue in both cases that there is more than analogy: the transmuting of verbally given problems into algebraic equations or logical formulas is itself a programming for something akin to machine computation, preparing the way as it does for the methodical manipulation of formulas according to fixed rules of algorithm.

In the programming of problems for genuine machines there is bound to be vast scope for the application of logical techniques of both of the sorts which I distinguished earlier: both the techniques of paraphrasing problems into efficiently manipulable formulas and the techniques of manipulating the results. Insofar as logical techniques bear on programming, moreover, they are bound to bear also on machine design; for programming and designing are reciprocal enterprises, each being slanted to the convenience of the other.

Such application of logical theory may be expected, moreover, to stimulate further progress in logical theory itself. This is a reasonable expectation in the application of any theory, but in the present instance it is especially strong. For programming demands utter explicitness and formality in the analysis of concepts; furthermore it thrives on conceptual economy; and it rewards novel lines of analysis, with never a backward glance at traditional forms of thought. It is a remarkable fact that programming provides a strictly monetary motive for very much the sort of rigor, imagination, and conceptual economy that have hitherto been cultivated by theoretical logicians for purely philosophical or aesthetic reasons. The extremes of abstract theory and practical application are seen converging here, much as they did in the technology of nuclear fission.

Between logical theory and machine computation there are connections yet more fundamental than these last considerations suggest. For let us recall the notions, lately touched upon, of effectiveness and constructiveness. I explained these notions by vague allusion to what I called routines of computation. And what counts as a routine of computation? The general notion of a routine of computation was made precise in 1936 and 1937 by the largely independent work of four mathematicians—Church, Kleene, Turing, Post; and the formulation of it turned out to constitute, at one and the same time, a formulation of the basic theoretical trait of any possible computing machine.

Early in this paper I cited Gödel's theorem, in proof theory, to illustrate a motive and a triumph of research in modern logic. A principal motive of modern logical research has been exploration of the nature, potentialities, and limits of mathematical proof. And now we see that the basic notions of proof theory converge with those of the theory of machine computing. Thus, take Gödel's theorem. It may be reformulated, I later remarked, as stating that number theory is not constructive. Here 'constructive' means, as I hinted, that a general routine of computation exists for generating proofs. Finally the notion of routine of computation, in turn, achieves its sharp formulation in a way that constitutes it the fundamental concept of machine computation. The utterly pure theory of mathematical proof and the utterly technological theory of machine computation are thus at bottom one, and the basic insights of each are henceforth insights of the other.

5

✌ *Homage to Rudolf Carnap*

Carnap is a towering figure. I see him as the dominant figure in philosophy from the 1930s onward, as Russell had been in the decades before. Russell's well-earned glory went on mounting afterward, as the evidence of his historical importance continued to pile up; but the leader of the continuing developments was Carnap. Some philosophers would assign this role rather to Wittgenstein; but many see the scene as I do.

Russell had talked of deriving the world from experience by logical construction. Carnap, in his *Aufbau*, undertook the task in earnest. It was a grand project, and yet a self-effacing one, when so few philosophers understood technical logic. Much ingenuity went into the constructions, much philosophical imagination, much understanding of psychology and physics. If the book did not achieve its exalted purpose, it did afford for the first time an example of what a scientific philosopher might aspire to in the way of rigor and explicitness. It afforded detailed glimpses also, and philosophically exciting ones, of how our knowledge of the external world could in considerable part turn out to be, in Eddington's phrase, a put-up job. And it provided techniques of construction that continue to be useful.

In his *Logical Syntax* Carnap again vigorously exploited the resources of modern logic for philosophical ends. The book is a mine of proof and opinion on the philosophy of logic and the logic

Presented in Boston, October 1970, at a memorial meeting under the auspices of the Philosophy of Science Association. Later it was read for me at a memorial meeting in Los Angeles. It appeared in *Boston Studies in the Philosophy of Science*, Volume 8.

of philosophy. During a critical decade it was the main inspiration of young scientific philosophers. It was the definitive work at the center, from which the waves of tracts and popularizations issued in ever widening circles. Carnap more than anyone else was the embodiment of logical positivism, logical empiricism, the Vienna Circle.

Ultimately Carnap saw limitations in his thesis of syntax. Thus came his third phase: books and papers on semantics, which have given Carnap a central place in the controversies over modal logic.

Meanwhile Carnap's *Logical Foundations of Probability* continued to develop, a monument to his unwavering concern with the logic of science. Two months ago I had a lively letter from him about some supplementary work that he was doing on this subject. Also he sent me a sheaf of material from the new work in progress.

Carnap was my greatest teacher. I got to him in Prague 38 years ago, just a few months after I had finished my formal studies and received my Ph.D. I was very much his disciple for six years. In later years his views went on evolving and so did mine, in divergent ways. But even where we disagreed he was still setting the theme; the line of my thought was largely determined by problems that I felt his position presented.

I first heard about Carnap and his *Aufbau* from John Cooley in 1931, when we were graduate students at Harvard. Herbert Feigl was then at Harvard as an International Rockefeller Fellow. He encouraged me to go to Vienna and to Carnap the following year if I got a traveling fellowship.

Carnap moved from Vienna to Prague that year, and I followed him. I attended his lectures and read his *Logische Syntax* page by page as it issued from Ina Carnap's typewriter. Carnap and Ina were a happy pair. He was 41, she even younger. Along with their intense productivity there was an almost gay informality. If you combine strong intellectual stimulation, easy laughter, and warm friendliness, you have an unbeatable recipe for good company; and such were the Carnaps. On a day when Carnap didn't have to come into the city to lecture, my wife and I would ride the trolley to the end of the line and walk the remaining few blocks to their little house in a suburb called Pod Homolkou. As the name implies, the place is at the foot of something; and Carnap and Ina would have just come in, likely as not, from an hour on skis on that very slope. Carnap and I would discuss logic and philosophy by the hour. My wife and I would stay to lunch, or maybe dinner; but, if dinner, that was the end of philosophy and logic until another meeting. Carnap's habits were already austere: no science after dinner, on pain of a sleepless night. No alcohol ever. No coffee.

I was then an unknown young foreigner of 23, with thirteen inconsequential pages in print and sixteen at press. It was extraordinary of anyone, and characteristic of Carnap, to have been so generous of his time and energy. It was a handsome gift. It was my first experience of sustained intellectual engagement with anyone of an older generation, let alone a great man. It was my first really considerable experience of being intellectually fired by a living teacher rather than by a dead book. I had not been aware of the lack. One goes on listening respectfully to one's elders, learning things, hearing things with varying degrees of approval, and expecting as a matter of course to have to fall back on one's own resources and those of the library for the main motive power. One recognizes that his professor has his own work to do, and that the problems and the approaches that appeal to him need not coincide in any very fruitful way with those that are exercising oneself. I could see myself in the professor's place, and I sought nothing different. I suppose most of us go through life with no brighter view than this of the groves of Academe. So might I have done, but for the graciousness of Carnap.

At Harvard the following year, I lectured on Carnap's philosophy. Our correspondence was voluminous. He would write in English, practicing up for a visit to America, and I in German; and we would enclose copies for correction. By Christmas 1935 he was with us in our Cambridge flat. Four of us drove with him from Cambridge to the Philosophical Association meeting in Baltimore. The others were David Prall, Mason Gross, and Nelson Goodman. We moved with Carnap as henchmen through the metaphysicians' camp. We beamed with partisan pride when he countered a diatribe of Arthur Lovejoy's in his characteristically reasonable way, explaining that if Lovejoy means A then p, and if he means B then q. I had yet to learn how unsatisfying this way of Carnap's could sometimes be.

Soon Carnap settled at Chicago. Two years later I took him to task for flirting with modal logic. His answer was characteristic: "I do not indulge in this vice generally and thoroughly ... Although we do not like to apply intensional languages, nevertheless I think we cannot help analyzing them. What would you think of an entomologist who refuses to investigate fleas and lice because he dislikes them?"

In 1939 Carnap came to Harvard as visiting professor. Those were historic months: Russell, Carnap, and Tarski were here together. Then it was that Tarski and I argued long with Carnap against his idea of analyticity.

Because of distances our later meetings were regrettably few. In 1949 my new and present wife and I spent some memorable days at the Carnaps' in New Mexico. In 1951 he and I held a symposium on ontology in Chicago. In 1958 a reunion in California was prevented by an illness of mine. Finally in 1965, to my delight, I saw him at Popper's colloquium in London. He looked well and was vigorous and alert. When Popper confronted him on induction his defense was masterly. It carried me back to his confrontation of Lovejoy thirty years before. It was the same old Carnap. His death, while still at the height of his powers, marks a sad date in the history of philosophy.

6

✌ *Logic as a Source of Syntactical Insights*

Mathematicians expedite their special business by deviating from ordinary language. Each such departure is prompted by specific considerations of utility for the mathematical venture afoot. Such reforms may be expected to reflect light on the ordinary language from which they depart, and the light reflected is all the brighter for the narrowly utilitarian character of the reforms. For in each case some special function which has hitherto been only incidentally and inconspicuously performed by a construction in ordinary language now stands boldly forth as the sole and express function of an artificial notation. As if by caricature, inconspicuous functions of common idioms are thus isolated and made conspicuous.

Thus consider the mathematician's use of parentheses to indicate grouping. Once this systematic device is in the forefront of our minds, we gain clearer insight into the purpose or survival value of certain related devices of ordinary language. We come to appreciate, for instance, that the pair of particles 'either–or' is not just a redundant elaboration of the simple 'or', but that the 'either' does the useful work of a left-hand parenthesis marking the beginning of the compound whose connective is 'or'. It is the

This paper was given by invitation of the American Mathematical Society at a symposium on mathematical methods in linguistics, held in New York in April 1960. © American Mathematical Society 1961 from the *Proceedings of Symposia in Applied Mathematics*, Volume 12, 1–5.

'either' that enables us verbally to resolve the ambiguity of 'p and q or r'. It enables us to draw the distinction between 'either p and q or r' and 'p and either q or r'—precisely the distinction which would be shown with parentheses as '$(p$ and $q)$ or r' versus 'p and $(q$ or $r)$'. The analogous purpose is served by the particle 'both' in connection with 'and'; thus '$(p$ or $q)$ and r' and 'p or $(q$ and $r)$' come out as 'both p or q and r' and 'p or both q and r'. This insight into the syntactical function of 'either' and 'both' could, of course, perfectly well have been vouchsafed us even if we had had no acquaintance with the method of parentheses; but they are likelier insights for the parenthesis-minded. Here, then, is a first crude instance of how the artificialities of mathematical notation may be expected to encourage syntactical insights into ordinary language.

For more persuasive examples, we do well to turn to mathematical logic. This branch of mathematics is especially rich in artifices that reflect light on the ordinary language from which they depart. My example of 'either–or' and 'both–and', indeed, was already drawn from logic; but there are also deeper examples to be drawn from that domain. Whereas most of the linguistic departures in mathematical developments other than logic have little to do with the very central devices of language, the departures in mathematical logic are as central as can be.

One distinction, obscure in ordinary English, that is brought into sharp relief by modern logical notation is the distinction of scopes of indefinite singular terms. Thus take the indefinite singular term 'every poem'. If I say 'I do not know every poem', am I to be construed as saying of every poem that I do not know it, or am I to be construed merely as denying the sentence 'I know every poem'? In the one case the scope of the indefinite singular term 'every poem' is the whole sentence 'I do not know every poem'. In the other case the scope is 'I know every poem', a subordinate sentence which the 'not' then denies.

Most of you are familiar with the modern logical notation which reduces indefinite singular terms and pronouns to so-called quantifiers and variables. It resolves questions of scope vividly and unambiguously. Ordinary language often resolves them too, but so unobtrusively that without benefit of the vivid rendering in modern logic one is unlikely to appreciate either the problem or the work which the locutions of ordinary language perform in resolving it. Once we have clearly appreciated the question of scope in the light of logical notation, we can return to ordinary language and see, as never before, what had been happening all along. What we find is an interplay of the apparent synonyms 'any' and 'every', as connoting wide and narrow scope respectively.

Let us return to our example. 'I do not know every poem' is definitely understood as confining the indefinite singular term 'every poem' to the narrower scope 'I know every poem', and then applying the 'not' to this subordinate sentence. The rule, implicit in usage but never brought to explicit attention until modern logic intervened, is that 'every' always calls for the narrowest available scope. 'Any' is subject to the contrary rule; it calls for the wider of two available scopes. Thus when we say 'I do not know any poem' the scope of the indefinite singular term 'any poem' is the whole sentence including the 'not'.

It is illuminating in this connection to compare 'I am ignorant of every poem'. This is equivalent, not to 'I do not know every poem', but to 'I do not know any poem', just because the scope is in this case the whole sentence merely for lack of any shorter; the 'i-' of 'ignorant', unlike 'not', happens to be inseparable, so that the scope of 'every' in 'I am ignorant of every poem' has to be the whole sentence.

The contrast between 'any' and 'every', in point of scope, holds not only in connection with negatives but generally. Thus compare 'If John knows any poem, he knows "The Raven"' and 'If John knows every poem, he knows "The Raven"'. The scope of 'any poem' is the whole conditional; the scope of 'every poem' is only the antecedent of the conditional. The one conditional says of each poem that if John knows it he knows "The Raven"; the other conditional says only that John knows "The Raven" if he knows them all.

We could have wondered alternately why English tolerates both of the apparent synonyms 'any' and 'every', and why they so often fail to be interchangeable. Chaos reduces to order once we gain a clear understanding of the scope of indefinite singular terms, through the regimented notation of mathematical logic. Retrospectively we appreciate that the difference in function between 'any' and 'every' is simply a matter of wide and narrow scope.

Questions of scope arise also apart from indefinite singular terms. Thus consider the phrase 'big European butterfly'; are we to take it as applying to all European butterflies that are big for European butterflies, or only to European butterflies that are big for butterflies? It is instructive to contrast with this example the formally similar one 'square black box', where the question of scope is irrelevant. The reason why the one example raises a question of scope and the other does not is that 'big' figures as a syncategorematic adjective, like 'poor' in 'poor sport' or 'mere' in 'mere child', while 'square' figures as a categorematic adjective. The keynote of the categorematic use is that a square so-and-so is simply anything that is square and a so-and-so; a mere child, in contrast, is not mere and a child, nor is a big butterfly simply big, absolutely, and a butterfly. This contrast is purely an affair of ordinary English, yet it is one that would have been less readily appreciated without the insights afforded by logical regimentation. In this case the notational departure of logic which may be expected to have fostered the relevant insight is a notation which resolves 'is a square so-and-so' into something like 'is square and is a so-and-so'; this susceptibility to resolution is what distinguishes the categorematic use of adjectives from the syncategorematic.

The analysis of linguistic compounds into their immediate constituents is another linguistic enterprise where modern logic can contribute occasional insights. Thus take 'the lady I saw you with'. Do we have here a singular term 'the lady' governed by a relative clause 'I saw you with', or do we have a general term 'lady I saw you with' governed by an article 'the'? The latter is definitely the preferable analysis, for it justifies the definiteness of the article by first incorporating all available determinants of uniqueness into the general term to which the article is applied. This insight would have been less likely without benefit of the theoretical study, in modern logic, of singular descriptions.

A modification of this example reveals, next, a curious anomaly. Let us paraphrase the example to read 'the lady such that I saw you with her'. By the preceding analysis, this phrase resolves into 'the' and a general term 'lady such that I saw you with her'. But then what, within this general term, is the grammatical antecedent of the final 'her'? Evidently 'lady'; and the anomaly is the occurrence of a general term as antecedent of a pronoun.

What intuitively sustains the use of the whole construction, surely, is the feeling rather that 'her' refers back to the singular term 'the lady'; yet this way of dividing the construction violates our previous point, that the article 'the' should be taken to govern a maximum description in the interests of uniqueness. Let me leave this quandary unresolved, remarking merely that it owes its very existence to insights from the side of modern logic.

Another insight which logic encourages is that pronouns are best classed with definite singular terms such as 'Henry', 'the man', and the like, rather than with indefinite singular terms such as 'a man' or 'every man'. The pronoun 'he', indeed, is roughly interchangeable with 'the man'; not with 'a man'. To say 'I saw a man and you saw him', for instance, is by no means equivalent to saying 'I saw a man and you saw a man'; the one implies identity and the other does not. To say 'I saw a man and you saw him' is equivalent rather to saying 'I saw a man and you saw the man'. Note the subtle contrast: in the sentence 'I saw a man and you saw him' the grammatical antecedent of 'him' is 'a man' but the appropriate substitute for 'him' is 'the man'. Pronouns do not stand for their grammatical antecedents; they may have indefinite singular terms as antecedents but they can be supplanted only by definite singular terms. And such they are.

This point about pronouns is clear enough, once enunciated, without appeal to subtleties of mathematical logic. Still, the regimented notation of logic is what is likeliest to suggest the point, because of the striking way in which that notation analyzes the work of pronouns and other singular terms, definite and indefinite.

And logic enables us to drive the point further. What our example revealed was only that the pronoun may have an indefinite singular term as antecedent, and can be supplanted only by a definite singular term. But modern developments in logic enable us to say further that in principle the pronoun is never needed with other than an indefinite singular term as antecedent, and that definite singular terms other than pronouns are needed not at all. We can systematically so paraphrase our sentences that the only definite singular terms to survive are variables used pronominally in apposition with indefinite singular terms, like the variable 'x' in 'Every region x contains a region smaller than x'. Such a reduction theorem can be of linguistic interest as affording a new perspective on the function of pronouns.

Let us next examine the basic role of pronouns according to this view. A typical sentence whose pronouns have indefinite singular terms as antecedents is this: 'Some whom none dislike do not appreciate themselves'. Now notice that the pronouns here are simply combinatorial devices for abstracting complex general terms from sentential clauses. An alternative device that would do the work of 'whom', in the complex general term 'whom some dislike', is the passive participial ending: thus 'disliked'. Similarly the complex general term 'whom none dislike' amounts to 'undisliked'. Again an alternative device that would do the work of the pronoun 'themselves', in the complex general term 'appreciate themselves', is the prefix 'self-': thus 'self-appreciators'. The whole sentence becomes 'There are undisliked non-self-appreciators'. No singular term remains, definite or indefinite, not even a pronoun.

The pronoun, in what may be viewed as its basic role, is thus seen as a device similar in purpose to the passive endings and the reflexive prefix. Its advantage over these latter lies merely in its flexibility, which spares us the trouble of such painstaking constructions as 'undisliked non-self-appreciators'.

I have brought out this point in an ordinary verbal example. The point comes, however, from mathematical logic, and it is there that the general proof exists. It is there proved that variables, which are the pronouns of logic, can in principle be dispensed with in favor of a few suitable chosen operators comparable to our passive ending and reflexive prefix. One way of dispensing with variables is due to Schönfinkel, whose ideas have been further developed by Curry under the name of combinatory logic; but that approach imports an excessively strong body of mathematical theory, tantamount to higher set theory. The half-dozen operators that I have in mind are, unlike Schönfinkel's, definable at the level of the elementary logic of predicates or quantifiers.[1] The point of them is not that they are handier than variables or pronouns, but that they suffice, however clumsily, to do the same job. To know this is to understand better than before just what the peculiar job of pronouns is.

[1]See "Algebraic logic and predicate functors," Essay 28 below.

7

❧ *Vagaries of Definition*

Mathematicians think more precisely than most of us. Yet there is a confusion to which they are more prone than most: the confusion of sign and object. Mathematicians attain precision because of the abstractness of their objects, and they confuse sign and object for the same reason. Physical things are palpably unlike their names; numbers and other mathematical objects, however, are not even palpable. Thus we read of reducing a *quantity* to its lowest *terms*. We read of *identity* of *unlike* expressions. The confusion takes also more serious, more tangled forms. Most mathematics texts abound in it. It is avoidable, and some recent texts avoid it. It is harmless for most mathematical purposes, and often even convenient. But in philosophy, in logic, and in a new branch of mathematics called proof theory, it spoils things.

Perhaps this confusion is coeval with language. Perhaps the ingenious stratagem of letting words stand for things would never have been hit upon without some supporting tendency to confuse the two. You and I never confuse physical things with their names, but primitive peoples do view the name as somehow the soul or essence of the thing. And there can be little doubt that an inverted form of the same confusion is to be thanked for all our useful talk of abstract objects. For the less careful one is of a distinction between a name and what it names, the less one is apt to observe a distinction between words that do name and words that do not. So, treating common nouns and adjectives on a par with names, one vaguely countenances dim new entities for these to name.

Presented in June 1972 at a colloquium on English lexicography in the New York Academy of Sciences. Published in the *Annals* of the Academy (1973).

Thus it must have been that properties, classes, kinds, and numbers made the scene. Science could not have got far without them, but to say this is not to deny their humble origin. They were conceived in sin.

The old vacillation between sign and object may still be seen in the way people talk of definition. They talk of defining a word, but they talk also of defining a thing or a kind of thing. They talk of the defining expression, but they talk also of the defining property of the thing or of the kind of thing. A *real* definition, according to the Aristotelian tradition, gives the essence of the kind of thing defined. This defining property is part of the essence of each thing of the kind. Man is defined as a rational animal, and thus rationality and animality are of the essence of each of us. Perhaps this notion of essence derives from the primitive view of the name as the soul or essence of the thing. If so, there has been considerable give-and-take between sign and object. For the essence comprises no longer the name, nor yet the common noun, nor yet the defining phrase, but rather the property that was posited for the phrase to designate.

We have outlived this doctrine of essences, we think, and have lived to patronize it, not appreciating that in a modified form it still deludes us. It lingers in the purported difference between meaning and collateral information. There is a feeling that the pure dictionary, if it existed, would attend strictly to meanings, thus leaving much of the content of actual dictionaries to the encyclopedia. The feeling is expressed only in a philosophical spirit; the existing so-called dictionary is admittedly a more useful book. But I say that the feeling is itself an unwarranted survival of the doctrine of essences. The distinction between what belongs to the meaning of a word and what counts as further information is scarcely clearer than the distinction between the essence of a thing and its accidents. Meaning is essence divorced from the thing and wedded to the word. We see here another nice case of give-and-take between sign and object. This divorce and re-marriage are indeed two good steps forward, but more are wanted.

Philosophers have made much capital of a distinction between *analytic* and *synthetic* statements. The distinction depends on the same uncritical notion of meaning. A true statement is analytic if its truth is due purely to the meanings of its words; otherwise synthetic. Definitions, we are told, should be analytic. Now such notions cannot be put on a scientific basis unless by shunning the mentalistic talk of meaning, the semantics of too, too common sense, and looking rather to speech dispositions and the behavioral psychology of language learning. We learn our words very largely by learning what contexts to affirm as true and in what circumstances; shall we say then that the analytic sentences are those that we learn to be true in learning their words? This criterion fits the popular examples of analyticity well enough, such as 'No bachelor is married', but it also fits many statements that philosophers would not want to include. In fact there is no telling what statements it would count as analytic for one or another speaker, since people learn the same words through different first contexts and even forget which contexts those were. Here is a better approximation: a statement is analytic if virtually *all* speakers of the language may be presumed to have learned the truth of the statement in the course of learning some of the words. This criterion wants some refining still, and even when refined it deviates somewhat in its coverage from the attributions of analyticity that philosophers are apt to make who have not defined the term. For my own part, I have no brief for the meaning game. The desire to keep one's definitions analytic, however that term be defined, is a vestige of essentialism that I would drop.

There is also in science a different and wholly respectable vestige of essentialism, or of real definition, but it is tangential to the lexicographer's concerns. It consists in picking out those minimum distinctive traits of a chemical, or of a species, or whatever, that link it most directly to the central laws of the science. Such definition has little air of semantics and is of a piece rather with the chemical or biological theory itself. Such definition conforms strikingly to the Aristotelian ideal of real definition, the Aristotelian quest for the essences of things. This vestige of essentialism is of course a vestige to prize.

Besides this special use in organizing natural science, definition has a distinctively philosophical use. Thus, imagine a philosopher in search of a phenomenalistic basis for natural science. His search is successful to the extent that he manages to find phenomenalistic definitions of the terms of science. He begins with an explicit phenomenalistic vocabulary, if he is rigorous, and then he defines each further term by showing how to eliminate it, how to paraphrase it away, in favor of that vocabulary. There happens actually to be no hope for phenomenalism, but it affords a convenient philosophical example. Other examples of this reductive use of definition abound in mathematics. It is shown, e.g., that the arithmetic of ratios and irrational and imaginary numbers can all be reduced by definition to the theory of classes of positive integers, and that this can be reduced in turn to pure set theory.

This reductive function of definition is by no means peculiar to philosophy and mathematics. It obtains equally in lexicography. The point is most evident in interlinguistic dictionaries: all the foreign words get paraphrased away in favor of the home vocabulary. The purpose of such a dictionary, for the layman, is clarification: reduction of the obscure foreign language to the clear home language.

The purpose of the domestic or English-to-English dictionary, for the layman, is likewise clarification: reduction of unfamiliar words to familiar ones. This reductive work on the part of the domestic dictionary could be made more vivid, and perhaps more efficient as well, by adopting a directional structure: defining each word by means exclusively of words of higher frequency. It has long seemed odd to me to clutter a popular domestic dictionary with idly compulsive definitions of words that all speakers of the language know; and the directional dictionary would omit all that. Words that are too common to admit of definition by words of higher frequency would go undefined; they would constitute a sort of basic English that would be used and not mentioned. This definitional criterion of basicity strikes me as interesting also apart from the question of the practical utility of the directional dictionary. And in the matter of utility I would have in any event to concede marginal exceptions to the directional rule. The public should continue to be apprised *both* that furze is gorse *and* that gorse is furze, and that they, or it, is of the genus *Ulex*.

But the directional idea has some virtue as a theoretical model. It enhances the affinity of the domestic dictionary to the interlinguistic dictionary and to the definitional reductions undertaken by the phenomenalist and the mathematician. Also a contrast obtrudes: the directional domestic dictionary reduces the rare words to the less rare grade by grade, while the interlinguistic dictionary plunges straight from foreign to English. This contrast, however, becomes purely superficial if we limit ourselves to the unrealistically theoretical case where all the definitions are elimina-

tive definitions, definitions *sensu stricto*, which serve to paraphrase their definienda away. For then each definition in the
directional domestic dictionary can be put into terms purely of the
core vocabulary of basic English, simply by paraphrasing each
intervening word according to its own definition. Conversely, the
interlinguistic dictionary could be given the structure of a grade-
by-grade reduction: each foreign word would be defined in terms of
more frequent foreign words, and then the residual foreign words,
too common for such further reduction, could be defined in English.
Not that I am recommending this. But it is the form that the
definitional reductions in mathematics generally do take: they
reduce in stages.

I alluded only now to the difference between definitions in the
strict sense, which are eliminative, and other sorts of dictionary
entries or definitions loosely so called. This is a clear and important
difference, unrelated to old oppositions of the analytic to the
synthetic or of essence to accident. To define 'gorse' as 'furze' is
eliminative, as far as it goes; or to define 'bachelor' as 'unmarried
man'. To explain 'gorse' by the phrase 'any of several spiny,
thickset shrubs' is not eliminative. This phrase cannot go proxy for
the word, being less specific. The point is familiar, and not meant
as a proposal of reform. Explanations of this noneliminative sort
are decidedly useful.

In definitions in the narrow sense, still, there are notable differences of liberality. Definition used to be thought of primarily as
equating a term outright to some expression. This view derived
from the old doctrine of real definition: the term would be a name
of some object or kind, and the definition would specify the essence.
Some words could not be viewed as naming objects or kinds; they
were called *syncategoremata*, and might be accounted for by including them in term phrases that were defined as wholes. It may
have been Jeremy Bentham who first appreciated that terms
generally might be handled like the syncategoremata. All we need
require of a definition, for full eliminability, is that it provide for
elimination of the defined word by paraphrasing all contexts in
which the word is to be used. Such was his theory of fictions, or
of paraphrasis, known later as the method of contextual definition.
It brought new power and freedom to philosophical enterprises of
reduction and analysis.

The contextual approach is common in dictionary definitions, when they are eliminative. Often, of course, as in the case of 'gorse' and 'bachelor', a substitute expression happens to be available for the word in isolation. Sometimes we are given a substitute expression along with stage directions: for 'addled' we are given 'spoiled, said of an egg'. This is a laconic contextual definition, telling how to eliminate 'addled' from certain contexts. The form of a definition is indifferent. What is required of an eliminative definition of a word W, on the basis of some accepted defining vocabulary V, is that it explain how to paraphrase every sentence S, in which the word W occurs, into a new sentence that contains only words of V and S other than W. If it is interlinguistic definition, the story has to be further complicated to avoid mixing languages. But in any event the way to view definitions, and truly eliminative definitions at that, is simply as clauses in a complex set of directions for translating whole sentences, or better perhaps whole texts.

I stressed the difference between definition, strictly so called, and other dictionary entries of a descriptive and noneliminative sort. I remarked that this was not a difference between analytic and synthetic, or essence and accident. And we observe now that it is also not a difference between direct substitutional definitions, like that of 'bachelor', and definitions that invoke stage directions or other indications of context. These latter, for all their chattiness, can be as strictly definitional as you please.

8

❧ *Linguistics and Philosophy*

Chomsky has expressed general doubts as to how much philosophy stands to gain from linguistics or linguistics from philosophy. But he did express the belief that linguistics contributes to philosophy in one quarter, by supporting rationalism as against empiricism.

With the following claim of Chomsky's, at least, we are all bound to agree:

> We must try to characterize innate structure in such a way as to meet two kinds of empirical conditions. First we must attribute to the organism, as an innate property, a structure rich enough to account for the fact that the postulated grammar is acquired on the basis of the given conditions of access to data; second, we must not attribute to the organism a structure so rich as to be incompatible with the data.

All this I find indisputable. If this is rationalism, and incompatible with Locke's empiricism, then so much the better for rationalism and so much the worse for Locke. The connection between this indisputable point about language, on the one hand, and the disagreements of seventeenth-century philosophers on the other, is a scholarly matter on which I have no interesting opinion. But what does require to be made clear is that this indisputable point about language is in no conflict with latter-day attitudes that are associated with the name of empiricism, or behaviorism.

Presented on April 13, 1968, at a symposium at New York University. Reprinted by permission of New York University Press from *Language and Philosophy* by Sidney Hook (ed.), © by New York University.

For, whatever we may make of Locke, the behaviorist is knowingly and cheerfully up to his neck in innate mechanisms of learning-readiness. The very reinforcement and extinction of responses, so central to behaviorism, depends on prior inequalities in the subject's qualitative spacing, so to speak, of stimulations. If the subject is rewarded for responding in a certain way to one stimulation, and punished for thus responding to another stimulation, then his responding in the same way to a third stimulation reflects an inequality in his qualitative spacing of the three stimulations; the third must resemble the first more than the second. Since each learned response presupposes some such prior inequalities, some such inequalities must be unlearned; hence innate. Innate biases and dispositions are the cornerstone of behaviorism, and have been studied by behaviorists. Chomsky mentioned some of that work himself, but still I feel I should stress the point.

This qualitative spacing of stimulations must therefore be recognized as an innate structure needed in accounting for any learning, and hence, in particular, language-learning. Unquestionably much additional innate structure is needed, too, to account for language-learning. The qualitative spacing of stimulations is as readily verifiable in other animals, after all, as in man; so the language-readiness of the human infant must depend on further endowments. It will be interesting to find out more and more, if we can, about what this additional innate structure is like and how it works. Such discoveries would illuminate not only language but learning processes generally.

It may well turn out that processes are involved that are very unlike the classical process of reinforcement and extinction of responses. This would be no refutation of behaviorism, in a philosophically significant sense of the term; for I see no interest in restricting the term 'behaviorism' to a specific psychological schematism of conditioned response.

Conditioned response does retain a key role in language-learning. It is the entering wedge to any particular lexicon, for it is how we learn observation terms (or, better, simple observation sentences) by ostension. Learning by ostension is learning by simple induction, and the mechanism of such learning is conditioning. But this method is notoriously incapable of carrying us far in language. This is why, on the translational side, we are soon

driven to what I have called analytical hypotheses. The as yet
unknown innate structures, additional to mere quality space,
that are needed in language-learning, are needed specifically to
get the child over this great hump that lies beyond ostension,
or induction. If Chomsky's antiempiricism or antibehaviorism
says merely that conditioning is insufficient to explain language-
learning, then the doctrine is of a piece with my doctrine of the
indeterminacy of translation.

When I dismiss a definition of behaviorism that limits it to
conditioned response, am I simply extending the term to cover
everyone? Well, I do think of it as covering all reasonable men.
What matters, as I see it, is just the insistence upon couching
all criteria in observation terms. By observation terms I mean
terms that are or can be taught by ostension, and whose application in each particular case can therefore be checked intersubjectively. Not to cavil over the word 'behaviorism', perhaps
current usage would be best suited by referring to this orientation to observation simply as empiricism; but it is empiricism in a
distinctly modern sense, for it rejects the naïve mentalism that
typified the old empiricism. It does still condone the recourse
to introspection that Chomsky has spoken in favor of, but it
condones it as a means of arriving at conjectures or conclusions
only insofar as these can eventually be made sense of in terms
of external observation.

Empiricism of this modern sort, or behaviorism broadly so
called, comes of the old empiricism by a drastic externaliza-
tion. The old empiricist looked inward upon his ideas; the new
empiricist looks outward upon the social institution of language.
Ideas dwindle to meanings, seen as adjuncts of words. The old
inner-directed empiricists—Hobbes, Gassendi, Locke, and their
followers—had perforce to formulate their empiricist standard
by reference to ideas; and they did so by exalting sense impressions and scouting innate ideas. When empiricism is externalized,
on the other hand, the idea itself passes under a cloud; talk of
ideas comes to count as unsatisfactory except insofar as it can
be paraphrased into terms of dispositions to observable behavior.
Externalized empiricism or behaviorism sees nothing uncongenial
in the appeal to innate dispositions to overt behavior, innate
readiness for language-learning. What would be interesting and
valuable to find out, rather, is just what these endowments are
in fact like in detail.

9

❧ *The Limits of Knowledge*

Are there things that man can never know?

I'm going to be concerned less with giving a straight answer to this question than with examining the question and ringing changes on it. Some variants of the question admit of obvious, uninteresting answers. Obviously there are things that man *will* never know. Man will never know how many cars will have entered your city between now and midnight tonight. He will never know and never care. But he *could* know this number if he cared enough and had the foresight to make arrangements for keeping count of the cars.

The serious question, rather, is whether there are things that man *could* never know, however foresighted he might be in setting out observers and cameras and tape recorders and Geiger counters and other detectors.

Well, we have touched up our question a little, in its auxiliary verb. We are asking if there are things that man *could* never know. Next, the noun needs some attention: *things*. We talk of knowing *things?* What sort of things? Stones, trees, birds, bees? No; *things* is a lame word in this connection. When we ask whether there are things that man could never know we are really asking whether there are *questions* that man could never *answer*. It is not a question of things, it is a question of questions.

It is a question of questions, so it depends partly on language. To suppose there are things we can never know is to suppose, more precisely, that there are questions that we can ask in our language but that we could never answer. Now our language is

Broadcast on Radio Canada, January 29, 1973.

a very rich language, and perhaps it *is* capable of supplying questions that man could never answer. But before we try to settle that issue regarding our language, we will do well to gain some perspective by standing off and viewing a simpler situation: the situation of a poverty-stricken language.

Imagine, then, a people who have never risen to the theoretical physics of hypothetical particles, nor to set theory or other abstract reaches of mathematics. Their language is adequate to the empirical mechanics of observable bodies: adequate to the laws of the lever and the pendulum and falling bodies and the laws of motion. It is adequate also to reporting the concrete facts of human history, and adequate to what used to be called natural history: to describing the observable traits of plants and the observable behavior of animals.

These people are a practical lot, not very imaginative perhaps, but as alert and observant as you please, and pretty knowledgeable in their down-to-earth sort of way. And within their language are there any questions that man *could* not answer?

In a rather uninteresting sense, someone might argue still that there are such questions. It is a legalistic point, having to do with generalizations. Thus take the general statement 'All men are mortal'. There is a big logical difference between the question how many cars will enter your city between now and midnight, and the question whether all men are mortal. We *could*, if we wished, arrange for a conclusive answer to the question of the cars, an answer based directly on observation; we could man all points of access. But we could never arrange for a similarly conclusive answer to the mortality question, based similarly on direct observation. Even if we cared so much about the answer that we were prepared to increase our observations by resorting to experimentation, which I find a rather lugubrious expedient in this instance, still there would be a difficulty in checking all instances. We could not check on ourselves, and live to report an affirmative answer to the question.

Other generalizations present somewhat similar difficulties, if less sanguinary ones. We felt we *could* answer the question how many cars will enter before midnight, because of the feasibility of a stakeout. But if a general question covers indefinitely many cases, including cases too remote in the future to be observed by living man, or too remote in the past to have been observed, then clearly it is a question that we cannot and *could* not conclusively answer on the basis directly of observation. Now there will be plenty of questions of this sort, even in the modest language of the practical people that we are imagining. Just about any generality about the care and use of one or another sort of plant, or the behavior of one or another sort of animal, or the mechanics of rigid bodies, will be a generality whose instances can be observed only by sampling and never exhausted.

Must we then conclude that even in the limited language of our hypothetical practical tribe there are questions that men could not answer? Yes, we must so conclude if we are going to be as stiff-necked as all this about what to count as answers. But we are demanding too much. We can know something, in a reasonable sense of the word, without having checked every instance by direct observation. If we have done a reasonable lot of sampling of instances, or if we have a plausible notion of an underlying mechanism that would account for the truth of the general statement in question, then we may reasonably be said to know the statement to be true. Sometime we may be surprised by a counterinstance, and compelled to conclude that we had not known the statement to be true after all; we only thought we did. This, however, is a risk we must run.

So let us relax our standard of what counts as the ability to answer a question. Belief well grounded in observation is what should count. But then how firmly grounded should a belief be in order to count as answering a question? How shaky an answer shall we allow? No general way is known of measuring the firmness of a scientific hypothesis; and if a way were known of measuring the firmness, still how would we decide where to draw the line?

Even in the limited language of our imagined tribe it must be possible to ask questions about remote places and events, questions admitting only of the most tenuous answers after the ablest research. But this is uninteresting; it is not what one has in mind when he asks if there are things that men can never know. It is uninteresting because of the continuity. The questions about broad generalities or about remote places and events and the questions about current local events differ only in degree; some respond more generously to our investigations than others. I think it would be to no purpose to try to draw a line. When one asks if there are things that man can never know, he is really wondering whether some questions are unanswerable *in principle*. By this he means that no answer could gain any support whatever from even the ablest research. He means at least that much and perhaps more; the question should also be somehow basically unlike the questions that we know how to find answers for. This further requirement is of course hard to formulate satisfactorily; basic unlikeness is a vague idea. However, given this strenuous standard of what to count as an unanswerable question, I think we can say of the imagined tribe that these people can raise no unanswerable questions.

Now let us take leave of the imaginary tribe and move nearer home. As we move nearer home we move farther from observation. We move into a conceptual scheme of electrons, neutrons, and other hypothetical particles that can never be directly observed; a conceptual scheme also of kinky four-dimensional space-time, and of mathematical abstractions—sets, relations, functions, integers, ratios, irrational numbers, imaginary numbers, infinite numbers. None of these extras are observable. We already allowed our imaginary tribe a language that was adequate for reporting anything observable, and a good deal more; it was adequate also for expressing generalities about any matters that were individually observable. What then is all this extra apparatus of ours? Is it sheer mythmaking, unwarranted by observational evidence?

Paradoxically, the purpose of all this extra apparatus is simplification. We are out to systematize and integrate the testimony of our senses by devising laws that relate the observable phenomena systematically to other observable phenomena; and the most systematic network of relations for this purpose turns out to be a network that links all these phenomena up with a lot of additional, unobserved, hypothetical entities that are only assumed for the purpose of integrating the system.

The consequence is a rich theoretical language—rich enough, perhaps, to formulate questions that man could in principle never answer. For a while let us assume that it is, so as to go on from that thought to some further ones. Afterward I'll come back to that question.

Very well, then: granted that we in our language can formulate questions that man could in principle never answer, what are we to say of the imagined tribe that knows no such limits? We are simply to say, it would seem, that there were always these things that man could never know, but the imagined people were unable to formulate them because their language was too weak. On the other hand it might be objected that in putting the matter thus we are holding too parochially to the point of view of our own language. It might be objected that the low-level language was already adequate to all possible objective data, after all, and that the extra richness of our language was added only to facilitate the systematization of all possible data. It might thus be objected that when we say there are things man could never know, when we say there are questions man could in principle never answer, we are merely pointing to an effect of our own artifact.

This objection gains some support from a remarkable theorem of logic due to William Craig. Consider again our rich language of scientific theory and the low-level language of the imagined tribe. We may think of the low-level language as a part of the rich language. It is a part that stays closer to observable matters. The richness of the theoretical language serves the purpose, I just now suggested, of enabling us to formulate manageably simple laws relating observations to observations. But all we care about as output of the theory, let us suppose, is its empirical output: we care about those consequences, predictions for instance, that can be expressed in the low-level language. We formulate our observations in the low-level language, we combine them with theoretical laws somewhere up in the richer language, and from the combination we deduce consequences in the low-level language. There is takeoff, flight, and landing. Now what Craig shows is that the flight into theory is logically dispensable. He shows that if we can get anywhere by plane, so to speak, we can also get there by laboriously slogging through on the ground. He shows that if you have found a way of deducing a sentence of the low-level language from other low-level sentences together with some theoretical truths, you can then also find a way of deducing that same sentence from those same other low-level sentences together with some further merely low-level truths.

Craig shows explicitly how we can find such a ground route, once we have the air route. If the deduction of the sentence from other low-level sentences and the theoretical truths is written out explicitly in symbolic logic, he shows how to find some low-level truths that can be used in place of the theoretical ones. Craig's reasoning is quite general; it does not depend on details of the low-level language and the theoretical language nor on how we draw the line between them.

Psychologically, granted, the flight into theory is indispensable. We would not find our way across the ground but for the aerial reconnaissance. On the ground we cannot see the woods for the trees. Theory brings system; system is simplicity; and simplicity is psychologically imperative. Very well, our objector pursues: theory is our heuristic crutch, if I may descend from your soaring metaphor of flight to my limping metaphor of the crutch. So our rich language differs from the low-level language of the imagined tribe in having this heuristic crutch, this handy artifact. The objector concludes by repeating himself, saying once more that those purported questions that man could never answer are merely an effect of his own artifact.

Even our objector is bound to recognize that this heuristic aid has worked wonders. It has had man soaring, not limping. Man's power over nature is awesome, staggering. It is due to scientific theory, and would have been humanly, psychologically impossible within the narrower language of the imagined tribe. But this is by the way.

I have given our objector his fair share of program time. He would like us to believe, I suppose, that the atoms and elementary particles and the sets and numbers and functions are unreal; mere heuristic fictions. Is he right? If we are looking for questions that man could in principle never answer, perhaps we have a shining candidate right here: are the hypothetical particles of physics and the abstract objects of mathematics real, or mere heuristic fictions? It would seem indeed that man can never know. Everything observable, everything that could be available as evidence, is expressible in the low-level language which shuns these controversial entities. Moreover, in view of Craig's theorem, all the inferential connections can in principle be held to that low level too; it is only to make the inferences easier that we venture higher. We might say of hypothetical particles and mathematical objects what Voltaire said of God: that if they hadn't existed they would have had to be invented. Who is to say, then, whether they exist or were invented? Have we here reached the limit of knowledge, the unanswerable question?

I think not. If we subscribe to our physical theory and our mathematics, as indeed we do, then we thereby accept these particles and these mathematical objects as real; it would be an empty gesture meanwhile to cross our fingers as if to indicate that what we are saying doesn't count. And if, rather than subscribing to our physical theory and mathematics, we were to adhere to the low-level language, then the question of the reality of the particles and the mathematical objects would simply not be there; it could not be phrased.

We have to work within some conceptual scheme or other; we can switch schemes, but we cannot stand apart from all of them. It is meaningless, while working within a theory, to question the reality of its objects or the truth of its laws, unless in so doing we are thinking of abandoning the theory and adopting another.

Let us then resume our accustomed stance at last, within the evolving conceptual scheme that we take seriously. We are swarms of particles, swarms of medium density, making our filtered way through thinner swarms and moving erratically between other swarms as dense as ourselves or denser still. This, by our present lights, is how things are; we may learn better, but meanwhile we do what we can. Cozily ensconced then in these familiar old digs, let us consider again our original question about questions. Are there, from this point of view, things that man could never know? Are there questions man could in principle never answer?

Possible cases in mathematics come to mind. There is something called the continuum hypothesis, having to do with the comparative sizes of certain infinite classes. Kurt Gödel and Paul J. Cohen have proved that this hypothesis can be neither proved nor disproved on the basis of the existing codifications of accepted mathematical laws. Still, this is not a clearly unanswerable question. For remember the role of theoretical entities, mathematical and otherwise: they are extras that serve to fill in and smooth out and simplify the comprehensive world system by which, ultimately, we link phenomena to one another. Now there may in time emerge new simplicity considerations, new plausibility considerations, that can reasonably supplement our existing codifications of accepted mathematical laws. These added laws just might suffice in the end for proving or disproving the continuum hypothesis.

A different sort of mathematical case that comes to mind is the celebrated theorem, due also to Gödel, to the effect that there can never be a complete formal proof procedure for what is called elementary number theory. This modest-seeming branch of mathematics treats of nothing more recondite than the positive integers. Yet Gödel has proved that any axiom system is bound to be inadequate to it: bound to leave some truths of elementary number theory unprovable. Any axiom system for it will be incomplete, and so will any other method of explicit proof; I am having to leave my statement a bit vague, for otherwise the story is long. Now this is a remarkable and startling result. I haven't time to explain how startling or why. But does it point to unanswerable questions? It does not. No truths of elementary number theory are set apart by Gödel's theorem as unprovable. Rather, each axiom system or proof procedure will miss some of those truths; other proof procedures can cover those, or some of them, and miss others. As I already suggested in connection with the continuum hypothesis, plausibility considerations can augment existing codifications of accepted mathematical laws. Gödel's theorem shows that such augmentation can never yield any one finished system in which every truth of elementary number theory admits of proof. But it does not show that any one truth of elementary number theory is forever inaccessible.

Turning now to natural science, one thinks of Werner Heisenberg's principle of indeterminacy. There is a strict limit to the accuracy with which man can know the position and velocity of an elementary particle. The accuracy of position can be increased, beyond a certain point, only by sacrificing accuracy of velocity. Physicists tell us that this is a hard and fast limitation, a limitation in principle not to be surmounted by any manner of observation and experiment. Man *could* in principle not answer the question of the position and velocity of the particle, except up to the prescribed band of tolerance. Here, then, is a really good example of the limits of knowledge?

New discoveries might, of course, lead to revisions of physical theory and upset Heisenberg's indeterminacy principle. But even short of such an event, opinion is divided regarding the interpretation of the principle. Some hold that the particle has indeed its exact position and velocity, and that these are in principle inscrutable. Those physicists, then, acknowledge that we have here a straightforward example of the limits of knowledge. Other physicists hold that the particle simply has no exact position and velocity. This claim raises obvious logical difficulties, and some physicists have gone so far as to revise logical theory to accommodate them.

One would hope for a less drastic remedy, but at any rate the motive is clear: there is a reluctance to assign meaning to strictly unanswerable questions. Questions, let us remember, are in language. Language is learned by people, from people, only in relation, ultimately, to observable circumstances of utterance. The relation of language to observation is often very devious, but observation is finally all there is for language to be anchored to. If a question could in principle never be answered, then, one feels that language has gone wrong; language has parted its moorings, and the question has no meaning. On this philosophy, of course, our central question has a sweeping answer. The question was whether there are things man could never know. The question was whether there are questions—meaningful questions—that man could in principle never answer. On this philosophy, the answer to this question of questions is *no*.

✥ *Necessary Truth*

If people thought that very little of what went on in the world happened by necessity, then surely they would have little occasion to use the adverb 'necessarily'. But the adverb is in fact frequently heard. So people must think that quite a lot happens by necessity.

But if people thought that almost everything that happened at all happened by necessity, then again they would have little occasion to use the adverb 'necessarily'; mostly it would go without saying. So people must think that while much of what goes on happens by necessity, much of it also does not. People must have some criterion which they keep using to sort the passing states and events into some that happened by necessity and others that happened without necessity. Otherwise the adverb 'necessarily' would not be heard so often. Or so it would seem.

Actually, of course, this is wrong. People have no such criterion. They would be hard put to it to classify any of the passing events outright as necessary or otherwise. For the fact is that the adverb 'necessarily', as it is most often used, does not mark a present or past event or state outright as necessary.

Future ones, yes; often we represent a future event or state as necessary, or not, according as we have or have not good reason to expect it. We say, "Surely she will worry"; that is, necessarily. We say, "The inhabitants are bound to be hostile"; they will

A Forum Lecture, broadcast by the Voice of America in 1963 and issued as one of a series of pamphlets of that organization in 1964.

necessarily be hostile. We ask, "Will it break?" and are told, "Not necessarily."

I have had to allow in these examples for a certain vernacular twist: generally 'necessarily' sounds well after a 'not' or 'then', whereas such synonyms as 'surely' and 'bound to' and 'must' are often preferred elsewhere.

These necessity idioms are not indeed confined to the future. But when they enter the present and past, they still tend to connote conjecture or inference; thus "As mayor he must have enriched himself"—necessarily did—"for look at his earlier record on the school board." It is paradoxical that these strong words, 'necessarily' and its synonyms, are used mainly where we are less than sure of the facts. What we really know we usually just affirm, without the intensive.

Should we in general dismiss the adverb 'necessarily', then, as a mere rhetorical device that people use to cover their uncertainty? No, there is a case for another account. To make it I shall turn to a more trivial example. Someone says, "Surely it has spots," "Necessarily it will have spots," when told that he is about to be shown a leopard. Now, instead of viewing the adverb 'necessarily' as governing outright the simple prediction of spots, we can understand it as governing, implicitly, the conditional sentence as a whole: "If it is a leopard, it has spots". In attributing a quality of necessity to this whole conditional compound, there is no air of paradox, certainly, nor of rhetorical subterfuge.

Something of the same may be done for the other future-tense examples. When we say, "The inhabitants are bound to be hostile," we are basing our prediction on something—perhaps the recent burning of their granary. So, instead of associating the necessity with the inhabitants' hostility outright, we can understand it as attaching to the conditional sentence as a whole: "Necessarily, if their granary was lately burned, the inhabitants will be hostile." Again, when we ask, "Will it break?" we mean, "If I use it, will it break?", so the reassuring answer, "Not necessarily," can be seen as applying not to the mere breaking but to the conditional sentence as a whole, as if to say, "It is not necessarily true that if you use it it will break."

This treatment works not only for the future-tense examples but also, of course, for the conjectures regarding the present and past. "As mayor he must have enriched himself": we may take the necessity as applying not to this conjectured self-enrichment as such, but to the whole implicit conditional, "If when on the school board he did thus and so, then also as mayor he will have enriched himself."

In a word the point is, in all cases, to seek the necessity not in the separate matters of fact but in the connections between them. No wonder people would be hard put to it to classify passing events as necessary or otherwise; it is a question rather of connections.

The next question is, "What does it take to qualify a connection as necessary?" Here we do well to return again to our trivial example of the leopard. Some leopard is announced, and we expect spots; what is the connection? Clearly, a generality: all leopards have spots.

In this I think there is the germ of an explanation of the less trivial examples as well. I submit that whenever one says, 'Necessarily if *p* then *q*', he has at least dimly in mind some fairly dependable generalization under which his particular 'if *p* then *q*' can be subsumed as a case. The leopard example is trivial only because there the relevant generalization is so easily recognized: Why should this newly heralded leopard necessarily have spots? Because they all have spots. Other examples, such as the one about the hostility of the natives, differ from the leopard example only in that the relevant generalization is less clearly hinted in the phrasing of the sentences. "Always or usually, when you burn their granary, people turn hostile"; the speaker is bound to have had some such generality in mind, and this it is that lends the force to his 'necessarily' when he says of his particular instance that necessarily, if *their* granary was lately burned, *these* inhabitants will be hostile.

A cautionary remark of a rather subtle kind is called for at this point. We must not suppose that a man is entitled to apply 'necessarily' to an assertion so long merely as he thinks there is *some* general truth that subsumes it. Thus, suppose I have lost my key. Then immediately we have this trivial generalization: It is true of everyone *x* without exception that if *x* is I, *x* lost his key. Just as on the strength of all leopards having spots we say that necessarily the upcoming leopard will have spots, so on the strength of this new generalization we might expect to be able to say that necessarily, I being indeed I, I lost my key. This line would allow us to attribute necessity to anything, however casual, that we are prepared to affirm at all.

I am therefore not suggesting that 'Necessarily if p then q' can be defined to mean 'There is a true generalization whereof an instance is that if p then q'. It is a matter rather of the speaker's having antecedently in mind some one actual generalization whose truth is, in his view, independent of particulars of the case in hand. It is this feeling, I suggest, that would normally prompt the speaker to attach a 'Necessarily' to his 'if p then q'. He might rather have attached 'So, in particular' if his antecedent generalization had actually been antecedently spoken.

What I have done thus far may be summed up as two steps. First, I have argued that the adverb 'necessarily' applies only by ellipsis to particular events or states, and properly rather to whole conditional connections: 'Necessarily if p then q.' Secondly, I have presented this 'necessarily' in turn, the 'necessarily' of 'Necessarily if p then q', as simply an allusion to some presently more or less hinted regularity, 'All A are B', which subsumes the particular link 'if p then q' as a case.

The doctrine that necessity is no more than regularity was expounded by David Hume more than two centuries ago. His, indeed, was the battle cry, "There are no necessary connections of matters of fact." He meant, of course, that there are none if 'necessary' is taken as claiming more than generality, or regularity. I am not taking it as claiming more.

One place in the philosophy of science where the idea of necessity comes in for special attention is in analyzing the so-called disposition terms, such as 'soluble'. To say of a particular lump of stuff that it is soluble in water is, as Carnap has stressed, to say more about it than just that whenever it is in water it dissolves. For perhaps this particular lump will never be in water. By default, then, even if the lump is quartz, it would be true that whenever the lump is in water it dissolves; but we cannot on that ground call it soluble in water. For a lump to be soluble we must be able to say of it that if it *were* in water it *would* dissolve; we need an 'if-then' connection governed by necessity, and by a necessity that goes beyond mere generality over time. To say merely that the lump dissolves at each time that it *is* in water is too weak.

Advances in chemistry eventually redeem the solubility idea, but only in terms of a full-blown theory. We come to understand just what there is about the submicroscopic form and composition of a solid that enables water to dissolve it. Thenceforward, solubility can simply be equated to these explanatory traits. When we say of a lump that it would necessarily dissolve if in water, we can be understood as attributing to the lump those supposedly enumerated details of submicroscopic structure— those explanatory traits with which we are imagining solubility to have been newly equated. A chemist can tell you what they are. I cannot.

Surely, it will be felt, something is wrong here. I seem to be talking intelligibly of solubility, yet by this account it is only the chemist, and neither you nor I, who knows its defining traits. Moreover, the term was already used just as freely and easily before even the chemists had arrived at those explanatory traits.

Still, I think we are on the right track. Early and late, solubility has been meant to be some causal agency or mechanism or arrangement in the lump, however little understood. From the start of a scientific attitude anyway, the term has been a sort of promissory note which one might hope eventually to redeem in terms of an explicit account of the working mechanism. What kind of account of a mechanism might pass as explanatory depends somewhat, of course, upon the general situation in science at the time. Nowadays, in general, one settles for an account in terms of the arrangement and movement of molecules, or of smaller particles when finer texture is relevant.

And meanwhile the promissory character of the unredeemed solubility idea was never an obstacle to glib use of the term. For, this much one is assured of early and late: whenever a soluble thing is in water it does dissolve. We intend in advance that solubility consist precisely in those explanatory traits of structure and composition, however ill-pictured or unpictured at the moment, that do make things dissolve when in water.

A disposition term that contrasts interestingly with 'soluble' is 'intelligent'. Solubility is the capacity to dissolve in water; intelligence is the capacity to learn, or to solve problems. Whereas chemists have redeemed the solubility idea by uncovering the explanatory traits, the intelligence idea is still as unredeemed as can be. We do not even know whether to seek the explanatory traits in the chemistry of the nerve cells or in the topology of the nerve net or in both or somewhere else. Intelligence today is where solubility was centuries ago. Still I think it is a promissory note. I do not think we would use the word 'intelligent' if we did not think there was an unidentified but some day identifiable causal agency or mechanism that sets one man above another in learning and in the solving of problems.

This account of disposition terms is not to deny that 'x is soluble' means that if x were in water it would dissolve. This equation is still good. Accordingly what I proceeded to say about disposition terms serves, insofar as it illuminates them, to illuminate also the subjunctive conditional idiom itself: 'If x were treated thus and so, it would do such and such'. This even is the general idiom for attributing dispositions; whether a single word like 'soluble' or 'intelligent' happens also to exist for the disposition is immaterial.

In general, when we say 'If x were treated thus and so, it would do such and such', we are attributing to x some theoretical explanatory trait or cluster of traits. Typically these would be traits of microscopic structure or substance. Sometimes they are analytically describable in all explicitness, by specialists if not by us, as in the case of solubility. Sometimes they are envisioned only as some day describable.

Such a conditional sentence may or may not flaunt the adverb 'necessarily'; in any event the subjunctive form connotes it. Now altogether the uses of the necessary conditional are varied and unsystematic. But this use, for imputing dispositions, is an important one among them.

Another use was seen in the example of the leopard and the spots, which so neatly fitted Hume's theory of necessity as generality. Now the conditional as used to impute dispositions may be said, in a sense, to come under Hume's theory too. If this lump were in water, it would dissolve; where is the underlying generality? It is in the explanatory trait which is solubility itself; *everything* that has that subtle trait of microstructure dissolves when in water.

In each of the necessity constructions, even the leopard example, the speaker has some one line of generalization in mind and not another. In the leopard example we easily guess: it is a question of all leopards. In the example of the inhabitants' being hostile we could not guess, but had to be told that the speaker was generalizing over peoples whose granaries were burned. And, in the necessity constructions that impute dispositions, the generality lies along some known or posited explanatory trait.

Thus the necessity constructions that impute dispositions do not depart from the Humean pattern. They turn, still, on generality. But they turn on theory, too, precisely because they fix upon explanatory traits for their domains of generality.

The uses of 'necessarily' that we have been considering up to now might loosely be spoken of as physical or natural necessity, as against the narrower notion of *logical* or *mathematical* necessity. A truth that might be cited rather under this latter category is that momentum is proportional to velocity. This might be said to be logically or mathematically necessary on the ground that the word 'momentum' is itself defined simply as short for 'mass times velocity'.

But now imagine a physicist with some unexpected experimental findings to provide for. They conflict with his physical theory. There is no specific point in his theory that they conflict with, for observations do not conflict with theoretical statements one by one. But they show that the theory taken conjunctively is false, and must be changed at one point or another to inactivate the false prediction. And now suppose the physicist hits upon a particularly neat repair, which involves revising slightly the law that momentum is proportional to velocity; he makes momentum proportional instead to, say, velocity divided by one minus the ratio of that velocity to the speed of light, which deviates negligibly for most purposes.

Will his colleagues protest that he is flying in the face of logical necessity? Will they protest that he is departing from the definition of 'momentum' and so depriving his theory of meaning? Will they protest that he is redefining momentum and so merely playing with words? I think they will do none of these things. His modification of the proportionality of momentum to velocity will strike them in no other way than a modification of any other time-honored proposition of physics might strike them. And this, I feel, is as it should be.

In supposing the contrary, we unduly exalt the act of definition. There are two ways in which we may learn a theoretical term: through context, by learning a network of laws in which the term occurs, and through definition, by learning what phrase to substitute the term for. But this difference may best be seen merely as a difference in the history of one's learning, and not as making for an enduring difference in status between the variously interlocking laws of the theory itself.

Thus, I am inclined to dismiss the idea that a special category of necessity, the logical or mathematical, is represented by the law that momentum is proportional to velocity. And my reason is that I attach no relevance to the status of definition.

The statement that momentum is proportional to velocity was supposed to be mathematically necessary because that definition, when expanded, turned the statement into a mathematical triviality. It may be well, then, if my skepticism is over the definition, to forget the definition and turn our attention to the mathematical triviality itself: "Mass times velocity is proportional to velocity." How is *this* for a case of mathematical necessity?

Admirable, certainly. But is even this necessity somehow different in kind from what can be attributed to ordinary truths of physical theory or other natural sciences? A long-standing doctrine says that it is; and I should like to conclude my remarks by questioning that doctrine. It depends, I think, upon a terminological boundary between physics and mathematics.

Thus, let us begin by supposing that we have somehow drawn a boundary across the face of physics, at some points perhaps quite arbitrary, so as to separate a more speculative and theoretical half of physics from a more experimental and empirical half. Let us call the one side theoretical physics and the other experimental physics. Now it strikes me that the contrasts that people are prone to draw between pure mathematics such as arithmetic, on the one hand, and physics on the other, can be drawn just as well between theoretical physics and experimental physics.

People say that physics is about the world, that it has empirical content, while arithmetic and other parts of pure mathematics do not. They grant that these mathematical disciplines have their motivation and their utility in the applications to physics and other natural sciences, but they call this a matter only of motivation and application, not content. Now why can we not say precisely this of theoretical physics, in relation to experimental? Certainly, it has its motivation and utility in applications to experimental physics; but why not say that this again is a matter only of motivation and not of content? I think our not saying this is an accident of nomenclature. Theoretical and experimental physics are both called physics; we see them as part of a single systematic enterprise, connecting ultimately with observation. Pure mathematics, on the other hand, partly because of its additional utility in natural sciences other than physics, is segregated in name; so we do not see it as just a further part of a broader systematic enterprise, still connecting ultimately with the observations of experimental physics and other natural sciences.

Boundaries between disciplines are useful for deans and librarians, but let us not overestimate them—the boundaries. When we abstract from them, we see all of science—physics, biology, economics, mathematics, logic, and the rest—as a single sprawling system, loosely connected in some portions but disconnected nowhere. Parts of it—logic, arithmetic, game theory, theoretical parts of physics—are farther from the observational or experimental edge than other parts. But the overall system, with all its parts, derives its aggregate empirical content from that edge; and the theoretical parts are good only as they contribute in their varying degrees of indirectness to the systematizing of that content.

In principle, therefore, I see no higher or more austere necessity than natural necessity; and in natural necessity, or our attributions of it, I see only Hume's regularities, culminating here and there in what passes for an explanatory trait or the promise of it.

11

❧ *Truth by Convention*

The less a science has advanced, the more its terminology tends to rest on an uncritical assumption of mutual understanding. With increase of rigor this basis is replaced piecemeal by the introduction of definitions. The interrelationships recruited for these definitions gain the status of analytic principles; what was once regarded as a theory about the world becomes reconstrued as a convention of language. Thus it is that some flow from the theoretical to the conventional is an adjunct of progress in the logical foundations of any science. The concept of simultaneity at a distance affords a stock example of such development: in supplanting the uncritical use of this phrase by a definition, Einstein so chose the definitive relationship as to verify conventionally the previously paradoxical principle of the absoluteness of the speed of light. But whereas the physical sciences are generally recognized as capable only of incomplete evolution in this direction, and as destined to retain always a non-conventional kernel of doctrine, developments of the past few decades have led to a widespread conviction that logic and mathematics are purely analytic or conventional. It is less the purpose of the present inquiry to question the validity of this contrast than to question its sense.

First published in O. H. Lee, ed., *Philosophical Essays for A. N. White-head* (New York: Longmans, 1936). It appears in H. Feigl and W. Sellars, eds., *Readings in Philosophical Analysis* (New York: Appleton, 1949), and in P. Benacerraf and H. Putnam, eds., *Readings in the Philosophy of Mathematics* (Englewood, N.J.: Prentice-Hall, 1964). Some corrections that I made in it for the latter anthology are incorporated here and a few slight further ones as well.

I

A definition, strictly, is a convention of notational abbreviation.[1] A *simple* definition introduces some specific expression, e.g., 'kilometer', or '*e*', called the *definiendum*, as arbitrary shorthand for some complex expression, e.g., 'a thousand meters' or 'lim
$\underset{n \to \infty}{}$

$(1 + \dfrac{1}{n})$"', called the *definiens*. A *contextual* definition sets up indefinitely many mutually analogous pairs of definienda and definientia according to some general scheme; an example is the definition whereby expressions of the form $\dfrac{\text{'sin} - - -\text{'}}{\cos - - -}$ are abbreviated as 'tan – – –'. From a formal standpoint the signs thus introduced are wholly arbitrary; all that is required of a definition is that it be theoretically immaterial, i.e., that the shorthand which it introduces admit in every case of unambiguous elimination in favor of the antecedent longhand.[2]

Functionally a definition is not a premise to theory, but a license for rewriting theory by putting definiens for definiendum or vice versa. By allowing such replacements a definition transmits truth: it allows true statements to be translated into new statements which are true by the same token. Given the truth of the statement 'The altitude of Kibo exceeds six thousand meters', the definition of 'kilometer' makes for the truth of the statement 'The altitude of Kibo exceeds six kilometers'; given the truth of the statement $\dfrac{\text{'sin } \pi}{\cos \pi} = \dfrac{\sin \pi}{\cos \pi}\text{'}$, of which logic assures us in its earliest pages, the contextual definition cited above makes for the truth of the statement $\text{'tan } \pi = \dfrac{\sin \pi}{\cos \pi}\text{'}$. In each case the statement inferred through the definition is true only because it is shorthand for another statement which was true independently of the definition. Considered

---

[1] Cf. Russell, *Principles of Mathematics*, p. 429.

[2] From the present point of view a contextual definition may be recursive, but can then count among its definienda only those expressions in which the argument of recursion has a constant value, since otherwise the requirement of eliminability is violated. Such considerations are of little consequence, however, since any recursive definition can be turned into a direct one by purely logical methods. Cf. Carnap, *Logische Syntax*, pp. 23, 79.

in isolation from all doctrine, including logic, a definition is incapable of grounding the most trivial statement; even 'tan $\pi = \frac{\sin \pi}{\cos \pi}$,' is a definitional transformation of an antecedent self-identity, rather than a spontaneous consequence of the definition.

What is loosely called a logical consequence of definitions is therefore more exactly describable as a logical truth definitionally abbreviated: a statement which becomes a truth of logic when definienda are replaced by definientia. In this sense 'tan $\pi = \frac{\sin \pi}{\cos \pi}$,' is a logical consequence of the contextual definition of the tangent.

Whatever may be agreed upon as the exact scope of logic, we may expect definitional abbreviations of logical truths to be reckoned as logical rather than extra-logical truths. This being the case, the preceding conclusion shows logical consequences of definitions to be themselves truths of logic. To claim that mathematical truths are conventional in the sense of following logically from definitions is therefore to claim that mathematics is part of logic. The latter claim does not represent an arbitrary extension of the term 'logic' to include mathematics; agreement as to what belongs to logic and what belongs to mathematics is supposed at the outset, and it is then claimed that definitions of mathematical expressions can so be framed on the basis of logical ones that all mathematical truths become abbreviations of logical ones.

Although signs introduced by definition are formally arbitrary, more than such arbitrary notational convention is involved in questions of definability; otherwise any expression might be said to be definable on the basis of any expressions whatever. When we speak of definability, or of finding a definition for a given sign, we have in mind some traditional usage of the sign antecedent to the definition in question. To be satisfactory in this sense a definition of the sign not only must fulfill the formal requirement of unambiguous eliminability, but must also conform to the traditional usage in question. For such conformity it is necessary and sufficient that every context of the sign which was true and every context which was false under traditional usage be construed by the definition as an abbreviation of some other statement which is correspondingly true or false under the established meanings of its signs. Thus when definitions of mathematical expressions on the basis of logical ones are said to have been framed, what is meant is that definitions have been set up whereby every statement which so involves those mathematical expressions as to be recognized traditionally as true, or as false, is construed as an abbreviation of another correspondingly true or false statement which lacks those mathematical expressions and exhibits only logical expressions in their stead.[3]

An expression will be said to occur *vacuously* in a given statement if its replacement therein by any and every other grammatically admissible expression leaves the truth or falsehood of the statement unchanged. Thus for any statement containing some expressions vacuously there is a class of statements, describable as *vacuous variants* of the given statement, which are like it in point of truth or falsehood, like it also in point of a certain skeleton of symbolic make-up, but diverse in exhibiting all grammatically possible variations upon the vacuous constituents of the given statement. An expression will be said to occur *essentially* in a statement if it occurs in all the vacuous variants of the statement, i.e., if it forms part of the aforementioned skeleton. (Note that though an expression occur non-vacuously in a statement it may fail of essential occurrence because some of its parts occur vacuously in the statement.)

Now let S be a truth, let the expressions E_i occur vacuously in S, and let the statements S_j be the vacuous variants of S. Thus the S_j will likewise be true. On the sole basis of the expressions belonging to a certain class α, let us frame a definition for one of the expressions F occurring in S outside the E_i. S and the S_i thereby become abbreviations of certain statements S' and S'_i which exhibit only members of α instead of those occurrences of F, but which remain so related that the S'_i are all the results of replacing the E_i in S' by any other grammatically admissible expressions. Now since our definition of F is supposed to conform to usage, S' and the S'_i will, like S and the S_i, be uniformly true; hence the S'_i will be vacuous variants of S', and the occurrences of the E_i in S' will be vacuous. The definition thus makes S an

---

[3] Note that an expression is said to be defined, in terms, e.g., of logic, not only when it is a single sign whose elimination from a context in favor of logical expressions is accomplished by a single application of one definition, but also when it is a complex expression whose elimination calls for successive application of many definitions.

abbreviation of a truth S' which, like S, involves the E_i vacuously, but which differs from S in exhibiting only members of α instead of the occurrences of F outside the E_i. Now it is obvious that an expression cannot occur essentially in a statement if it occurs only within expressions which occur vacuously in the statement; consequently F, occurring in S' as it does only within the E_i if at all, does not occur essentially in S'; members of α occur essentially in its stead. Thus if we take F as any non-member of α occurring essentially in S, and repeat the above reasoning for each such expression, we see that, through definitions of all such expressions in terms of members of α, S becomes an abbreviation of a truth S'' involving only members of α essentially.

Thus if in particular we take α as the class of all logical expressions, the above tells us that if logical definitions be framed for all non-logical expressions occurring essentially in the true statement S, S becomes an abbreviation of a truth S'' involving only logical expressions essentially. But if S'' involves only logical expressions essentially, and hence remains true when everything except that skeleton of logical expressions is changed in all grammatically possible ways, then S'' depends for its truth upon those logical constituents alone, and is thus a truth of logic. It is therefore established that if all non-logical expressions occurring essentially in a true statement S be given definitions on the basis solely of logic, then S becomes an abbreviation of a truth S'' of logic. In particular, then, if all mathematical expressions be defined in terms of logic, all truths involving only mathematical and logical expressions essentially become definitional abbreviations of truths of logic.

Now a mathematical truth, for example, 'Smith's age plus Brown's equals Brown's age plus Smith's', may contain non-logical, non-mathematical expressions. Still any such mathematical truth, or another whereof it is a definitional abbreviation, will consist of a skeleton of mathematical or logical expressions filled in with non-logical, non-mathematical expressions all of which occur vacuously. Every mathematical truth either is a truth in which only mathematical and logical expressions occur essentially, or is a definitional abbreviation of such a truth. Hence, granted definitions of all mathematical expressions in terms of logic, the preceding conclusion shows that all mathemat-

ical truths become definitional abbreviations of truths of logic—
therefore truths of logic in turn. For the thesis that mathematics
is logic it is thus sufficient that all mathematical notation be
defined on the basis of logical notation.

If on the other hand some mathematical expressions resist
definition on the basis of logical ones, then every mathematical
truth containing such recalcitrant expressions must contain them
only inessentially, or be a definitional abbreviation of a truth
containing such expressions only inessentially, if all mathematics
is to be logic: for though a logical truth may involve non-logical
expressions, it or some other logical truth whereof it is an
abbreviation must involve only logical expressions essentially. It
is of this alternative that those[4] avail themselves who regard
mathematical truths, insofar as they depend upon non-logical
notions, as elliptical for hypothetical statements containing as
tacit hypotheses all the postulates of the branch of mathematics
in question. Thus, suppose the geometrical terms 'sphere' and
'includes' to be undefined on the basis of logical expressions, and
suppose all further geometrical expressions defined on the basis of
logical expressions together with 'sphere' and 'includes', as with
Huntington. Let Huntington's postulates for (Euclidean) geometry, and all the theorems, be expanded by thoroughgoing replacement of definienda by definientia, so that they come to contain
only logical expressions and 'sphere' and 'includes', and let the
conjunction of the thus expanded postulates be represented as
'Hunt (sphere, includes)'. Then, where 'Φ (sphere, includes)' is
any of the theorems, similarly expanded into primitive terms, the
point of view under consideration is that 'Φ (sphere, includes)',
insofar as it is conceived as a mathematical truth, is to be
construed as an ellipsis for 'If Hunt (sphere, includes) then Φ
(sphere, includes)'. Since 'Φ (sphere, includes)' is a logical
consequence of Huntington's postulates, the above hypothetical
statement is a truth of logic; it involves the expressions 'sphere'
and 'includes' inessentially, in fact vacuously, since the logical
deducibility of the theorems from the postulates is independent of
the meanings of 'sphere' and 'includes' and survives the replacement of those expressions by any other grammatically admissible
expressions whatever. Since, granted the fitness of Huntington's

---

[4] E.g., Russell, *Principles*, pp. 429f; Behmann, pp. 8–10.

postulates, all and only those geometrical statements are truths of geometry which are logical consequences in this fashion of 'Hunt (sphere, includes)', all geometry becomes logic when interpreted in the above manner as a conventional ellipsis for a body of hypothetical statements.

But if, as a truth of mathematics, 'Φ (sphere, includes)' is short for 'If Hunt (sphere, includes) then Φ (sphere, includes)', still there remains, as part of this expanded statement, the original statement 'Φ (sphere, includes)'; this remains as a presumably true statement within some body of doctrine, say for the moment "non-mathematical geometry," even if the title of mathematical truth be restricted to the entire hypothetical statement in question. The body of all such hypothetical statements, describable as the "theory of deduction of non-mathematical geometry," is of course a part of logic; but the same is true of any "theory of deduction of sociology," "theory of deduction of Greek mythology," etc., which we might construct in parallel fashion with the aid of any set of postulates suited to sociology or to Greek mythology. The point of view toward geometry which is under consideration thus reduces merely to an exclusion of geometry from mathematics, a relegation of geometry to the status of sociology or Greek mythology; the labeling of the "theory of deduction of non-mathematical geometry" as "mathematical geometry" is a verbal *tour de force* which is equally applicable in the case of sociology or Greek mythology. To incorporate mathematics into logic by regarding all recalcitrant mathematical truths as elliptical hypothetical statements is thus in effect merely to restrict the term 'mathematics' to exclude those recalcitrant branches. But we are not interested in renaming. Those disciplines, geometry and the rest, which have traditionally been grouped under mathematics are the objects of the present discussion, and it is with the doctrine that mathematics in this sense is logic that we are here concerned.[5]

Discarding this alternative and returning, then, we see that if some mathematical expressions resist definition on the basis of logical ones, mathematics will reduce to logic only if, under a literal reading and without the gratuitous annexation of hypotheses, every mathematical truth contains (or is an abbreviation of

[5] Obviously the foregoing discussion has no bearing upon postulate method as such, nor upon Huntington's work.

one which contains) such recalcitrant expressions only inessentially if at all. But a mathematical expression sufficiently troublesome to have resisted trivial contextual definition in terms of logic can hardly be expected to occur thus idly in all its mathematical contexts. It would thus appear that for the tenability of the thesis that mathematics is logic it is not only sufficient but also necessary that all mathematical expressions be capable of definition on the basis solely of logical ones.

Though in framing logical definitions of mathematical expressions the ultimate objective be to make all mathematical truths logical truths, attention is not to be confined to mathematical and logical truths in testing the conformity of the definitions to usage. Mathematical expressions belong to the general language, and they are to be so defined that all statements containing them, whether mathematical truths, historical truths, or falsehoods under traditional usage, come to be construed as abbreviations of other statements which are correspondingly true or false. The definition introducing 'plus' must be such that the mathematical truth 'Smith's age plus Brown's equals Brown's age plus Smith's' becomes an abbreviation of a logical truth, as observed earlier; but it must also be such that 'Smith's age plus Brown's age equals Jones' age' becomes an abbreviation of a statement which is empirically true or false in conformity with the county records and the traditional usage of 'plus'. A definition which fails in this latter respect is no less Pickwickian than one which fails in the former; in either case nothing is achieved beyond the transient pleasure of a verbal recreation.

But for these considerations, contextual definitions of any mathematical expressions whatever could be framed immediately in purely logical terms, on the basis of any set of postulates adequate to the branch of mathematics in question. Thus, consider again Huntington's systematization of geometry. It was remarked that, granted the fitness of Huntington's postulates, a statement will be a truth of geometry if and only if it is logically deducible from 'Hunt (sphere, includes)' without regard to the meanings of 'sphere' and 'includes'. Thus 'Φ(sphere, includes)' will be a truth of geometry if and only if the following is a truth of logic: 'If α is any class and R any relation such that Hunt (α, R), then $\Phi(\alpha, R)$'. For 'sphere' and 'includes' we might then adopt the following contextual definition: Where '---' is any

statement containing 'α' or 'R' or both, let the statement 'If
α is any class and R any relation such that Hunt (α, R), then
---' be abbreviated as that expression which is got from
'---' by putting 'sphere' for 'α' and 'includes' for 'R' throughout.
(In the case of a compound statement involving 'sphere' and
'includes', this definition does not specify whether it is the entire statement or each of its constituent statements that is to be
accounted as shorthand in the described fashion; but this ambiguity can be eliminated by stipulating that the convention
apply only to whole contexts.) 'Sphere' and 'includes' thus receive contextual definition in terms exclusively of logic, for any
statement containing one or both of those expressions is construed by the definition as an abbreviation of a statement containing only logical expressions (plus whatever expressions the
original statement may have contained other than 'sphere' and
'includes'). The definition satisfies past usage of 'sphere' and
'includes' to the extent of verifying all truths and falsifying all
falsehoods of geometry; all those statements of geometry which
are true, and only those, become abbreviations of truths of logic.

The same procedure could be followed in any other branch of
mathematics, with the help of a satisfactory set of postulates for
the branch. Thus nothing further would appear to be wanting for
the thesis that mathematics is logic. And the royal road runs
beyond that thesis, for the described method of logicizing a
mathematical discipline can be applied likewise to any non-
mathematical theory. But the whole procedure rests on failure to
conform the definitions to usage; what is logicized is not the
intended subject matter. It is readily seen, e.g., that the suggested
contextual definition of 'sphere' and 'includes', though transforming purely geometrical truths and falsehoods respectively into
logical truths and falsehoods, transforms certain empirical truths
into falsehoods and vice versa. Consider, e.g., the true statement
'A baseball is roughly a sphere', more rigorously 'The whole of a
baseball, except for a certain very thin, irregular peripheral
layer, constitutes a sphere'. According to the contextual definition, this statement is an abbreviation for the following: 'If α is
any class and R any relation such that Hunt (α, R), then the
whole of a baseball, except for a thin peripheral layer, constitutes
an [a member of] α'. This tells us that the whole of a baseball,
except for a thin peripheral layer, belongs to every class α for

which a relation R can be found such that Huntington's postulates are true of α and R. Now it happens that 'Hunt (α, includes)' is true not only when α is taken as the class of all spheres, but also when α is restricted to the class of spheres a foot or more in diameter;[6] yet the whole of a baseball, except for a thin peripheral layer, can hardly be said to constitute a sphere a foot or more in diameter. The statement is therefore false, whereas the preceding statement, supposedly an abbreviation of this one, was true under ordinary usage of words. The thus logicized rendering of any other discipline can be shown in analogous fashion to yield the sort of discrepancy observed just now for geometry, provided only that the postulates of the discipline admit, like those of geometry, of alternative applications; and such multiple applicability is to be expected of any postulate set.[7]

Definition of mathematical notions on the basis of logical ones is thus a more arduous undertaking than would appear from a consideration solely of the truths and falsehoods of pure mathematics. Viewed *in vacuo*, mathematics is trivially reducible to logic through erection of postulate systems into contextual definitions; but *"cette science n'a pas uniquement pour objet de contempler éternellement son propre nombril."*[8] When mathematics is recognized as capable of use, and as forming an integral part of general language, the definition of mathematical notions in terms of logic becomes a task whose completion, if theoretically possible at all, calls for mathematical genius of a high order. It was primarily to this task that Whitehead and Russell addressed themselves in their *Principia Mathematica*. They adopt a meager logical language as primitive, and on its basis alone they undertake to endow mathematical expressions with definitions which conform to usage in the full sense described above: definitions which not only reduce mathematical truths and falsehoods to logical ones, but reduce *all* statements, containing the mathematical expressions in question, to equivalent statements involving logical expressions instead of the mathe-

[6] Cf. Huntington, p. 540.

[7] Note that a postulate set is superfluous if it *demonstrably* admits of one and only one application: for it then embodies an adequate defining property for each of its constituent primitive terms. Cf. Tarski, "Einige methodologische Untersuchungen," Satz 2.

[8] Poincaré, p. 199.

matical ones. Within *Principia* the program has been advanced to
such a point as to suggest that no fundamental difficulties stand
in the way of completing the process. The foundations of
arithmetic are developed in *Principia*,' and therewith those
branches of mathematics are accommodated which, like analysis
and theory of number, spring from arithmetic. Abstract algebra
proceeds readily from the relation theory of *Principia*. Only
geometry remains untouched, and this field can be brought into
line simply by identifying n-dimensional figures with those n-
adic arithmetical relations ("equations in n variables") with
which they are correlated through analytic geometry.[9] Some
question Whitehead and Russell's reduction of mathematics to
logic,[10] on grounds for whose exposition and criticism there is not
space; the thesis that all mathematics reduces to logic is,
however, substantiated by *Principia* to a degree satisfactory to
most of us. There is no need here to adopt a final stand in the
matter.

If for the moment we grant that all mathematics is thus
definitionally constructible from logic, then mathematics becomes true by convention in a relative sense: mathematical
truths become conventional transcriptions of logical truths.
Perhaps this is all that many of us mean to assert when we assert
that mathematics is true by convention; at least, an *analytic*
statement is commonly explained merely as one which proceeds
from logic and definitions, or as one which, on replacement of
definienda by definientia, becomes a truth of logic.[11] But in
strictness we cannot regard mathematics as true purely by
convention unless all those logical principles to which mathematics is supposed to reduce are likewise true by convention. And the
doctrine that mathematics is *analytic* accomplishes a less fundamental simplification for philosophy than would at first appear, if
it asserts only that mathematics is a conventional transcription
of logic and not that logic is convention in turn: for if in the end
we are to countenance any a priori principles at all which are
independent of convention, we should not scruple to admit a few
more, nor attribute crucial importance to conventions which

[9] Cf. Study, pp. 86–92.

[10] Cf., e.g., Dubislav; also Hilbert, pp. 73, 82.

[11] Cf. Frege, *Grundlagen*, p. 4; Behmann, p. 5. Carnap uses the term in
Logische Syntax in essentially the same sense but subject to more subtle
and rigorous treatment.

serve only to diminish the number of such principles by reducing some to others.

But if we are to construe logic also as true by convention, we must rest logic ultimately upon some manner of convention other than definition: for it was noted earlier that definitions are available only for transforming truths, not for founding them. The same applies to any truths of mathematics which, contrary to the supposition of a moment ago, may resist definitional reduction to logic; if such truths are to proceed from convention, without merely being reduced to antecedent truths, they must proceed from conventions other than definitions. Such a second sort of convention, generating truths rather than merely transforming them, has long been recognized in the use of postulates.[12] Application of this method to logic will occupy the next section; customary ways of rendering postulates and rules of inference will be departed from, however, in favor of giving the whole scheme the explicit form of linguistic convention.

II

Let us suppose an approximate maximum of definition to have been accomplished for logic, so that we are left with about as meager as possible an array of primitive notational devices. There are indefinitely many ways of framing the definitions, all conforming to the same usage of the expressions in question; apart from the objective of defining much in terms of little, choice among these ways is guided by convenience or chance. Different choices involve different sets of primitives. Let us suppose our procedure to be such as to reckon among the primitive devices the *not*-idiom, the *if*-idiom ('If . . . then . . . '), the *every*-idiom ('No matter what x may be, $--- x ---$'), and one or two more as required. On the basis of this much, then, all further logical notation is to be supposed defined; all statements involving any further logical notation become construed as abbreviations of statements whose logical constituents are limited to those primitives.

---

[12] The function of postulates as conventions seems to have been first recognized by Gergonne. His designation of them as "implicit definitions," which has had some following in the literature, is avoided here.

'Or', as a connective joining statements to form new statements, is amenable to the following contextual definition in terms of the *not*-idiom and the *if*-idiom: A pair of statements with 'or' between is an abbreviation of the statement made up successively of these ingredients: first, 'If'; second, the first statement of the pair, with 'not' inserted to govern the main verb (or, with 'it is false that' prefixed); third, 'then'; fourth, the second statement of the pair. The convention becomes clearer if we use the prefix '∼' as an artificial notation for denial, thus writing '∼ ice is hot' instead of 'Ice is not hot' or 'It is false that ice is hot'. Where '−−−' and '−−−−' are any statements, our definition then introduces '−−− or −−−−' as an abbreviation of 'If ∼−−− then −−−−'. Again 'and', as a connective joining statements, can be defined contextually by construing '−−− and −−−−' as an abbreviation for '∼ if −−− then ∼−−−−'. Every such idiom is what is known as a *truth function*, and is characterized by the fact that the truth or falsehood of the complex statement which it generates is uniquely determined by the truth or falsehood of the several statements which it combines. All truth functions are known to be constructible in terms of the *not*- and *if*-idioms as in the above examples.[13] On the basis of the truth functions, then, together with our further primitives—the *every*-idiom *et al.* —all further logical devices are supposed defined.

A word may, through historical or other accidents, evoke a train of ideas bearing no relevance to the truth or falsehood of its context; in point of *meaning*, however, as distinct from connotation, a word may be said to be determined to whatever extent the truth or falsehood of its contexts is determined. Such determination of truth or falsehood may be outright, and to that extent the meaning of the word is absolutely determined; or it may be relative to the truth or falsehood of statements containing other words, and to that extent the meaning of the word is determined relatively to those other words. A definition endows a word with complete determinacy of meaning relative to other words. But the alternative is open to us, on introducing a new word, of determining its meaning *absolutely* to whatever

[13] Sheffer has shown ways of constructing these two, in turn, in terms of one; strictly, therefore, such a one should supplant the two in our ostensibly minimal set of logical primitives. Exposition will be facilitated, however, by retaining the redundancy.

extent we like by specifying contexts which are to be true and contexts which are to be false. In fact, we need specify only the former: for falsehood may be regarded as a derivative property depending on the word '∼', in such wise that falsehood of '---' means simply truth of '∼ ---'. Since all contexts of our new word are meaningless to begin with, neither true nor false, we are free to run through the list of such contexts and pick out as true such ones as we like; those selected become true by fiat, by linguistic convention. For those who would question them we have always the same answer, "You use the word differently." The reader may protest that our arbitrary selection of contexts as true is subject to restrictions imposed by the requirement of *consistency*—e.g., that we must not select both '---' and '∼---'; but this consideration, which will receive a clearer status a few pages hence, will be passed over for the moment.

Now suppose in particular that we abstract from existing usage of the locutions 'if–then', 'not' (or '∼'), and the rest of our logical primitives, so that for the time being these become meaningless marks, and the erstwhile statements containing them lose their status as statements and become likewise meaningless, neither true nor false; and suppose we run through all those erstwhile statements, or as many of them as we like, segregating various of them arbitrarily as true. To whatever extent we carry this process, we to that extent determine meaning for the initially meaningless marks 'if', 'then', '∼', and the rest. Such contexts as we render true are true by convention.

We saw earlier that if all expressions occurring essentially in a true statement S and not belonging to a class α are given definitions in terms solely of members of α, then S becomes a definitional abbreviation of a truth S'' involving only members of α essentially. Now let α comprise just our logical primitives, and let S be a statement which, under ordinary usage, is true and involves only logical expressions essentially. Since all logical expressions other than the primitives are defined in terms of the primitives, it then follows that S is an abbreviation of a truth S'' involving only the primitives essentially. But if one statement S is a definitional abbreviation of another S'', the truth of S proceeds wholly from linguistic convention if the truth of S'' does so. Hence if, in the above process of arbitrarily segregating statements as true by way of endowing our logical primitives with meaning, *we assign truth to those statements which, according to ordinary usage, are true and involve only our primitives essentially,* then not only will the latter statements be true by convention, but so will all statements which are true under ordinary usage and involve only logical expressions essentially. Since, as remarked earlier, every logical truth involves (or is an abbreviation of another which involves) only logical expressions essentially, the described scheme of assigning truth makes all logic true by convention.

Not only does such assignment of truth suffice to make all those statements true by convention which are true under ordinary usage and involve only logical expressions essentially, but it serves also to make all those statements false by convention which are false under ordinary usage and involve only logical expressions essentially. This follows from our explanation of the falsehood of '---' as the truth of '~---', since '---' will be false under ordinary usage if and only if '~---' is true under ordinary usage. The described assignment of truth thus goes far toward fixing all logical expressions in point of meaning, and fixing them in conformity with usage. Still many statements containing logical expressions remain undecided by the described assignments: all those statements which, from the standpoint of ordinary usage, involve some non-logical expressions essentially. There is hence room for supplementary conventions of one sort or another, over and above the described truth assignments, by way of completely fixing the meanings of our primitives—and fixing them, it is to be hoped, in conformity with ordinary usage. Such supplementation need not concern us now; the described truth assignments provide partial determinations which, as far as they go, conform to usage, and which go far enough to make all logic true by convention.

But we must not be deceived by schematism. It would appear that we sit down to a list of expressions and check off as arbitrarily true all those which, under ordinary usage, are true statements involving only our logical primitives essentially; but this picture wanes when we reflect that the number of such statements is infinite. If the convention whereby those statements are singled out as true is to be formulated in finite terms, we must avail ourselves of conditions finite in length which determine infinite classes of expressions.[14]

Such conditions are ready at hand. One, determining an infinite class of expressions all of which, under ordinary usage, are true statements involving only our primitive *if*-idiom essentially, is the condition of being obtainable from:

(1)   If if p then q then if if q then r then if p then r

by putting a statement for 'p', a statement for 'q', and a statement for 'r'. In more customary language the form (1) would be expanded, for clarity, in some such fashion as this: 'If it is the case that if p then q, then, if it is the case further that if q then r, then, if p, r'. The form (1) is thus seen to be the principle of the syllogism. Obviously it is true under ordinary usage for all substitutions of statements for 'p', 'q', and 'r'; hence such results of substitution are, under ordinary usage, true statements involving only the *if*-idiom essentially. One infinite part of our program of assigning truth to all expressions which, under ordinary usage, are true statements involving only our logical primitives essentially, is thus accomplished by the following convention:

(I) *Let all results of putting a statement for 'p', a statement for 'q', and a statement for 'r' in (1) be true.*

Another infinite part of the program is disposed of by adding this convention:

(II) *Let any expression be true which yields a truth when put for 'q' in the result of putting a truth for 'p' in 'If p then q'.*

Given truths '——' and 'If —— then ——', (II) yields the truth of '——'. That (II) conforms to usage, i.e., that from statements which are true under ordinary usage (II) leads only to statements which are likewise true under ordinary usage, is seen from the fact that under ordinary usage a statement '——' is always true if statements '——' and 'If —— then ——' are true. Given all the truths yielded by (I), (II) yields another infinity of truths which, like the former, are under ordinary usage truths involving only the *if*-idiom essentially.

[14] Such a condition is all that constitutes a *formal system*. Usually we assign such meanings to the signs as to construe the expressions of the class as statements, specifically true statements, theorems; but this is neither intrinsic to the system nor necessary in all cases for a useful application of the system.

How this comes about is seen roughly as follows. The truths
yielded by (I), being of the form of (1), are complex statements of the form 'If --- then ——'. The statement '---'
here may in particular be of the form (1) in turn, and hence
likewise be true according to (I). Then, by (II), '——' becomes true. In general '——' will not be of the form (1),
hence would not have been obtainable by (I) alone. Still
'——' will in every such case be a statement which, under
ordinary usage, is true and involves only the *if*-idiom essentially; this follows from the observed conformity of (I) and
(II) to usage, together with the fact that the above derivation if '——' demands nothing of '——' beyond proper structure
in terms of 'if–then'.

Now our stock of truths embraces not only those yielded by
(I) alone, i.e., those having the form (1), but also all those
thence derivable by (II) in the manner in which '——' has just
now been supposed derived.[15] From this increased stock we can
derive yet further ones by (II), and these likewise will, under
ordinary usage, be true and involve only the *if*-idiom essentially.
The generation proceeds in this fashion ad infinitum.

When provided only with (I) as an auxiliary source of truth,
(II) thus yields only truths which under ordinary usage are
truths involving only the *if*-idiom essentially. When provided
with further auxiliary sources of truths, however, e.g., the convention (III) which is to follow, (II) yields truths involving
further locutions essentially. Indeed, the effect of (II) is not even
confined to statements which, under ordinary usage, involve only
logical locutions essentially; (II) also legislates regarding other
statements, to the extent of specifying that no two statements
'---' and 'If --- then ——' can both be true unless '——' is
true. But this overflow need not disturb us, since it also conforms
to ordinary usage. In fact, it was remarked earlier that room re-
mained for supplementary conventions, over and above the
described truth assignments, by way of further determining the
meanings of our primitives. This overflow accomplishes just that
for the *if*-idiom; it provides, with regard even to a statement 'If
--- then ——' which from the standpoint of ordinary usage in-

---

[15] The latter in fact comprise all and only those statements which have
the form 'If if if if q then r then if p then r then s then if if p then q
then s'.

volves non-logical expressions essentially, that the statement is
not to be true if '–––' is true and '––––' not.

But present concern is with statements which, under ordinary
usage, involve only our logical primitives essentially; by (I) and
(II) we have provided for the truth of an infinite number of such
statements, but by no means all. The following convention
provides for the truth of another infinite set of such statements;
these, in contrast to the preceding, involve not only the *if*-idiom
but also the *not*-idiom essentially (under ordinary usage).

(III) *Let all results of putting a statement for 'p' and a
statement for 'q', in 'If p then if* $\sim$ *p then q' or 'If if* $\sim$ *p then p
then p', be true.*[16]

Statements generated thus by substitution in 'If p then if $\sim p$
then q' are statements of hypothetical form in which two
mutually contradictory statements occur as premises; obviously
such statements are trivially true, under ordinary usage, no
matter what may figure as conclusion. Statements generated by
substitution in 'If [it is the case that] if $\sim p$ then p, then p' are
likewise true under ordinary usage, for one reasons as follows:
Grant the hypothesis, viz., that if $\sim p$ then p; then we must admit
the conclusion, viz., that p, since even denying it we admit it.
Thus all the results of substitution referred to in (III) are true
under ordinary usage no matter what the substituted statements
may be; hence such results of substitution are, under ordinary
usage, true statements involving nothing essentially beyond the
if-idiom and the *not*-idiom ('$\sim$').

From the infinity of truths adopted in (III), together with
those already at hand from (I) and (II), infinitely more truths
are generated by (II). It happens, curiously enough, that (III)
adds even to our stock of statements which involve only the *if*-
idiom essentially (under ordinary usage); there are truths of that
description which, though lacking the *not*-idiom, are reached by
(I)–(III) and not by (I) and (II). This is true, e.g., of any
instance of the principle of identity, say:

(2)   If time is money then time is money.

It will be instructive to derive (2) from (I)–(III), as an
illustration of the general manner in which truths are generated

[16] (1) and the two formulae in (III) are Łukasiewicz's three postulates
for the propositional calculus.

by those conventions. (III), to begin with, directs that we adopt these statements as true:

(3) If time is money then if time is not money then time is money.

(4) If if time is not money then time is money then time is money.

(I) directs that we adopt this as true:

(5) If if time is money then if time is not money then time is money then if if if time is not money then time is money then time is money then if time is money then time is money.

(II) tells us that, in view of the truth of (5) and (3), this is true:

(6) If if if time is not money then time is money then time is money then if time is money then time is money.

Finally (II) tells us that, in view of the truth of (6) and (4), (2) is true.

If a statement S is generated by (I)–(III), obviously only the structure of S in terms of 'if–then' and '$\sim$' was relevant to the generation; hence all those variants S_i of S which are obtainable by any grammatically admissible substitutions upon constituents of S not containing 'if', 'then', or '$\sim$', are likewise generated by (I)–(III). Now it has been observed that (I)–(III) conform to usage, i.e., generate only statements which are true under ordinary usage; hence S and all the S_i are uniformly true under ordinary usage, the S_i are therefore vacuous variants of S, and hence only 'if', 'then', and '$\sim$' occur essentially in S. Thus (I)–(III) generate only statements which under ordinary usage are truths involving only the *if*-idiom and the *not*-idiom essentially.

It can be shown also that (I)–(III) generate *all* such statements.[17] Consequently (I)–(III), aided by our definitions of

---

[17] The proof rests essentially upon Łukasiewicz's proof that his three postulates for the propositional calculus, viz., (1) and the formulae in (III), are *complete*. Adaptation of his result to present purposes depends upon the fact, readily established, that any formula generable by his two rules of inference (the so-called rule of substitution and a rule answering to (II)) can be generated by applying the rules in such order that all applications

logical locutions in terms of our primitives, are adequate to the generation of all statements which under ordinary usage are truths which involve any of the so-called truth functions but nothing else essentially: for it has been remarked that all the truth functions are definable on the basis of the *if*-idiom and the *not*-idiom. All such truths thus become true by convention. They comprise all those statements which are instances of any of the principles of the so-called propositional calculus.

To (I)–(III) we may now add a further convention or two to cover another of our logical primitives—say the *every*-idiom. A little more in this direction, by way of providing for our remaining primitives, and the program is completed; all statements which under ordinary usage are truths involving only our logical primitives essentially become true by convention. Therewith, as observed earlier, all logic becomes true by convention. The conventions with which (I)–(III) are thus to be supplemented will be more complex than (I)–(III), and considerable space would be needed to present them. But there is no need to do so, for (I)–(III) provide adequate illustration of the method; the complete set of conventions would be an adaptation of one of various existing systematizations of general logistic, in the same way in which (I)–(III) are an adaptation of a systematization of the propositional calculus.

The systematization chosen must indeed leave some logical statements undecided, by Gödel's theorem, if we set generous bounds to the logical vocabulary. But logic still becomes true by convention insofar as it gets reckoned as true on any account.

Let us now consider the protest which the reader raised earlier, viz. that our freedom in assigning truth by convention is subject to restrictions imposed by the requirement of consistency.[18] Under the fiction, implicit in an earlier stage of

---

of the rule of substitution precede all applications of the other rule. This fact is relevant because of the manner in which the rule of substitution has been absorbed, here, into (I) and (III). The adaptation involves also two further steps, which however present no difficulty: we must make connection between Łukasiewicz's *formulae*, containing variables '*p*', '*q*', etc., and the concrete *statements* which constitute the present subject matter; also between *completeness*, in the sense (Post's) in which Łukasiewicz uses the term, and the generability of all statements which under ordinary usage are truths involving only the *if*-idiom or the *not*-idiom essentially.

[18] So, e.g., Poincaré, pp. 162–163, 195–198; Schlick, pp. 36, 327.

our discussion, that we check off our truths one by one in an exhaustive list of expressions, consistency in the assignment of truth is nothing more than a special case of conformity to usage. If we make a mark in the margin opposite an expression '---', and another opposite '∼---', we sin only against the established usage of '∼' as a denial sign. Under the latter usage '---' and '∼---' are not both true; in taking them both by convention as true we merely endow the sign '∼', roughly speaking, with a meaning other than denial. Indeed, we might so conduct our assignments of truth as to allow no sign of our language to behave analogously to the denial locution of ordinary usage; perhaps the resulting language would be inconvenient, but conventions are often inconvenient. It is only the objective of ending up with our mother tongue that dissuades us from marking both '---' and '∼---', and this objective would dissuade us also from marking 'It is always cold on Thursday'.

The requirement of consistency still retains the above status when we assign truth wholesale through general conventions such as (I)–(III). Each such convention assigns truth to an infinite sheaf of the entries in our fictive list, and in this function the conventions cannot conflict; by overlapping in their effects they reinforce one another, by not overlapping they remain indifferent to one another. If some of the conventions specified entries to which truth was *not* to be assigned, genuine conflict might be apprehended; such negative conventions, however, have not been suggested. (II) was, indeed, described earlier as specifying that 'If --- then ——' is not to be true if '---' is true and '——' not; but within the framework of the conventions of truth assignment this apparent proscription is ineffectual without antecedent proscription of '——'. Thus any inconsistency among the general conventions will be of the sort previously considered, viz. the arbitrary adoption of both '---' and '∼---' as true; and the adoption of these was seen merely to impose some meaning other than denial upon the sign '∼'. As theoretical restrictions upon our freedom in the conventional assignment of truth, requirements of consistency thus disappear. Preconceived usage may lead us to stack the cards, but does not enter the rules of the game.

III

Circumscription of our logical primitives in point of meaning, through conventional assignment of truth to various of their contexts, has been seen to render all logic true by convention. Then if we grant the thesis that mathematics is logic, i.e., that all mathematical truths are definitional abbreviations of logical truths, it follows that mathematics is true by convention.

If on the other hand, contrary to the thesis that mathematics is logic, some mathematical expressions resist definition in terms of logical ones, we can extend the foregoing method into the domain of these recalcitrant expressions: we can circumscribe the latter through conventional assignment of truth to various of their contexts, and thus render mathematics conventionally true in the same fashion in which logic has been rendered so. Thus, suppose some mathematical expressions to resist logical definition, and suppose them to be reduced to as meager as possible a set of mathematical primitives. In terms of these and our logical primitives, then, all further mathematical devices are supposed defined; all statements containing the latter become abbreviations of statements containing by way of mathematical notation only the primitives. Here, as remarked earlier in the case of logic, there are alternative courses of definition and therewith alternative sets of primitives; but suppose our procedure to be such as to count 'sphere' and 'includes' among the mathematical primitives. So far we have a set of conventions, (I)–(III) and a few more, let us call them (IV)–(VII), which together circumscribe our logical primitives and yield all logic. By way of circumscribing the further primitives 'sphere' and 'includes', let us now add this convention to the set:

(VIII) *Let 'Hunt (sphere, includes)' be true.*

Now we saw earlier that where 'Φ (sphere, includes)' is any theorem of geometry, supposed expanded into primitive terms, the statement:

(7) If Hunt (sphere, includes) then Φ (sphere, includes)

is a truth of logic. Hence (7) is one of the expressions to which truth is assigned by the conventions (I)–(VII). Now (II) instructs us, in view of convention (VIII) and the truth of (7), to adopt 'Φ (sphere, includes)' as true. In this way each theorem of geometry is seen to be present among the statements to which truth is assigned by the conventions (I)–(VII).

We have considered four ways of construing geometry. One way consisted of straightforward definition of geometrical expressions in terms of logical ones, within the direction of development represented by *Principia Mathematica;* this way, presumably, would depend upon identification of geometry with algebra through the correlations of analytic geometry, and definition of algebraic expressions on the basis of logical ones as in *Principia Mathematica.* By way of concession to those who have fault to find with certain technical points in *Principia,* this possibility was allowed to retain a tentative status. The other three ways all made use of Huntington's postulates, but are sharply to be distinguished from one another. The first was to include geometry in logic by construing geometrical truths as elliptical for hypothetical statements bearing 'Hunt (sphere, includes)' as hypothesis; this was seen to be a mere evasion, tantamount, under its verbal disguise, to the concession that geometry is not logic after all. The next procedure was to define 'sphere' and 'includes' contextually in terms of logical expressions by construing 'Φ (sphere, includes)' in every case as an abbreviation of 'If α is any class and R any relation such that Hunt (α, R), then Φ (α, R)'. This definition was condemned on the grounds that it fails to yield the intended usage of the defined terms. The last procedure finally, just now presented, renders geometry true by convention without making it part of logic. Here 'Hunt (sphere, includes)' is made true by fiat, by way of conventionally delimiting the meanings of 'sphere' and 'includes'. The theorems of geometry then emerge not as truths of logic, but in parallel fashion to the truths of logic.

This last method of accommodating geometry is available also for any other branch of mathematics which may resist definitional reduction to logic. In each case we merely set up a conjunction of postulates for that branch as true by fiat, as a conventional circumscription of the meanings of the constituent primitives, and all the theorems of the branch thereby become true by convention: the convention thus newly adopted together with the conventions (I)–(VII). In this way mathematics becomes conventionally true, not by becoming a definitional transcription of logic, but by proceeding from linguistic convention in the same way as does logic.

But the method can even be carried beyond mathematics, into the so-called empirical sciences. Having framed a maximum of definitions in the latter realm, we can circumscribe as many of our "empirical" primitives as we like by adding further conventions to the set adopted for logic and mathematics; a corresponding portion of "empirical" science then becomes conventionally true in precisely the manner observed above for geometry.

The impossibility of defining any of the "empirical" expressions in terms exclusively of logical and mathematical ones may be recognized at the outset: for if any proved to be so definable, there can be no question but that it would thenceforward be recognized as belonging to pure mathematics. On the other hand vast numbers of "empirical" expressions are of course definable on the basis of logical and mathematical ones together with other "empirical" ones. Thus 'momentum' is defined as 'mass times velocity'; 'event' may be defined as 'referent of the *later*-relation', i.e., 'whatever is later than something'; 'instant' may be defined as 'maximal class of events no one of which is later than any other event of the class';[19] 'time' may be defined as 'the class of all instants'; and so on. In these examples 'momentum' is defined on the basis of mathematical expressions together with the further expressions 'mass' and 'velocity'; 'event', 'instant', and 'time' are all defined on the basis ultimately of logical expressions together with the one further expression 'later than'.

Now suppose definition to have been performed to the utmost among such non-logical, non-mathematical expressions, so that the latter are reduced to as few "empirical" primitives as possible.[20] *All* statements then become abbreviations of statements containing nothing beyond the logical and mathematical primitives and these "empirical" ones. Here, as before, there are

[19] Russell, *Our Knowledge of the External World*, p. 126.
[20] In *Der Logische Aufbau der Welt* Carnap has pursued this program with such amazing success as to provide grounds for expecting all the expressions to be definable ultimately in terms of logic and mathematics plus just one "empirical" primitive, representing a certain dyadic relation described as *recollection of resemblance*. But for the present cursory considerations no such spectacular reducibility need be presupposed.

alternatives of definition and therewith alternative sets of primitives; but suppose our primitives to be such as to include 'later than', and consider the totality of the known truths which under ordinary usage are truths involving only 'later than' and mathematical or logical expressions essentially. Examples of such statements are 'Nothing is later than itself'; 'If Pompey died later than Brutus and Brutus died later than Caesar then Pompey died later than Caesar'. All such statements will be either very general-principles, like the first example, or else instances of such principles, like the second example. Now it is a simple matter to frame a small set of general statements from which all and only the statements under consideration can be derived by means of logic and mathematics. The conjunction of these few general statements can then be adopted as true by fiat, as 'Hunt (sphere, includes)' was adopted in (VIII); their adoption is a conventional circumscription of the meaning of the primitive 'later than'. Adoption of this convention renders all the known truths conventionally true which under ordinary usage are truths essentially involving any logical or mathematical expressions, or 'later than', or any of the expressions which, like 'event', 'instant', and 'time', are defined on the basis of the foregoing, and inessentially involving anything else.

Now we can pick another of our "empirical" primitives, perhaps 'body' or 'mass' or 'energy', and repeat the process. We can continue in this fashion to any desired point, circumscribing one primitive after another by convention, and rendering conventionally true all known truths which under ordinary usage are truths essentially involving only the locutions treated up to that point. If in disposing successively of our "empirical" primitives in the above fashion we take them up in an order roughly describable as leading from the general to the special, then as we progress we may expect to have to deal more and more with statements which are true under ordinary usage only with reservations, only with a probability recognized as short of certainty. But such reservations need not deter us from rendering a statement true by convention; so long as under ordinary usage the presumption is rather for than against the statement, our convention conforms to usage in verifying it. In thus elevating the statement from putative to conventional truth, we still retain the right to falsify the statement tomorrow if those events should be observed which would have occasioned its repudiation while it was still putative: for conventions are commonly revised when new observations show the revision to be convenient.

If in describing logic and mathematics as true by convention what is meant is that the primitives *can* be conventionally circumscribed in such fashion as to generate all and only the accepted truths of logic and mathematics, the characterization is empty; our last considerations show that the same might be said of any other body of doctrine as well. If on the other hand it is meant merely that the speaker adopts such conventions for those fields but not for others, the characterization is uninteresting; while if it is meant that it is a general practice to adopt such conventions explicitly for those fields but not for others, the first part of the characterization is false.

Still, there is the apparent contrast between logico-mathematical truths and others that the former are a priori, the latter a posteriori; the former have "the character of an inward necessity," in Kant's phrase, the latter do not. Viewed behavioristically and without reference to a metaphysical system, this contrast retains reality as a contrast between more and less firmly accepted statements; and it obtains antecedently to any *post facto* fashioning of conventions. There are statements which we choose to surrender last, if at all, in the course of revamping our sciences in the face of new discoveries; and among these there are some which we will not surrender at all, so basic are they to our whole conceptual scheme. Among the latter are to be counted the so-called truths of logic and mathematics, regardless of what further we may have to say of their status in the course of a subsequent sophisticated philosophy. Now since these statements are destined to be maintained independently of our observations of the world, we may as well make use here of our technique of conventional truth assignment and thereby forestall awkward metaphysical questions as to our a priori insight into necessary truths. On the other hand this purpose would not motivate extension of the truth-assignment process into the realm of erstwhile contingent statements. On such grounds, then, logic and mathematics may be held to be conventional while other fields are not; it may be held that it is philosophically important to circumscribe the logical and mathematical primitives by conventions of truth assignment but that it is idle elaboration to carry the process further. Such a characterization of logic and mathematics is perhaps neither empty nor uninteresting nor false.

In the adoption of the very conventions (I)–(III), etc., whereby logic itself is set up, however, a difficulty remains to be faced. Each of these conventions is general, announcing the truth of every one of an infinity of statements conforming to a certain description; derivation of the truth of any specific statement from the general convention thus requires a logical inference, and this involves us in an infinite regress. E.g., in deriving (6) from (3) and (5) on the authority of (II) we *infer*, from the general announcement (II) and the specific premise that (3) and (5) are true statements, the conclusion that

(7)   (6) is to be true.

An examination of this inference will reveal the regress. For present purposes it will be simpler to rewrite (II) thus:

(II') *No matter what x may be, no matter what y may be, no matter what z may be, if x and z are true [statements] and z is the result of putting x for 'p' and y for 'q' in 'If p then q' then y is to be true.*

We are to take (II') as a premise, then, and in addition the premise that (3) and (5) are true. We may also grant it as known that (5) is the result of putting (3) for 'p' and (6) for 'q' in 'If p then q'. Our second premise may thus be rendered compositely as follows:

(8) (3) and (5) are true and (5) is the result of putting (3) for 'p' and (6) for 'q' in 'If p then q'.

From these two premises we propose to infer (7). This inference is obviously sound logic; as logic, however, it involves use of (II') and others of the conventions from which logic is supposed to spring. Let us try to perform the inference on the basis of those conventions. Suppose that our convention (IV), passed over earlier, is such as to enable us to infer specific instances from statements which, like (II'), involve the *every*-idiom; i.e., suppose that (IV) entitles us in general to drop the prefix 'No matter what x [or y, etc.] may be' and simultaneously to introduce a concrete designation instead of 'x' [or 'y', etc.] in the sequel. By invoking (IV) three times, then, we can infer the following from (II'):

(9) If (3) and (5) are true and (5) is the result of putting (3)
for 'p' and (6) for 'q' in 'If p then q' then (6) is to be true.

It remains to infer (7) from (8) and (9). But this is an inference
of the kind for which (II') is needed; from the fact that

(10) (8) and (9) are true and (9) is the result of putting (8)
for 'p' and (7) for 'q' in 'If p then q'

we are to infer (7) with help of (II'). But the task of getting (7)
from (10) and (II') is exactly analogous to our original task of
getting (6) from (8) and (II'); the regress is thus under way.[21]
(Incidentally the derivation of (9) from (II') by (IV), granted
just now for the sake of argument, would encounter a similar
obstacle; so also the various unanalyzed steps in the derivation of
(8).)

In a word, the difficulty is that if logic is to proceed *mediately*
from conventions, logic is needed for inferring logic from the
conventions. Alternatively, the difficulty which appears thus as a
self-presupposition of doctrine can be framed as turning upon a
self-presupposition of primitives. It is supposed that the *if*-idiom,
the *not*-idiom, the *every*-idiom, and so on, mean nothing to us
initially, and that we adopt the conventions (I)–(VII) by way of
circumscribing their meaning; and the difficulty is that communication of (I)–(VII) themselves depends upon free use of those
very idioms which we are attempting to circumscribe, and can
succeed only if we are already conversant with the idioms. This
becomes clear as soon as (I)–(VII) are rephrased in rudimentary
language, after the manner of (II').[22] It is important to note that
this difficulty besets only the method of wholesale truth assignment, not that of definition. It is true, e.g., that the contextual
definition of 'or' presented at the beginning of the second section

---

[21] Cf. Lewis Carroll, "What the tortoise said to Achilles."

[22] Incidentally the conventions presuppose also some further locutions,
e.g., 'true' ('a true statement'), 'the result of putting . . . for . . . in . . .',
and various nouns formed by displaying expressions in quotation marks.
The linguistic presuppositions can of course be reduced to a minimum by
careful rephrasing; (II'), e.g., can be improved to the following extent:

(II") *No matter what x may be, no matter what y may be, no matter
what z may be, if x is true then if z is true then if z is the result of putting
x for 'p' in the result of putting y for 'q' in 'If p then q' then y is true.*

This involves just the *every*-idiom, the *if*-idiom, 'is', and the further locutions mentioned above.

was communicated with the help of logical and other expressions which cannot be expected to have been endowed with meaning at the stage where logical expressions are first being introduced. But a definition has the peculiarity of being theoretically dispensable; it introduces a scheme of abbreviation, and we are free, if we like, to forego the brevity which it affords until enough primitives have been endowed with meaning, through the method of truth assignment or otherwise, to accommodate full exposition of the definition. On the other hand the conventions of truth assignment cannot be thus withheld until preparations are complete, because they are needed in the preparations.

If the truth assignments were made one by one, rather than an infinite number at a time, the above difficulty would disappear; truths of logic such as (2) would simply be asserted severally by fiat, and the problem of inferring them from more general conventions would not arise. This course was seen to be closed to us, however, by the infinitude of the truths of logic.

It may still be held that the conventions (I)–(VIII), etc., are *observed* from the start, and that logic and mathematics thereby become conventional. It may be held that we can adopt conventions through behavior, without first announcing them in words; and that we can return and formulate our conventions verbally afterward, if we choose, when a full language is at our disposal. It may be held that the verbal formulation of conventions is no more a prerequisite of the adoption of the conventions than the writing of a grammar is a prerequisite of speech; that explicit exposition of conventions is merely one of many important uses of a completed language. So conceived, the conventions no longer involve us in vicious regress. Inference from general conventions is no longer demanded initially, but remains to the subsequent sophisticated stage where we frame general statements of the conventions and show how various specific conventional truths, used all along, fit into the general conventions as thus formulated.

It must be conceded that this account accords well with what we actually do. We discourse without first phrasing the conventions; afterwards, in writings such as this, we formulate them to fit our behavior. On the other hand it is not clear wherein an adoption of the conventions, antecedently to their formulation, consists; such behavior is difficult to distinguish from that in which conventions are disregarded. When we first agree to understand 'Cambridge' as referring to Cambridge in England, failing a suffix to the contrary, and then discourse accordingly, the role of linguistic convention is intelligible; but when a convention is incapable of being communicated until after its adoption, its role is not so clear. In dropping the attributes of deliberateness and explicitness from the notion of linguistic convention we risk depriving the latter of any explanatory force and reducing it to an idle label. We may wonder what one adds to the bare statement that the truths of logic and mathematics are a priori, or to the still barer behavioristic statement that they are firmly accepted, when he characterizes them as true by convention in such a sense.

The more restricted thesis discussed in the first section, viz., that mathematics is a conventional transcription of logic, is far from trivial; its demonstration is a highly technical undertaking and an important one, irrespectively of what its relevance may be to fundamental principles of philosophy. It is valuable to show the reducibility of any principle to another through definition of erstwhile primitives, for every such achievement reduces the number of our presuppositions and simplifies and integrates the structure of our theories. But as to the larger thesis that mathematics and logic proceed wholly from linguistic conventions, only further clarification can assure us that this asserts anything at all.

12

❦ *Carnap and Logical Truth*

I

Kant's question "How are synthetic judgments a priori possible?" precipitated the *Critique of Pure Reason*. Question and answer notwithstanding, Mill and others persisted in doubting that such judgments were possible at all. At length some of Kant's own clearest purported instances, drawn from arithmetic, were sweepingly disqualified (or so it seemed; but see §II) by Frege's reduction of arithmetic to logic. Attention was thus forced upon the less tendentious and indeed logically prior question, "How is logical certainty possible?" It was largely this latter question that precipitated the form of empiricism which we associate with between-war Vienna—a movement which began with Wittgenstein's *Tractatus* and reached its maturity in the work of Carnap.

Mill's position on the second question had been that logic and mathematics were based on empirical generalizations, despite their superficial appearance to the contrary. This doctrine may well have been felt to do less than justice to the palpable surface

Written early in 1954 for P. A. Schilpp, ed., *The Philosophy of Rudolf Carnap* (La Salle, Ill.: Open Court, 1963) at the request of the editor. It appeared in Italian translation in *Rivista di Filosofia*, 1957, and selected portions amounting to somewhat less than half appeared also in Sidney Hook, ed., *American Philosophers at Work* (New York: Criterion, 1956). Its first appearance whole in English was in the Carnap jubilee issue of *Synthese* (Volume 12, 1960), which was subsequently reissued as a book: B. H. Kazemier and D. Vuysje, eds., *Logic and Language* (Dordrecht, Holland: D. Reidel Publishing Co., 1962).

differences between the deductive sciences of logic and mathematics, on the one hand, and the empirical sciences ordinarily socalled on the other. Worse, the doctrine derogated from the certainty of logic and mathematics; but Mill may not have been one to be excessively disturbed by such a consequence. Perhaps classical mathematics did lie closer to experience then than now; at any rate the infinitistic reaches of set theory, which are so fraught with speculation and so remote from any possible experience, were unexplored in his day. And it is against just these latter-day mathematical extravagances that empiricists outside the Vienna Circle have since been known to inveigh,[1] in much the spirit in which the empiricists of Vienna and elsewhere have inveighed against metaphysics.

What now of the empiricist who would grant certainty to logic, and to the whole of mathematics, and yet would make a clean sweep of other non-empirical theories under the name of metaphysics? The Viennese solution of this nice problem was predicated on language. Metaphysics was meaningless through misuse of language; logic was certain through tautologous use of language.

As an answer to the question "How is logical certainty possible?" this linguistic doctrine of logical truth has its attractions. For there can be no doubt that sheer verbal usage is in general a major determinant of truth. Even so factual a sentence as 'Brutus killed Caesar' owes its truth not only to the killing but equally to our using the component words as we do. Why then should a logically true sentence on the same topic, e.g., 'Brutus killed Caesar or did not kill Caesar', not be said to owe its truth *purely* to the fact that we use our words (in this case 'or' and 'not') as we do?—for it depends not at all for its truth upon the killing.

The suggestion is not, of course, that the logically true sentence is a contingent truth about verbal usage; but rather that it is a sentence which, given the language, automatically becomes true, whereas 'Brutus killed Caesar', given the language, becomes true only contingently on the alleged killing.

Further plausibility accrues to the linguistic doctrine of logical truth when we reflect on the question of alternative logics. Suppose someone puts forward and uses a consistent logic the

[1] See Bridgman.

principles of which are contrary to our own. We are then clearly free to say that he is merely using the familiar particles 'and', 'all', or whatever, in other than the familiar senses, and hence that no real contrariety is present after all. There may of course still be an important failure of intertranslatability, in that the behavior of certain of our logical particles is incapable of being duplicated by paraphrases in his system or vice versa. If the translation in this sense is possible, from his system into ours, then we are pretty sure to protest that he was wantonly using the familiar particles 'and' and 'all' (say) where we might unmisleadingly have used such-and-such other familiar phrasing. This reflection goes to support the view that the truths of logic have no content over and above the meanings they confer on the logical vocabulary.

Much the same point can be brought out by a caricature of a doctrine of Lévy-Bruhl, according to which there are pre-logical peoples who accept certain simple self-contradictions as true. Oversimplifying, no doubt, let us suppose it claimed that these natives accept as true a certain sentence of the form 'p and not p'. Or—not to oversimplify too much—that they accept as true a certain heathen sentence of the form 'q ka bu q' the English translation of which has the form 'p and not p'. But now just how good a translation is this, and what may the lexicographer's method have been? If any evidence can count against a lexicographer's adoption of 'and' and 'not' as translations of 'ka' and 'bu', certainly the natives' acceptance of 'q ka bu q' as true counts overwhelmingly. We are left with the meaninglessness of the doctrine of there being pre-logical peoples; pre-logicality is a trait injected by bad translators. This is one more illustration of the inseparability of the truths of logic from the meanings of the logical vocabulary.

We thus see that there is something to be said for the naturalness of the linguistic doctrine of logical truth. But before we can get much further we shall have to become more explicit concerning our subject matter.

II

Without thought of any epistemological doctrine, either the linguistic doctrine or another, we may mark out the intended scope of the term 'logical truth', within that of the broader term 'truth', in the following way. First we suppose indicated, by enumeration if not otherwise, what words are to be called logical words; typical ones are 'or', 'not', 'if', 'then', 'and', 'all', 'every', 'only', 'some'. The logical truths, then, are those true sentences which involve only logical words *essentially*. What this means is that any other words, though they may also occur in a logical truth (as witness 'Brutus', 'kill', and 'Caesar' in 'Brutus killed or did not kill Caesar'), can be varied at will without engendering falsity.[2]

Though formulated with reference to language, the above clarification does not of itself hint that logical truths owe their truth to language. What we have thus far is only a delimitation of the class, *per accidens* if you please. Afterward the linguistic doctrine of logical truth, which is an epistemological doctrine, goes on to say that logical truths are true by virtue purely of the intended meanings, or intended usage, of the logical words. Obviously if logical truths *are* true by virtue purely of language, the logical words are the only part of the language that can be concerned in the matter; for these are the only ones that occur essentially.

Elementary logic, as commonly systematized nowadays, comprises truth-function theory, quantification theory, and identity theory. The logical vocabulary for this part, as commonly rendered for technical purposes, consists of truth-function signs (corresponding to 'or', 'and', 'not', etc.), quantifiers and their variables, and '='.

The further part of logic is set theory, which requires there to be classes among the values of its variables of quantification. The one sign needed in set theory, beyond those appropriate to elementary logic, is the connective 'ϵ' of membership. Additional

---

[2] Substantially this formulation is traced back a century and a quarter, by Bar-Hillel, to Bolzano. But note that the formulation fails of its purpose unless the phrase "can be varied at will," above, is understood to provide for varying the words not only singly but also two or more at at time. E.g., the sentence 'If some men are angels some animals are angels' can be turned into a falsehood by simultaneous substitution for 'men' and 'angels', but not by any substitution for 'angels' alone, nor for 'men', nor for 'animals' (granted the non-existence of angels). For this observation and illustration I am indebted to John R. Myhill, who expresses some indebtedness in turn to Benson Mates. —I added most of this footnote in May 1955, a year after the rest of the essay left my hands.

signs, though commonly used for convenience, can be eliminated in well-known ways.

In this dichotomy I leave metatheory, or logical syntax, out of account. For, either it treats of special objects of an extralogical kind, viz., notational expressions, or else, if these are made to give way to numbers by arithmetization, it is reducible via number theory to set theory.

I will not here review the important contrasts between elementary logic and set theory, except for the following one. Every truth of elementary logic is obvious (whatever this really means), or can be made so by some series of individually obvious steps. Set theory, in its present state anyway, is otherwise. I am not alluding here to Gödel's incompleteness principle, but to something right on the surface. Set theory was straining at the leash of intuition ever since Cantor discovered the higher infinites; and with the added impetus of the paradoxes of set theory the leash was snapped. Comparative set theory has now long been the trend; for, so far as is known, no consistent set theory is both adequate to the purposes envisaged for set theory and capable of substantiation by steps of obvious reasoning from obviously true principles. What we do is develop one or another set theory by obvious reasoning, or elementary logic, from unobvious first principles which are set down, whether for good or for the time being, by something very like convention.

Altogether, the contrasts between elementary logic and set theory are so fundamental that one might well limit the word 'logic' to the former (though I shall not), and speak of set theory as mathematics in a sense exclusive of logic. To adopt this course is merely to deprive 'ϵ' of the status of a logical word. Frege's derivation of arithmetic would then cease to count as a derivation from logic; for he used set theory. At any rate we should be prepared to find that the linguistic doctrine of logical truth holds for elementary logic and fails for set theory, or vice versa. Kant's readiness to see logic as analytic and arithmetic as synthetic, in particular, is not superseded by Frege's work (as Frege supposed[3]) if 'logic' be taken as elementary logic. And for Kant logic certainly did not include set theory.

[3] See §§87f., §109 of Frege, *Foundations of Arithmetic*.

III

Where someone disagrees with us as to the truth of a sentence, it often happens that we can convince him by getting the sentence from other sentences, which he does accept, by a series of steps each of which he accepts. Disagreement which cannot be thus resolved I shall call *deductively irresoluble.* Now if we try to warp the linguistic doctrine of logical truth around into something like an experimental thesis, perhaps a first approximation will run thus: *Deductively irresoluble disagreement as to a logical truth is evidence of deviation in usage (or meanings) of words.* This is not yet experimentally phrased, since one term of the affirmed relationship, viz., 'usage' (or 'meanings'), is in dire need of an independent criterion. However, the formulation would seem to be fair enough within its limits; so let us go ahead with it, not seeking more sublety until need arises.

Already the obviousness or potential obviousness of elementary logic can be seen to present an insuperable obstacle to our assigning any experimental meaning to the linguistic doctrine of elementary logical truth. Deductively irresoluble dissent from an elementary logical truth *would* count as evidence of deviation over meanings if anything can, but simply because dissent from a logical truism is as extreme as dissent can get.

The philosopher, like the beginner in algebra, works in danger of finding that his solution-in-progress reduces to '$0 = 0$'. Such is the threat to the linguistic theory of elementary logical truth. For, that theory now seems to imply nothing that is not already implied by the fact that elementary logic is obvious or can be resolved into obvious steps.

The considerations which were adduced in §I, to show the naturalness of the linguistic doctrine, are likewise seen to be empty when scrutinized in the present spirit. One was the circumstance that alternative logics are inseparable practically from mere change in usage of logical words. Another was that illogical cultures are indistinguishable from ill-translated ones. But both of these circumstances are adequately accounted for by mere obviousness of logical principles, without help of a linguistic doctrine of logical truth. For, there can be no stronger evidence of a change in usage than the repudiation of what had been obvious, and no stronger evidence of bad translation than that it translates earnest affirmations into obvious falsehoods.

Another point in §I was that true sentences generally depend for their truth on the traits of their language in addition to the traits of their subject matter; and that logical truths then fit neatly in as the limiting case where the dependence on traits of the subject matter is nil. Consider, however, the logical truth 'Everything is self-identical', or '$(x)(x = x)$'. We *can* say that it depends for its truth on traits of the language (specifically on the usage of ' $=$ '), and not on traits of its subject matter; but we can also say, alternatively, that it depends on an obvious trait, viz., self-identity, of its subject matter, viz., everything. The tendency of our present reflections is that there is no difference.

I have been using the vaguely psychological word "obvious" non-technically, assigning it no explanatory value. My suggestion is merely that the linguistic doctrine of elementary logical truth likewise leaves explanation unbegun. I do not suggest that the linguistic doctrine is false and some doctrine of ultimate and inexplicable insight into the obvious traits of reality is true, but only that there is no real difference between these two pseudo-doctrines.

Turning away now from elementary logic, let us see how the linguistic doctrine of logical truth fares in application to set theory. As noted in §II, we may think of 'ϵ' as the one sign for set theory in addition to those of elementary logic. Accordingly the version of the linguistic doctrine which was italicized at the beginning of the present section becomes, in application to set theory, this: Among persons who are already in agreement on elementary logic, any deductively irresoluble disagreement as to a truth of set theory is evidence of deviation in usage (or meaning) of 'ϵ'.

This thesis is not trivial in quite the way in which the parallel thesis for elementary logic was seen to be. It is not indeed experimentally significant as it stands, simply because of the lack, noted earlier, of a separate criterion for usage or meaning. But it does seem reasonable, by the following reasoning.

Any acceptable evidence of usage or meaning of words must

reside surely either in the observable circumstances under which the words are uttered (in the case of concrete terms referring to observable individuals) or in the affirmation and denial of sentences in which the words occur. Only the second alternative is relevant to 'ϵ'. Therefore any evidence of deviation in usage or meaning of 'ϵ' must reside in disagreement on sentences containing 'ϵ'. This is not, of course, to say of *every* sentence containing 'ϵ' that disagreement over it establishes deviation in usage or meaning of 'ϵ'. We have to assume in the first place that the speaker under investigation agrees with us on the meanings of words other than 'ϵ' in the sentences in question. And it might well be that, even from among the sentences containing only 'ϵ' and words on whose meanings he agrees with us, there is only a select species S which is so fundamental that he cannot dissent from them without betraying deviation in his usage or meaning of 'ϵ'. But S may be expected surely to include some (if not all) of the sentences which contain *nothing* but 'ϵ' and the elementary logical particles; for it is these sentences, insofar as true, that constitute (pure, or unapplied) set theory. But it is difficult to conceive of how to be other than democratic toward the truths of set theory. In exposition we may select some of these truths as so-called postulates and deduce others from them, but this is subjective discrimination, variable at will, expository and not set-theoretic. We do not change our meaning of 'ϵ' between the page where we show that one particular truth is deducible by elementary logic from another and the page where we show the converse. Given this democratic outlook, finally, the law of sufficient reason leads us to look upon S as including *all* the sentences which contain only 'ϵ' and the elementary logical particles. It then follows that anyone in agreement on elementary logic and in irresoluble disagreement on set theory is in deviation with respect to the usage or meaning of 'ϵ'; and this was the thesis.

The effect of our effort to inject content into the linguistic doctrine of logical truth has been, up to now, to suggest that the doctrine says nothing worth saying about elementary logical truth, but that when applied to set-theoretic truth it makes for a reasonable partial condensation of the otherwise vaporous notion of meaning as applied to 'ϵ'.

IV

The linguistic doctrine of logical truth is sometimes expressed by saying that such truths are true by linguistic convention. Now if this be so, certainly the conventions are not in general explicit. Relatively few persons, before the time of Carnap, had ever seen any convention that engendered truths of elementary logic. Nor can this circumstance be ascribed merely to the slipshod ways of our predecessors. For it is impossible in principle, even in an ideal state, to get even the most elementary part of logic exclusively by the explicit application of conventions stated in advance. The difficulty is the vicious regress, familiar from Lewis Carroll, which I have elaborated elsewhere.[4] Briefly the point is that the logical truths, being infinite in number, must be given by general conventions rather than singly; and logic is needed then to begin with, in the metatheory, in order to apply the general conventions to individual cases.

"In dropping the attributes of deliberateness and explicitness from the notion of linguistic convention," I went on to complain in the aforementioned paper, "we risk depriving the latter of any explanatory force and reducing it to an idle label." It would seem that to call elementary logic true by convention is to add nothing but a metaphor to the linguistic doctrine of logical truth which, as applied to elementary logic, has itself come to seem rather an empty figure (cf. §III).

The case of set theory, however, is different on both counts. For set theory the linguistic doctrine has seemed less empty (cf. §III) ; in set theory, moreover, convention in quite the ordinary sense seems to be pretty much what goes on (cf. §II). Conventionalism has a serious claim to attention in the philosophy of mathematics, if only because of set theory. Historically, though, conventionalism was encouraged in the philosophy of mathematics rather by the non-Euclidean geometries and abstract algebras, with little good reason. We can contribute to subsequent purposes by surveying this situation. Further talk of set theory is deferred to §V.

In the beginning there was Euclidean geometry, a compendium

---

[4] Late in the preceding essay.

of truths about form and void; and its truths were not based on convention (except as a conventionalist might, begging the present question, apply this tag to everything mathematical). Its truths were in practice presented by deduction from so-called postulates (including axioms; I shall not distinguish); and the selection of truths for this role of postulate, out of the totality of truths of Euclidean geometry, was indeed a matter of convention. But this is not *truth* by convention. The truths were there, and what was conventional was merely the separation of them into those to be taken as starting point (for purposes of the exposition at hand) and those to be deduced from them.

The non-Euclidean geometries came of artificial deviations from Euclid's postulates, without thought (to begin with) of true interpretation. These departures were doubly conventional; for Euclid's postulates were a conventional selection from among the truths of geometry, and then the departures were arbitrarily or conventionally devised in turn. But still there was no truth by convention, because there was no truth.

Playing within a non-Euclidean geometry, one might conveniently make believe that his theorems were interpreted and true; but even such conventional make-believe is not truth by convention. For it is not really truth at all; and what is conventionally pretended is that the theorems are true by non-convention.

Non-Euclidean geometries have, in the fullness of time, received serious interpretations. This means that ways have been found of so construing the hitherto unconstrued terms as to identify the at first conventionally chosen set of non-sentences with some genuine truths, and truths presumably not by convention. The status of an interpreted non-Euclidean geometry differs in no basic way from the original status of Euclidean geometry, noted above.

Uninterpreted systems became quite the fashion after the advent of non-Euclidean geometries. This fashion helped to cause, and was in turn encouraged by, an increasingly formal approach to mathematics. Methods had to become more formal to make up for the unavailability, in uninterpreted systems, of intuition. Conversely, disinterpretation served as a crude but useful device (until Frege's syntactical approach came to be appreciated) for achieving formal rigor uncorrupted by intuition.

The tendency to look upon non-Euclidean geometries as true

by convention applied to uninterpreted systems generally, and then carried over from these to mathematical systems generally. A tendency indeed developed to look upon all mathematical systems as, qua mathematical, uninterpreted. This tendency can be accounted for by the increase of formality, together with the use of disinterpretation as a heuristic aid to formalization. Finally, in an effort to make some sense of mathematics thus drained of all interpretation, recourse was had to the shocking quibble of identifying mathematics merely with the elementary logic which leads from uninterpreted postulates to uninterpreted theorems.[5] What is shocking about this is that it puts arithmetic qua interpreted theory of number, and analysis qua interpreted theory of functions, and geometry qua interpreted theory of space, outside mathematics altogether.

The substantive reduction of mathematics to logic by Frege, Whitehead, and Russell is of course quite another thing. It is a reduction not to elementary logic but to set theory; and it is a reduction of genuine interpreted mathematics, from arithmetic onward.

V

Let us then put aside these confusions and get back to set theory. Set theory is pursued as interpreted mathematics, like arithmetic and analysis; indeed, it is to set theory that those further branches are reducible. In set theory we discourse about certain immaterial entities, real or erroneously alleged, viz., sets, or classes. And it is in the effort to make up our minds about genuine truth and falsity of sentences about these objects that we find ourselves engaged in something very like convention in an ordinary non-metaphorical sense of the word. We find ourselves making deliberate choices and setting them forth unaccompanied by any attempt at justification other than in terms of elegance and convenience. These adoptions, called postulates, and their logical consequences (via elementary logic), are true until further notice.

So here is a case where postulation can plausibly be looked on

[5] See §I of the preceding essay.

as constituting truth by convention. But in §IV we have seen how
the philosophy of mathematics can be corrupted by supposing
that postulates always play that role. Insofar as we would
epistemologize and not just mathematize, we might divide
postulation as follows. Uninterpreted postulates may be put
aside, as no longer concerning us; and on the interpreted side we
may distinguish between *legislative* and *discursive* postulation.
Legislative postulation institutes truth by convention, and seems
plausibly illustrated in contemporary set theory. On the other
hand discursive postulation is mere selection, from a pre-existing
body of truths, of certain ones for use as a basis from which to
derive others, initially known or unknown. What discursive
postulation fixes is not truth, but only some particular ordering of
the truths, for purposes perhaps of pedagogy or perhaps of
inquiry into logical relationships (logical in the sense of elementary logic). All postulation is of course conventional, but only
legislative postulation properly hints of *truth* by convention.

It is well to recognize, if only for its distinctness, yet a further
way in which convention can enter; viz., in the adoption of new
notations for old ones, without, as one tends to say, change of
theory. Truths containing the new notation are conventional
transcriptions of sentences true apart from the convention in
question. They depend for their truth partly on language, but
then so did 'Brutus killed Caesar' (cf. §I). They come into being
through a conventional adoption of a new sign, and they become
true through conventional definition of that sign *together with*
whatever made the corresponding sentences in the old notation
true.

Definition, in a properly narrow sense of the word, is convention in a properly narrow sense of the word. But the phrase 'true
by definition' must be taken cautiously; in its strictest usage it
refers to a transcription, by the definition, of a truth of
elementary logic. Whether such a sentence is true by convention
depends on whether the logical truths themselves be reckoned as
true by convention. Even an outright equation or biconditional
connection of the definiens and the definiendum is a definitional
transcription of a prior logical truth of the form '$x = x$' or
'$p \equiv p$'.

Definition commonly so-called is not thus narrowly conceived,
and must for present purposes be divided, as postulation was

divided, into legislative and discursive. Legislative definition introduces a notation hitherto unused, or used only at variance with the practice proposed, or used also at variance, so that a convention is wanted to settle the ambiguity. Discursive definition, on the other hand, sets forth a pre-existing relation of interchangeability or coextensiveness between notations in already familiar usage. A frequent purpose of this activity is to show how some chosen part of language can be made to serve the purposes of a wider part. Another frequent purpose is language instruction.

It is only legislative definition, and not discursive definition or discursive postulation, that makes a conventional contribution to the truth of sentences. Legislative postulation, finally, affords truth by convention unalloyed.

Increasingly the word 'definition' connotes the formulas of definition which appear in connection with formal systems, signaled by some extra-systematic sign such as '$=_{df}$'. Such definitions are best looked upon as correlating two systems, two notations, one of which is prized for its economical lexicon and the other for its brevity or familiarity of expression.[6] Definitions so used can be either legislative or discursive in their inception. But this distinction is in practice left unindicated, and wisely; for it is a distinction only between particular acts of definition, and not germane to the definition as an enduring channel of inter-translation.

The distinction between the legislative and the discursive refers thus to the act, and not to its enduring consequence, in the case of postulation as in the case of definition. This is because we are taking the notion of truth by convention fairly literally and simple-mindedly, for lack of an intelligible alternative. So conceived, conventionality is a passing trait, significant at the moving front of science but useless in classifying the sentences behind the lines. It is a trait of events and not of sentences.

Might we not still project a derivative trait upon the sentences themselves, thus speaking of a sentence as forever true by convention if its first adoption as true was a convention? No; this, if done seriously, involves us in the most unrewarding historical conjecture. Legislative postulation contributes truths

[6] See my *From a Logical Point of View,* pp. 26f.

which become integral to the corpus of truths; the artificiality of
their origin does not linger as a localized quality, but suffuses the
corpus. If a subsequent expositor singles out those once legislatively postulated truths again as postulates, this signifies nothing; he is engaged only in discursive postulation. He could as well
choose his postulates from elsewhere in the corpus, and will if he
thinks this serves his expository ends.

VI

Set theory, currently so caught up in legislative postulation,
may some day gain a norm—even a strain of obviousness,
perhaps—and lose all trace of the conventions in its history. A
day could likewise have been when our elementary logic was
itself instituted as a deliberately conventional deviation from
something earlier, instead of evolving, as it did, mainly by
unplanned shifts of form and emphasis coupled with casual
novelties of notation.

Today indeed there are dissident logicians even at the elementary level, propounding deviations from the law of the excluded
middle. These deviations, insofar as meant for serious use and not
just as uninterpreted systems, are as clear cases of legislative
postulation as the ones in set theory. For here we have again,
quite as in set theory, the propounding of a deliberate choice
unaccompanied (conceivably) by any attempt at justification
other than in terms of convenience.

This example from elementary logic controverts no conclusion
we have reached. According to §§I and III, the departure from
the law of the excluded middle would count as evidence of revised
usage of 'or' and 'not'. (This judgment was upheld in §III, though
disqualified as evidence for the linguistic doctrine of logical
truth.) For the deviating logician the words 'or' and 'not' are
unfamiliar, or defamiliarized; and his decisions regarding truth
values for their proposed contexts can then be just as genuinely a
matter of deliberate convention as the decisions of the creative
set theorist regarding contexts of 'ϵ'.

The two cases are indeed much alike. Not only is departure
from the classical logic of 'or' and 'not' evidence of revised usage
of 'or' and 'not'; likewise, as argued at length in §III, divergences

between set theorists may reasonably be reckoned to revised usage of 'ε'. Any such revised usage is conspicuously a matter of convention, and can be declared by legislative postulation.

We have been at a loss to give substance to the linguistic doctrine, particularly of elementary logical truth, or to the doctrine that the familiar truths of logic are true by convention. We have found some sense in the notion of truth by convention, but only as attaching to a process of adoption, viz., legislative postulation, and not as a significant lingering trait of the legislatively postulated sentence. Surveying current events, we note legislative postulation in set theory and, at a more elementary level, in connection with the law of the excluded middle.

And do we not find the same continually in the theoretical hypotheses of natural science itself? What seemed to smack of convention in set theory (§V), at any rate, was "deliberate choice, set forth unaccompanied by any attempt at justification other than in terms of elegance and convenience"; and to what theoretical hypothesis of natural science might not this same character be attributed? For surely the justification of any theoretical hypothesis can, at the time of hypothesis, consist in no more than the elegance or convenience which the hypothesis brings to the containing body of laws and data. How then are we to delimit the category of legislative postulation, short of including under it every new act of scientific hypothesis?

The situation may seem to be saved, for ordinary hypotheses in natural science, by there being some indirect but eventual confrontation with empirical data. However, this confrontation can be remote; and, conversely, some such remote confrontation with experience may be claimed even for pure mathematics and elementary logic. The semblance of a difference in this respect is largely due to overemphasis of departmental boundaries. For a self-contained theory which we can check with experience includes, in point of fact, not only its various theoretical hypotheses of so-called natural science but also such portions of logic and mathematics as it makes use of. Hence I do not see how a line is to be drawn between hypotheses which confer truth by convention and hypotheses which do not, short of reckoning all hypotheses to the former category save perhaps those actually derivable or refutable by elementary logic from what Carnap used to call protocol sentences. But this version, besides depending to an unwelcome degree on the debatable notion of protocol sentences, is far too inclusive to suit anyone.

Evidently our troubles are waxing. We had been trying to make sense of the role of convention in a priori knowledge. Now the very distinction between a priori and empirical begins to waver and dissolve, at least as a distinction between sentences. (It could of course still hold as a distinction between factors in one's adoption of a sentence, but both factors might be operative everywhere.)

VII

Whatever our difficulties over the relevant distinctions, it must be conceded that logic and mathematics do seem qualitatively different from the rest of science. Logic and mathematics hold conspicuously aloof from any express appeal, certainly, to observation and experiment. Having thus nothing external to look to, logicians and mathematicians look closely to notation and explicit notational operations: to expressions, terms, substitution, transposition, cancellation, clearing of fractions, and the like. This concern of logicians and mathematicians with syntax (as Carnap calls it) is perennial, but in modern times it has become increasingly searching and explicit, and has even prompted, as we see, a linguistic philosophy of logical and mathematical truth.

On the other hand an effect of these same formal developments in modern logic, curiously, has been to show how to divorce mathematics (other than elementary logic) from any peculiarly notational considerations not equally relevant to natural science. By this I mean that mathematics can be handled (insofar as it can be handled at all) by axiomatization, outwardly quite like any system of hypotheses elsewhere in science; and elementary logic can then be left to extract the theorems.

The consequent affinity between mathematics and systematized natural science was recognized by Carnap when he propounded his P-rules alongside his L-rules or meaning postulates. Yet he did not look upon the P-rules as engendering analytic sentences, sentences true purely by language. How to sustain this distinction has been very much our problem in these pages, and one on which we have found little encouragement.

Carnap appreciated this problem, in *Logical Syntax*, as a problem of finding a difference in kind between the P-rules (or the truths thereby specified) and the L-rules (or the L-truths, analytic sentences, thereby specified). Moreover he proposed an ingenious solution.[7] In effect he characterized the logical (including mathematical) vocabulary as the largest vocabulary such that (1) there are sentences which contain only that vocabulary and (2) all such sentences are determinable as true or false by a purely syntactical condition—i.e., by a condition which speaks only of concatenation of marks. Then he limited the L-truths in effect to those involving just the logical vocabulary essentially.[8]

Truths given by P-rules were supposedly excluded from the category of logical truth under this criterion, because, though the rules specifying them are formally stated, the vocabulary involved can also be recombined to give sentences whose truth values are not determinate under any set of rules formally formulable in advance.

At this point one can object (pending a further expedient of Carnap's, which I shall next explain) that the criterion based on (1) and (2) fails of its purpose. For, consider to begin with the totality of those sentences which are expressed purely within what Carnap (or anyone) would want to count as logical (and mathematical) vocabulary. Suppose, in conformity with (2), that the division of this totality into the true and the false is reproducible in purely syntactical terms. Now surely the adding of one general term of an extra-logical kind, say 'heavier than', is not going to alter the situation. The truths which are expressible in terms of just 'heavier than', together with the logical vocabulary, will be truths of only the most general kind, such as '$(\exists x)(\exists y)(x$ is heavier than $y)$', '$(x) \sim (x$ is heavier than $x)$', and '$(x)(y)(z)(x$ is heavier than $y \cdot y$ is heavier than $z \cdot \supset \cdot x$ is heavier than $z)$'. The division of the truths from the falsehoods in this supplementary domain can probably be reproduced in syntactical terms if the division of the original totality could. But then, under the criterion based on (1) and (2), 'heavier than' qualifies for the logical vocabulary. And it is hard to

[7] Carnap, *Logical Syntax*, §50.
[8] Cf. §I above. Also, for certain reservations conveniently postponed at the moment, see §IX on "essential predication."

see what whole collection of general terms of natural science might not qualify likewise.

The further expedient, by which Carnap met this difficulty, was his use of Cartesian co-ordinates.[9] Under this procedure, each spatio-temporal particular c becomes associated with a class K of quadruples of real numbers, viz., the class of those quadruples which are the co-ordinates of component point events of c. Further let us write $K[t]$ for the class of triples which with t appended belong to K; thus $K[t]$ is that class of triples of real numbers which is associated with the momentary state of object c at time t. Then, in order to say, e.g., that c_1 is heavier than c_2 at time t, we say '$H(K_1[t], K_2[t])$', which might be translated as 'The momentary object associated with $K_1[t]$ is heavier than that associated with $K_2[t]$'. Now $K_1[t]$ and $K_2[t]$ are, in every particular case, purely mathematical objects; viz., classes of triples of real numbers. So let us consider all the true and false sentences of the form '$H(K_1[t], K_2[t])$' where, in place of '$K_1[t]$' and '$K_2[t]$', we have purely logico-mathematical designations of particular classes of triples of real numbers. There is no reason to suppose that all the truths of *this* domain can be exactly segregated in purely syntactical terms. Thus inclusion of 'H' does violate (2), and therefore 'H' fails to qualify as logical vocabulary. By adhering to the method of co-ordinates and thus reconstruing all predicates of natural science in the manner here illustrated by 'H', Carnap overcomes the objection noted in the preceding paragraph.

To sum up very roughly, this theory characterizes logic (and mathematics) as the largest part of science within which the true–false dichotomy *can* be reproduced in syntactical terms. This version may seem rather thinner than the claim that logic and mathematics are somehow true by linguistic convention, but at any rate it is more intelligible, and, if true, perhaps interesting and important. To become sure of its truth, interest, and importance, however, we must look more closely at this term 'syntax'.

As used in the passage: "The terms 'sentence' and 'direct consequence' are the two primitive terms of logical syntax,"[10] the

---

[9] *Logical Syntax*, §§3, 15.
[10] Carnap, *Philosophy and Logical Syntax*, p. 47.

term 'syntax' is of course irrelevant to a thesis. The relevant sense is that rather in which it connotes discourse about marks and their succession. But here still we must distinguish degrees of inclusiveness; two different degrees are exemplified in *Logical Syntax,* according as the object language is Carnap's highly restricted Language I or his more powerful Language II. For the former, Carnap's formulation of logical truth is narrowly syntactical in the manner of familiar formalizations of logical systems by axioms and rules of inference. But Gödel's proof of the incompletability of elementary number theory shows that no such approach can be adequate to mathematics in general, nor in particular to set theory, nor to Language II. For Language II, in consequence, Carnap's formulation of logical truth proceeded along the lines rather of Tarski's technique of truth definition.[11] The result was still a purely syntactical specification of the logical truths, but only in this more liberal sense of 'syntactical': it was couched in a vocabulary consisting (in effect) of (a) names of signs, (b) an operator expressing concatenation of expressions, and (c), by way of auxiliary machinery, the whole logical (and mathematical) vocabulary itself.

So construed, however, the thesis that logico-mathematical truth is syntactically specifiable becomes uninteresting. For, what it says is that logico-mathematical truth is specifiable in a notation consisting solely of (a), (b), *and* the whole logico-mathematical vocabulary itself. But *this* thesis would hold equally if 'logico-mathematical' were broadened (at *both* places in the thesis) to include physics, economics, and anything else under the sun; Tarski's routine of truth definition would still carry through just as well. No special trait of logic and mathematics has been singled out after all.

Strictly speaking, the position is weaker still. The mathematics appealed to in (c) must, as Tarski shows, be a yet more inclusive mathematical theory in certain respects than that for which truth is being defined. It was largely because of his increasing concern

---

[11] *Logical Syntax,* especially §§34a–i, 60a–d, 71a–d. These sections had been omitted from the German edition, but only for lack of space; cf. p. xi of the English edition. Meanwhile they had appeared as articles: "Die Antinomien . . ." and "Ein Gültigkeitskriterium . . ." At that time Carnap had had only partial access to Tarski's ideas (cf. "Gültigkeitskriterium," footnote 3), the full details of which reached the non-Slavic world in 1936 in Tarski's "Wahrheitsbegriff."

over this self-stultifying situation that Carnap relaxed his stress
on syntax, in the years following *Logical Syntax,* in favor of
semantics.

VIII

Even if logical truth were specifiable in syntactical terms, this
would not show that it was grounded in language. Any *finite* class
of truths (to take an extreme example) is clearly reproducible by
a membership condition couched in as narrowly syntactical terms
as you please; yet we certainly cannot say of every finite class of
truths that its members are true purely by language. Thus the ill-
starred doctrine of syntactical specifiability of logical truth was
always something other than the linguistic doctrine of logical
truth, if this be conceived as the doctrine that logical truth is
grounded in language. In any event the doctrine of syntactical
specifiability, which we found pleasure in being able to make
comparatively clear sense of, has unhappily had to go by the
board. The linguistic doctrine of logical truth, on the other hand,
goes sturdily on.

The notion of logical truth is now counted by Carnap as
semantical. This of course does not of itself mean that logical
truth is grounded in language; for note that the general notion of
truth is also semantical, though truth in general is not grounded
purely in language. But the semantical attribute of logical truth,
in particular, *is* one which, according to Carnap, is grounded in
language: in convention, fiat, meaning. Such support as he hints
for this doctrine, aside from ground covered in §§I–VI, seems to
depend on an analogy with what goes on in the propounding of
artificial languages; and I shall now try to show why I think the
analogy mistaken.

I may best schematize the point by considering a case, not
directly concerned with logical truth, where one might typically
produce an artificial language as a step in an argument. This is
the imaginary case of a logical positivist, say Ixmann, who is out
to defend scientists against the demands of a metaphysician. The
metaphysician argues that science presupposes metaphysical
principles, or raises metaphysical problems, and that the scientists should therefore show due concern. Ixmann's answer consists

in showing in detail how people (on Mars, say) might speak a language quite adequate to all of our science but, unlike our language, incapable of expressing the alleged metaphysical issues. (I applaud this answer, and think it embodies the most telling component of Carnap's own anti-metaphysical representations; but here I digress.) Now how does our hypothetical Ixmann specify that doubly hypothetical language? By telling us, at least to the extent needed for his argument, what these Martians are to be imagined as uttering and what they are thereby to be understood to mean. Here is Carnap's familiar duality of formation rules and transformation rules (or meaning postulates), as rules of language. But these rules are part only of Ixmann's narrative machinery, not part of what he is portraying. He is not representing his hypothetical Martians themselves as somehow explicit on formation and transformation rules. Nor is he representing there to be any intrinsic difference between those truths which happen to be disclosed to us by his partial specifications (his transformation rules) and those further truths, hypothetically likewise known to the Martians of his parable, which he did not trouble to sketch in.

The threat of fallacy lurks in the fact that Ixmann's rules are indeed arbitrary fiats, as is his whole Martian parable. The fallacy consists in confusing levels, projecting the conventional character of the rules into the story, and so misconstruing Ixmann's parable as attributing truth legislation to his hypothetical Martians.

The case of a non-hypothetical artificial language is in principle the same. Being a new invention, the language has to be explained; and the explanation will proceed by what may certainly be called formation and transformation rules. These rules will hold by arbitrary fiat, the artifex being boss. But all we can reasonably ask of these rules is that they enable us to find corresponding to each of his sentences a sentence of like truth value in familiar ordinary language. There is no (to me) intelligible additional decree that we can demand of him as to the boundary between analytic and synthetic, logic and fact, among his truths. We may well decide to extend our word 'analytic' or 'logically true' to sentences of his language which he in his explanations has paired off fairly directly with English sentences so classified by us; but this is our decree, regarding our word 'analytic' or 'logically true'.

IX

We had in §II to form some rough idea of what logical truth was supposed to take in, before we could get on with the linguistic doctrine of logical truth. This we did, with help of the general notion of truth[12] together with a partial enumeration of the logical vocabulary of a particular language. In §VII we found hope of a less provincial and accidental characterization of logical vocabulary; but it failed. Still, the position is not intolerable. We well know from modern logic how to devise a technical notation which is admirably suited to the business of 'or', 'not', 'and', 'all', 'only', and such other particles as we would care to count as logical; and to enumerate the signs and constructions of that technical notation, or a theoretically adequate subset of them, is the work of a moment (cf. §II). Insofar as we are content to think of all science as fitted within that stereotyped logical framework—and there is no hardship in so doing—our notion of logical vocabulary is precise. And so, derivatively, is our notion of logical truth. But only in point of extent. There is no epistemological corollary as to the *ground* of logical truth (cf. §II).

Even this halfway tolerable situation obtains only for logical truth in a relatively narrow sense, omitting truths by "essential predication" (Aristotle) such as 'No bachelor is married'. I tend to reserve the term 'logically true' for the narrower domain, and to use the term 'analytic' for the more inclusive domain which includes truths by essential predication. Carnap on the contrary has used both terms in the broader sense. But the problems of the two subdivisions of the analytic class differ in such a way that it has been convenient up to now in this essay to treat mainly of logical truth in the narrower sense.

The truths by essential predication are sentences which can be turned into logical truths by supplanting certain simple predicates (e.g., 'bachelor') by complex synonyms (e.g., 'man not married'). This formulation is not inadequate to such further examples as 'If A is part of B and B is part of C then A is part of C'; this case can be managed by using for 'is part of' the

---

[12] In defense of this general notion, in invidious contrast to that of analyticity, see my *From a Logical Point of View*, pp. 137f.

synonym 'overlaps nothing save what overlaps'.[13] The relevant notion of synonymy is simply *analytic* co-extensiveness (however circular this might be as a definition).

To count analyticity a genus of logical truth is to grant, it may seem, the linguistic doctrine of logical truth; for the term 'analytic' directly suggests truth by language. But this suggestion can be adjusted, in parallel to what was said of 'true by definition' in §V. 'Analytic' means true by synonymy and logic, hence no doubt true by language and logic, and simply true by language *if* the linguistic doctrine of logical truth is right. Logic itself, throughout these remarks, may be taken as including or excluding set theory (and hence mathematics), depending on further details of one's position.

What has made it so difficult for us to make satisfactory sense of the linguistic doctrine is the obscurity of 'true by language'. Now 'synonymous' lies within that same central obscurity; for, about the best we can say of synonymous predicates is that they are somehow "co-extensive by language." The obscurity extends, of course, to 'analytic'.

One quickly identifies certain seemingly transparent cases of synonymy, such as 'bachelor' and 'man not married', and senses the triviality of associated sentences such as 'No bachelor is married'. Conceivably the mechanism of such recognition, when better understood, might be made the basis of a definition of synonymy and analyticity in terms of linguistic behavior. On the other hand such an approach might make sense only of something like degrees of synonymy and analyticity. I see no reason to expect that the full-width analyticity which Carnap and others make such heavy demands upon can be fitted to such a foundation in even an approximate way. In any event, we at present lack any tenable general suggestion, either rough and practical or remotely theoretical, as to what it is to be an analytic sentence. All we have are purported illustrations, and claims that the truths of elementary logic, with or without the rest of mathematics, should be counted in. Wherever there has been a semblance of a general criterion, to my knowledge, there has been either some drastic failure such as tended to admit all or no sentences as analytic, or there has been a circularity of the kind

[13] After Goodman.

noted three paragraphs back, or there has been a dependence on terms like 'meaning', 'possible', 'conceivable', and the like, which are at least as mysterious (and in the same way) as what we want to define. I have expatiated on these troubles elsewhere,[14] as has White.

Logical truth (in my sense, excluding the additional category of essential predication) is, we saw, well enough definable (relatively to a fixed logical notation). *Elementary* logical truth can even be given a narrowly syntactical formulation, such as Carnap once envisaged for logic and mathematics as a whole (cf. §VII); for the deductive system of elementary logic is known to be complete. But when we would supplement the logical truths by the rest of the so-called analytic truths, true by essential predication, then we are no longer able even to say what we are talking about. The distinction itself, and not merely an epistemological question concerning it, is what is then in question.

What of settling the limits of the broad class of analytic truths by fixing on a standard language as we did for logical truth? No, the matter is very different. Once given the logical vocabulary, we have a means of clearly marking off the species logical truth within the genus truth. But the intermediate genus analyticity is not parallel, for it does not consist of the truths which contain just a certain vocabulary essentially (in the sense of §II). To segregate analyticity we should need rather some sort of accounting of synonymies throughout a universal or all-purpose language. No regimented universal language is at hand, however, for consideration; what Carnap has propounded in this direction have of course been only illustrative samples, fragmentary in scope. And even if there were one, it is not clear by what standards we would care to settle questions of synonymy and analyticity within it.

X

Carnap's present position[15] is that one has specified a language quite rigorously only when he has fixed, by dint of so-called meaning postulates, what sentences are to count as analytic. The

14 "Two dogmas."
15 See particularly "Meaning postulates."

proponent is supposed to distinguish between those of his declarations which count as meaning postulates, and thus engender analyticity, and those which do not. This he does, presumably, by attaching the label 'meaning postulate'.

But the sense of this label is far less clear to me than four causes of its seeming to be clear. Which of these causes has worked on Carnap, if any, I cannot say; but I have no doubt that all four have worked on his readers. One of these causes is misevaluation of the role of convention in connection with artificial language; thus note the unattributed fallacy described in §VIII. Another is misevaluation of the conventionality of postulates: failure to appreciate that postulates, though they are postulates always by fiat, are not *therefore* true by fiat (cf. §§IV–V). A third is over-estimation of the distinctive nature of postulates, and of definitions, because of conspicuous and peculiar roles which postulates and definitions have played in situations not really relevant to present concerns: postulates in uninterpreted systems (cf. §IV), and definitions in double systems of notation (cf. §V). A fourth is misevaluation of legislative postulation and legislative definition themselves, in two respects: failure to appreciate that this legislative trait is a trait of scientific hypotheses very generally (cf. §VI), and failure to appreciate that it is a trait of the passing event rather than of the truth which is thereby instituted (cf. end of §V).

Suppose a scientist introduces a new term, for a certain substance or force. He introduces it by an act either of legislative definition or of legislative postulation. Progressing, he evolves hypotheses regarding further traits of the named substance or force. Suppose now that some such eventual hypothesis, well attested, identifies this substance or force with one named by a complex term built up of other portions of his scientific vocabulary. We all know that this new identity will figure in the ensuing developments quite on a par with the identity which first came of the act of legislative definition, if any, or on a par with the law which first came of the act of legislative postulation. Revisions, in the course of further progress, can touch any of these affirmations equally. Now I urge that scientists, proceeding thus, are not thereby slurring over any meaningful distinction. Legislative acts occur again and again; on the other hand a dichotomy of the resulting truths themselves into analytic and synthetic, truths by meaning postulate and truths by force of nature, has been given no tolerably clear meaning even as a methodological ideal.

One conspicuous consequence of Carnap's belief in this dichotomy may be seen in his attitude toward philosophical issues as to what there is.[16] It is only by assuming the cleavage between analytic and synthetic truths that he is able to declare the problem of universals to be a matter not of theory but of linguistic decision. Now I am as impressed as anyone with the vastness of what language contributes to science and to one's whole view of the world; and in particular I grant that one's hypothesis as to what there is, e.g., as to there being universals, is at bottom just as arbitrary or pragmatic a matter as one's adoption of a new brand of set theory or even a new system of bookkeeping. Carnap in turn recognizes that such decisions, however conventional, "will nevertheless usually be influenced by theoretical knowledge."[17] But what impresses me more than it does Carnap is how well this whole attitude is suited also to the theoretical hypotheses of natural science itself, and how little basis there is for a distinction.

The lore of our fathers is a fabric of sentences. In our hands it develops and changes, through more or less arbitrary and deliberate revisions and additions of our own, more or less directly occasioned by the continuing stimulation of our sense organs. It is a pale gray lore, black with fact and white with convention. But I have found no substantial reasons for concluding that there are any quite black threads in it, or any white ones.

[16] See next essay.
[17] "Empiricism, semantics, and ontology," §2.

13

❧ *Implicit Definition Sustained*

The characterization of axioms as implicit definitions can be found as far back as 1818, in Gergonne, and it was still vigorous thirty years ago. What is exasperating about the doctrine is its facility, or cheapness, as a way of endowing statements with the security of analytic truths without ever having to show that they follow from definitions properly so called, definitions with eliminable definienda.

Russell gave the doctrine its due, I felt, though he did not mention it by name, when he wrote in 1919 that "the method of 'postulating' what we want has many advantages; they are the same as the advantages of theft over honest toil."

I am shocked now to find that the view of axioms as implicit definitions can be defended, and with a literalness that its own proponents can scarcely have thought possible. To discharge this somber duty is the purpose of the present note.

Briefly, the point is that there is a mechanical routine whereby, given an assortment of interpreted undefined predicates 'F_1', 'F_2', . . . , 'F_n' governed by a true axiom or a finite list of such, we can switch to a new and equally economical set of undefined predicates and define 'F_1', . . . , 'F_n' in terms of them, plus auxiliary arithmetical notations, in such a way that the old axioms

This first appeared in the *Journal of Philosophy* (Volume 61, 1964). For helpful remarks on a first draft I am indebted to Burton Dreben and Dagfinn Føllesdal.

become true by arithmetic. The predicates 'F_1', . . . , 'F_n' do not become predicates of numbers, but continue under the definitions to be true of precisely the things that they were true of under their original interpretations.

This will not surprise readers who encountered the central idea in a 1940 paper by Goodman and me. The link with the doctrine of implicit definition is an added thought, but the technical point itself, as formulated in the foregoing paragraph, merely improves on our 1940 result in these three ways: it is geared to predicates instead of singular terms, thus conforming to a more modern theory of theories; it draws specifically on arithmetic, in fact elementary number theory, rather than on set theory generally; and it assures a mechanical routine for finding the definitions.

This last improvement depends on a strengthened form of Löwenheim's theorem given by Hilbert and Bernays in 1939. Löwenheim's theorem dates from 1915 and says that every satisfiable schema that can be written in the notation of the logic of quantification can be satisfied by an interpretation in the universe of natural numbers. The strengthened version in Hilbert and Bernays specifies the interpretation in arithmetical notation. Hilbert and Bernays show how, given any schema in the notation of the logic of quantification, to find arithmetical predicates (better: open sentences of elementary number theory) which, when adopted as interpretations of the predicate letters of the schema, will make the schema come out true if it was satisfiable.[1]

In the remaining pages we shall see how, granted the ability thus conferred by Hilbert and Bernays, we can convert axioms to definitions as promised above. Imagine an interpreted deductive theory θ that presupposes elementary logic and treats of some extra-logical subject matter, say chemistry. Suppose it set forth in the standard way using primitive predicates 'F_1', . . . , 'F_n', truth functions, quantifiers, and general variables. The exclusion of singular terms, function signs, and multiple sorts of variables is no real restriction, for these accessories are reducible to the narrower basis in familiar ways.

By a slight and innocuous reinterpretation, the range of values of the variables of a theory can be extended to take in any desired supplementary objects. We just pick one of the values

[1] Hilbert and Bernays, Vol. 2, p. 253. For exposition and additional references see my "Interpretations of sets of conditions," pp. 101f.

originally available, say a, and then extend the original interpretation of each predicate by counting true of the supplementary objects whatever was true of a, and false of them what was false of a. The new objects thus enter undetectably, indiscriminable from a. This maneuver, which I shall call *hidden inflation*, is not new.[2]

In particular, then, let us understand the variables of θ as ranging not just over physical objects or other special objects of chemistry, but over the natural numbers too—all these things being pooled in a single universe of discourse. For the natural numbers, if they were not there, could always be incorporated by hidden inflation.

Let the axioms of θ be finite in number, and true. Think of '$A(F_1, \ldots, F_n)$' as abbreviating the conjunction of them all. This is a schema of the logic of quantification if we forget the chemical interpretations of 'F_1', ..., 'F_n'; and it is a satisfiable one, since under the chemical interpretations it was true. So by Hilbert and Bernays' method we can find predicates in elementary number theory, abbreviated say as 'K_1', ..., 'K_n', such that $A(K_1, \ldots, K_n)$. Nor must the quantified variables thereupon be narrowed in range to the natural numbers; by hidden inflation we can still let them range over the whole universe of θ, numerical and otherwise.

Adopt, next, a new interpreted theory, having again the same inclusive universe of discourse as θ. Give it primitive predicates sufficient for elementary number theory, and in addition give it the primitive predicates 'G_1', ..., 'G_n', subject to the same chemical interpretations that 'F_1', ..., 'F_n' enjoyed in θ. But give the new theory no axioms involving 'G_1', ..., 'G_n'. Now in the new theory let us introduce 'F_1', ..., 'F_n' as defined predicates, as follows. For each i, explain '$F_i(x_1, \ldots, x_j)$, (with the appropriate number j of places) as short for:

$$A(G_1, \ldots, G_n) . G_i(x_1, \ldots, x_j) . \lor .$$
$$\sim A(G_1, \ldots, G_n) . K_i(x_1, \ldots, x_j).$$

It will be recalled that the axioms of θ are chemically true. Hence also, as a chemical matter of unaxiomatized fact, $A(G_1, \ldots, G_n)$. Therefore the above definition makes 'F_i' in fact coextensive with 'G_i'. Therefore it agrees with the chemical inter-

[2] E.g., see Hilbert and Ackermann, p. 92.

pretation of 'F_i' in θ, for each i. Yet, under the above definition, '$A(F_1, \ldots, F_n)$' is logically deducible from just the arithmetical truth '$A(K_1, \ldots, K_n)$'. (Proof: 'F_1', $\ldots$, 'F_n' are equated by the definition to 'K_1', $\ldots$, 'K_n' unless $A(G_1, \ldots, G_n)$, and in this event they are equated to 'G_1', $\ldots$, 'G_n', so that again $A(F_1, \ldots, F_n)$.)

The shift of system was of course farcical. We merely rewrote the primitive predicates of θ as new letters, keeping the old chemical interpretations, and then pleonastically defined the old predicate letters anew in terms of these so that their chemical interpretations were again preserved (extensionally anyway). Yet the erstwhile chemical axioms of θ became, under this definitional hocus pocus, arithmetically true.

I do not speak of arithmetical demonstrability, for a question there arises of choosing among incomplete systems of number theory. I speak of arithmetical truth.

The doctrine that axioms are implicit definitions thus gains support. If axioms are satisfiable at all, they can be viewed as a shorthand instruction to adopt definitions as above, rendering one's theory true by arithmetic. And, if the axioms were true on a literal reading, the interpretation of their predicates remains undisturbed.

The doctrine of implicit definition has been deplored as a too facile way of making any desired truth analytic: just call it an axiom. Now we see that such claims to analyticity are every bit as firm as can be made for sentences whose truth follows by definition from arithmetic. So much the worse, surely, for the notion of analyticity.

14

❧ *Mr. Strawson*
on Logical Theory

A philosopher of ordinary language has brought his limpid vernacular to bear on formal logic.[1] Step by unhurried step he explains the terms of logical appraisal and what the logician's business is, and sets the logician's artifacts over against the speech of natural man. '⊃' emerges at page 34, the truth tables at page 68, the quantifiers at page 131, and the syllogism at page 158. The intervening and ensuing space is given over not to theorems and proofs and decision procedures (except for some sketchy examples), but to interpretation and criticism. A ninth chapter, the last, is an excellent little philosophical essay on induction.

The division of the present review into sections will correspond to the structure not of the book, but of the critical reflections which the book has stimulated in this reader.

I. ENTAILMENT, ANALYTICITY, AND COMPANY

First Mr. Strawson undertakes to explain, in an ordinary-language setting, the notions of inconsistency and entailment.

This was written as a review, but was run instead as the opening article in *Mind* (Volume 62, October 1953) to launch my year as George Eastman Visiting Professor at Oxford. Reprinted by permission of the editor of *Mind*.

[1] Strawson, *Introduction to Logical Theory*.

The devices at his disposal are analogy and example; and even the method of example offers difficulties, since he is at pains to withhold the stigma of inconsistency from speech fads like "Well, I do and I don't."

Engineers have been known to work wonders with the differential calculus without ever having been given an account of its foundations more intelligible than the notion of an actual infinitesimal; and there are philosophers who have, through use and custom, grown to feel equally at home with the notion of entailment which so pervades G. E. Moore's philosophical analyses. There are philosophers of ordinary language who have grown so inured to the philosophical terms 'entails' and 'inconsistent' as to look upon them, perhaps, as ordinary language. But the reader without such benefits of use and custom is apt to feel, even after Mr. Strawson's painstaking discussion of the notions of inconsistency and entailment, somewhat the kind of insecurity over these notions that many engineers must have felt, when callow, over derivatives and differentials. At the risk of seeming unteachable, I go on record as one such reader.

Turning away from Mr. Strawson's book for a bit, let us seek perspective on the general problem. The terms 'entail' and 'inconsistent' belong to a group other members of which are 'analytic' and 'synonymous'. Because of the easy interdefinability of these terms, one of them suffices to represent the group; and a handy choice is 'analytic'. In recent classical philosophy the usual gesture toward explaining 'analytic' amounts to something like this: a statement is analytic if it is true by virtue solely of meanings of words and independently of matters of fact. It can be objected, in a somewhat formalistic and unsympathetic spirit, that the boundary which this definition draws is vague or that the definiens is as much in need of clarification as the definiendum. This is an easy level of polemic in philosophy, and no serious philosophical effort is proof against it. But misgivings over the notion of analyticity are warranted also at a deeper level, where a sincere attempt has been made to guess the unspoken *Weltanschauung* from which the motivation and plausibility of a division of statements into analytic and synthetic arise. My guess is that that *Weltanschauung* is a more or less attenuated holdover of phenomenalistic reductionism.

A philosopher may have rejected phenomenalism in the full reductionistic sense, in favor of admitting that statements for the most part are laden with an irreducibly extra-phenomenal burden over and above their phenomenal import. But he may continue to hold (a) that the statements do still possess their phenomenal import, what there is of it, as separate statements one by one; or he may hold rather (b) that the statements are tied to the testimony of the senses only in a systematic or holistic way which defies any statement-by-statement distribution of sensory certificates. If he holds so much as the vestige (a) of phenomenalistic reductionism, then he will find it natural to accept in principle a division between analytic and synthetic truths, the former being those in which the phenomenal content is null. If on the other hand his position is (b), he may be expected to find no way of putting some truths into empirical quarantine and judging the remainder free of infection. For him the contribution which linguistic meaning makes to knowledge and the contribution which sensory evidence makes to knowledge are too inextricably intertwined to admit of a sentence-by-sentence separation.

My own position is (b). I do grant that any given sensory event seems more relevant to some statements than to others; also that some statements seem less directly touched than others by sensory events in general; but I think these variations can be accounted for as sporadic surface effects, without prejudice to (b) as underlying principle.[2] My misgivings over the notion of analyticity are thus misgivings in principle. But those also who espouse the notion espouse it mainly in principle, granting freely that the boundary between the analytic and synthetic can be troublesome and indecisive in application.

The purpose of the foregoing excursion is not to invoke my philosophy in criticism of another man's book. There are rather three other points. One is that misgivings over analyticity and related notions are not just a caviling over fuzzy boundaries. A second is that these notions are too bound up with a debatable philosophical position to be well suited to the very prominent roles which Mr. Strawson assigns to them in his project of clarifying elementary logic from the standpoint of ordinary

[2] See my "Two dogmas of empiricism," pp. 40ff.

language. A third is that I should think Mr. Strawson himself, with his stress on the realities of common-sense language, would incline rather to (*b*) than to (*a*).

He frequently shows awareness that there are difficulties in applying analyticity and related notions. On page 5 he writes:

What makes predicates incompatible? . . . It is we, the makers of a language, who make predicates incompatible. . . . A boundary must be drawn, limiting the applicability of a word used in describing things; and it is we who decide where the boundaries are to be drawn.

This metaphor of drawing boundaries is in some ways misleading. I do not mean by it that we often make conscious decisions of this kind . . . nor that the decisions we make, when we make them, are purely verbal decisions.

On page 91 he writes:

What we are suffering from here is perhaps a crudity in our notion of entailment.

On page 231 he writes:

We may very often hesitate to say whether a given sentence is analytic or synthetic; and the imprecision of this distinction, as applied to ordinary speech, reflects an imprecision in the application of the notion of entailment to ordinary speech.

The laudable observation last quoted might well have caused a philosopher of ordinary language to wonder about his use of the notion of analyticity as a keystone. But, as I have urged in earlier pages, the notion has yet a more serious fault than vagueness.

II. LOGICAL TRUTH

If the author has chosen too soft and friable a keystone in analyticity, then it is fair to ask what he could have used in its place. Insofar as he uses the notion of analyticity in defining the province of logic, my answer is as follows: he could have used, instead, the notion of truth and the notion of logical vocabulary. Given these, the business of formal logic is describable as that of finding statement forms which are *logical,* in the sense of containing no constants beyond the logical vocabulary, and (extensionally) *valid,* in the sense that all statements exemplifying the form in question are true. Statements exemplifying such forms may be called *logically true.* Here there is no hint of a doctrine as to the epistemological grounds of logical truth; no affirmation or denial of conventionalism (whatever that would be), nor any effort to separate the analytic from the synthetic.

Mr. Strawson observes (pp. 40ff.), and rightly (if for the moment we set aside any misgivings over the notion of analyticity), that not all analytic statements are instances of logical forms all of whose instances are analytic. As examples to the contrary he cites statements of the non-logical form:

$$x \text{ is a younger son} \supset x \text{ is a brother.}[3]$$

However, he recognizes that instances of the latter kind are not supposed to be provided for by rules of logic. The forms which the logician wants as theorems are, by Mr. Strawson's own account, just those logical forms all of whose instances are analytic. This account matches that in my preceding paragraph, except that it has 'analytic' instead of 'true'. In net resultant scope these two accounts of logic differ little if any. They may differ in that certain logical forms whose validity depends on the size of the universe would qualify as theorems for my logic book and not for his; but I should need to understand analyticity better to be sure even of this.

I have urged, above, that Mr. Strawson's characterization of the scope of logic in terms of the notion of analyticity be dropped in favor of a characterization in terms of the notions of logical vocabulary and truth. Logical vocabulary is specified only, I suppose, by enumeration. If this element of apparent arbitrariness is a shortcoming, it is a shortcoming also in Mr. Strawson's characterization; for this also depends on the notion of logical vocabulary, via logical form. He may still feel that he brings out the essential nature of logic more fully than my characterization would do, in that the logical truths turn out for him to be some (though not all) of the analytic statements. However, one who rejects the notion of analyticity is less averse than others to finding that the boundaries of logic, like those of biochemistry and other disciplines, are to some degree capricious.

The notion of analyticity, as used in Mr. Strawson's charac-

[3] For further discussion of this contrast see my "Two dogmas."

terization of logic, gave way to the notion of truth in my
alternative characterization. The notion of truth is also of course
one of which Mr. Strawson avails himself frequently in the course
of his book. Possibly he considers the notion intelligible only as a
sum of analyticity and empirical truth; if so, reluctance to do
without the notion of analyticity is the more understandable. But
in fact the inclusive notion of truth is a far less dubious starting
point than that of analyticity; for we understand under what
circumstances to say of *any* given statement that it is true, just
as clearly as we understand the statement itself.

The group of notions to which that of analyticity gives rise,
viz., entailment, inconsistency, and synonymy, are paralleled by
a group of notions issuing from logical truth in the sense defined a
few paragraphs back. Thus, just as one statement entails another
if the corresponding conditional ('⊃') is analytic, so for me one
statement (logically) implies another if that conditional is
logically true. Just as a statement is inconsistent for Mr.
Strawson if its negation is analytic, so for me it is inconsistent, or
logically false, if its negation is logically true. It is noteworthy,
for my strictures against the notion of analyticity, that much of
Mr. Strawson's use of analyticity and entailment in the course of
his logical expositions strongly resembles my use of logical truth
and implication in *Methods of Logic*. On the other hand there
also are long and inconclusive passages in Mr. Strawson's book
which would drop out if the recommended shift were made.

III. WORDS INTO SYMBOLS. TRUTH-VALUE GAPS

Logic, under either of the accounts contrasted above, is *formal*
logic in a narrow sense which excludes those preparatory operations, in applied logic, whereby sentences of ordinary language
are fitted to logical forms by interpretation and paraphrase. Mr.
Strawson stresses the magnitude of these applicational maneuvers, and in this I am in full agreement. The considerations
involved in them deserve attention in logic texts, and have been
given attention in some; rarely, however, with the sympathetic
care and subtlety which Mr. Strawson bestows on them.

One conspicuous divergence between language as used and
language as depicted in logical forms is the correspondence of

many idioms on the one hand to few on the other. Reduction of the rich variety of more or less interchangeable grammatical constructions and logical locutions of ordinary language to a conveniently standardized minimum is imperative for algorithmic purposes; for the power and simplicity of an algorithm, or indeed of any theory, depend on there being many occurrences of few elements rather than few occurrences of many.

Further divergence between languages as used and language as reflected in logical forms remains after reductions of the kind just alluded to have been completed; for, the surviving logical particles have uses in ordinary language which diverge from the laws formulated by logicians. The well-known failure of the ordinary statement operators 'or', 'if–then', 'and', and 'not' to conform in all cases to the precepts of truth-functional logic is well expounded by Mr. Strawson. Because 'and' and 'not' deviate less radically than the others, I have found it pedagogically helpful (in *Elementary Logic*) to treat the translation of ordinary language into logical form, at the truth-functional level, as funneled through 'and' and 'not'; and Mr. Strawson follows suit.

Such failures of correspondence are not, of course, confined to the truth-function level. They recur with 'every' and 'some', in relation to the logic of quantification. Mr. Strawson also develops these details with much sensitivity.

Another conspicuous way in which ordinary language diverges from language as reflected in logical forms is in the existence of what I have called truth-value gaps. One illustration in my *Methods of Logic* is the conditional, under ordinary usage in the indicative mood. Ordinarily the conditional is not thought of as true or false at all, but rather the consequent is thought of as conditionally true or false given the antecedent. Another example, *op. cit.*, is provided by the singular description; if the object which it purports to describe does not exist, then commonly the contexts of the description are accorded no truth values under ordinary usage. "The question of their truth," as Mr. Strawson phrases it in his able exposition of the topic, "does not arise."

Mr. Strawson exploits this idea in a detailed defense of the traditional syllogistic logic apropos of the famous question, raised by Leibniz and others, of existential import. Mr. Strawson's method is to construe the categorical forms, for purposes of

traditional logic, in such a way that where a term is empty of
extension the question of the truth of the containing categorical
statement does not arise. He argues plausibly that this view does
considerable justice to ordinary language. His is, I expect, the
best way of defending the traditional syllogistic.

A substantial offshoot of Mr. Strawson's reflexions on truth-
value gaps is a theory, expounded earlier in an article by
Strawson[4] and reminiscent also of Aquinas and Geach, in which a
distinction is made between the referential and the predicative
role of a singular term. This distinction, little heeded in logical
literature, is important for an appreciation of ordinary language;
and, as Mr. Strawson well brings out, it reveals a marked failure
on the part of Russell's theory of descriptions to correspond to
the ordinary use of 'the'.

Normally, if the role of a singular term in a given statement is
referential, the question of the truth of the statement does not
arise in case the purported object of the term is found not to
exist. Since modern formal logic closes all such truth-value gaps,
it is not to be wondered that there is nothing in modern logic to
correspond to the referential role, in Mr. Strawson's sense, of
terms. Mr. Strawson is at pains to point out that proper names,
so-called by formal logicians, are therefore far from corresponding to the singular terms of ordinary language.

On this point he thinks to find modern logic in a difficulty. For,
he writes (p. 216):

Now the whole structure of quantificational logic, with its apparatus
of individual variables, seems, or has seemed to most of its exponents,
to require, for its application to ordinary speech to be possible at all,
that there should exist individual referring expressions that could
appear as values of the individual variables.

It is therefore important to emphasize, in contrariety to what the
above quotation suggests, that anything even remotely analogous
to proper names or singular terms is systematically eliminable
from modern logic altogether, both in theory and in application.[5]

Granted the value of the distinction between referential and
predicative roles as a means of capturing the genius of ordinary
language, it would be a mistake to infer that modern logic errs in

[4] "On referring."
[5] Cf. my *Methods of Logic*, pp. 215–224 (3d ed., pp. 227–234).

not keeping the idiosyncrasy of ordinary language which that distinction brings out. We shall recur to the general question of the function of formal logic in §V, below. Meanwhile let us rest with this analogy: Weierstrass did not define the infinitesimal, but showed rather how to get on without it.

IV. INSTABILITY OF TRUTH VALUE. TENSE

Another important respect in which language as used diverges from language as reflected in logical forms is the variation of truth value from occurrence to occurrence of a single sentence. Such variation can result from the use of indices ('I', 'here', 'now') or tensed verbs; also it can result from casual ambiguities, variously resolved by varying contexts and situations. Formal logic, on the other hand, developing arguments as it does in which a schematic letter 'p' keeps recurring, is misapplied unless the sentence represented by 'p' is thought of as keeping a fixed truth value at all points in the argument.

In describing these matters, Mr. Strawson adopts a double terminology: 'sentence' versus 'statement'. One and the same sentence can be used in ordinary language to make any of various statements, whereas a sentence to which formal logic is applied must be thought of as making one fixed statement and no other. In appealing thus to "statements," not as a kind of sentence but as acts performed by uttering sentences, or perhaps contents conveyed by sentences, Mr. Strawson gains a certain expository ease and also runs a certain risk. The risk is that of hypostatizing obscure entities, akin perhaps to "propositions" or "meanings" or "facts" or "states of affairs," and reading into them an explanatory value which is not there.

Terminological questions aside, the variation of truth values in ordinary language and the insistence on fixed truth values for purposes of formal logic are points which are no less important than they are familiar. Mr. Strawson overstates the consequent limitation on the uses of formal logic, however, when he writes (p. 223):

(1) that when we inquire what use can be made of the symbolic apparatus of logic we find that for certain general reasons it seems best adapted to the role of systematically exhibiting the logical relationships

between sentences which answer to the ideal of independence of contextual conditions;
(2) that the actually occurring sentences of this type are analytic sentences and law-sentences.

Formal logic would be a pretty idle luxury if its applicability were limited thus severely. In explanation of why formal logic is not really thus limited, let me quote myself (*Methods of Logic*, p. 43):

> Insofar as the interpretation of ambiguous expressions depends on circumstances of the argument as a whole—speaker, hearer, scene, date, and underlying problem and purpose—the fallacy of equivocation is not to be feared; for, those background circumstances may be expected to influence the interpretation of an ambiguous expression uniformly wherever the expression recurs in the course of the argument. . . .
>
> The fallacy of equivocation arises rather when the interpretation of the ambiguous expression is influenced in varying ways by immediate contexts . . . so that the expression undergoes changes of meaning within the limits of the argument. In such cases we have to rephrase . . . to the extent of resolving such part of the ambiguity as might, if left standing, end up by being resolved in different ways by different immediate contexts within the proposed logical argument.

Mr. Strawson's dim view of the scope of applicability of formal logic is perhaps attributable in part to the fact that he gets into trouble over tensed and tenseless verbs on pages 150f.:

> For example, we might try writing the sentence 'There was at least one woman among the survivors' in the form '$(\exists x)$ (x is a woman . x was among the survivors)'. But to say 'There *is* at least one person who is a woman and was among the survivors' is at least to suggest that the person is alive at the time the sentence is uttered . . . Changing the second ' is ' to ' was ' will not help; it will merely prompt the question 'What became of her then? Has she changed her sex?' Nor can the difficulty be evaded by declaring '$(\exists x)$' in this sentence to be timeless; it is not true that when we speak of persons and incidents the question of time-reference does not arise.

Mr. Strawson's error occurs where he says "Nor can the difficulty be evaded . . .". The only tenable attitude toward quantifiers and other notations of modern logic is to construe them always, in all contexts, as timeless. This does not mean that the values of 'x' may not themselves be thing-events, four-dimensional beings in space-time; it means only that date is to

be treated on a par with location, color, specific gravity, etc.—
hence not as a qualification on '∃', but merely as one of sundry
attributes of the thing-events which are values of 'x'. When
'x' ranges rather over numbers, Mr. Strawson appreciates that
'$(\exists x)$' is best read 'There [is] in the number series a number
x such that', with tenseless '[is]'; but he does not appreciate
that '$(\exists x)$' is likewise to be read 'There [is] in space-time a
thing-event x such that' when 'x' ranges over the four-dimensional denizens of the ages and galaxies of space-time. Any value
of 'x' in this latter or spatio-temporal universe of discourse will
in fact have a time, just as any value of 'x' in the former or
numerical universe of discourse will in fact have a highest prime
factor; but the '[is]' or '∃' itself speaks no more of time than of
prime factors.

The way to render Mr. Strawson's example is '$(\exists x)(x$ [is] a
woman . x was among the survivors)', with tenseless '[is]' and,
as always, tenseless '∃'. The 'was' here involves reference presumably to some time or occasion implicit in the missing context;
if we suppose it given by some constant 'D' (e.g., 'the sinking of
the *Lusitania*'), then the whole amounts to '$(\exists x)(x$ [is] a woman
. x [is] among the survivors of $D)$', tenseless throughout.

The above example is not odd, but typical. The four-dimensional view of space-time is part and parcel of the use of modern
formal logic, and in particular the use of quantification theory, in
application to temporal affairs. It may be felt to be a criticism of
modern logic that it calls for so drastic a departure from the
time-slanted Indo-European language structure. But the better
way of looking at the matter is to recognize both in the four-
dimensional approach, with its notable technical advantages, and
in quantification theory, with its notable technical advantages,
two interrelated contributions to scientific method.

It would be hard to exaggerate the importance of recognizing
the tenselessness of quantification over temporal entities. The
precept has been followed as a matter of course by anyone who
has been serious about applying modern logic to temporal
entities.[6] I see no reason to expect a coherent application of
quantification theory to temporal matters on any other basis.

Earlier I suggested that Mr. Strawson's failure to appreciate

---

[6] Examples: Carnap, *Der logische Aufbau der Welt*; Woodger, *The
Axiomatic Method in Biology*; Woodger, *Biology and Language*.

the tenselessness of quantification over temporal entites might be
a factor in his underestimation of the scope of modern logic. I
should like to go further and say that I do not see how, failing to
appreciate the tenselessness of quantification over temporal
entities, one could reasonably take modern logic very seriously.
From having perhaps wondered at Mr. Strawson's doubts over
logic, one comes to wonder rather at his forbearance.

V. THE PLACE OF FORMAL LOGIC

Reduction of ordinary language to logical form is, as noted in
§III above, a reduction in at least two ways: reduction of the
variety of idioms and grammatical constructions, and reduction
of each surviving idiom to one fixed and convenient interpretation. That fixed interpretation is bound to be, moreover, a pretty
Pickwickian one, as is evident from §§III–IV above. Now Mr.
Strawson represents this Procrustean activity somewhat as a
hobby:

Logicians like to present a tidy system of interconnected rules. The
neatness of a system might suffer if it had too many constants in it
[p. 49].
And it is this ideal of systematization which has most profoundly
influenced the modern development of logic; so profoundly that the
original conception of simply codifying the most general principles we
appeal to in making our logical appraisals has pretty well been lost
sight of. . . . The formal logician, in relation to ordinary language,
might be compared with a man ostensibly mapping a piece of country
of which the main contours are highly irregular and shifting. But the
man is passionately addicted to geometry. . . . Naturally his maps will
never quite fit [pp. 57f.].

The pleasures of science are not to be denied, but the tendency
to equate those pleasures with the pleasures of games can be
seriously misleading. There are those, certainly, who have ap-
proached mathematics and logic in the same spirit in which they
approach chess; but my suspicion, undissipated still by the
fashionable tendency to cite quaternions as a case to the
contrary, is that those playful spirits have been less productive of
important results than those whose pleasure in science is the
pleasure of working toward fundamentals. There is no deciding

whether ibn-Tahir and al-Khwarizmi devised Arabic numeration and algebraic notation in a gaming spirit, but at any rate the motivation of the Procrustean treatment of ordinary language at the hands of logicians has been rather that of achieving theoretical insights comparable to those which Arabic numeration and algebra made possible. That their hope has not been forlorn is attested by such discoveries as Gödel's of the impossibility of a complete system of number theory, and Church's of the impossibility of a decision procedure for quantification theory.

Nor need one set one's sights so high; even the humdrum spinning out of elementary logical principles in modern logic brings insights, concerning the general relation of premise to conclusion in actual science and common sense, which are denied to men who scruple to disturb a particle of natural language in its full philological concreteness. The naturalist who observes nature only with his hands clasped behind him may gain poetic inspiration, and he may even contribute a little something to taxonomy; but he is not to be looked to for a basic contribution to scientific theory.

The ancillary activity of analyzing and paraphrasing scientific sentences of ordinary language, so as to abstract out their logical form and explore the formal consequences, is comparable in principle to the activity of the physicist who reworks and rethinks his data and hypotheses into a stereotyped mathematical form so as to be able to bring the techniques of tensor analysis or differential equations to bear upon them. It is an important activity, and deserving of all the space and acumen which Mr. Strawson expends upon it. My only quarrel is with the notion, hinted now and again, that it is somehow wrong to have to undertake this activity, and that formal logicians have been generally seduced by hobbyism into making mistakes about language—as if Frenchmen betrayed ignorance of French when they depart from the pattern of 'soixante-dix-neuf' and 'quatre-vingts' by writing '79' and '80'.

The long and perceptive passages in which Mr. Strawson traces out something like a logic of ordinary language have all the interest and value of an able philological inquiry. But it is a mistake to think of Mr. Strawson as doing here, realistically, a job which the dream-beset formal logician had been trying to do in his unrealistic way. Actually the formal logician's job is very different, and may be schematized as follows. To begin with let us picture formal logic as one phase of the activity of a hypothetical individual who is also physicist, mathematician, *et al*. Now this overdrawn individual is interested in ordinary language, let us suppose, only as a means of getting on with physics, mathematics, and the rest of science; and he is happy to depart from ordinary language whenever he finds a more convenient device of extraordinary language which is equally adequate to his need of the moment in formulating and developing his physics, mathematics, or the like. He drops 'if–then' in favor of '⊃' without ever entertaining the mistaken idea that they are synonymous; he makes the change only because he finds that the purposes for which he had been *needing* 'if–then', in connection with his particular scientific work, happen to be satisfactorily manageable also by a somewhat different use of '⊃' and other devices. He makes this and other shifts with a view to streamlining his scientific work, maximizing his algorithmic facility, and maximizing his understanding of what he is doing. He does not care how inadequate his logical notation is as a reflexion of the vernacular, as long as it can be made to serve all the particular needs for which he, in his scientific program, would have otherwise to depend on that part of the vernacular. He does not even need to paraphrase the vernacular into his logical notation, for he has learned to think directly in his logical notation, or even (which is the beauty of the thing) to let it think for him.

Not that this logical language is independent of ordinary language. It has its roots in ordinary language, and these roots are not to be severed. Everyone, even to our hypothetical logician-scientist and his pupils' pupils, grows up in ordinary language, and can learn the logician-scientist's technical jargon, from '⊃' to $\frac{dy}{dx}$ to 'neutrino', only by learning how, in principle at least, to paraphrase it into ordinary language. But for this purpose no extensive analysis of the logic of ordinary language is required. It is enough that we show how to reduce the logical notations to a few primitive notations (say '∼', '.', 'ε', and universal quantification) and then explain just *these* in ordinary language, availing ourselves of ample paraphrases and scholia as needed for precision. These explanations would be such as to exclude, explicitly, any unwanted vagaries of the 'not', 'and', 'is', and 'every' of ordinary language; such also as to provide for the tenselessness, the eternal invariance of truth value, which classical logical theory presupposes in the statements to which it is applied (cf. §IV above).

Let it not be inferred from the above account that formal logic is a scientific tool without philosophical relevance; nor let it be supposed that its philosophical relevance must consist in a point-by-point application to the recorded speech behavior of the man in the street. Philosophy is in large part concerned with the theoretical, non-genetic underpinnings of scientific theory; with what science could get along with, could be reconstructed by means of, as distinct from what science has historically made use of. If certain problems of ontology, say, or modality, or causality, or contrary-to-fact conditionals, which arise in ordinary language, turn out not to arise in science as reconstituted with the help of formal logic, then those philosophical problems have in an important sense been solved: they have been shown not to be implicated in any necessary foundation of science. Such solutions are good to just the extent that (a) philosophy of science is philosophy enough and (b) the refashioned logical underpinnings of science do not engender new philosophical problems of their own.

One example of such elimination of philosophical perplexities is Frege's "definition" of number. Another is the avoidance, by means of quantification theory, of the misleading substantive 'nothing'. Another is the recourse to '⊃' and quantification to avoid the vernacular 'if–then', with the problems of cause and modality to which it gives rise. And the classic case is Russell's theory of descriptions. Mr. Strawson (to get back to him after an absence of a page and a half) ably shows the failure of Russell's theory of descriptions as an analysis of the vernacular usage of the singular 'the', but he shows no appreciation of the value of Russell's theory as a means of getting on in science without use of any real equivalent of the vernacular 'the'. Russell's '$(\imath x)$' is to the vernacular 'the x such that' as '⊃' is to the vernacular 'if–then'; in neither case do we have a *translation*, but in both cases we have an important means of *avoidance* for scientific purposes. And in both cases we therefore have solutions of philosophical problems, in one important sense of this phrase.

VI. PERPLEXITY OVER TRANSITIVITY

Mr. Strawson compares (pp. 40–46) the forms of inference:

(1)   all f's are g and x is an f $\therefore$ x is a g,

(2) x is a younger son $\therefore$ x has a brother,

(3) xRy and yRz $\therefore$ xRz.

He observes that all inferences of forms (1) and (2) are valid (indeed analytically so), whereas only some inferences of the form (3) are valid. In particular those inferences of the form (3) are valid (analytically so) which have, e.g., the more special forms:

(4) x is congruent with y and y is congruent with z $\therefore$ x is congruent with z,

(5) x is an ancestor of y and y is an ancestor of z $\therefore$ x is an ancestor of z,

(6) x is faster than y and y is faster than z $\therefore$ x is faster than z.

He observes further that the forms (1) and (3) are logical (cf. §II, above), while the forms (2), (4), (5), and (6) are not. So far all is in order. But then he continues his discussion with a perplexing air of perplexity over (3). "Some logicians," he writes, "have felt that all those words which, substituted for 'R' [in (3)], would yield valid inference patterns *ought* to have some common verbal feature." He goes on to urge, rightly, that those logicians (whoever they may be) are mistaken. But he recurs to (3) in extended passages later in the book (pp. 53–55, 203, 207–208, 210); and the reader gets a sense of there still being a puzzle in the author's mind, both from the disproportionate use of space and from two particular subsequent passages.

In one of these passages (pp. 207f.) he cites "transitively relational inference" as an example of what the traditional formal logic could not do. "Attempts," he continues, ". . . to maintain the reducibility of, e.g. transitively relational inferences to syllogistic form have a certain interest . . . The cruder kind of attempt merely introduces the principle . . . as a further premise, to be added to those of the original inference." But what more than this can modern logic do for "transitively relational inference"? (3) is not a law of any logic, as the author himself has stressed in other pages. *Any* logic will need to bolster (3) with an appropriate further premise of the form:

(7) $xRy \cdot yRz \mathbin{.} \supset xRz,$

except in those special examples whose transitivity happens to be logically demonstrable. This remark is indeed a flat tautology.

In the other passage (p. 204) he classifies as transitive those relational predicates which, if substituted in (7), yield *analytic* formulae. But standard usage requires only, for "transitivity," that (7) come out *true* for all x, y, and z. This discrepancy may suggest a clue to the author's very special concern over transitivity: is it traceable to a notion that whenever (7) holds for all x, y, and z it holds analytically? And if he thinks this, does he think it because (7) is a logical formula? But this would be a mistake. Transitivity is indeed a logical trait, in that (7) is a logical formula. Likewise nullity is a logical trait, in that '$(x) \sim fx$' is a logical formula; but the possession of nullity (or fulfillment of '$(x) \sim fx$') by the predicate of griffinhood is a matter of empirical zoology. The fulfillment of (7), for all x, y, and z, by a given predicate can be equally accidental. Example: Take 'xRy' in (7) as 'x and y are residents of the western Azores and live within ten miles of each other'. (Here the relevant facts are that the western Azores are eleven miles apart and the longer of them is ten miles long.)

For the mistaken ideas which I have attributed to Mr. Strawson in the psychological speculations of the foregoing paragraph, he is not responsible beyond having led me to speculate. There are passages, e.g., in the lower part of page 54 and the next page, where his views on transitivity seem quite in order; yet the extensive further passages make one wonder. Actually the matter of transitivity need not have occupied him much beyond the observations noted in the first paragraph of the present section of this review. (7) is on a par, in logical status, with '$\sim fx$' or '$(x) \sim fx$' (as lately noted), and (3) is on a par with:

(8) $fx \mathbin{\therefore} gx.$

They are on a par in the sense of being logical and non-valid and having some valid cases. Some cases of (3) are analytically valid, e.g., (4)–(6), and others not; some cases of (8) are analytically valid, e.g., (2), and others not. For some choices of '*R*', moreover, (3) is not analytically valid but still leads from true premises always to true conclusions; witness the Azores example. Correspondingly, of course, for (8).

VII. FURTHER CRITICAL OBSERVATIONS

The direct value of the book is very considerable, and lies in the realm of logical analysis of ordinary language. The book also has additional value in an ironically negative way: the very misconceptions which I have been warring against in this review are philosophically significant enough so that it is important to have got them out into the open, particularly as they are probably not peculiar to Mr. Strawson. Finally it is scarcely to be denied that various proponents of modern logic have labored from time to time under misconceptions of their own; and some of those Mr. Strawson usefully sets right.

The value of the book in this last respect would have been enhanced if the author had made references to the literature. The anonymity of his "formal logicians say" engenders an air of *Strawson* v. *Strawman*. The discipline of documenting his adversary might also have operated now and again as a corrective, by leading him to wonder whether formal logicians do think quite the way he supposed they did, on certain points, after all. The almost total absence of citations has also other disadvantages, apart from the polemical point. Finding so much in the book that is familiar but unattributed, a less than omnivorous reader is in danger of supposing that the unfamiliar parts are old too, thus giving the author less than his due. Perhaps the ultimate in noncitation occurs on page 99, where it is said that Whitehead and Russell's fifth truth-functional axiom is superfluous; mere mention of Bernays would have enabled the curious reader to look up the proof, with help say of Church's *Bibliography*.

The remainder of this review will be given over to a series of miscellaneous points of criticism, each of which can be covered in briefer space than those belabored in the foregoing sections.

There is a recurrent notion among philosophers that a predicate can be significantly denied only of things that are somehow homogeneous in point of category with the things to which the predicate applies; or that the complement of a class comprises just those things, other than members of the class, which are somehow of the same category as members of the class. This point of view turns up on pages 6, 112, and elsewhere. It is part and parcel of the doctrine that 'This stone is thinking about Vienna' (Carnap's example) is meaningless rather than false. This attitude is no doubt encouraged by Russell's theory of types, to which, by the way, Mr. Strawson seems to think modern logic is firmly committed (cf. p. 227). It is well, in opposition to this attitude, to note three points: the obscurity of the notion of category involved, the needlessness for formal logic of any such strictures on negation and complement, and the considerable theoretical simplifications that are gained by lifting such bans. This is not to deny the importance for linguistics of what the linguists call substitution classes, and at points Mr. Strawson has essentially that notion in mind (cf. p. 226); but the needs and purposes of linguistics are very different from those of formal logic.

On page 16, the author writes: "To say of two statements that they are contradictories is to say that they are inconsistent with each other and that no statement is inconsistent with both of them." But this is unsatisfactory where S is by itself inconsistent, and hence inconsistent with every statement. The definition of 'contraries', on the same page, is subject to a similar difficulty. My criticism depends indeed on assuming that a self-inconsistent S counts as a statement, but I think I am authorized in this by the foot of page 8.

A related difficulty occurs on page 87, where 'if' is being contrasted with '$\supset$': "As an example of a law which holds for 'if', but not for '$\supset$', we may give the analytic formula '$\sim[(\text{if } p, \text{ then } q) . (\text{if } p, \text{ then not } q)]$'." But how does this supposedly analytic formula fare when 'p' is taken as '$q . \sim q$'? Presumably 'if $q . \sim q$ then q' holds, as a case of 'if $q . r$ then q'; and similarly for 'if $q . \sim q$ then $\sim q$'. Maybe the author's defense would be that my instance is one where, for ordinary 'if', the question of truth "does not arise" (cf. §III of this review); if so, then the passage needs expanding.

Whether or not the above two paragraphs bring out two genuine cases of failure to allow for an always-false component, at any rate just such an oversight does unequivocally occur on page 204. An assertion on that page hinges on incompatibility of:

$$(x)(y)(z)(fxy . fyz . \supset fxz), \qquad (x)(y)(z)(fxy . fyz . \supset \sim fxz),[7]$$

whereas actually both of these formulae come out true if $(x)(y) \sim fxy$.

On page 17, line 18, "both" should be read "each of" to avoid ambiguity.

In the italicized definition of 'truth-functional' on page 66, the words *"and only"* should be dropped. If they add anything, what they add is wrong; for we can often know the truth of a truth-functional compound without knowing the truth value of any component. A similar remark applies to "solely" in the middle of page 69.

On page 66, and again on page 216 (quoted in III above), the idiom 'value of a variable' is used, contrary to custom, to refer to substitutable constant expressions rather than to the objects in the universe of discourse over which a quantification ranges. The latter, more orthodox usage occurs at the foot of page 112. On page 66 the "variables" are unquantifiable statement letters; so in this case it would be more natural not to think of them as taking "values" at all, but to speak of them as standing for (i.e., in place of) sentences.

Mr. Strawson is good on '$\supset$' and 'if–then'. He rightly observes the divergences between the two, and stresses that '$p \supset q$' is more accurately read as 'not $(p$ and not $q)$' than 'if p then q'. He also shows awareness that such correspondence as '$\supset$' does bear to 'if–then' is better than its correspondence to 'implies'. But both ideas languish. Pages 218ff. would seem less strange and more obvious if he would there revive the reading 'not $(p$ and not $q)$'. Again the terminology 'material implication and equivalence', which he rightly deplores on page 94 but continues to use, could easily have been omitted from the book altogether in favor of the less objectionable terminology 'material conditional and biconditional', whose currency in the literature is encouragingly on the increase.

On page 106, "or doctors" should be changed twice to "and

[7] Here and elsewhere, even in quotation, I depart slightly from the author's dot conventions.

doctors." The reason is that the logical sum of classes is represented rather by 'and' than 'or' in ordinary language, as the author has correctly noted on the preceding page.

In the small print of page 124 the author speculates on the possibility of a mechanical routine for testing validity of truth functions of formulae of Boolean class algebra, without remarking that the literature contains various.[8] Mostly these techniques, as published, are geared to the notation of monadic quantification theory but they are easily adapted to the other notation. Actually the author is speculating on the possibility of a test of a somewhat special form; still the reader should be informed that tests are at hand.

On page 140, 'Nobody loves without somebody else suffering' is wrongly rendered '$(x)(\exists y)[\sim(x = y) . fx .\supset gy]$'. It should be '$(x)(\exists y)[fx \supset .\sim (x = y) . gy]$'. Mr. Strawson's formula is a logical truism, provable thus: $x = x$; therefore $\sim(x = x) . fx .\supset gx$; therefore $(\exists y)[\sim(x = y) . fx .\supset gy]$.

On page 149, where the author explains Russell's theory of descriptions, the paraphrase which he gives of 'the King of England smiled' is redundant: 'x is King of England' can be deleted, for it follows from the ensuing quantification. Or, if he wants to keep the redundant clause for perspicuity, he might as well weaken '$\equiv$' to '$\supset$' in the ensuing quantification. The same criticism applies to page 185 and again to page 186.

[8] For one and reference to others see my *Methods of Logic*, p. 116 and preceding pages (or see 3d ed., pp. 102–110).

ꝯ *Three Grades of Modal Involvement*

There are several closely interrelated operators, called *modal* operators, which are characteristic of modal logic. There are the operators of *necessity, possibility, impossibility, non-necessity.* Also there are the binary operators, or connectives, of *strict implication* and *strict equivalence.* These various operators are easily definable in terms of one another. Thus impossibility is necessity of the negation; possibility and non-necessity are the negations of impossibility and necessity; and strict implication and strict equivalence are necessity of the material conditional and biconditional. In a philosophical examination of modal logic we may therefore conveniently limit ourselves for the most part to a single modal operator, that of *necessity.* Whatever may be said about necessity may be said also, with easy and obvious adjustments, about the other modes.

There are three different degrees to which we may allow our logic, or semantics, to embrace the idea of necessity. The first or least degree of acceptance is this: necessity is expressed by a *semantical predicate* attributable to statements as notational forms—hence attachable to names of statements. We write, e.g.:

From the *Proceedings of the XIth International Congress of Philosophy,* Brussels, 1953, Volume 14 (Amsterdam: North-Holland Publishing Co.).

(1)   Nec '9 > 5',

(2)   Nec (Sturm's theorem),

(3)   Nec 'Napoleon escaped from 'Elba',

in each case attaching the predicate 'Nec' to a noun, a singular term, which is a *name of* the statement which is affirmed to be necessary (or necessarily true). Of the above examples, (1) and (2) would presumably be regarded as true and (3) as false; for the necessity concerned in modal logic is generally conceived to be of a logical or a priori sort.

A second and more drastic degree in which the notion of necessity may be adopted is in the form of a *statement operator*. Here we have no longer a predicate, attaching to names of statements as in (1)–(3), but a logical operator 'nec', which attaches to statements themselves, in the manner of the negation sign. Under this usage, (1) and (3) would be rendered rather as:

(4)   nec (9 > 5),

(5)   nec (Napoleon escaped from Elba),

and (2) would be rendered by prefixing 'nec' to Sturm's actual theorem rather than to its name. Thus whereas 'Nec' is a predicate or verb, 'is necessary', which attaches to a noun to form a statement, 'nec' is rather an adverb, 'necessarily', which attaches to a statement to form a statement.

Finally the third and gravest degree is expression of necessity by a sentence operator. This is an extension of the second degree, and goes beyond it in allowing the attachment of 'nec' not only to statements but also to open sentences, such as '$x > 5$', preparatory to the ultimate attachment of quantifiers:

(6) (x) nec $(x > 5)$,

(7) $(\exists x)$ nec $(x > 5)$,

(8) $(x)[x = 9 . \supset$ nec $(x > 5)]$.

The example (6) would doubtless be rated as false, and perhaps (7) and (8) as true.

I shall be concerned in this paper to bring out the logical and philosophical significance of these three degrees of acceptance of a necessity device.

I

I call an occurrence of a singular term in a statement *purely referential*[1] (Frege: *gerade*[2]), if, roughly speaking, the term serves in that particular context simply to refer to its object. Occurrences within quotation are not in general referential; e.g., the statements:

(9)   'Cicero' contains six letters,

(10)   '9 > 5' contains just three characters

say nothing about the statesman Cicero or the number 9. Frege's criterion for referential occurrence is substitutivity of identity. Since

(11)   Tully = Cicero,

(12)   the number of planets = 9,

whatever is true of Cicero is true *ipso facto* of Tully (these being one and the same) and whatever is true of 9 is true of the number of planets. If by putting 'Tully' for 'Cicero' or 'the number of planets' for '9' in a truth, e.g., (9) or (10), we come out with a falsehood:

(13)   'Tully' contains six letters,

(14)   'the number of planets > 5' contains just three characters,

we may be sure that the position on which the substitution was made was not purely referential.

(9) must not be confused with:

(15)   Cicero has a six-letter name,

which *does* say something about the man Cicero, and—unlike (9) —remains true when the name 'Cicero' is supplanted by 'Tully'.

Taking a hint from Russell,[3] we may speak of a context as *referentially opaque* when, by putting a statement ϕ into that context, we can cause a purely referential occurrence in ϕ to be not purely referential in the whole context. E.g., the context:

'. . .' contains just three characters

---

[1] *From a Logical Point of View*, pp. 75f, 139ff, 145.
[2] "Über Sinn und Bedeutung."
[3] Whitehead and Russell, 2d ed., Vol. 1, Appendix C.

is referentially opaque; for, the occurrence of '9' in '9 > 5' is purely referential, but the occurence of '9' in (10) is not. Briefly, a context is referentially opaque if it can render a referential occurrence non-referential.

Quotation is the referentially opaque context par excellence. Intuitively, what occurs inside a referentially opaque context may be looked upon as an orthographic accident, without logical status, like the occurrence of 'cat' in 'cattle'. The quotational context ' '9 > 5' ' of the statement '9 > 5' has, perhaps, unlike the context 'cattle' of 'cat', a deceptively systematic air which tempts us to think of its parts as somehow logically germane. Insofar as this temptation exists, it is salutary to paraphrase quotations by the following expedient. We may adopt names for each of our letters and other characters, and Tarski's '⌢' to express concatenation. Then, instead of naming a notational form by putting that notational form itself bodily between quotation marks, we can name it by spelling it. E.g., since 'μ' is mu, 'ϵ' is epsilon, and 'ν' is nu, the word '$\mu\epsilon\nu$' is mu⌢epsilon⌢nu. Similarly the statement '9 > 5' is n⌢g⌢f, if we adopt the letters 'n', 'g', and 'f' as names of the characters '9', '>', and '5'. The example (10) can thus be transcribed as:

(16)   n⌢g⌢f contains just three characters.

Here there is no non-referential occurrence of the numeral '9', for there is no occurrence of it all; and here there is no referentially opaque containment of one statement by another, because there is no contained statement at all. Paraphrasing (10) into (16), so as to get rid altogether of the opaquely contained statement '9 > 5', is like paraphrasing 'cattle' into 'kine' so as to rid it of the merely orthographic occurrence of the term 'cat'. Neither paraphrase is mandatory, but both are helpful when the irreferential occurrences draw undue attention.

An occurrence of a statement as a part of a longer statement is called *truth-functional* if, whenever we supplant the contained statement by another statement having the same truth value, the containing statement remains unchanged in truth value. Naturally one would not expect occurrences of statements within referentially opaque contexts, such as quotations, to be truth-functional. E.g., the truth (10) becomes false when the contained statement '9 > 5' is supplanted by another, 'Napoleon escaped from Elba', which has the same truth value as '9 > 5'. Again the truth (1) is carried, by that same substitution, into the falsehood (3). One might not expect occurrences of statements within statements to be truth-functional, in general, even when the contexts are not referentially opaque; certainly not when the contexts are referentially opaque.

In mathematical logic, however, a policy of *extensionality* is widely espoused: a policy of admitting statements within statements truth-functionally only (apart of course from such contexts as quotation, which are referentially opaque). Note that the semantical predicate 'Nec' as of (1)–(3) is reconcilable with this policy of extensionality, since whatever breach of extensionality it *prima facie* involves is shared by examples like (10) and attributable to the referential opacity of quotation. We can always switch to the spelling expedient, thus rewriting (1) as:

(17)   Nec (n⌢g⌢f).

(17), like (16) and indeed (2) and unlike (1) and (3), contains no component statement but only a name of a statement.

The statement operator 'nec', on the other hand, is a premeditated departure from extensionality. The occurrence of the truth '9 > 5' in (4) is non-truth-functional, since by supplanting it by a different truth we can turn the true context (4) into a falsehood such as (5). Such occurrences, moreover, are not looked upon as somehow spurious or irrelevant to logical structure, like occurrences in quotation or like 'cat' in 'cattle'. On the contrary, the modal logic typified in (4) is usually put forward as a corrective of extensionality, a needed supplementation of an otherwise impoverished logic. Truth-functional occurrence is by no means the rule in ordinary language, as witness occurrences of statements governed by 'because', 'thinks that', 'wishes that', etc., as well as 'necessarily'. Modal logicians, adopting 'nec', have seen no reason to suppose that an adequate logic might adhere to a policy of extensionality.

But, for all the willingness of modal logicians to flout the policy of extensionality, is there really any difference—on the score of extensionality—between their statement operator 'nec' and the extensionally quite admissible semantical predicate 'Nec'? The latter was excusable, within a policy of extensionality, by citing the referential opacity of quotation. But the statement operator 'nec' is likewise excusable, within a policy of extensionality, by citing the referential opacity of 'nec' itself! To see the referential opacity of 'nec' we have only to note that (4) and (12) are true and yet this is false:

(18)   nec (the number of planets > 5).

The statement operator 'nec' is, in short, on a par with quotation. (1) happens to be written with quotation marks and (4) without, but from the point of view of a policy of extensionality one is no worse than the other. (1) might be preferable to (4) only on the score of a possible ancillary policy of trying to reduce referentially opaque contexts to uniformly quotational form.

Genuine violation of the extensionality policy, by admitting non-truth-functional occurrences of statements within statements *without* referential opacity, is less easy than one at first supposes. Extensionality does not merely recommend itself on the score of simplicity and convenience; it rests on somewhat more compelling grounds, as the following argument will reveal. Think of 'p' as short for some statement, and think of '$F(p)$' as short for some containing true statement, such that the context represented by 'F' is not referentially opaque. Suppose further that the context represented by 'F' is such that logical equivalents are interchangeable, within it, *salvâ veritate*. (This is true in particular of 'nec'.) What I shall show is that the occurrence of 'p' in '$F(p)$' is then truth-functional. I.e., think of 'q' as short for some statement having the same truth value as 'p'; I shall show that '$F(q)$' is, like '$F(p)$', true.

What 'p' represents is a statement, hence true or false (and devoid of free 'x'). If 'p' is true, then the conjunction '$x = \Lambda \cdot p$' is true of one and only one object x, viz., the empty class Λ; whereas if 'p' is false the conjunction '$x = \Lambda \cdot p$' is true of no object x whatever. The class $\hat{x}(x = \Lambda \cdot p)$, therefore, is the unit class $\iota\Lambda$ or Λ itself according as 'p' is true or false. Moreover, the equation:

$$\hat{x}(x = \Lambda \cdot p) = \iota\Lambda$$

is, by the above considerations, *logically* equivalent to 'p'. Then, since '$F(p)$' is true and logical equivalents are interchangeable within it, this will be true:

(19) $F[\hat{x}(x = \Lambda \cdot p) = \iota\Lambda]$.

Since 'p' and 'q' are alike in truth value, the classes $\hat{x}(x = \Lambda . p)$ and $\hat{x}(x = \Lambda . q)$ are both $\iota\Lambda$ or both Λ; so

(20) $\hat{x}(x = \Lambda . p) = \hat{x}(x = \Lambda . q).$

Since the context represented by 'F' is not referentially opaque, the occurrence of '$\hat{x}(x = \Lambda . p)$' in (19) is a purely referential occurrence and hence subject to the substitutivity of identity; so from (19) by (20) we can conclude that

$$F[\hat{x}(x = \Lambda . q) = \iota\Lambda].$$

Thence in turn, by the logical equivalence of '$\hat{x}(x = \Lambda . q) = \iota\Lambda$' to '$q$', we conclude that $F(q)$.

The above argument cannot be evaded by denying (20), as long as the notation in (20) is construed, as usual, as referring to classes. For classes, properly so-called, are one and the same if their members are the same—regardless of whether that sameness be a matter of logical proof or of historical accident. But the argument could be contested by one who does not admit class names '$\hat{x}(\ . \ . \ . \ )$'. It could also be contested by one who, though admitting such class names, does not see a final criterion of referential occurrence in the substitutivity of identity, as applied to constant singular terms. These points will come up, perforce, when we turn to 'nec' as a sentence operator under quantification. Meanwhile the above argument does serve to show that the policy of extensionality has more behind it than its obvious simplicity and convenience, and that any real departure from the policy (at least where logical equivalents remain interchangeable) must involve revisions of the logic of singular terms.

The simpler earlier argument for the referential opacity of the statement operator 'nec', viz., observation of the truths (4) and (12) and the falsehood (18), could likewise be contested by one who either repudiates constant singular terms or questions the criterion of referential opacity which involves them. Short of adopting 'nec' as a full-fledged *sentence* operator, however, no such searching revisions of classical mathematical logic are required. We can keep to a classical theory of classes and singular terms, and even to a policy of extensionality. We have only to recognize, in the *statement* operator 'nec', a referentially opaque context comparable to the thoroughly legitimate and very convenient context of quotation. We can even look upon (4) and (5) as elliptical renderings of (1) and (3).

II

Something very much to the purpose of the semantical predicate 'Nec' is regularly needed in the theory of proof. When, e.g., we speak of the completeness of a deductive system of quantification theory, we have in mind some concept of *validity* as norm with which to compare the class of obtainable theorems. The notion of validity in such contexts is not identifiable with truth. A true statement is not a valid statement of quantification theory unless not only it but all other statements similar to it in quantificational structure are true. Definition of such a notion of validity presents no problem, and the importance of the notion for proof theory is incontestable.

A conspicuous derivative of the notion of quantificational validity is that of quantificational implication. One statement quantificationally implies another if the material conditional composed of the two statements is valid for quantification theory.

This reference to quantification theory is only illustrative. There are parallels for truth-function theory: a statement is valid for truth-function theory if it and all statements like it in truth-functional structure are true, and one statement truth-functionally implies another if the material conditional formed of the two statements is valid for truth-function theory.

And there are parallels, again, for logic taken as a whole: a statement is logically valid if it and all statements like it in logical structure are true, and one statement logically implies another if the material conditional formed of the two statements is logically valid.

Modal logic received special impetus years ago from a confused reading of '⊃', the material 'if-then', as 'implies': a confusion of the material conditional with the relation of implication.[4] Properly, whereas '⊃' or 'if-then' connects statements, 'implies' is a verb which connects names *of* statements and thus expresses a relation of the named statements. Carelessness over the distinction of use and mention having allowed this intrusion of 'implies' as a reading of '⊃', the protest thereupon arose that '⊃' in its material sense was too weak to do justice to 'implies', which connotes some-

[4] Notably in Whitehead and Russell.

thing like logical implication. Accordingly an effort was made to repair the discrepancy by introducing an improved substitute for '⊃', written '⥽' and called strict implication.[5] The initial failure to distinguish use from mention persisted; so ⥽ ', though read 'implies' and motivated by the connotations of the word 'implies', functioned actually not as a verb but as a statement connective, a much strengthened 'if–then'. Finally, in recognition of the fact that logical implication is validity of the material conditional, a validity operator 'nec' was adopted to implement the definition of 'p ⥽ q' as 'nec $(p \supset q)$'. Since '⥽' had been left at the level of a statement connective, 'nec' in turn was of course rendered as an operator directly attachable to statements—whereas 'is valid', properly, is a verb attachable to a name of a statement and expressing an attribute of the statement named.[6]

In any event, the use of 'nec' as statement operator is easily converted into use of 'Nec' as semantical predicate. We have merely to supply quotation marks, thus rewriting (4) and (5) as (1) and (3). The strong 'if–then', '⥽', can correspondingly be rectified to a relation of implication properly so-called. What had been:

(21)　　the witness lied ⥽. the witness lied ∨ the owner is liable,

explained as:

(22) nec (the witness lied ⊃. the witness lied ∨ the owner is liable),

becomes:

(23)

'the witness lied' implies 'the witness lied ∨ the owner is liable',

explained as:

(24)

Nec 'the witness lied ⊃. the witness lied ∨ the owner is liable'.

Typically, in modal logic, laws are expressed with help of schematic letters 'p', 'q', etc., thus:

(25)　　　　　　　　p ⥽. $p \lor q$,

(26)　　　　　　　　nec $(p \supset. p \lor q)$.

---

[5] Lewis, *A Survey of Symbolic Logic*, Chap. 5.

[6] On the concerns of this paragraph and the next, see also §69 of Carnap, *Logical Syntax*, and §5 of my *Mathematical Logic*.

The schematic letters are to be thought of as supplanted by any specific statements so as to yield actual cases like (21) and (22). Now just as (21) and (22) are translatable into (23) and (24), so the schemata (25) and (26) themselves might be supposed translatable as:

(27)   'p' implies '$p \lor q$',

(28)   Nec '$p \supset . \, p \lor q$'.

Here, however, we must beware of a subtle confusion. A quotation names precisely the expression inside it; a quoted 'p' names the sixteenth letter of the alphabet and nothing else. Thus whereas (25) and (26) are schemata or diagrams which depict the forms of actual statements, such as (21) and (22), on the other hand (27) and (28) are *not* schemata depicting the forms of actual statements such as (23) and (24). On the contrary, (27) and (28) are not schemata at all, but actual statements: statements *about* the specific schemata 'p', '$p \lor q$', and '$p \supset . \, p \lor q$' (with just those letters). Moreover, the predicates 'implies' and 'Nec' have thus far been looked upon as true only of statements, not of schemata; so in (27) and (28) they are misapplied (pending some deliberate extension of usage).

The letters 'p' and 'q' in (25) and (26) stand in place of statements. For translation of (25) and (26) into semantical form, on the other hand, we need some special variables which refer *to* statements and thus stand in place of names of statements. Let us use 'ϕ', 'ψ', etc., for that purpose. Then the analogues of (25) and (26) in semantical form can be rendered:

(29) ϕ implies the alternation of ϕ and ψ,

(30)   Nec (the conditional of ϕ with the alternation of ϕ and ψ).

We can condense (29) and (30) by use of a conventional notation which I have elsewhere[7] called *quasi-quotation*, thus:

(31) ϕ implies $\ulcorner \phi \lor \psi \urcorner$,

(32)   Nec $\ulcorner \phi \supset . \, \phi \lor \psi \urcorner$.

The relationship between the modal logic of statement operators and the semantical approach, which was pretty simple and obvious when we compared (21)–(22) with (23)–(24), is thus seen to take on some slight measure of subtlety at the stage of

[7] *Mathematical Logic*, §6.

(25)–(26); these correspond not to (27)–(28) but to (31)–(32). It is schemata like (25)–(26), moreover, and not actual statements like (21)–(22), that fill the pages of works on modal logic. However, be that as it may, it is in actual statements such as (21)–(24) that the point of modal logic lies, and it is the comparison of (21)–(22) with (23)–(24) that reflects the true relationship between the use of statement operators and that of semantical predicates. Schemata such as (25)–(26) are mere heuristic devices, useful in expounding the theory of (21)–(22) and their like; and the heuristic devices which bear similarly on (23)–(24) are (31)–(32).

Seeing how modal statement operators can be converted into semantical predicates, one may of course just note the conversion as a principle and leave it undone in practice. But there are five reasons why it is important to note it in principle. One is that the inclination to condemn '⊃' unduly, through a wrong association of 'if–then' with 'implies', is thereby removed. A second reason is that it is at the semantical or proof-theoretic level, where we talk *about* expressions and their truth values under various substitutions, that we make clear and useful sense of logical validity; and it is logical validity that comes nearest to being a clear explication of 'Nec', taken as a semantical predicate. A third reason is that in using 'Nec' as a semantical predicate we flaunt a familiar reminder of referential opacity, in the form of quotation marks. A fourth reason is that the adoption of 'nec' as a statement operator tempts one to go a step further and use it as a sentence operator subject to quantification. The momentousness of this further step—whereof more anon—tends to be overlooked save as one expressly conceives of the 'nec', in its use as statement operator, as shorthand for the semantical usage.

A fifth reason has to do with iteration. Since 'nec' attaches to a statement and produces a statement, 'nec' can then be applied again. On the other hand 'Nec' attaches to a name and yields a statement, to which, therefore, it cannot be applied again. An iterated 'nec', e.g.:

(33)   nec nec(x)(x is red ⊃ x is red),

can of course be translated by our regular procedure into semantical form thus:

(34)   Nec 'Nec '(x)(x is red ⊃ x is red)' ',

and we are thereby reminded that 'Nec' can indeed be iterated if we insert new quotation marks as needed. But the fact remains that (34) is, in contrast with (33), an unlikely move. For, suppose we have made fair sense of 'Nec' as logical validity, relative say to the logic of truth functions, quantification, and perhaps classes. The statement:

(35) $(x)(x$ is red $\supset x$ is red$)$,

then, is typical of the statements to which we would attribute such validity; so

(36)   Nec $'(x)(x$ is red $\supset x$ is red$)'$.

The validity of (35) resides in the fact that (35) is true and so are all other statements with the same quantificational and truth-functional structure as (35). Thus it is that (36) is *true*. But if (36) in turn is also *valid*, it is valid only in an extended sense with which we are not likely to have been previously concerned: a sense involving not only quantificational and truth-functional structure but also the semantical structure, somehow, of quotation and 'Nec' itself.

Ordinarily we work in a metalanguage, as in (36), treating of an object language, exemplified by (35). We would not rise to (34) except in the rare case where we want to treat the metalanguage by means of itself, and want furthermore to extend the notion of validity beyond the semantics of logic to the semantics of semantics. When on the other hand the statement operator 'nec' is used, iteration as in (33) is the most natural of steps; and it is significant that in modal logic there has been some question as to just what might most suitably be postulated regarding such iteration.[8]

The iterations need not of course be consecutive. In the use of modal statement operators we are led also into complex iterations such as:

(37) $p \dashv q \cdot \dashv . \sim q \dashv \sim p,$

short for:

(38)   nec [nec $(p \supset q) \supset$ nec $(\sim q \supset \sim p)]$.

---

[8] Cf. Lewis and Langford, pp. 497ff.

Or, to take an actual example:

(39) $(x)(x$ has mass) $\dashv3$ $(\exists x)(x$ has mass) . $\dashv3$.
                $\sim (\exists x)(x$ has mass) $\dashv3$ $\sim (x)(x$ has mass),

(40)   nec $\{$nec $[(x)(x$ has mass$) \supset (\exists x)(x$ has mass$)] \supset$
                nec $[\sim(\exists x)(x$ has mass$) \supset \sim (x)(x$ has mass$)]\}$.

In terms of semantical predicates the correspondents of (39) and (40) are:

(41)   ' '$(x)(x$ has mass)' implies '$(\exists x)(x$ has mass)' ' implies
                ' '$\sim(\exists x)(x$ has mass)' implies '$\sim(x)(x$ has mass)' ',

(42)   Nec 'Nec '$(x)(x$ has mass)' $\supset (\exists x)(x$ has mass)' $\supset$
                Nec '$\sim(\exists x)(x$ has mass)' $\supset \sim (x)(x$ has mass)' '.

But (41)–(42), like (34), have singularly little interest or motivation when we think of necessity semantically.

It is important to note that we must not translate the schemata (37)–(38) into semantical form in the manner:

$$' 'p' \text{ implies } 'q' ' \text{ implies, etc.}$$

To do so would be to compound, to an altogether horrifying degree, the error noted earlier of equating (25)–(26) to (27)–(28). The analogues of (37)–(38) in semantical application should be rendered rather:

(43) $\ulcorner\phi$ implies $\psi\urcorner$ implies $\ulcorner\ulcorner\sim\psi\urcorner$ implies $\ulcorner\sim\phi\urcorner\urcorner$,

(44)   Nec $\ulcorner$Nec $\ulcorner\phi \supset \psi\urcorner \supset$ Nec $\ulcorner\sim\psi \supset \sim\phi\urcorner\urcorner$,

subject to some special conventions governing the nesting of quasi-quotations. Such conventions would turn on certain subtle considerations which will not be entered upon here. Suffice it to recall that the sort of thing formulated in (33)–(34) and (37)–(44) is precisely the sort of thing we are likely to see least point in formulating when we think of necessity strictly as a semantical predicate rather than a statement operator. It is impressive and significant that *most* of modal logic (short of quantified modal logic, to which we shall soon turn) is taken up with iterated cases like (33) and (37)–(40) which would simply not recommend themselves to our attention if necessity were held to the status of a semantical predicate and not depressed to the level of a statement operator.

Our reflections have favored the semantical side immensely,

but they must not be allowed to obscure the fact that even as a semantical predicate necessity can raise grave questions. There is no difficulty as long as necessity is construed as validity relative say to the logic of truth functions and quantification and perhaps classes. If we think of arithmetic as reduced to class theory, then such validity covers also the truths of arithmetic. But one tends to include further territory still; cases such as 'No bachelor is married', whose truth is supposed to depend on "meanings of terms" or on "synonymy" (e.g., the synonymy of 'bachelor' and 'man not married'). The synonymy relation on which such cases depend is supposedly a narrower relation than that of the mere coextensiveness of terms, and it is not known to be amenable to any satisfactory analysis. In short, necessity in semantical application tends to be identified with what philosophers call analyticity; and analyticity, I have argued elsewhere,[9] is a pseudo-concept which philosophy would be better off without.

As long as necessity in semantical application is construed simply as explicit truth-functional validity, on the other hand, or quantificational validity, or set-theoretic validity, or validity of any other well-determined kind, the logic of the semantical necessity predicate is a significant and very central strand of proof theory. But it is not modal logic, even unquantified modal logic, as the latter ordinarily presents itself; for it is a remarkably meager thing, bereft of all the complexities which are encouraged by the use of 'nec' as a statement operator. It is unquantified modal logic minus all principles which, explicitly or implicitly (via '-3', etc.), involve iteration of necessity; and plus, if we are literal-minded, a pair of quotation marks after each 'Nec'.

III

Having adopted the operator '~' of negation as applicable to statements, one applies it without second thought to open sentences as well: sentences containing free variables ripe for quantification. Thus we can write not only '~(Socrates is mortal)' but also '~(x is mortal)', from which, by quantification

---

[9] "Two dogmas of empiricism."

and further negation, we have '$\sim (x) \sim (x$ is mortal)' or briefly '$(\exists x)(x$ is mortal)'. With negation this is as it should be. As long as 'nec' is used as a statement operator, on a par with negation, the analogous course suggests itself again: we write not only 'nec $(9 > 5)$' but also 'nec $(x > 5)$', from which by quantification we can form (6)–(8) and the like.

This step brings us to 'nec' as sentence operator, Given 'nec' as statement operator, the step is natural. Yet it is a drastic one, for it suddenly obstructs the earlier expedient of translation into terms of 'Nec' as semantical predicate. We can reconstrue (4) and (5) at will as (1) and (3), but we cannot reconstrue:

$$(45) \qquad\qquad \text{nec } (x > 5)$$

correspondingly as:

$$(46) \qquad\qquad \text{Nec '}x > 5\text{'}.$$

'Nec' has been understood up to now as a predicate true only of statements, whereas (46) attributes it rather to an open sentence and is thus trivially false, at least pending some deliberate extension of usage. More important, whereas (45) is an open sentence with free 'x', (46) has no corresponding generality; (46) is simply a statement *about* a specific open sentence. For, it must be remembered that '$x > 5$' in quotation marks is a name of the specific quoted expression, with fixed letter 'x'. The 'x' in (46) cannot be reached by a quantifier. To write:

$$(47) \qquad (x)(\text{Nec '}x > 5\text{'}), \quad (\exists x)(\text{Nec '}x > 5\text{'})$$

is like writing:

$$(48) \qquad (x)(\text{Socrates is mortal}), \quad (\exists x)(\text{Socrates is mortal});$$

the quantifier is followed by no germane occurrence of its variable. In a word, necessity as sentence operator does not go over into terms of necessity as semantical predicate.

Moreover, acceptance of necessity as a sentence operator implies an attitude quite opposite to our earlier one (in §§I–II above), which was that 'nec' as statement operator is referentially opaque. For, one would clearly have no business quantifying into a referentially opaque context; witness (47) above. We can reasonably infer '$(\exists x)$ nec $(x > 5)$' from 'nec $(9 > 5)$' only if we regard the latter as telling us something about the *object* 9, a number, viz. that it necessarily exceeds 5. If 'nec $(\ldots > 5)$'

can turn out true or false "of" the number 9 depending merely on how that number is referred to (as the falsity of (18) suggests), then evidently 'nec $(x > 5)$' expresses no genuine condition on objects of any kind. If the occurrence of '9' in 'nec $(9 > 5)$' is not purely referential, then putting 'x' for '9' in 'nec $(9 > 5)$' makes no more sense than putting 'x' for 'nine' within the context 'canine'.

But isn't it settled by the truth of (4) and (12) and the falsity of (18) that the occurrence of '9' in question is irreferential, and more generally that 'nec' is referentially opaque, and hence that 'nec' as a sentence operator under quantifiers is a mistake? No, not if one is prepared to accede to certain pretty drastic departures, as we shall see.

Thus far we have tentatively condemned necessity as general sentence operator on the ground that 'nec' is referentially opaque. Its referential opacity has been shown by a breakdown in the operation of putting one constant singular term for another which names the same object. But it may justly be protested that constant singular terms are a notational accident, not needed at the level of primitive notation.

For it is well known that primitively nothing in the way of singular terms is needed except the variables of quantification themselves. Derivatively all manner of singular terms may be introduced by contextual definition in conformity with Russell's theory of singular descriptions. Class names, in particular, which figured in the general argument for extensionality in §I above, may be got either by explaining '$\hat{x}(\ldots)$' as short for the contextually defined description '$(\imath y)(x)(x \epsilon y . \equiv \ldots)$' or by adopting a separate set of contextual definitions for the purpose.[10]

Now the modal logician intent on quantifying into 'nec' sentences may say that 'nec' is not referentially opaque, but that it merely interferes somewhat with the contextual definition of singular terms. He may argue that '$(\exists x)$ nec $(x > 5)$' is not meaningless but true, and in particular that the number 9 is one of the things of which 'nec $(x > 5)$' is true. He may blame the real or apparent discrepancy in truth value between (4) and (18) simply on a queer behavior of contextually defined singular terms. Specifically he may hold that (18) is true if construed as:

<hr>

[10] Cf. my *Methods of Logic*, §§36–38 (3d ed., §§41–43); *Mathematical Logic*, §§24, 26.

(49)   (∃x)[there are exactly x planets . nec (x > 5)]

and false if construed as:

(50)   nec (∃x)(there are exactly x planets . x > 5),

and that (18) as it stands is ambiguous for lack of a distinguishing mark favoring (49) or (50).[11] No such ambiguity arises in the contextual definition of a singular term in extensional logic (as long as the named object exists), and our modal logician may well deplore the complications which thus issue from the presence of 'nec' in his primitive notation. Still he can fairly protest that the erratic behavior of contextually defined singular terms is no reflection on the meaningfulness of his primitive notation, including his open 'nec' sentences and his quantification of them.

Looking upon quantification as fundamental, and constant singular terms as contextually defined, one must indeed concede the inconclusiveness of a criterion of referential opacity that rests on interchanges of constant singular terms. The objects of a theory are not properly describable as the things named by the singular terms; they are the values, rather, of the variables of quantification.[12] Fundamentally the proper criterion of referential opacity turns on quantification rather than naming, and is this: a referentially opaque context is one that cannot properly be *quantified into* (with quantifier outside the context and variable inside). Quotation, again, is the referentially opaque context par excellence; cf. (47). However, to object to necessity as sentence operator on the grounds of referential opacity so defined would be simply to beg the question.

Frege's criterion of referential occurrence, viz., substitutivity of identity, underlay the notion of referential opacity as developed in §I above. The statements of identity there concerned were formed of constant singular terms; cf. (11), (12). But there is a more fundamental form of the law of substitutivity of identity, which involves no constant singular terms, but only variables of quantification; viz.:

(51) $(x)(y)(x = y . \supset . Fx \equiv Fy)$.

This law is independent of any theory of singular terms, and cannot properly be challenged. For, to challenge it were simply to

---

[11] Thus Smullyan.
[12] See *From a Logical Point of View*, pp. 12ff, 75f, 102–110, 113ff, 148ff.

use the sign '=' in some unaccustomed way irrelevant to our inquiry. In any theory, whatever the shapes of its symbols, an open sentence whose free variables are 'x' and 'y' is an expression of identity only in case it fulfills (51) in the role of '$x = y$'. The generality of 'F' in (51) is this: 'Fx' is to be interpretable as any open sentence of the system in question, having 'x' as free (quantifiable) variable; and 'Fy', of course, is to be a corresponding context of 'y'.

If 'nec' is not referentially opaque, 'Fx' and 'Fy' in (51) can in particular be taken respectively as 'nec $(x = x)$' and 'nec $(x = y)$'. From (51), therefore, since surely 'nec $(x = x)$' is true for all x, we have:

(52) \qquad\qquad $(x)(y)[x = y . \supset \text{nec } (x = y)]$.

I.e., identity holds necessarily if it holds at all.

Let us not jump to the conclusion, just because (12) is true, that

(53) \qquad\qquad nec (the number of planets $= 9$).

This does not follow from (12) and (52) except with help of a law of universal instantiation, allowing us to put singular terms 'the number of planets' and '9' for the universally quantified 'x' and 'y' of (52). Such instantiation is allowable, certainly, in extensional logic; but it is a question of good behavior of constant singular terms, and we have lately observed that such behavior is not to be counted on when there is a 'nec' in the woodpile.

So our observations on necessity in quantificational application are, up to now, as follows. Necessity in such application is not *prima facie* absurd if we accept some interference in the contextual definition of singular terms. The effect of this interference is that constant singular terms cannot be manipulated with the customary freedom, even when their objects exist. In particular they cannot be used to instantiate universal quantifications, unless special supporting lemmas are at hand. A further effect of necessity in quantificational application is that objects come to be necessarily identical if identical at all.

There is yet a further consequence, and a particularly striking one: Aristotelian essentialism. This is the doctrine that some of the attributes of a thing (quite independently of the language in

which the thing is referred to, if at all) may be essential to the
thing, and others accidental. E.g., a man, or talking animal, or
featherless biped (for they are in fact all the same *things*), is
essentially rational and accidentally two-legged and talkative,
not merely qua man but qua itself. More formally, what
Aristotelian essentialism says is that you can have open sentences—which I shall represent here as '*Fx*' and '*Gx*'—such that

(54) $(\exists x)(\text{nec } Fx \cdot Gx \cdot \sim \text{nec } Gx).$

An example of (54) related to the falsity of (53) might be:

$(\exists x)[\text{nec}(x > 5) \cdot \text{there are just } x \text{ planets} \cdot$
$\qquad\qquad \sim\text{nec (there are just } x \text{ planets})],$

such an object x being the number (by whatever name) which is
variously known as 9 and the number of planets.

How Aristotelian essentialism as above formulated is required
by quantified modal logic can be quickly shown. Actually
something yet stronger can be shown: that there are open
sentences '*Fx*' and '*Gx*' fulfilling not merely (54) but:

$(x)(\text{nec } Fx \cdot Gx \cdot \sim \text{nec } Gx),$

i.e.:

$(x) \text{ nec } Fx \cdot (x) Gx \cdot (x) \sim \text{nec } Gx.$

An appropriate choice of '*Fx*' is easy: '$x = x$'. And an appropriate
choice of '*Gx*' is '$x = x \cdot p$', where in place of 'p' any statement is
chosen which is true but not necessarily true. Surely there *is* such
a statement, for otherwise 'nec' would be a vacuous operator and
there would be no point in modal logic.

Necessity as semantical predicate reflects a non-Aristotelian
view of necessity: necessity resides in the way in which we say
things, and not in the things we talk about. Necessity as
statement operator is capable, we saw, of being reconstrued in
terms of necessity as a semantical predicate, but has, nevertheless, its special dangers; it makes for an excessive and idle
elaboration of laws of iterated modality, and it tempts one to a
final plunge into quantified modality. This last complicates the
logic of singular terms; worse, it leads us back into the metaphysical jungle of Aristotelian essentialism.

16

❧ *Reply to Professor Marcus*

Professor Marcus struck the right note when she represented me as suggesting that modern modal logic was conceived in sin: the sin of confusing use and mention. She rightly did not represent me as holding that modal logic *requires* confusion of use and mention. My point was a historical one, having to do with Russell's confusion of 'if–then' with 'implies'.

Lewis founded modern modal logic, but Russell provoked him to it. For whereas there is much to be said for the material conditional as a version of 'if–then', there is nothing to be said for it as a version of 'implies'; and Russell called it implication, thus apparently leaving no place open for genuine deductive connections between sentences. Lewis moved to save the connections. But his way was not, as one could have wished, to sort out Russell's confusion of 'implies' with 'if–then'. Instead, preserving that confusion, he propounded a strict conditional and called *it* implication.

It is logically possible to like modal logic without confusing use and mention. You could like it because, apparently at least, you can quantify into a modal context by a quantifier outside the modal context, whereas you obviously cannot coherently quantify into a mentioned sentence from outside the mention of it. Still, man is a sense-making animal, and as such he derives little

This was presented as a commentary at a meeting of the Boston Colloquium for the Philosophy of Science, February 8, 1962. With the rest of the proceedings of that meeting it was published in *Synthese* (Volume 20, 1961), and in M. W. Wartofsky, ed., *Boston Studies in the Philosophy of Science* (Dordrecht, Holland: D. Reidel Publishing Co., 1963).

comfort from quantifying into modal contexts that he does not think he understands. On this score, confusion of use and mention seems to have more than genetic significance for modal logic. It seems to be also a sustaining force, engendering an illusion of understanding.

I am speaking empirically. There was a period twenty-five years ago when I kept being drawn into arguments with C. I. Lewis and E. V. Huntington over interpretation of modal logic; and in those arguments I found it necessary to harp continually on the theme of use versus mention. And now points that Professor Marcus has urged this evening, in favor of modal logic, force me back to that same theme again.

Thus consider her "informal argument:

(12)   If p is a tautology, and p eq q, then q is a tautology."

Her adoption of the letters 'p' and 'q', rather than say 'S_1' and 'S_2', suggests that she intends them to occupy sentence positions. Also her 'eq' is perhaps intended as a sentence *connective,* despite her saying that it names some equivalence relation; for she says that it could be taken as '$\equiv$'. On the other hand her clauses 'p is a tautology' and 'q is a tautology' do not show 'p' and 'q' in sentence position. These clauses show 'p' and 'q' in name positions, as if they were replaceable not by sentences but by names of sentences.

Or try the opposite interpretation. Suppose that Professor Marcus, contrary to custom, is using 'p' and 'q' as variables whose values are sentences, and whose proper substitutes are therefore names of sentences. Then 'eq' is indeed to be seen as naming some equivalence *relation,* just as she says; and the mention of '$\equiv$' must be overlooked as an inadvertency. On this interpretation, (12) is unexceptionable. But on this interpretation (12) is no part of modal logic; it is ordinary non-modal metalogic. For on this interpretation 'eq' is not a non-truth-functional sentence connective at all, but an ordinary non-truth-functional two-place sentence predicate, like 'implies'. I have no objection to these. In my logical writings early and late I have used them constantly.

Twenty-five years ago, in arguing much the same matter with Lewis and Huntington at vastly greater length, I was forced to recognize my inability to make people aware of confusing use and mention. Nor have the passing years brought me the ability; they have only vindicated my despair of it. By now perhaps I should have concluded that I must be the confused one, were it not for people who do turn out to see the distinction my way.

I have said that modal logic does not require confusion of use and mention. But there is no denying that confusion of use and mention engenders an irresistible case for modal logic, as witness (12).

I should not leave (12) without touching upon a third interpretation. Perhaps 'p' and 'q' are to be seen as propositional variables, whose values are propositions (or meanings of sentences) and whose appropriate substitutions are therefore names of propositions, hence names of meanings of sentences. Then again (12) is in order, if we countenance these subtle entities. But, on this interpretation, 'eq' comes to name a relation between propositions; again it is no connective of sentences. To suppose it were would be to confuse meaning with reference, and thus to view sentences as names of their meanings.

Let me move now to Professor Marcus's discussion of her identity predicate 'I'. Suppose that aIb. Then, she argues, anything true of a is true of b. I agree. But, she says, 'aIa' is a tautology. Again I agree, not quarreling over the term. So, she concludes, 'aIb' must be a tautology too. Why? The reasoning is as follows. We are trying to prove this about b: not just that aIb, but that tautologously aIb. Now this thing that we are trying to prove about b, viz., that tautologously aIb, is true of a; so, since b is a, it is true of b.

Again our troubles condense about the distinction between use and mention. If we take 'tautologously' as a modal operator attachable directly to sentences, then the argument is all right, but pointless so long as the merits of modal logic are under debate. If on the other hand we accept only 'tautologous', as a predicate attributable to sentences and therefore attachable to quotations of sentences, then the argument breaks down. For, the property that was to be proved about b—viz., that tautologously aIb—has to be seen now as a quotation-breaking pseudo-property on which the substitutivity of identity has no bearing. What I mean by a quotation-breaking pseudo-property will be evident if we switch for a moment to the truth ' 'Cicero' has three syllables'. Obviously we cannot infer that 'Tully' has three syllables, even though Tully is Cicero. And from '*'aIa'* is tautologous' there is no more reason to infer that '*aIb*' is tautologous, even granted that *b* is *a*.

Professor Marcus's reflections on identity led her to conclude that identity, substitutivity, and extensionality are things that come in grades. I have just now objected to some of the reasoning. I also do not accept the conclusion. My position is that we can settle objectively and absolutely what predicate of a theory to count as the identity predicate, if any, once we have settled what notations to count as quantifiers, variables, and the truth functions. Until we have found how to handle quantification in a given theory, of course we have no way even of telling what expressions of the theory to count as predicates and what signs to count as their subject variables; and, not being able to spot predicates, we cannot spot the identity predicate. But show me the quantifiers and the variables and the truth functions, and I can show you when to read an open sentence 'ϕxy' as '$x = y$'. The requirements are strong reflexivity and substitutivity, thus:

$$(x)\phi xx, \qquad (x)(y)(\phi xy . \ldots x \ldots . \supset . \ldots y \ldots).$$

If these requirements are met, then, as is well known, 'ϕxy' meets all the formal requirements of '$x = y$'; and otherwise not.

The requirements fix identity uniquely. That is, if 'ϕ' and 'ψ' both meet the requirements of strong reflexivity and substitutivity, then they are coextensive. Let me quickly prove this. By substitutivity of 'ϕ',

$$(x)(y)(\phi xy . \psi xx . \supset \psi xy).$$

But, by reflexivity of ψ, we can drop the 'ψxx'. So 'ψ' holds wherever 'ϕ' does. By the same argument with 'ϕ' and 'ψ' interchanged, 'ϕ' holds wherever 'ψ' does.

There are a couple of tangents that I would just mention and not use. One is that there is no assurance, given a theory with recognized notations for quantification and the truth functions, that there is an identity predicate in it. It can happen that no open sentence in 'x' and 'y', however complex, is strongly reflexive and substitutive. But this is unusual.

The other is that if an open sentence in 'x' and 'y' does meet these two requirements, we may still find it to be broader than true identity when we interpret it in the light of prior interpretations of the primitive predicates of the theory. But this sort of discrepancy is always traceable to some gratuitous distinctions in those prior interpretations of the primitive predicates. The effect of our general rule for singling out an identity predicate is a mild kind of identification of indiscernibles.[1]

Tangents aside, my point is that we have an objective and unequivocal criterion whereby to spot the identity predicate of a given theory, if such there be. The criterion is independent of what the author of the theory may do with '$=$' or 'I' or the word 'identity'. What it does depend on is recognition of the notations of quantification and the truth functions. The absoluteness of this criterion is important, as giving a fixed point of reference in the comparison of theories. Questions of universe, and individuation, take on a modicum of intersystematic significance that they would otherwise lack.

In particular the criterion makes no doubt of Professor Marcus's law for modal logic:

$$(x)(y)(x = y \,.\supset. \text{ necessarily } x = y).$$

It follows from 'necessarily $x = x$' by substitutivity.

Notice that my substitutivity condition was absolute. There was no question what special positions to exempt from substitutivity, and no question what special names or descriptions to exempt in special positions. Hence there was no scope for gradations of identity or substitutivity. What enabled me to cut so clean was that I talked in terms not of names or descriptions but of 'x' and 'y': variables of quantification. The great philosophical value of the eliminability of singular terms other than variables is that we can sometimes thus spare ourselves false leads and lost motion.

In her own continuing discussion, Professor Marcus developed a contrast between proper names and descriptions. Her purpose was, I gather, to shed further light on supposed grades or alternatives in the matter of identity and substitutivity. I have urged just now that we can cut through all this by focusing on the bindable variable. And I am glad, for I think I see trouble anyway in the contrast between proper names and descriptions as Professor Marcus draws it. Her paradigm of the assigning of

[1] See my *Word and Object*, p. 230.

proper names is tagging. We may tag the planet Venus, some fine evening, with the proper name 'Hesperus'. We may tag the same planet again, some day before sunrise, with the proper name 'Phosphorus'. When at last we discover that we have tagged the same planet twice, our discovery is empirical. And not because the proper names were descriptions.

In any event, this is by the way. The contrast between description and name need not concern us if we take rather the variables of quantification as our ultimate singular terms. Already for the second time we note the philosophical value of the eliminability of singular terms other than variables: again it spares us false leads and lost motion.

Let us look then to Professor Marcus's next move. Alarmingly, her next move was to challenge quantification itself, or my object-oriented interpretation of it. Here she talks of values of variables in a sense that I must sharply separate from my own. For me the values, e.g., of number variables in algebra are not the numerals that you can substitute, but the numbers that you talk about. For Professor Marcus, the values are the expressions you can substitute. I think my usage has the better history, but hers has a history too. Ryle objected somewhere to my dictum that to be is to be the value of a variable, arguing that the values of variables are expressions and hence that my dictum repudiates all things except expressions. Clearly, then, we have to distinguish between values of variables in the *real* sense and values of variables in the *Ryle* sense. To confuse these is, again, to confuse use and mention. Professor Marcus is not, so far as I observe, confusing them. She simply speaks of values of variables in the Ryle sense. But to forestall confusion I should like to say 'substitutes for variables' rather than 'values of variables' in this sense, thus reserving 'values of variables' for values of variables in the real sense.

Thus paraphrased, Professor Marcus's proposed reinterpretation of existential quantification is this: The quantification is to be true if and only if the open sentence after the quantifier is true for some substitute for the variable of quantification. Now this is, I grant, an intelligible reinterpretation, and one that does not require objects, in any sense, as values, in the real sense, of the variables of quantification. Note only that it deviates from the ordinary interpretation of quantification in ways that can matter. For one thing, there is a question of unspecifiable objects. Thus take the real numbers. On the classical theory, at any rate, they are indenumerable, whereas the expressions, simple and complex, available to us in any given language are denumerable. There are therefore, among the real numbers, infinitely many none of which can be separately specified by any expression, simple or complex. Consequently an existential quantification can come out true when construed in the ordinary sense, thanks to the existence of appropriate real numbers, and yet be false when construed in Professor Marcus's sense, if by chance those appropriate real numbers all happen to be severally unspecifiable.

But the fact remains that quantification can indeed be thus reinterpreted, if not altogether *salvâ veritate,* so as to dissociate it from objective reference and real values of variables. Why should this be seen as desirable? As an answer, perhaps, to the charge that quantified modal logic can tolerate only intensions and not classes or individuals as values of its variables? But it is a puzzling answer. For it abstracts from reference altogether. Quantification ordinarily so-called is purely and simply the logical idiom of objective reference. When we reconstrue it in terms of substituted expressions rather than real values, we waive reference. We preserve distinctions between true and false, as in truth-function logic itself, but we cease to depict the referential dimension. Now anyone who is willing to abstract thus from questions of universe of discourse cannot have cared much whether there were classes and individuals or only intensions in the universe of discourse. But then why the contortions? In short, if reference matters, we cannot afford to waive it as a category; and if it does not, we do not need to.

As a matter of fact, the worrisome charge that quantified modal logic can tolerate only intensions and not classes or individuals was a mistake to begin with. It goes back to 1943: my "Notes on existence and necessity" and Church's review of it. To illustrate my misgivings over quantifying into modal contexts I used, in that article, the example of 9 and the number of the planets. They are the same thing, yet 9 necessarily exceeds 7 whereas the number of the planets only contingently exceeds 7. So, I argued, necessarily exceeding 7 is no trait of the neutral thing itself, the number, which is the number of the planets as

well as 9. And so it is nonsense to say neutrally that there is
something, x, that necessarily exceeds 7. Church countered that
my argument worked only for things like numbers, bodies,
classes, that we could specify in contingently coincident ways:
thus 9 is what succeeds 8, and is what numbers the planets, and
these two specifications only contingently coincide. If we limit
our objects to intensions, Church urged, this will not happen.

Now on this latter point Church was wrong. I have been slow
to see it, but the proof is simple. Anything x, even an intension,
is specifiable in contingently coincident ways if specifiable at all.
For suppose x is determined uniquely by the condition 'ϕx'. Then
it is also determined uniquely by the conjunctive condition '$p . \phi x$'
where 'p' is any truth, however irrelevant. Take 'p' as an arbitrary
truth not implied by 'ϕx', and these two specifications of x are seen
to be contingently coincident: 'ϕx' and '$p . \phi x$'.

Contrary to what Church thought, therefore, my 1943 strictures were cogent against quantification over any sorts of objects
if cogent at all; nothing is gained by limiting the universe to
intensions. The only course open to the champion of quantified
modal logic is to meet my strictures head on: to argue in the case
of 9 and the number of the planets that this number is, of itself
and independently of mode of specification, something that
necessarily, not contingently, exceeds 7. This means adopting a
frankly inequalitarian attitude toward the various ways of
specifying the number. One of the determining traits, the succeeding of 8, is counted as a necessary trait of the number. So are
any traits that follow from that one, notably the exceeding of 7.
Other uniquely determining traits of the number, notably its
numbering the planets, are discounted as contingent traits of the
number and held not to belie the fact that the number does still
necessarily exceed 7.

This is how essentialism comes in: the invidious distinction
between some traits of an object as essential to *it* (by whatever
name) and other traits of it as accidental. I do not say that such
essentialism, however uncongenial to me, should be uncongenial
to the champion of quantified modal logic. On the contrary, it
should be every bit as congenial as quantified modal logic
itself.[2]

---

[2] For more in the vein of these last few paragraphs see my *From a Logical Point of View*, 2d ed., pp. 148–157.

17

❧ *Quantifiers and Propositional Attitudes*

I

The incorrectness of rendering 'Ctesias is hunting unicorns' in the fashion:

$$(\exists x)(x \text{ is a unicorn . Ctesias is hunting } x)$$

is conveniently attested by the non-existence of unicorns, but is not due simply to that zoological lacuna. It would be equally incorrect to render 'Ernest is hunting lions' as:

(1) $(\exists x)(x$ is a lion . Ernest is hunting $x)$,

where Ernest is a sportsman in Africa. The force of (1) is rather that there is some individual lion (or several) which Ernest is hunting; stray circus property, for example.

The contrast recurs in 'I want a sloop'. The version:

(2) $(\exists x)(x$ is a sloop . I want $x)$

is suitable insofar only as there may be said to be a certain sloop that I want. If what I seek is mere relief from slooplessness, then (2) gives the wrong idea.

The contrast is that between what may be called the *relational* sense of lion-hunting or sloop-wanting, viz., (1)–(2), and the

This paper appeared in the *Journal of Philosophy* (Volume 53, 1956), summing up some points which I had made in lectures at Harvard and Oxford from 1952 onward. It is reprinted here minus fifteen lines.

likelier or *notional* sense. Appreciation of the difference is evinced in Latin and Romance languages by a distinction of mood in subordinate clauses; thus *'Procuro un perro que habla'* has the relational sense:

$$(\exists x)(x \text{ is a dog . } x \text{ talks . I seek } x)$$

as against the notional *'Procuro un perro que hable':*

I strive that $(\exists x)(x$ is a dog . x talks . I find x).

Pending considerations to the contrary in later pages, we may represent the contrast strikingly in terms of permutations of components. Thus (1) and (2) may be expanded (with some violence to both logic and grammar) as follows:

(3) $(\exists x)(x$ is a lion . Ernest strives that Ernest finds x),

(4) $(\exists x)(x$ is a sloop . I wish that I have x),

whereas 'Ernest is hunting lions' and 'I want a sloop' in their notional senses may be rendered rather thus:

(5)   Ernest strives that $(\exists x)(x$ is a lion . Ernest finds x),

(6)   I wish that $(\exists x)(x$ is a sloop . I have x).

The contrasting versions (3)–(6) have been wrought by so paraphrasing 'hunt' and 'want' as to uncover the locutions 'strive that' and 'wish that', expressive of what Russell has called *propositional attitudes*. Now of all examples of propositional attitudes, the first and foremost is *belief;* and, true to form, this example can be used to point up the contrast between relational and notional senses still better than (3)–(6) do. Consider the relational and notional senses of believing in spies:

(7) $(\exists x)(\text{Ralph believes that } x \text{ is a spy}),$

(8)   Ralph believes that $(\exists x)(x$ is a spy).

Both may perhaps be ambiguously phrased as 'Ralph believes that someone is a spy', but they may be unambiguously phrased respectively as 'There is someone whom Ralph believes to be a spy' and 'Ralph believes there are spies'. The difference is vast; indeed, if Ralph is like most of us, (8) is true and (7) false.

In moving over to propositional attitudes, as we did in (3)–(6), we gain not only the graphic structural contrast between (3)–(4) and (5)–(6) but also a certain generality. For we can now multiply examples of striving and wishing, unrelated to hunting and wanting. Thus we get the relational and notional senses of wishing for a president:

(9) $(\exists x)$(Witold wishes that x is president),

(10) Witold wishes that $(\exists x)(x$ is president).

According to (9), Witold has his candidate; according to (10) he merely wishes the appropriate form of government were in force. Also we open other propositional attitudes to similar consideration—as witness (7)–(8).

However, the suggested formulations of the relational senses— viz., (3), (4), (7), and (9)—all involve quantifying into a propositional-attitude idiom from outside. This is a dubious business, as may be seen from the following example.

There is a certain man in a brown hat whom Ralph has glimpsed several times under questionable circumstances on which we need not enter here; suffice it to say that Ralph suspects he is a spy. Also there is a gray-haired man, vaguely known to Ralph as rather a pillar of the community, whom Ralph is not aware of having seen except once at the beach. Now Ralph does not know it, but the men are one and the same. Can we say of this *man* (Bernard J. Ortcutt, to give him a name) that Ralph believes him to be a spy? If so, we find ourselves accepting a conjunction of the type:

(11) w sincerely denies '. . .' . w believes that . . .

as true, with one and the same sentence in both blanks. For, Ralph is ready enough to say, in all sincerity, 'Bernard J. Ortcutt is no spy'. If, on the other hand, with a view to disallowing situations of the type (11), we rule simultaneously that

(12) Ralph believes that the man in the brown hat is a spy,

(13) Ralph does not believe that the man seen at the beach is a spy,

then we cease to affirm any relationship between Ralph and any man at all. Both of the component 'that'-clauses are indeed about the man Ortcutt; but the 'that' must be viewed in (12) and (13) as sealing those clauses off, thereby rendering (12) and (13) compatible because not, as wholes, about Ortcutt at all. It then becomes improper to quantify as in (7); 'believes that' becomes, in a word, referentially opaque.[1]

No question arises over (8); it exhibits only a quantification *within* the 'believes that' context, not a quantification *into* it. What goes by the board, when we rule (12) and (13) both true, is just (7). Yet we are scarcely prepared to sacrifice the relational construction 'There is someone whom Ralph believes to be a spy', which (7) as against (8) was supposed to reproduce.

The obvious next move is to try to make the best of our dilemma by distinguishing two senses of belief: $belief_1$, which disallows (11), and $belief_2$, which tolerates (11) but makes sense of (7). For $belief_1$, accordingly, we sustain (12)–(13) and ban (7) as nonsense. For $belief_2$, on the other hand, we sustain (7); and for *this* sense of belief we must reject (13) and acquiesce in the conclusion that Ralph $believes_2$ that the man at the beach is a spy even though he *also* $believes_2$ (and $believes_1$) that the man at the beach is not a spy.

II

But there is a more suggestive treatment. Beginning with a single sense of belief, viz., $belief_1$ above, let us think of this at first as a relation between the believer and a certain *intension*, named by the 'that'-clause. Intensions are creatures of darkness, and I shall rejoice with the reader when they are exorcised, but first I want to make certain points with the help of them. Now intensions named thus by 'that'-clauses, without free variables, I shall speak of more specifically as intensions of degree 0, or propositions. In addition I shall (for the moment) recognize intensions of degree 1, or attributes. These are to be named by prefixing a variable to a sentence in which it occurs free; thus z (z is a spy) is spyhood. Similarly we may specify intensions of higher degrees by prefixing multiple variables.

Now just as we have recognized a dyadic relation of belief between a believer and a proposition, thus:

(14)   Ralph believes that Ortcutt is a spy,

[1] See *From a Logical Point of View*, pp. 142–159; also "Three grades of modal involvement," Essay 15 above.

so we may recognize also a triadic relation of belief among a believer, an object, and an attribute, thus:

(15)   Ralph believes $z(z$ is a spy) of Ortcutt.

For reasons which will appear, this is to be viewed not as dyadic belief between Ralph and the proposition *that* Ortcutt has $z(z$ is a spy), but rather as an irreducibly triadic relation among the three things Ralph, $z(z$ is a spy), and Ortcutt. Similarly there is tetradic belief:

(16) Tom believes $yz(y$ denounced $z)$ of Cicero and Catiline,

and so on.

Now we can clap on a hard and fast rule against quantifying into propositional-attitude idioms; but we give it the form now of a rule against quantifying into names of intensions. Thus, though (7) as it stands becomes unallowable, we can meet the needs which prompted (7) by quantifying rather into the triadic belief construction, thus:

(17) $(\exists x)$(Ralph believes $z(z$ is a spy) of x).

Here then, in place of (7), is our new way of saying that there is someone whom Ralph believes to be a spy.

Belief$_1$ was belief so construed that a proposition might be believed when an object was specified in it in one way, and yet not believed when the same object was specified in another way; witness (12)–(13). Hereafter we can adhere uniformly to this narrow sense of belief, both for the dyadic case and for triadic and higher; in each case the term which names the intension (whether proposition or attribute or intension of higher degree) is to be looked on as referentially opaque.

The situation (11) is thus excluded. At the same time the effect of belief$_2$ can be gained, simply by ascending from dyadic to triadic belief as in (15). For (15) does relate the men Ralph and Ortcutt precisely as belief$_2$ was intended to do. (15) does remain true of Ortcutt under any designation; and hence the legitimacy of (17).

Similarly, whereas from:

Tom believes that Cicero denounced Catiline

we cannot conclude:

Tom believes that Tully denounced Catiline,

on the other hand we can conclude from:

>   Tom believes $y(y$ denounced Catiline$)$ of Cicero

that

>   Tom believes $y(y$ denounced Catiline$)$ of Tully,

and also that

(18) $(\exists x)$(Tom believes $y(y$ denounced Catiline$)$ of x).

From (16), similarly, we may infer that

(19) $(\exists w)(\exists x)$(Tom believes $yz(y$ denounced $z)$ of w and x).

Such quantifications as:

> $(\exists x)$(Tom believes that x denounced Catiline),

> $(\exists x)$(Tom believes $y(y$ denounced $x)$ of Cicero)

still count as nonsense, along with (7); but such legitimate purposes as these might have served are served by (17)–(19) and the like. Our names of intensions, and these only, are what count as referentially opaque.

Let us sum up our findings concerning the seven numbered statements about Ralph. (7) is now counted as nonsense, (8) as true, (12)–(13) as true, (14) as false, and (15) and (17) as true. Another that is true is:

(20)   Ralph believes that the man seen at the beach is not a spy,

which of course must not be confused with (13).

The kind of exportation which leads from (14) to (15) should doubtless be viewed in general as implicative. [Correction: see Sleigh, p. 397.] Under the terms of our illustrative story, (14) happens to be false; but (20) is true, and it leads by exportation to:

(21)   Ralph believes $z(z$ is not a spy$)$ of the man seen at the beach.

The man at the beach, hence Ortcutt, does not receive reference in (20), because of referential opacity; but he does in (21), so we may conclude from (21) that

(22)   Ralph believes $z(z$ is not a spy$)$ of Ortcutt.

Thus (15) and (22) both count as true. This is not, however, to charge Ralph with contradictory beliefs. Such a charge might reasonably be read into:

(23) Ralph believes $z(z$ is a spy . z is not a spy) of Ortcutt,

but this merely goes to show that it is undesirable to look upon (15) and (22) as implying (23).

It hardly needs be said that the barbarous usage illustrated in (15)–(19) and (21)–(23) is not urged as a practical reform. It is put forward by way of straightening out a theoretical difficulty, which, summed up, was as follows: Belief contexts are referentially opaque; therefore it is *prima facie* meaningless to quantify into them; how then to provide for those indispensable relational statements of belief, like 'There is someone whom Ralph believes to be a spy'?

Let it not be supposed that the theory which we have been examining is just a matter of allowing unbridled quantification into belief contexts after all, with a legalistic change of notation. On the contrary, the crucial choice recurs at each point: quantify if you will, but pay the price of accepting near-contraries like (15) and (22) at each point at which you choose to quantify. In other words: distinguish as you please between referential and non-referential positions, but keep track, so as to treat each kind appropriately. The notation of intensions, of degree one and higher, is in effect a device for inking in a boundary between referential and non-referential occurrences of terms.

III

Striving and wishing, like believing, are propositional attitudes and referentially opaque. (3) and (4) are objectionable in the same way as (7), and our recent treatment of belief can be repeated for these propositional attitudes. Thus, just as (7) gave way to (17), so (3) and (4) give way to:

(24) $(\exists x)(x$ is a lion . Ernest strives z(Ernest finds z) of x),

(25) $(\exists x(x$ is a sloop . I wish z(I have z) of x),

a certain breach of idiom being allowed for the sake of analogy in the case of 'strives'.

These examples came from a study of hunting and wanting. Observing in (3)–(4) the quantification into opaque contexts, then, we might have retreated to (1)–(2) and forborne to paraphrase them into terms of striving and wishing. For (1)–(2) were quite straightforward renderings of lion-hunting and sloop-wanting in their relational senses; it was only the notional senses that really needed the breakdown into terms of striving and wishing, (5)–(6).

Actually, though, it would be myopic to leave the relational senses of lion-hunting and sloop-wanting at the unanalyzed stage (1)–(2). For, whether or not we choose to put these over into terms of wishing and striving, there are other relational cases of wishing and striving which require our consideration anyway—as witness (9). The untenable formulations (3)–(4) may indeed be either corrected as (24)–(25) or condensed back into (1)–(2); on the other hand we have no choice but to correct the untenable (9) on the pattern of (24)–(25), viz., as:

$$(\exists x)(\text{Witold wishes } y(y \text{ is president}) \text{ of } x).$$

The untenable versions (3)–(4) and (9) all had to do with wishing and striving in the relational sense. We see in contrast that (5)–(6) and (10), on the notional side of wishing and striving, are innocent of any illicit quantification into opaque contexts from outside. But now notice that exactly the same trouble begins also on the notional side, as soon as we try to say not just that Ernest hunts lions and I want a sloop, but that *someone* hunts lions or wants a sloop. This move carries us, ostensibly, from (5)–(6) to:

(26) $(\exists w)(w \text{ strives that } (\exists x)(x \text{ is a lion} \,.\, w \text{ finds } x))$,

(27) $(\exists w)(w \text{ wishes that } (\exists x)(x \text{ is a sloop} \,.\, w \text{ has } x))$,

and these do quantify unallowably into opaque contexts.

We know how, with help of the attribute apparatus, to put (26)–(27) in order; the pattern, indeed, is substantially before us in (24)–(25). Admissible versions are:

$$(\exists w)(w \text{ strives } y(\exists x)(x \text{ is a lion} \,.\, y \text{ finds } x) \text{ of } w),$$

$$(\exists w)(w \text{ wishes } y(\exists x)(x \text{ is a sloop} \,.\, y \text{ has } x) \text{ of } w),$$

or briefly:

(28) $(\exists w)(w \text{ strives } y(y \text{ finds a lion}) \text{ of } w)$,

(29) $(\exists w)(w \text{ wishes } y(y \text{ has a sloop}) \text{ of } w)$.

Such quantification of the subject of the propositional attitude can of course occur in belief as well; and, if the subject is mentioned in the belief itself, the above pattern is the one to use. Thus 'Someone believes he is Napoleon' must be rendered:

$$(\exists w)(w \text{ believes } y(y = \text{Napoleon}) \text{ of } w).$$

For concreteness I have been discussing belief primarily, and two other propositional attitudes secondarily: striving and wishing. The treatment is, we see, closely parallel for the three; and it will pretty evidently carry over to other propositional attitudes as well—e.g., hope, fear, surprise. In all cases my concern is, of course, with a special technical aspect of the propositional attitudes: the problem of quantifying in.

IV

There are good reasons for being discontent with an analysis that leaves us with propositions, attributes, and the rest of the intensions. Intensions are less economical than extensions (truth values, classes, relations), in that they are more narrowly individuated. The principle of their individuation, moreover, is obscure.

Commonly logical equivalence is adopted as the principle of individuation of intensions. More explicitly: if S and S' are any two sentences with n (≥ 0) free variables, the same in each, then the respective intensions which we name by putting the n variables (or 'that', if $n = 0$) before S and S' shall be one and the same intension if and only if S and S' are logically equivalent. But the relevant concept of logical equivalence raises serious questions in turn.[2] The intensions are at best a pretty obscure lot.

Yet it is evident enough that we cannot, in the foregoing treatment of propositional attitudes, drop the intensions in favor of the corresponding extensions. Thus, to take a trivial example, consider 'w is hunting unicorns'. On the analogy of (28), it becomes:

$$w \text{ strives } y(y \text{ finds a unicorn}) \text{ of } w.$$

[2] See my "Two dogmas"; also "Carnap and logical truth," which is Essay 12 above.

Correspondingly for the hunting of griffins. Hence, if anyone w is
to hunt unicorns without hunting griffins, the attributes

$$y(y \text{ finds a unicorn}),$$
$$y(y \text{ finds a griffin})$$

must be distinct. But the corresponding classes are identical,
being empty. So it is indeed the attributes, and not the classes,
that were needed in our formulation. The same moral could be
drawn, though less briefly, without appeal to empty cases.

But there is a way of dodging the intensions which merits
serious consideration. Instead of speaking of intensions we can
speak of sentences, naming these by quotation. Instead of:

$$w \text{ believes that . . .}$$

we may say:

$$w \text{ believes-true '. . .'.}$$

Instead of:

(30) w believes $y(\ldots y \ldots)$ of x

we may say:

(31) w believes '. . . y . . .' satisfied by x.

The words 'believes satisfied by' here, like 'believes of' before,
would be viewed as an irreducibly triadic predicate. A similar
shift can be made in the case of the other propositional attitudes,
of course, and in the tetradic and higher cases.

This semantical reformulation is not, of course, intended to
suggest that the subject of the propositional attitude speaks the
language of the quotation, or any language. We may treat a
mouse's fear of a cat as his fearing true a certain English
sentence. This is unnatural without being therefore wrong. It is a
little like describing a prehistoric ocean current as clockwise.

How, where, and on what grounds to draw a boundary between
those who believe or wish or strive that p, and those who do not
quite believe or wish or strive that p, is undeniably a vague and
obscure affair. However, if anyone does approve of speaking of
belief of a proposition at all and of speaking of a proposition in
turn as meant by a sentence, then certainly he cannot object to
our semantical reformulation 'w believes-true S' on any special
grounds of obscurity; for, 'w believes-true S' is explicitly defin-

able in *his* terms as '*w* believes the proposition meant by *S*.' Similarly for the semantical reformulation (31) of (30); similarly for the tetradic and higher cases; and similarly for wishing, striving, and other propositional attitudes.

Our semantical versions do involve a relativity to language, however, which must be made explicit. When we say that *w* believes-true *S*, we need to be able to say what language the sentence *S* is thought of as belonging to; not because *w* needs to understand *S*, but because *S* might by coincidence exist (as a linguistic form) with very different meanings in two languages.[3] Strictly, therefore, we should think of the dyadic 'believes-true *S*' as expanded to a triadic '*w* believes-true *S* in *L*'; and correspondingly for (31) and its suite.

As noted two paragraphs back, the semantical form of expression:

(32)   *w* believes-true '. . .' in *L*

can be explained in intensional terms, for persons who favor them, as:

(33)   *w* believes the proposition meant by '. . .' in *L*,

thus leaving no cause for protest on the score of relative clarity. Protest may still be heard, however, on a different score: (32) and (33), though equivalent to each other, are not strictly equivalent to the '*w* believes that . . .' which is our real concern. For, it is argued, in order to infer (33) we need not only the information about *w* which '*w* believes that . . .' provides, but also some extraneous information about the language *L*. Church[4] brings the point out by appeal to translations, substantially as follows. The respective statements:

> *w* believes that there are unicorns,
> *w* believes the proposition meant by 'There are unicorns'
> in English

go into German as:

(34)   *w glaubt, dass es Einhörne gibt,*

(35)   *w glaubt diejenige Aussage, die* ,,There are unicorns"
          auf Englisch bedeutet,

---

[3] This point is made by Church, "On Carnap's analysis."
[4] *Ibid.*, with an acknowledgment to Langford.

and clearly (34) does not provide enough information to enable a German ignorant of English to infer (35).

The same reasoning can be used to show that 'There are unicorns' is not strictly or analytically equivalent to:

'There are unicorns' is true in English.

Nor, indeed, was Tarski's truth paradigm intended to assert analytic equivalence. Similarly, then, for (32) in relation to 'w believes that . . .'; a systematic agreement in truth value can be claimed, and no more. This limitation will prove of little moment to persons who share my skepticism about analyticity.

What I find more disturbing about the semantical versions, such as (32), is the need of dragging in the language concept at all. What is a language? What degree of fixity is supposed? When do we have one language and not two? The propositional attitudes are dim affairs to begin with, and it is a pity to have to add obscurity to obscurity by bringing in language variables too. Only let it not be supposed that any clarity is gained by restituting the intensions.

18

ᕤ *A Logistical Approach to the Ontological Problem*[1]

What does it mean to ask, e.g., whether there is such an entity as roundness? Note that we can use the word 'roundness' without acknowledging any such entity. We can maintain that the word is *syncategorematic*, like prepositions, conjunctions, articles, commas, etc.: that though it occurs as an essential part of various meaningful sentences it is not a *name* of anything. To ask whether there is such an entity as roundness is thus not to question the meaningfulness of 'roundness'; it amounts rather to asking whether this word is a name or a syncategorematic expression.

Ontological questions can be transformed, in this superficial way, into linguistic questions regarding the boundary between names and syncategorematic expressions. Now where, in fact, does this boundary fall? The answer is to be found, I think, by turning our attention to variables. If in the statement:

(1)   Pebbles have roundness

Presented at the fifth International Congress for the Unity of Science, Cambridge, Mass., September 1939, and printed for distribution at the congress as an advance extract from the *Journal of Unified Science,* which had been established in Holland as the successor to *Erkenntnis* after the German annexation of Austria. The *Journal* itself, containing this and the other congress papers, was destined never to appear, owing to the German invasion of Holland.

[1] Acknowledgment is due Mr. H. Nelson Goodman for valuable criticism of an earlier draft.

the word 'roundness' is regarded as a merely syncategorematic
fragment of its context, like 'have' or indeed 'bles' or 'ness', then
the truth of (1) does not entitle us to infer:

Pebbles have something,

i.e.:

(2) $(\exists x)$ (pebbles have x).

Where 'have' is understood as in the context 'have roundness',
and 'roundness' is understood syncategorematically, the use of
the variable 'x' after 'have' as in (2) would be simply ungrammatical—like its use after 'peb' in:

$(\exists x)$ (peb$x$ have roundness).

Variables are pronouns, and make sense only in positions
which are available to names. Thus it would seem that admission
of the inference of (2) from (1) is tantamount to recognizing
'roundness' as a name rather than a syncategorematic expression;
tantamount, in other words, to recognizing an entity roundness.

The same conclusion can be reached through less explicitly
syntactical channels. (2) says that there is an entity which
pebbles "have"; hence, if we allow ourselves to infer (2) from
(1), we have countenanced an entity roundness and construed
(1) as saying that pebbles "have" it. Some may protest, however,
that the quantifier '$(\exists x)$' in (2) says nothing of entities nor of
existence; that the meaning of so-called existential quantification
is completely described merely by the logical rules which govern
it. Now I grant that the meaning of quantification is covered by
the logical rules; but the meaning which those rules determine is
still that which ordinary usage accords to the idioms 'there is an
entity such that', 'an entity exists such that', etc. Such conformity was the logistician's objective when he codified quantification; existential quantification was designed for the role of those
common idioms. It is in just this usual sense of 'there is' that we
mean to inquire whether there is such an entity as roundness; and
it in just this sense that an affirmative answer is implicit in the
inference of (2) from (1).

We seem to have found a formal basis for distinguishing names
from syncategorematic expression. To say that 'roundness' is a
name, i.e., that there is such an entity as roundness, is to say that
from a context '. . . roundness . . .' we may infer '$(\exists x)$
(. . . x . . .)'. But if such inferences are valid, then in par-

ticular from a negative context '$\sim$(. . . roundness . . .)' it will be valid to infer '$(\exists x) \sim (\ldots x \ldots)$', i.e., '$\sim (x) (\ldots x \ldots)$'; wherefore, by contraposition, it will be valid conversely to infer '. . . roundness . . .' from '$(x)(\ldots x \ldots)$'. The law whereby the existential statement follows from the singular is indeed equivalent to the law whereby the singular follows from the universal.

It thus appears suitable to describe *names* simply as those constant expressions which replace variables and are replaced by variables according to the usual laws of quantification. Other meaningful expressions (other expressions capable of occurring in statements) are *syncategorematic*. It is to names, in this sense, that the words 'There is such an entity as' may truthfully be prefixed. Elliptically stated: We may be said to countenance such and such an entity if and only if we regard the range of our variables as including such an entity. To *be* is to be a value of a variable.

The formulation at which we have arrived is adapted only to those familiar forms of language in which quantification figures as primitive and variables figure solely as adjuncts to quantification.[2] Ensuing considerations will likewise be limited to languages of that sort. Superficial revisions would be needed to adapt these developments to languages in which abstraction is primitive;[3] and basic revisions would be needed for adaptation to languages in which variables are eliminated in favor of combinators.[4]

One sometimes chooses to speak *as if* certain syncategorematic expressions were names of entities, though still holding that this is merely a manner of speaking, that the expressions are not actually names, and that the alleged entities are convenient *fictions*. This notion of fiction can be given a clear meaning from the point of view of the present developments. To speak as if certain expressions were names is, we have seen, to allow those expressions to replace and be replaced by variables according to the laws of quantification. But if this is to be merely a convenient and theoretically avoidable manner of speaking, we must be able

[2] E.g., Tarski's "Wahrheitsbegriff," pp. 363–366, and my "Set-theoretic foundations" and "New foundations."

[3] E.g., my *System of Logistic* and "Logic based on inclusion and abstraction."

[4] Schönfinkel; Curry. [See Essay 28, below.]

to translate such usage into another idiom which does *not* require
the expressions in question to replace and be replaced by
variables. The expressions in question must be syncategorematic
to begin with, and the use of variables of quantification in the
position of such expressions must be explained by definitions,
conventions of notational abbreviation. It is in such definitional
extensions of quantification that the introduction of fictitious
entities may be regarded as consisting.

Suppose, e.g., that our language does not, at the primitive level,
make use of variables in positions appropriate to statements.
Statements are then syncategorematic; they name nothing. Suppose further that our language is such as to allow one statement
to occur in another only by way of the truth-functional modes of
statement composition; i.e., suppose that statements with like
truth values are interchangeable in every context without affecting the truth value of the context. This condition is met by the
usual logical languages, and presumably it can be met likewise
by languages adequate to science in general.[5] Now the use of
variables in our language can be extended to statement positions
by the following definitions.[6] Where '. . . p . . .' has the form of
a statement but contains the variable 'p' in places where
constituent statements would normally occur, we explain the
quantification '$(p)(. . . p . . .)$' and '$(\exists p)(. . . p . . .)$' respectively as short for the conjunction:

$$(. . . 0 = 0 . . .) . (. . . 0 = 1 . . .)$$

and the alternation:

$$(. . . 0 = 0 . . .) \vee (. . . 0 = 1 . . .).$$

Statements now become names; propositions—designata of
statements—become recognized as entities. But this is only a
manner of speaking, resting on abbreviations; so we rate the
statements as fake names, and the alleged propositions as
fictions. The difference between fiction and reality may be
regarded thus as reducing to the difference between defined
quantification and quantification belonging to the primitive
notation.

By extending quantification definitionally we accomplish the
introduction of fictions; but we may still add further definitions

[5] Carnap, *Logical Syntax*, pp. 240–260.
[6] After Tarski, "Sur les truth-functions."

in order to make our fictions behave more like real entities—i.e., in order to make our fake names amenable to various contexts in which genuine names occur. One important context is identity. The equation formed from fake names α and β must have as its definiens some primitively meaningful context of the syncategorematic expressions α and β; and this context should be of such kind that it holds as a true statement for just those choices of α and β which are interchangeable in all other contexts *salvâ veritate*. This canon combines preservation of the substitutivity of identity with preservation of the converse principle, the identity of indiscernibles. Thus in the system considered earlier, where statements of like truth value are interchangeable in all contexts *salvâ veritate*, the present canon would single out the truth-functional biconditional ('$\equiv$', 'if and only if') as the appropriate way of defining '$=$' between statements. Our fictitious propositions would then turn out to be just two in number.

What entities there are, from the point of view of a given language, depends on what positions are accessible to variables in that language. What are fictions, from the point of view of a given language, depends on what positions are accessible to variables definitionally rather than primitively. Shift of language ordinarily involves a shift of ontology. There is one important sense, however, in which the ontological question transcends linguistic convention: How economical an ontology *can* we achieve and still have a language adequate to all purposes of science? In this form the question of the ontological presuppositions of science survives.

It is known that logic and mathematics are expressible in a language comprising only alternative denial (Sheffer's stroke), universal quantification, and the predicate 'ϵ' of class membership.[7] A language adequate to science in general can presumably be formed on this nucleus by annexing an indefinite number of empirical predicates. For this entire language the only ontology required—the only range of values for the variables of quantification—consists of concrete individuals of some sort or other, plus all classes of such entities, plus all classes formed from the thus supplemented totality of entities, and so on.

---

[7] See references in note 2 above.

But this is no meager universe. It is of a kind which I will call *transcendent;* in von Neumann's set theory it would be called a II-*Ding.* A transcendent totality is one every combination of whose members determines a further member. Such a universe is worse than infinite: to speak of its cardinal number at all entails revision of the classical infinite arithmetic,[8] since either the number is the highest of all numbers or else parts of the universe have higher cardinal numbers than the whole.

The above phrase "every combination" is vague. We cannot, even in our transcendent universe, allow a new entity to be determined by every formulable *condition* on entities; this is known to lead to contradiction in the case of the condition '$\sim(x \epsilon x)$' and certain others. Such illusory combinations of entities can be ruled out by one or another stipulation; but it is significant that such stipulations are *ad hoc,* unsupported by intuition. A transcendent universe transcends the controls of common sense.

Nominalism is in essence, perhaps, a protest against a transcendent universe. The nominalist would like to suppress "universals"—the *classes* of our universe—and keep only the concrete individuals (whatever these may be). The effective consummation of nominalism in this sense would consist in starting with an immanent (non-transcendent) universe and then extending quantification to classes by some indirect sort of contextual definition. The transcendent side of our universe then reduces to fictions, under the control of the definitions. Such a construction would presumably involve certain semantic primitives as auxiliaries to the logical primitives. If, as is likely, it turns out that fragments of classical mathematics must be sacrificed under all such constructions, still one resort remains to the nominalist: he may undertake to show that those recalcitrant fragments are inessential to science.

[8] See my paper "On Cantor's theorem."

19

On Carnap's Views on Ontology

Though no one has influenced my philosophical thought more than Carnap, an issue has persisted between us for years over questions of ontology and analyticity. These questions prove to be interrelated; their interrelations come out especially clearly in Carnap's paper "Empiricism, semantics, and ontology." I shall devote particular attention to that one paper in an effort to isolate and reduce our divergences.

When I inquire into the *ontological commitments* of a given doctrine or body of theory, I am merely asking what, according to that theory, there is. I might say in passing, though it is no substantial point of disagreement, that Carnap does not much like my terminology here. Now if he had a better use for this fine old word 'ontology,' I should be inclined to cast about for another word for my own meaning. But the fact is, I believe, that he disapproves of my giving meaning to a word which belongs to traditional metaphysics and should therefore be meaningless. Now my ethics of terminology demand, on occasion, the avoidance of a word for given purposes when the word has been preempted in a prior meaning; meaningless words, however, are precisely the words which I feel freest to specify meanings for. But actually my adoption of the word 'ontology' for the purpose

Part of a paper presented at a colloquium with Carnap at the University of Chicago, February 1, 1951. This portion went to *Philosophical Studies* at the editors' request and was published later that year (Volume 2, 1951).

described is not as arbitrary as I make it sound. Though no
champion of traditional metaphysics, I suspect that the sense in
which I use this crusty old word has been nuclear to its usage all
along.

Let us agree, for the space of my remarks, on the word. The
question of the ontological commitments of a theory, then, is the
question what, according to that theory, there is. Carnap thinks
—and here is a more than terminological issue—that the question
what a theory presupposes that there is should be divided into
two questions in a certain way; and I disagree. What he thinks
the division should be, and why I disagree, will appear soon; but
first let us examine the undivided idea a bit.

It has not always been clear how to decide whether or not a
given discourse involves commitment to a given alleged entity.
When we say that all fish are aquatic, do we commit ourselves to
the acceptance of two abstract entities, two classes or properties,
named by the words 'fish' and 'aquatic'? When we use the word
'similar,' without defining it in any anterior terms, do we thereby
commit ourselves to the acceptance of an abstract entity which is
the relation of similarity? Russell has said that we do. But no
nominalist would agree.

Every nominalist, every user of language, avails himself freely
of general terms such as 'fish' and 'aquatic' and 'similar'; but
only anti-nominalists imagine in such usage any allusion to
abstract entities. The nominalist holds that the word 'fish' is *true
of* each concrete fish, but that it does not, in addition, *name* an
abstract fishhood or class of fish; and that the word 'similar' is
true of each alligator with respect to each crocodile, and true of
each Pontiac with respect to each Pontiac, but that it does not, in
addition, name a relation of similarity. Why should 'fish' or
'aquatic' or 'similar' be put on a par with names such as 'Chicago'
and 'Truman' and 'Parthenon'? Many words are admissible in
significant sentences without claiming to name; witness 'the' and
'of' and 'sake' and 'kilter.' Why not 'fish' and 'aquatic' and
'similar'?

Perhaps we can convict a speaker of commitment to abstract
entities not through his general terms, but only through his
abstract terms such as 'fishhood,' 'aquaticity,' 'similarity'? But
this is no feasible resting place. If you grant the nominalist his
general terms, he can excuse his use of abstract terms as

picturesque paraphrasing of what could be said in general terms.

All this tolerance of language and waiving of commitments is reasonable enough, but is there no end to it? The words 'Chicago' and 'Truman' and 'Parthenon' could themselves be excused in the same spirit, as admissible in sentences without claiming to name. There would appear to be no such thing as commitment to entities through discourse.

I think it is true that there is no commitment to entities through use of alleged *names* of them; other things being equal, we can always deny the allegation that the words in question are names. But still there is certainly commitment to entities through discourse; for we are quite capable of saying in so many words that *there are* black swans, that *there is* a mountain more than 8800 meters high, and that *there are* prime numbers above a hundred. Saying these things, we also say by implication that there are physical objects and abstract entities; for all the black swans are physical objects and all the prime numbers above a hundred are abstract entities.

Thus I consider that the essential commitment to entities of any sort comes through the variables of quantification and not through the use of alleged names. The entities to which a discourse commits us are the entities over which our variables of quantification have to range in order that the statements affirmed in that discourse be true.

Names are a red herring. The use of alleged names, we have seen, is no commitment to corresponding entities. Conversely, through our variables of quantification we are quite capable of committing ourselves to entities which cannot be named individually at all in the resources of our language; witness the real numbers, which, according to classical theory, constitute a larger infinity than does the totality of constructible names in any language. Names, in fact, can be dispensed with altogether in favor of *un*naming general terms, plus quantification and other logical devices; the trick of accomplishing this elimination is provided, in its main lines, by Russell's theory of descriptions. Thenceforward the variable of quantification becomes the sole channel of reference. For ontological commitment it is the variable that counts.

If I understand correctly, Carnap accepts my standard for judging whether a given theory accepts given alleged entities.

The test is whether the variables of quantification have to include those entities in their range in order to make the theory true. Allow, of course, for a shudder between the word 'ontological' and the word 'commitment'.

Now to determine what entities a given theory presupposes is one thing, and to determine what entities a theory should be allowed to presuppose, what entities there really are, is another. It is especially in the latter connection that Carnap urges the dichotomy which I said I would talk about. On one side of his dichotomy he puts the question of there being black swans, or mountains more than 8800 meters, or prime numbers above a hundred; on the other side the question of there being physical objects or abstract entities. The distinction depends on what he calls a *framework:*

If someone wishes to speak in his language about a new kind of entities, he has to introduce a system of new ways of speaking, subject to new rules; we shall call this procedure the construction of a *framework* for the new entities in question. And now we must distinguish two kinds of questions of existence: first, questions of the existence of certain entities of the new kind *within the framework;* we call them *internal questions;* and second, questions concerning the existence or reality of *the framework itself,* called *external questions.* . . . Let us consider as an example the simplest framework dealt with in the everyday language: the spatio-temporally ordered system of observable things and events. Once we have accepted this thing language and thereby the framework of things, we can raise and answer internal questions, e. g., 'Is there a white piece of paper on my desk?', 'Did King Arthur actually live?', 'Are unicorns and centaurs real or merely imaginary?', and the like. These questions are to be answered by empirical investigations. . . . From these questions we must distinguish the external question of the reality of the thing world itself. In contrast to the former questions, this question is raised neither by the man in the street nor by scientists, but only by philosophers. . . . Those who raise the question of the reality of the thing world itself have perhaps in mind not a theoretical question as their formulation seems to suggest, but rather a practical question, a matter of a practical decision concerning the structure of our language. We have to make the choice whether or not to accept and use the forms of expression for the framework in question. . . . If someone decides to accept the thing language, there is no objection against saying that he has accepted the world of things. But this must not be interpreted as if it meant his acceptance of a *belief* in the reality of the thing world; there is no such belief or assertion or assumption, because it is not a theoretical question. To accept the thing world means nothing more than to accept a certain form of language.[1]

Let us recall now my account of wherein the countenancing of entities consists. It consists in the inclusion of them within the range or ranges of the variables of quantification. Accordingly Carnap describes the introduction of a framework as consisting essentially in these two steps:

> First, the introduction of a general term, a predicate of higher level, for the new kind of entities, permitting us to say of any particular entity that it belongs to this kind (e. g., 'Red is a *property*', 'Five is a *number*'). Second, the introduction of variables of the new type. The new entities are values of these variables; the constants (and the closed compound expressions, if any) are substitutable for the variables. With the help of the variables, general sentences concerning the new entities can be formulated.[2]

It begins to appear, then, that Carnap's dichotomy of questions of existence is a dichotomy between questions of the form "Are there so-and-so's?" where the so-and-so's purport to exhaust the range of a particular style of bound variables, and questions of the form "Are there so-and-so's?" where the so-and-so's do not purport to exhaust the range of a particular style of bound variables. Let me call the former questions *category* questions, and the latter ones *subclass* questions. I need this new terminology because Carnap's terms 'external' and 'internal' draw a somewhat different distinction which is derivative from the distinction between category questions and subclass questions. The external questions are the category questions conceived as propounded before the adoption of a given language; and they are, Carnap holds, properly to be construed as questions of the desirability of a given language form. The internal questions comprise the subclass questions and, in addition, the category questions when these are construed as treated within an adopted language as questions having trivially analytic or contradictory answers.[3]

But now I want to examine the dichotomy which, as we see, underlies Carnap's distinction of external and internal, and which I am phrasing as the distinction between category questions and

---

[1] Carnap, "Empiricism, semantics, and ontology," pp. 21–23.
[2] *Ibid.*, p. 30.
[3] This is clearly intended, *ibid.*, p. 24.

subclass questions. It is evident that the question whether there are numbers will be a category question only with respect to languages which appropriate a separate style of variables for the exclusive purpose of referring to numbers. If our language refers to numbers through variables which also take classes other than numbers as values, then the question whether there are numbers becomes a subclass question, on a par with the question whether there are primes over a hundred. This will be the situation in the language of *Principia Mathematica* and in the languages of all the other familiar set theories.

Even the question whether there are classes, or whether there are physical objects, becomes a subclass question if our language uses a single style of variables to range over both sorts of entities. Whether the statement that there are physical objects and the statement that there are black swans should be put on the same side of the dichotomy, or on opposite sides, comes to depend on the rather trivial consideration of whether we use one style of variables or two for physical objects and classes.

I must now explain why I call this a rather trivial consideration. The use of different styles of variables for different ranges is common in mathematics, but can usually be explained as a casual and eliminable shorthand: instead of prefacing various of our statements with the words 'If x is a real number between 0 and 1, then,' we may find it convenient for the space of a chapter or a book of probability theory to reserve special letters 'p', 'q', 'r' to the real numbers between 0 and 1. The difference between using the explicit hypothesis 'x is a real number between 0 and 1' and introducing the restricted variables is so negligible that at the level of ordinary mathematical writing it cannot usually be detected; nor is there any reason why it should be detected.

But Carnap does not have just this trivial distinction in mind. He is thinking of languages which contain fundamentally segregated styles of variables before any definitional abbreviations; and he is thinking of styles of variables which are sealed off from one another so utterly that it is commonly ungrammatical to use a variable of one style where a variable of another style would be grammatical. A language which exploits this sort of basic compartmentalization of variables is that of Russell's theory of logical types. However, I think many of us overstress the theory of types to the neglect of its coeval alternative, Zermelo's set theory, and its descendants. In a notation of the latter tradition, carrying no distinctions in styles of variables, all questions regarding the acceptance not only of numbers in general but of abstract entities in general, or of physical objects in general, would become subclass questions—just as genuinely so as the question of there being black swans and prime numbers above a hundred. Thus Carnap's distinction between internal and external, based as it is upon a distinction between category questions and subclass questions, is of little concern to us apart from the adoption of something like the theory of types. I am one of those who have tended for many years not to adopt the theory of types.

Actually the case is a little worse than I have thus far represented it. Even if we adopt the theory of types we remain free to adopt the course which Russell himself adopted under the name of *typical ambiguity*—thus abandoning the use of a distinctive style of variables for every type. Russell uses his device in moderation, but we can go farther and use just a single style of variables for all types. The theory of types remains in force in this way: only those formulas are admitted as grammatical which *could*, by a one-to-one rewriting of variables, be turned into meaningful formulas of explicit type theory with distinctive styles of variables for all types.

This sort of indirect conformity to the theory of types, on the part of formulas written with a single style of variables, is a feature which I have called *stratification;* and it can be defined also directly, without any appeal to a supposedly more fundamental notation involving distinctive styles of variables. Stratification is simply freedom, on the part of the variables in a formula, from certain repetition patterns in connection with the symbol of class membership.

Next we can even abandon Russell's notion of a hierarchical universe of entities disposed into logical types; nothing remains of type theory except an ultimate grammatical restriction on the sorts of repetition patterns which variables are allowed to exhibit in formulas. Yet formally our logic, refurbished as described, is indistinguishable from Russell's theory of types plus Russell's convention of typical ambiguity. Now the point of this logical digression is that even under the theory of types the use of distinctive styles of variables, explicitly or even implicitly, is the most casual editorial detail.

I argued before that the distinction between category questions and subclass questions is of little concern apart from the adoption of something like the theory of types. But what I now think to have shown is that it is of little concern even under the theory of types. It is a distinction which is not invariant under logically irrelevant changes of typography.

I have doubly warranted hopes of persuading Carnap to abandon this particular distinction. First, as argued, I find it ill grounded. But second, also, I think it is a distinction which he can perfectly well discard compatibly with the philosophical purpose of the paper under discussion. No more than the distinction between *analytic* and *synthetic* is needed in support of Carnap's doctrine that the statements commonly thought of as ontological, viz., statements such as 'There are physical objects', 'There are classes', 'There are numbers', are analytic or contradictory given the language. No more than the distinction between analytic and synthetic is needed in support of his doctrine that the statements commonly thought of as ontological are proper matters of contention only in the form of linguistic proposals. The contrast which he wants between those ontological statements and empirical existence statements such as 'There are black swans' is clinched by the distinction of analytic and synthetic. True, there is in these terms no contrast between analytic statements of an ontological kind and other analytic statements of existence such as 'There are prime numbers above a hundred'; but I don't see why he should care about this.

However, this is not an end of my dissent. On the contrary, the basic point of contention has just emerged: the distinction between analytic and synthetic itself. Carnap correctly states in a footnote:

Quine does not acknowledge the distinction which I emphasize above [viz., the distinction between ontological questions and factual questions of existence], because according to his general conception there are no sharp boundary lines between logical and factual truth, between questions of meaning and questions of fact, between the acceptance of a language structure and the acceptance of an assertion formulated in the language.

I have set down my misgivings regarding the distinction between analytic and synthetic in a recent paper "Two dogmas of empiricism," and will not retrace those steps here. Let me merely stress the consequence: if there is no proper distinction between analytic and synthetic, then no basis at all remains for the contrast which Carnap urges between ontological statements and empirical statements of existence. Ontological questions then end up on a par with questions of natural science.

Within natural science there is a continuum of gradations, from the statements which report observations to those which reflect basic features say of quantum theory or the theory of relativity. The view which I end up with, in the paper last cited, is that statements of ontology or even of mathematics and logic form a continuation of this continuum, a continuation which is perhaps yet more remote from observation than are the central principles of quantum theory or relativity. The differences here are in my view differences only in degree and not in kind. Science is a unified structure, and in principle it is the structure as a whole, and not its component statements one by one, that experience confirms or shows to be imperfect. Carnap maintains that ontological questions, and likewise questions of logical or mathematical principle, are questions not of fact but of choosing a convenient conceptual scheme or framework for science; and with this I agree only if the same be conceded for every scientific hypothesis.

20

✌ Ontological Reduction and the World of Numbers

One conspicuous concern of analytical or scientific philosophy has been to reduce some notions to others, preferably to less dubious ones. A familiar case of such reduction is Frege's definition of number. Each natural number n became, if I may speak in circles, the class of all n-member classes. As is also well known, Frege's was not the only good way. Another was von Neumann's. Under it, if I may again speak in circles, each natural number n became the class of all numbers less than n.

In my judgment we have satisfactorily reduced one predicate to others, certainly, if in terms of these others we have fashioned an open sentence that is *co-extensive* with the predicate in question as originally interpreted; i.e., that is satisfied by the same values of the variables. But this standard does not suit the Frege and von Neumann reductions of number; for these reductions are both good, yet not co-extensive with each other.

Again consider Carnap's clarification of measure, or impure number, where he construes 'the temperature of x is $n°C$' in the fashion 'the temperature-in-degrees-Centigrade of x is n' and so dispenses with the impure numbers $n°C$ in favor of the pure numbers n.[1] There had been, we might say, a two-place predicate

Presented at meetings of the Princeton Graduate Seminar and the Harvard Philosophy Club in February 1964. Reprinted from the *Journal of Philosophy* (Volume 61, 1964), with substantial changes. I am grateful to Kenneth F. Schaffner for a letter of inquiry that sparked the revision.

[1] Carnap, *Physikalische Begriffsbildung.*

'H' of temperature such that '$H(x, \alpha)$' meant that the temperature of x was α. We end up with a new two-place predicate 'H_c' of temperature in degrees Centigrade. '$H(x, n°C)$' is explained away as '$H_c(x, n)$'. But 'H' is not co-extensive with 'H_c', nor indeed with any surviving open sentence at all; 'H' had applied to putative things α, impure numbers, which come to be banished from the universe. Their banishment was Carnap's very purpose. Such reduction is in part *ontological*, as we may say, and co-extensiveness here is clearly not the point.

The definitions of numbers by Frege and von Neumann are best seen as ontological reductions too. Carnap, in the last example, showed how to skip the impure numbers and get by with pure ones. Just so, we might say, Frege and von Neumann showed how to skip the natural numbers and get by with what we may for the moment call *Frege classes* and *von Neumann classes*. There is only this difference of detail: Frege classes and von Neumann classes simulate the behavior of the natural numbers to the point where it is convenient to call them natural numbers, instead of saying that we have contrived to dispense with the natural numbers as Carnap dispensed with impure numbers.

Where reduction is in part ontological, we see, co-extensiveness is not the issue. What then is? Consider again Frege's way and von Neumann's of construing natural number. And there is yet a third well-known way, Zermelo's. Why are these all good? What have they in common? Each is a structure-preserving model of the natural numbers. Each preserves arithmetic, and that is enough. It has been urged that we need more: we need also to provide for translating mixed contexts in which the arithmetical idioms occur in company with expressions concerning physical objects and the like. Specifically, we need to be able to say what it means for a class to have n members. But in fact this is no added requirement. We can say what it means for a class to have n members no matter how we construe the numbers, as long as we have them in order. For to say that a class has n members is simply to say that the members of the class can be correlated with the natural numbers up to n, whatever they are.

The real numbers, like the natural numbers, can be taken in a variety of ways. The Dedekind cut is the central idea, but you can use it to explain real numbers either as certain classes of ratios, or as certain relations of natural numbers, or as certain

classes of natural numbers. Under the first method, if I may
again speak in circles, each real number x becomes the class of all
ratios less than x. Under the second method, x becomes this
relation of natural numbers: m bears the relation to n if m stands
to n in a ratio less than x. For the third version, we change this
relation of natural numbers to a class of natural numbers by
mapping the ordered pairs of natural numbers into the natural
numbers.

All three alternatives are admissible, and what all three
conspicuously have in common is, again, just the relevant
structure: each is a structure-preserving model of the real
numbers. Again it seems that no more is needed to assure
satisfactory translation also of any mixed contexts. When real
numbers are applied to magnitudes in the physical world, any
model of the real numbers could be applied as well.

The same proves true when we come to the imaginary numbers
and the infinite numbers, cardinal and ordinal: the problem of
construing comes to no more, again, than modeling. Once we find
a model that reproduces the formal structure, there seems to be
no difficulty in translating any mixed contexts as well.

These cases suggest that what justifies the reduction of one
system of objects to another is preservation of relevant structure.
Since, according to the Löwenheim–Skolem theorem, any theory
that admits of a true interpretation at all admits of a model in
the natural numbers, G. D. W. Berry concluded that only
common sense stands in the way of adopting an all-purpose
Pythagorean ontology: natural numbers exclusively.

There is an interesting reversal here. Our first examples of
ontological reduction were Frege's and von Neumann's reductions
of natural number to set theory. These and other examples
encouraged the thought that what matters in such reduction is
the discovery of a model. And so we end up saying, in view of the
Löwenheim–Skolem theorem, that theories about objects of any
sort can, when true, be reduced to theories of natural numbers.
Instead of reducing talk of numbers to talk of sets, we may
reduce talk of sets—and of all else—to talk of natural numbers.
And here there is an evident gain, since the natural numbers are
relatively clear and, as infinite sets go, economical.

But is it true that all that matters is a model? Any interpretable theory can, in view of the Löwenheim–Skolem theorem, be

modeled in the natural numbers, yes; but does this entitle us to say that it is once and for all *reducible* to that domain, in a sense that would allow us thenceforward to repudiate the old objects for all purposes and recognize just the new ones, the natural numbers? Examples encouraged in us the impression that modeling assured such reducibility, but we should be able to confirm or remove the impression with a little analysis.

What do we require of a reduction of one theory to another? Here is a complaisant answer: any effective mapping of closed sentences on closed sentences will serve if it preserves truth. If we settle for this, then what of the thesis that every true theory θ can be reduced to a theory about natural numbers? It can be proved, even without the Löwenheim–Skolem theorem. For we can translate each closed sentence S of θ as 'Tx' with x as the Gödel number of S and with 'T' as the *truth predicate* for θ, a predicate satisfied by all and only the Gödel numbers of true sentences of θ.

Of this trivial way of reducing an ontology to natural numbers, it must be said that whatever it saves in ontology it pays for in *ideology:* we have to strengthen the primitive predicates. For we know from Gödel and Tarski that the truth predicate of θ is expressible only in terms that are stronger in essential ways than any originally available in θ itself.[2]

Nor is this a price that can in general be saved by invoking the Löwenheim–Skolem theorem. I shall explain why not. When, in conformity with the proof of the Löwenheim–Skolem theorem, we reinterpret the primitive predicates of a theory θ so as to make them predicates of natural numbers, we do not in general make them arithmetical predicates. That is, they do not in general go over into predicates that can be expressed in terms of sum, product, equality, and logic. If we are modeling merely the *theorems* of a deductive system—the implicates of an effective if not finite set of axioms—then certainly we can get arithmetical reinterpretations of the predicates.[3] But that is not what we are about. We are concerned rather to accommodate all the *truths* of θ—all the sentences, regardless of axiomatizability, that were true under the original interpretation of the predicates of θ. There

---

[2] See Tarski, *Logic, Semantics, Metamathematics,* p. 273. There are exceptions where θ is especially weak; see Myhill, p. 194.

[3] See Wang; also Kleene, pp. 389–398 and more particularly p. 431. For exposition see also my "Interpretations of sets of conditions."

is, under the Löwenheim–Skolem theorem, a reinterpretation that carries all these truths into truths about natural numbers; but there may be no such interpretation in arithmetical terms. There will be if θ admits of complete axiomatization, of course, and there will be under some other circumstances, but not under all. In the general case the most that can be said is, again, that the numerical reinterpretations are expressible in the notation of arithmetic plus the truth predicate for θ.[4]

So on the whole the reduction to a Pythagorean ontology exacts a price in ideology whether we invoke the truth predicate directly or let ourselves be guided by the argument of the Löwenheim–Skolem theorem. Still there is a reason for preferring the latter, longer line. When I suggested simply translating S as 'Tx' with x as Gödel number of S, I was taking advantage of the liberal standard: reduction was just any effective and truth-preserving mapping of closed sentences on closed sentences. Now the virtue of the longer line is that it works also for a less liberal standard of reduction. Instead of accepting just any and every mapping of closed sentences on closed sentences so long as it is effective and truth-preserving, we can insist rather that it preserve predicate structure. That is, instead of mapping just whole sentences of θ on sentences, we can require that each of the erstwhile primitive predicates of θ carry over into a predicate or open sentence about the new objects (the natural numbers).

Whatever its proof and whatever its semantics, a doctrine of blanket reducibility of ontologies to natural numbers surely trivializes most further ontological endeavor. If the universe of discourse of every theory can as a matter of course be standardized as the Pythagorean universe, then apparently the only special ontological reduction to aspire to in any particular theory is reduction to a finite universe. Once the size is both finite and specified, of course, ontological considerations lose all force; for we can then reduce all quantifications to conjunctions and alternations and so retain no recognizably referential apparatus.

Some further scope for ontological endeavor does still remain, I suppose, in the relativity to ideology. One can try to reduce a given theory to the Pythagorean ontology without stepping up its

---

[4] This can be seen by examining the general construction in §1 of "Interpretations of sets of conditions."

ideology. This endeavor has little bearing on completely axiomatized theories, however, since they reduce to pure arithmetic, or elementary number theory.[5]

Anyway we seem to have trivialized most ontological contrasts. Perhaps the trouble is that our standard of ontological reduction is still too liberal. We narrowed it appreciably when we required that the predicates be construed severally. But we still did not make it very narrow. We continued to allow the several predicates of a theory θ to go over into any predicates or open sentences concerning natural numbers, so long merely as the truth values of closed sentences were preserved.

Let us return to the Carnap case of impure number for a closer look. We are initially confronted with a theory whose objects include place-times x and impure numbers α and whose primitive predicates include 'H'. We reduce the theory to a new one whose objects include place-times and pure numbers, and whose predicates include 'H_c'. The crucial step consists of explaining '$H(x, n°C)$' as '$H_c(x, n)$'.

Now this is successful, if it is, because three conditions are met. One is, of course, that '$H_c(x, n)$' under the intended interpretation agrees in truth value with '$H(x, n°C)$', under its originally intended interpretation, for all values of x and n. A second condition is that, in the original theory, all mention of impure numbers α was confined or confinable to the specific form of context '$H(x, \alpha)$'. Otherwise the switch to '$H_c(x, n)$' would not eliminate such mention. But if this condition were to fail, through there being further predicates (say a predicate of length or of density) and further units (say meters) along with 'H' and degrees, we could still win through by just treating them similarly. A third condition, finally, is that an impure number α can always be referred to in terms of a pure number and a unit: thus $n°C$, n meters. Otherwise explaining '$H(x, n°C)$' as '$H_c(x, n)$' would not take care of '$H(x, \alpha)$'.

This third condition is that we be able to specify what I shall call a *proxy function*: a function which assigns one of the new things, in this example a pure number, to each of the old things—each of the impure numbers of temperature. In this example the

---

[5] Thus far in this paper I have been recording things that I said in the Shearman Lectures at University College, London, February 1954. Not so from here on.

proxy function is the function "how many degrees centigrade"—
the function f such that $f(n°C) = n$. It is not required that such a
function be expressible in the original theory θ to which 'H'
belonged, much less that it be available in the final theory θ' to
which 'H_c' belongs. It is required rather of *us*, out in the
metatheory where we are explaining and justifying the discontin-
uance of θ in favor of θ', that we have some means of expressing a
proxy function. Only upon us, who explain '$H(x, \alpha)$' away by
'$H_c(x, n)$', does it devolve to show how every α that was intended
in the old θ determines an n of the new θ'.

In these three conditions we have a further narrowing of what
had been too liberal a standard of what to count as a reduction of
one theory or ontology to another. We have in fact narrowed it to
where, as it seems to me, the things we should like to count as
reduction do so count and the rest do not. Carnap's elimination of
impure number so counts; likewise Frege's and von Neumann's
reduction of natural arithmetic to set theory; likewise the various
essentially Dedekindian reductions of the theory of real numbers.
Yet the general trivialization of ontology fails; there ceases to be
any evident way of arguing, from the Löwenheim–Skolem theorem, that ontologies are generally reducible to the natural
numbers.

The three conditions came to us in an example. If we restate
them more generally, they lose their tripartite character. The
standard of reduction of a theory θ to a theory θ' can now be put
as follows. We specify a function, not necessarily in the notation
of θ or θ', which admits as arguments all objects in the universe
of θ and takes values in the universe of θ'. This is the proxy
function. Then to each n-place primitive predicate of θ, for each
n, we effectively associate an open sentence of θ' in n free
variables, in such a way that the predicate is fulfilled by an n-
tuple of arguments of the proxy function always and only when
the open sentence is fulfilled by the corresponding n-tuple of
values.

For brevity I am supposing that θ has only predicates,
variables, quantifiers, and truth functions. The exclusion of
singular terms, function signs, abstraction operators, and the like
is no real restriction, for these accessories are reducible to the
narrower basis in familiar ways.

Let us try applying the above standard of reduction to the

Frege case: Frege's reduction of number to set theory. Here the proxy function f is the function which, applied, e.g., to the "genuine" number 5, gives as value the class of all five-member classes (Frege's so-called 5). In general fx is describable as the class of all x-member classes.

When the real numbers are reduced (by what I called the first method) to classes of ratios, fx is the class of all ratios less than the "genuine" real number x.

I must admit that my formulation suffers from a conspicuous element of make-believe. Thus, in the Carnap case I had to talk as if there *were* such things as $x°$C, much though I applaud Carnap's repudiation of them. In the Frege case I had to talk as if the "genuine" number 5 were really something over and above Frege's, much though I applaud his reduction. My formulation belongs, by its nature, in an inclusive theory that admits the objects of θ, as unreduced, and the objects of θ' on an equal footing.

But the formulation seems, if we overlook this imperfection, to mark the boundary we want. Ontological reductions that were felt to be serious do conform. Another that conforms, besides those thus far mentioned, is the reduction of an ontology of place-times to an ontology of number quadruples by means of Cartesian co-ordinates. And at the same time any sweeping Pythagoreanization on the strength of the Löwenheim–Skolem theorem is obstructed. The proof of the Löwenheim–Skolem theorem is such as to enable us to give the predicates of the numerical model; but the standard of ontological reduction that we have now reached requires more than that. Reduction of a theory θ to natural numbers—true reduction by our new standard, and not mere modeling—means determining a proxy function that actually assigns numbers to all the objects of θ and maps the predicates of θ into open sentences of the numerical model. Where this can be done, with preservation of truth values of closed sentences, we may well speak of reduction to natural numbers. But the Löwenheim–Skolem argument determines, in the general case, no proxy function. It does not determine which numbers are to go proxy for the respective objects of θ. Therein it falls short of our standard of ontological reduction.

It emerged early in this paper that what justifies an ontological reduction is, vaguely speaking, preservation of relevant structure.

What we now perceive is that this relevant structure runs deep; the objects of the one system must be assigned severally to objects of the other.

Goodman argued along other lines to this conclusion and more;[6] he called for isomorphism, thereby requiring one-to-one correspondence between the old objects and their proxies. I prefer to let different things have the same proxy. For consider again hidden inflation, as described in the preceding essay. Relieving such inflation is a respectable brand of ontological reduction, and it consists precisely in taking one thing as proxy for all the things that were indiscriminable from it.[7]

---

[6] Pp. 5–19.

[7] I am indebted for this observation to Paul Benacerraf. On such deflation see further my discussion of identification of indiscernibles in *Word and Object*, p. 230; in *From a Logical Point of View*, pp. 71f; and in "Reply to Professor Marcus," Essay 16 above.

21

‌ *On Mental Entities*

A question which is very much in the air is whether we should affirm or deny that there are such things as *sensations*, these being conceived as immediate, subjective experiences. I shall touch on this question, but not just yet. For a while it will be convenient to talk as if there are.

Falling in thus uncritically with the usage of old-fashioned epistemology and introspective psychology, let us consider, to begin with, the process of language. It has been the fashion in recent philosophy, both that of some of the English analysts and that of some of the logical positivists, to think of the terms of science and ordinary language as having some sort of hidden or implicit definitions which carry each such term back finally to terms relating to immediate experience. Now this view is clearly unrealistic. A better description, though countenancing the notion of immediate experience still, is as follows. On the one hand we have language, as an infinite totality of said or appropriately sayable phrases and sentences. On the other hand we have our sense experience, which, by a process of psychological association or conditioned response, is keyed in with the linguistic material at numerous and varied places. The linguistic material is an interlocked system which is tied here and there to experience; it is not a society of separately established terms and statements, each with its separate empirical definition. There is no separate

Presented at Cambridge, Mass., November 18, 1952, in a colloquium of the Institute for the Unity of Science, and published 1953 in *Contributions to the Analysis and Synthesis of Knowledge,* which was Vol. 80 of the *Proceedings* of the American Academy of Arts and Sciences.

meaning, in terms of direct experience, for the statement that there is a table here, or that there is a planet somewhere in outer space. The statement that there is the planet may be keyed with our sense experience by our seeing the planet, or by our merely noting perturbations in the orbits of other planets. And even the statement that there is a table right here may be keyed with our sense experience through touch *or* sight *or* hearsay. Again the statement that I have cut my finger may be tied with experience either by sight or by pain or both. I have often argued that it is mistaken to try to distinguish even between those scientific statements which are true by virtue of the meanings of our terms and those which are true or probable by inductive evidence. As Pierre Duhem urged, it is the system as a whole that is keyed to experience. It is taught by exploitation of its heterogeneous and sporadic links with experience, and it stands or falls, is retained or modified, according as it continues to serve us well or ill in the face of continuing experience.

We get the system, in its main lines, from our forebears. As children learning the language, we get on to various simple terms and key phrases by direct association with appropriate experiences. When we have progressed a bit with this kind of learning, we learn further usages contextually. Eventually we are in a position to receive traditional doctrine a whole chapter at a time. Finally some men venture to revise the tradition here and there, for the sake of greater simplicity or better experiential links; and these are scientists.

So much for the individual's mastery of language and lore; but what of the origins of all this in the race? It would be irrational to suppose that those origins were rational. The prehistory of science was probably a composite of primitive unconscious symbolism of the Freudian kind, confusions of sign and object, word magic, wishful thinking, and a lazy acquiescence in forms whose motivation had been long forgotten. Biases in our conceptual schemes may have great utility in the systematizing of science, and therewith high survival value, despite humble origins in the random workings of unreason—just as chance mutations in the chromosome may launch a sturdy and efficient new race. Natural selection through the ages tends to favor the happy accidents at the expense of the unpropitious ones, in the evolution of ideas as in the evolution of living species.

As scientists we accept provisionally our heritage from the dim past, with intermediate revisions by our more recent forebears; and then we continue to warp and revise. As Neurath has said, we are in the position of a mariner who must rebuild his ship plank by plank while continuing to stay afloat on the open sea.

How do we decide on such retentions and revisions? To be more specific: how do we decide, apropos of the real world, what things there *are?* Ultimately, I think, by considerations of simplicity plus a pragmatic guess as to how the overall system will continue to work in connection with experience. We posit molecules, and eventually electrons, even though these are not given to direct experience, merely because they contribute to an overall system which is simpler as a whole than its known alternatives; the empirical relevance of the notion of molecules and electrons is indirect, and exists only by virtue of the links with experience which exist at *other* points of the system. Actually I expect that tables and sheep are, in the last analysis, on much the same footing as molecules and electrons. Even these have a continuing right to a place in our conceptual scheme only by virtue of their indirect contribution to the overall simplicity of our linguistic or conceptual organization of experience; for note that even tables and sheep are not direct sensations.

The notion of macroscopic objects, tables and sheep, differs from that of molecules and electrons mainly, from an epistemological point of view, in point of degree of antiquity. Molecules were posited consciously in historic times, whereas the positing of the external objects of common sense is an original trait of human nature. Men have believed in something very like our common-sense world of external objects as long, surely, as anything properly describable as language has existed; for the teaching of language and the use of it for communication depend on investing linguistic forms with intersubjectively fixed references. It would be senseless to speak of a motive for this archaic and unconscious posit, but we can significantly speak of its function and its survival value; and in these respects the hypothesis of common-sense external objects is quite like that of molecules and electrons.

Because the notion of external macroscopic objects is so fundamental both to the origins of language and to the continued learning of language, we may be pretty sure that it is here to stay, though electrons and other more hypothetical entities may, with the continued revisions of science, come and go. Experience is continually reminding us that it is over the external macroscopic objects that there is least semantical misunderstanding between speakers; it is naturally to tables and sheep and the like that we keep returning when there is trouble about new concepts.

Epistemologists, put off by the fact that macroscopic objects are epistemologically on the same footing as molecules and electrons, have looked to sense data—the raw content of sensation itself—as a more ultimate realm of entities. The ensuing difficulties are notorious. They may be seen most vividly if to begin with we think about memory. Our present data of our own past experiences are, on this theory, some sort of faint present replicas of past sense impressions; faint echoes of past sensation accompanying the blare of present sensation. Now it takes little soul-searching to persuade oneself that such double impressions, dim against bright, are rather the exception than the rule. Ordinarily we do not remember the trapezoidal sensory surface of a desk, as a color patch extending across the lower half of the visual field; what we remember is *that* there was a desk meeting such-and-such approximate specifications of form and size in three-dimensional space. Memory is just as much a product of the past positing of extra-sensory objects as it is a datum for the positing of past sense data.

What has been said just now of memory applies in some degree to the stream of sensory experience generally. It would be increasingly apparent from the findings of the Gestalt psychologists, if it were not quite apparent from everyday experience, that our selective awareness of present sensory surfaces is a function of present purposes and past conceptualizations. The contribution of reason cannot be viewed as limited merely to conceptualizing a presented pageant of experience and positing objects behind it; for this activity reacts, by selection and emphasis, on the qualitative make-up of the pageant itself in its succeeding portions. It is not an instructive oversimplification, but a basic falsification, to represent cognition as a discernment of regularities in an unadulterated stream of experience. Better to conceive of the stream itself as polluted, at each succeeding point of its course, by every prior cognition.

So the notion of pure sense datum is a pretty tenuous abstraction, a good deal more conjectural than the notion of an external object, a table or a sheep. It is significant that when we try to talk of the subjective we borrow our terminology from the objective: I feel as if I were falling, I have a sinking sensation, I feel on top of the world, I see pink elephants (better: I feel as if I were really seeing real pink elephants), etc. Even the terms which we have come to regard as strictly and immediately sensory, like 'red', are obviously objective in reference in the first instance: we learn the word 'red' by being confronted with an external object which our parent calls red, just as we learn the word 'sheep' by being confronted with an external object which our parent calls a sheep. When, at a certain stage of epistemological sophistication, we transfer the word 'red' to an alleged datum of immediate subjective sense experience, we are doing just what we do when we say we have a sinking sensation: I feel *as if* I were really, externally falling, and I feel *as if* I were really confronted by an external red object.

I suggest that it is a mistake to seek an immediately evident reality, somehow more immediately evident than the realm of external objects. Unbemused by philosophy, we would all go along with Dr. Johnson, whose toe was his touchstone of reality. Sheep are real, unicorns not. Clouds are real, the sky (as a solid canopy) not. Odd numbers are perhaps real, but prime even numbers other than 2 not. Everything, of course, is real; but there are sheep and there are no unicorns, there are clouds and there is (in the specified sense of the term) no sky, there are odd numbers and there are no even primes other than 2. Such is the ordinary usage of the word 'real', a separation of the sheep from the unicorns. Failing some aberrant definition which is certainly not before us, this is the only usage we have to go on.

The crucial insight of empiricism is that any evidence for science has its end points in the senses. This insight remains valid, but it is an insight which comes after physics, physiology, and psychology, not before. Epistemologists have wanted to posit a realm of sense data, situated somehow just me-ward of the physical stimulus, for fear of circularity: to view the physical stimulation rather than the sense datum as the end point of scientific evidence would be to make physical science rest for its evidence on physical science. But if with Neurath we accept this circularity, simply recognizing that the science of science is a science, then we dispose of the epistemological motive for assuming a realm of sense data. May we then make a clean sweep of mental entities?

I urged earlier that we decide what things there are, or what things to treat as there being, by considerations of simplicity of the overall system and its utility in connection with experience, so to speak. I say "so to speak" because I do not want to force the issue of recognizing experience as an entity or composite of entities. I have talked up to now as if there were such entities; I had to talk some language, and I uncritically talked this one. But the history of the mind–body problem bears witness to the awkwardness of the practice. We are virtually bound, as re-marked earlier, to hold to an ontology of external objects; but it is moot indeed whether the positing of additional objects of a mental kind is a help or a hindrance to science. Or perhaps not so moot. At any rate it is moot or else it is clear that they are a hindrance.

To repudiate mental entities is not to deny that we sense or even that we are conscious; it is merely to report and try to describe these facts without assuming entities of a mental kind. What is spoken of in terms of the residual posited objects of science and common sense as my cut finger is keyed into our nervous responses in various ways; nerves from my eye and other eyes are involved, and nerves from my finger. Some persons are so situated as to be accessible to the stimuli which are most closely relevant to the phrase 'Quine's cut finger' and some are not. A dozen of us are in a position for the appropriate stimulation of the eye, and one of us for the appropriate stimulation of the finger.

None of us is oriented to external objects quite like anyone else, for we occupy different positions, and while we exchange positions the objects age. None of us learned his words quite like anyone else. But we use them in sufficient systematic agreement for fair communication—which is no accident, since language is subject to the law of survival of the fittest. We manage to talk effectively about other people's cut fingers because of a pattern of habits connecting with present and past stimulation of the eye together with past stimulation, under optically similar circum-stances, of our own fingers. The same is true of pain—but no argument against construing pain as a state of the physical organism. If we repudiate mental entities as entities, there ceases to be an iron curtain between the private and the public; there remains only a smoke screen, a matter of varying degrees of privacy of events in the physical world. Consciousness still retains a place, as a state of a physical object, if—following the suggestion made by Professor Deutsch in addressing this institute last year—we construe consciousness as a faculty of responding to one's own responses. The responses here are, or can be construed as, physical behavior. It is not the purpose of this view to leave any aspect of life out of account. The issue is merely whether, in an ideal last accounting of everything or a present practical accounting of everything we can, it is efficacious so to frame our conceptual scheme as to mark out a range of entities or units of a so-called mental kind in addition to the physical ones. My hypothesis, put forward in the spirit of a hypothesis of natural science, is that it is not efficacious.

22

✺ The Scope and Language of Science

I

I am a physical object sitting in a physical world. Some of the forces of this physical world impinge on my surface. Light rays strike my retinas; molecules bombard my eardrums and finger-tips. I strike back, emanating concentric air waves. These waves take the form of a torrent of discourse about tables, people, molecules, light rays, retinas, air waves, prime numbers, infinite classes, joy and sorrow, good and evil.

My ability to strike back in this elaborate way consists in my having assimilated a good part of the culture of my community, and perhaps modified and elaborated it a bit on my own account. All this training consisted in turn of an impinging of physical forces, largely other people's utterances, upon my surface, and of gradual changes in my own constitution consequent upon these physical forces. All I am or ever hope to be is due to irritations of my surface, together with such latent tendencies to response as may have been present in my original germ plasm. And all the

Presented as an invited address in one of the Bicentennial Conferences at Columbia University, October 1954, and published with the editor's re-visions in Lewis Leary, ed., *The Unity of Knowledge* (New York: Double-day, 1955). My original text appeared afterward in the *British Journal for the Philosophy of Science,* 1957, and that is what is reprinted here, with negligible emendations, with the permission of the Columbia trustees and with the approval of the editor of the *British Journal.*

lore of the ages is due to irritation of the surfaces of a succession of persons, together, again, with the internal initial conditions of the several individuals.

Now how is it that we know that our knowledge must depend thus solely on surface irritation and internal conditions? Only because we know in a general way what the world is like, with its light rays, molecules, men, retinas, and so on. It is thus our very understanding of the physical world, fragmentary though that understanding be, that enables us to see how limited the evidence is on which that understanding is predicated. It is our understanding, such as it is, of what lies beyond our surfaces, that shows our evidence for that understanding to be limited to our surfaces. But this reflection arouses certain logical misgivings: for is not our very talk of light rays, molecules, and men then only sound and fury, induced by irritation of our surfaces and signifying nothing? The world view which lent plausibility to this modest account of our knowledge is, according to this very account of our knowledge, a groundless fabrication.

To reason thus is, however, to fall into fallacy: a peculiarly philosophical fallacy, and one whereof philosophers are increasingly aware. We cannot significantly question the reality of the external world, or deny that there is evidence of external objects in the testimony of our senses; for, to do so is simply to dissociate the terms 'reality' and 'evidence' from the very applications which originally did most to invest those terms with whatever intelligibility they may have for us.

We imbibe an archaic natural philosophy with our mother's milk. In the fullness of time, what with catching up on current literature and making some supplementary observations of our own, we become clearer on things. But the process is one of growth and gradual change: we do not break with the past, nor do we attain to standards of evidence and reality different in kind from the vague standards of children and laymen. Science is not a substitute for common sense, but an extension of it. The quest for knowledge is properly an effort simply to broaden and deepen the knowledge which the man in the street already enjoys, in moderation, in relation to the commonplace things around him. To disavow the very core of common sense, to require evidence for that which both the physicist and the man in the street accept as platitudinous, is no laudable perfectionism; it is a pompous confusion, a failure to observe the nice distinction between the baby and the bath water.

Let us therefore accept physical reality, whether in the manner of unspoiled men in the street or with one or another degree of scientific sophistication. In so doing we constitute ourselves recipients and carriers of the evolving lore of the ages. Then, pursuing in detail our thus accepted theory of physical reality, we draw conclusions concerning, in particular, our own physical selves, and even concerning ourselves as lorebearers. One of these conclusions is that this very lore which we are engaged in has been induced in us by irritation of our physical surfaces and not otherwise. Here we have a little item of lore about lore. It does not, if rightly considered, tend to controvert the lore it is about. On the contrary, our initially uncritical hypothesis of a physical world gains pragmatic support from whatever it contributes towards a coherent account of lorebearing or other natural phenomena.

Once we have seen that in our knowledge of the external world we have nothing to go on but surface irritation, two questions obtrude themselves—a bad one and a good one. The bad one, lately dismissed, is the question whether there is really an external world after all. The good one is this: Whence the strength of our notion that there is an external world? Whence our persistence in representing discourse as somehow *about* a reality, and a reality beyond the irritation?

It is not as though the mere occurrence of speech itself were conceived somehow as *prima facie* evidence of there being a reality as subject matter. Much of what we say is recognized even by the man in the street as irreferential: 'Hello', 'Thank you', 'Ho hum', these make no claims upon reality. These are physical responses on a par, semantically, with the patellar reflex. Whence then the idea of scientific objectivity? Whence the idea that language is occasionally descriptive in a way that other quiverings of irritable protoplasm are not?

This is a question for the natural science of the external world: in particular, for the psychology of human animals. The question has two not quite separate parts: whence the insistence on a world of reference, set over against language? and whence the insistence on a world of external objects, set over against oneself? Actually we can proceed to answer this twofold question plausibly enough, in a general sort of way, without any very elaborate psychologizing.

II

Let us suppose that one of the early words acquired by a particular child is 'red'. How does he learn it? He is treated to utterances of the word simultaneously with red presentations; further, his own babbling is applauded when it approximates to 'red' in the presence of red. At length he acquires the art of applying the word neither too narrowly nor too broadly for his mother's tastes. This learning process is familiar to us under many names: association, conditioning, training, habit formation, reinforcement and extinction, induction.

Whatever our colleagues in the laboratory may discover of the inner mechanism of that process, we may be sure of this much: the very possibility of it depends on a prior tendency on the child's part to weight qualitative differences unequally. Logically, as long as a, b, and c are three and not one, there is exactly as much difference between a and b as between a and c; just as many classes, anyway, divide a from b (i.e., contain one and not the other) as a from c. For the child, on the other hand, some differences must count for more than others if the described process of learning 'red' is to go forward at all. Whether innately or as a result of pre-linguistic learning, the child must have more tendency to associate a red ball with a red ball than with a yellow one; more tendency to associate a red ball with a red ribbon than with a blue one; and more tendency to dissociate the ball from its surroundings than to dissociate its parts from one another. Otherwise no training could mold the child's usage of the word 'red', since no future occasion would be more strongly favored by past applications of the word than any other. A working appreciation of something like 'natural kinds', a tendency anyway to respond in different degrees to different differences, has to be there before the word 'red' can be learned.

At the very beginning of one's learning of language, thus, words are learned in relation to such likenesses and contrasts as are already appreciated without benefit of words. No wonder we attribute those likenesses and contrasts to real stuff, and think of language as a superimposed apparatus for talking *about* the real.

The likenesses and contrasts which underlie one's first learning of language must not only be pre-verbally appreciable; they must, in addition, be intersubjective. Sensitivity to redness will avail the child nothing, in learning 'red' from the mother, except insofar as the mother is in a position to appreciate that the child is confronted with something red. Hence, perhaps, our first glimmerings of an external world. The most primitive sense of externality may well be a sense of the mother's reinforcement of likenesses and contrasts in the first phases of word learning. The real is thus felt, first and foremost, as prior to language and external to oneself. It is the stuff that mother vouches for and calls by name.

This priority of the non-linguistic to the linguistic diminishes as learning proceeds. *Scholarship* sets in; i.e., the kind of learning which depends on prior learning of words. We learn 'mauve' at an advanced age, through a verbal formula of the form 'the color of' or 'a color midway between'. And the scholarly principle takes hold early; the child will not have acquired many words before his vocabulary comes to figure as a major agency in its own increase. By the time the child is able to sustain rudimentary conversation in his narrow community, his knowledge of language and his knowledge of the world are a unitary mass.

Nevertheless, we are so overwhelmingly impressed by the initial phase of our education that we continue to think of language generally as a secondary or superimposed apparatus for talking about real things. We tend not to appreciate that most of the things, and most of the supposed traits of the so-called world, are learned through language and believed in by a projection from language. Some uncritical persons arrive thus at a copy theory of language: they look upon the elements of language as names of elements of reality, and true discourse as a map of reality. They project vagaries of language indiscriminately upon the world, stuffing the universe with ands and ors, singulars and plurals, definites and indefinites, facts and states of affairs, simply on the ground that there are parallel elements and distinctions on the linguistic side.

The general task which science sets itself is that of specifying how reality "really" is: the task of delineating the structure of reality as distinct from the structure of one or another traditional language (except, of course, when the science happens to be grammar itself). The notion of reality independent of language is carried over by the scientist from his earliest impressions, but the facile reification of linguistic features is avoided or minimized.

But how is it possible for scientists to be thus critical and discriminating about their reifications? If all discourse is mere response to surface irritation, then by what evidence may one man's projection of a world be said to be sounder than another's? If, as suggested earlier, the terms 'reality' and 'evidence' owe their intelligibility to their applications in archaic common sense, why may we not then brush aside the presumptions of science?

The reason we may not is that science is itself a continuation of common sense. The scientist is indistinguishable from the common man in his sense of evidence, except that the scientist is more careful. This increased care is not a revision of evidential standards, but only the more patient and systematic collection and use of what anyone would deem to be evidence. If the scientist sometimes overrules something which a superstitious layman might have called evidence, this may simply be because the scientist has other and contrary evidence which, if patiently presented to the layman bit by bit, would be conceded superior. Or it may be that the layman suffers from some careless chain of reasoning of his own whereby, long since, he came wrongly to reckon certain types of connection as evidential: wrongly in that a careful survey of his own ill-observed and long-forgotten steps would suffice to disabuse him. (A likely example is the "gambler's fallacy"—the notion that the oftener black pays the likelier red becomes.)

Not that the layman has an explicit standard of evidence—nor the scientist either. The scientist begins with the primitive sense of evidence which he possessed as layman, and uses it carefully and systematically. He still does not reduce it to rule, though he elaborates and uses sundry statistical methods in an effort to prevent it from getting out of hand in complex cases. By putting nature to the most embarrassing tests he can devise, the scientist makes the most of his lay flair for evidence; and at the same time he amplifies the flair itself, affixing an artificial proboscis of punch cards and quadrille paper.

Our latest question was, in brief, how science gets ahead of common sense; and the answer, in a word, is 'system'. The scientist introduces system into his quest and scrutiny of evidence. System, moreover, dictates the scientist's hypotheses themselves: those are most welcome which are seen to conduce most to simplicity in the overall theory. Predictions, once they have been deduced from hypotheses, are subject to the discipline of evidence in turn; but the hypotheses have, at the time of hypothesis, only the considerations of systematic simplicity to recommend them. Insofar, simplicity itself—in some sense of this difficult term—counts as a kind of evidence; and scientists have indeed long tended to look upon the simpler of the two hypotheses as not merely the more likable, but the more likely. Let it not be supposed, however, that we have found at last a type of evidence that is acceptable to science and foreign to common sense. On the contrary, the favoring of the seemingly simpler hypothesis is a lay habit carried over by science. The quest of systematic simplicity seems peculiarly scientific in spirit only because science is what it issues in.

III

The notion of a reality independent of language is derived from earliest impressions, if the speculations in the foregoing pages are right, and is then carried over into science as a matter of course. The stress on externality is likewise carried over into science, and with a vengeance. For the sense of externality has its roots, if our speculations are right, in the intersubjectivity which is so essential to the learning of language; and intersubjectivity is vital not only to language but equally to the further enterprise, likewise a social one, of science. All men are to qualify as witnesses to the data of science, and the truths of science are to be true no matter who pronounces them. Thus it is that science has got on rather with masses and velocities than with likes and dislikes. And thus it is that when science does confront likes and dislikes it confronts them as behavior, intersubjectively observable. Language in general is robustly extravert, but science is more so.

It would be unwarranted rationalism to suppose that we can stake out the business of science in advance of pursuing science and arriving at a certain body of scientific theory. Thus consider, for the sake of analogy, the smaller task of staking out the business of chemistry. Having got on with chemistry, we can describe it *ex post facto* as the study of the combining of atoms in molecules. But no such clean-cut delimitation of the business of chemistry was possible until that business was already in large measure done. Now the situation is similar with science generally. To describe science as the domain of cognitive judgment avails us nothing, for the definiens here is in as urgent need of clarification as the definiendum. Taking advantage of existing scientific work, however, and not scrupling to identify ourselves with a substantive scientific position, we can then delineate the scientific objective, or the cognitive domain, to some degree. It is a commonplace predicament to be unable to formulate a task until half done with it.

Thought, if of any considerable complexity, is inseparable from language—in practice surely and in principle quite probably. Science, though it seeks traits of reality independent of language, can neither get on without language nor aspire to linguistic neutrality. To some degree, nevertheless, the scientist can enhance objectivity and diminish the interference of language, by his very choice of language. And we, concerned to distill the essence of scientific discourse, can profitably purify the language of science beyond what might reasonably be urged upon the practicing scientist. To such an operation we now turn.

In a spirit thus not of practical language reform but of philosophical schematism, we may begin by banishing what are known as *indicator words* (Goodman) or *egocentric particulars* (Russell): 'I', 'you', 'this', 'that', 'here', 'there', 'now', 'then', and the like. This we clearly must do if the truths of science are literally to be true independently of author and occasion of utterance. It is only thus, indeed, that we come to be able to speak of sentences, i.e., certain linguistic forms, as true and false. As long as the indicator words are retained, it is not the sentence but only the several events of its utterance that can be said to be true or false.

Besides indicator words, a frequent source of fluctuation in point of truth and falsity is ordinary ambiguity. One and the same sentence, qua linguistic form, may be true in one occurrence and false in another because the ambiguity of a word in it is differently resolved by attendant circumstances on the two occasions. The ambiguous sentence 'Your mothers bore you' is likely to be construed in one way when it follows on the heels of a sentence of the form '*x* bore *y*', and in another when it follows on the heels of a sentence of the form '*x* bores *y*'.

In Indo-European languages there is also yet a third conspicuous source of fluctuation in point of truth and falsity; viz., tense. Actually tense is just a variant of the phenomenon of indicator words; the tenses can be paraphrased in terms of tenseless verbs governed by the indicator word 'now', or by 'before now', etc.

How can we avoid indicator words? We can resort to personal names or descriptions in place of 'I' and 'you', to dates or equivalent descriptions in place of 'now', and to place names or equivalent descriptions in place of 'here'. It may indeed be protested that something tantamount to the use of indicator words is finally unavoidable, at least in the teaching of the terms which are to be made to supplant the indicator words. But this is no objection; all that matters is the *subsequent* avoidability of indicator words. All that matters is that it be possible in principle to couch science in a notation such that none of *its* sentences fluctuates between truth and falsity from utterance to utterance. Terms which are primitive or irreducible, from the point of view of that scientific notation, may still be intelligible to us only through explanations in an ordinary language rife with indicator words, tense, and ambiguity. Scientific language is in any event a splinter of ordinary language, not a substitute.

Granted then that we can rid science of indicator words, what would be the purpose? A kind of objectivity, to begin with, appropriate to the aims of science: truth becomes invariant with respect to speaker and occasion. At the same time a technical purpose is served: that of simplifying and facilitating a basic department of science, viz., deductive logic. For, consider, e.g., the very elementary canons of deduction which lead from '*p* and *q*' to '*p*', and from '*p*' to '*p* or *q*', and from '*p* and if *p* then *q*' to '*q*'. The letter '*p*', standing for any sentence, turns up twice in each of these rules; and clearly the rules are unsound if the sentence which we put for '*p*' is capable of being true in one of its occurrences and false in the other. But to formulate logical laws in such a way as not to depend thus upon the assumption of fixed truth and falsity would be decidedly awkward and complicated, and wholly unrewarding.

In practice certainly one does not explicitly rid one's scientific work of indicator words, tense, and ambiguity, nor does one limit one's use of logic to sentences thus purified. In practice one merely *supposes* all such points of variation fixed for the space of one's logical argument; one does not need to resort to explicit paraphrase, except at points where local shifts of context *within* the logical argument itself threaten equivocation.

This practical procedure is often rationalized by positing abstract entities, 'propositions', endowed with all the requisite precision and fixity which is wanting in the sentences themselves; and then saying that it is with propositions, and not their coarse sentential embodiments, that the laws of logic really have to do. But this posit achieves only obscurity. There is less mystery in imagining an idealized form of scientific language in which sentences are so fashioned as never to vacillate between truth and falsity. It is significant that scientific discourse actually does tend toward this ideal, in proportion to the degree of development of the science. Ambiguities and local and epochal biases diminish. Tense, in particular, gives way to a four-dimensional treatment of space-time.

IV

A basic form for sentences of science may be represented as 'Fa', where 'a' stands in place of a singular term referring to some object, from among those which exist according to the scientific theory in question, and 'F' stands in place of a general term or predicate. The sentence 'Fa' is true if and only if the object fulfills the predicate. No tense is to be read into the predication 'Fa'; any relevant dating is to be integral rather to the terms represented by 'F' and 'a'.

Compound sentences are built up of such predications with help of familiar logical connectives and operators: 'and', 'not', the universal quantifier '(x)' ('each object x is such that'), and the existential quantifier '$(\exists x)$' ('at least one object x is such that'). An example is '(x) not $(Fx$ and not $Gx)$', which says that no object x is such that Fx and not Gx; briefly, every F is a G.

A given singular term and a given general term or predicate will be said to *correspond* if the general term is true of just one object, viz., the object to which the singular term refers. A general term which thus corresponds to a singular term will of course be "of singular extension," i.e., true of exactly one object; but it belongs nevertheless to the grammatical category of general terms, represented by the '*F*' rather than the '*a*' of '*Fa*'. Now the whole category of singular terms can, in the interests of economy, be swept away in favor of general terms, viz., the general terms which correspond to those singular terms. For let '*a*' represent any singular term, '*F*' any corresponding general term, and '. . . *a* . . .' any sentence we may have cared to affirm containing '*a*'. Then we may instead dispense with '*a*' and affirm '$(\exists x)(Fx$ and . . . x . . .)'. Clearly this will be true if and only if '. . . *a* . . .' was true. If we want to go on explicitly to remark that the object fulfilling '*F*' is unique, we can easily do that too, thus:

$$(x)(y) \text{ not } [Fx \text{ and } Fy \text{ and not } (x = y)]$$

provided that the identity sign '=' is in our vocabulary.

How, it may be asked, can we be sure there will be a general term corresponding to a given singular term? The matter can be viewed thus: we merely *reparse* what had been singular terms as general terms of singular extension, and what had been reference-to as truth-of, and what had been '. . . *a* . . .' as '$(\exists x)(Fx$ and . . . x . . .)'. If the old singular term was a proper name learned by ostension, then it is reparsed as a general term similarly learned.

The recent reference to '=' comes as a reminder that relative general terms, or polyadic predicates, must be allowed for along with the monadic ones; i.e., the atomic sentences of our regimented scientific language will comprise not only '*Fx*', '*Fy*', '*Gx*', etc., but also '*Hxy*', '*Hzx*', '*Jyz*', '*Kxyz*', and the like, for appropriately interpreted predicates '*F*', '*G*', '*H*', '*J*', '*K*', etc. (whereof '*H*' might in particular be interpreted as '='). The rest of the sentences are built from these atomic ones by 'and,' 'not,' '(x)', '(y)', etc. Singular terms '*a*', '*b*', etc., can, we have seen, be left out of account. So can the existential quantifiers '$(\exists x)$', '$(\exists y)$', etc., since '$(\exists x)$' can be paraphrased 'not (x) not'.

Besides simple singular terms there are operators to reckon with, such as '+', which yield complex singular terms such as '$x + y$'. But it is not difficult to see how these can be got rid of in favor of corresponding polyadic predicates—e.g., a predicate 'Σ' such that 'Σzxy' means that z is $x + y$.

This pattern for a scientific language is evidently rather confining. There are no names of objects. Further, no sentences occur within sentences save in contexts of conjunction, negation, and quantification. Yet it suffices very generally as a medium for scientific theory. Most or all of what is likely to be wanted in a science can be fitted into this form, by dint of constructions of varying ingenuity which are familiar to logic students. To take only the most trivial and familiar example, consider the 'if–then' idiom; it can be managed by rendering 'if p then q' as 'not (p and not q)'.

It may be instructive to dwell on this example for a moment. Notoriously, 'not (p and not q)' is no translation of 'if p then q'; and it need not pretend to be. The point is merely that in the places where, at least in mathematics and other typical scientific work, we would ordinarily use the 'if–then' construction, we find we can get on perfectly well with the substitute form 'not (p and not q)', sometimes eked out with a universal quantifier. We do not ask whether our reformed idiom constitutes a genuine semantical analysis, somehow, of the old idiom; we simply find ourselves ceasing to depend on the old idiom in our technical work. Here we see, in paradigm, the contrast between linguistic analysis and theory construction.

V

The variables 'x', 'y', etc., adjuncts to the notation of quantification, bring about a widening of the notion of sentence. A sentence which contains a variable without its quantifier (e.g., 'Fx' or '$(y)Fxy$', lacking '(x)') is not a sentence in the ordinary true-or-false sense; it is true *for* some values of its free variables, perhaps, and false for others. Called an *open* sentence, it is akin rather to a predicate: instead of having a *truth value* (truth or falsity) it may be said to have an *extension*, this being conceived as the class of those evaluations of its free variables for which it is true. For convenience one speaks also of the extension of a closed sentence, but what is then meant is simply the truth value.

A compound sentence which contains a sentence as a component clause is called an *extensional* context of that component sentence if, whenever you supplant the component by any sentence with the same extension, the compound remains unchanged in point of its own extension. In the special case where the sentences concerned are closed sentences, then, contexts are extensional if all substitutions of truths for true components and falsehoods for false components leave true contexts true and false ones false. In the case of closed sentences, in short, extensional contexts are what are commonly known as truth functions.

It is well known, and easily seen, that the conspicuously limited means which we have lately allowed ourselves for compounding sentences—viz., 'and', 'not', and quantifiers—are capable of generating only extensional contexts. It turns out, on the other hand, that they confine us no more than that; the *only* ways of embedding sentences within sentences which ever obtrude themselves, and resist analysis by 'and', 'not', and quantifiers, prove to be contexts of other than extensional kind. It will be instructive to survey them.

Clearly *quotation* is, by our standards, non-extensional; we cannot freely put truths for truths and falsehoods for falsehoods within quotation, without affecting the truth value of a broader sentence whereof the quotation forms a part. Quotation, however, is always dispensable in favor of spelling. Instead, e.g., of:

> Heraclitus said '$\pi\acute{a}\nu\tau\alpha$ $\hat{\rho}\epsilon\iota$',
>
> '$\pi\acute{a}\nu\tau\alpha$ $\hat{\rho}\epsilon\iota$' contains three syllables,

we can say (following Tarski):

Heraclitus said pi-alpha-nu-tau-alpha-space-rho-epsilon-iota,

and correspondingly for the other example, thus availing ourselves of names of letters together with a hyphen by way of concatenation sign. Now, whereas the quotational version showed a sentence (the Greek one) embedded within a sentence, the version based on spelling does not; here, therefore, the question of extensionality no longer arises.

Under either version, we are talking about a certain object—a linguistic form—with help, as usual, of a singular term which refers to that object. Quotation produces one singular term for the purpose; spelling another. Quotation is a kind of picture-writing, convenient in practice; but it is rather spelling that provides the proper analysis for purposes of the logical theory of signs.

We saw lately that singular terms are never finally needed. The singular terms involved in spelling, in particular, can of course finally be eliminated in favor of a notation of the sort envisaged in recent pages, in which there are just predicates, quantifiers, variables, 'and', and 'not'. The hyphen of concatenation then gives way to a triadic predicate analogous to the 'Σ' of §IV, and the singular terms 'pi', 'alpha', etc., give way to general terms which "correspond" to them in the sense of §IV.

A more seriously non-extensional context is indirect discourse: "Heraclitus said that all is flux." This is not, like the case of quotation, a sentence about a specific and namable linguistic form. Perhaps, contrary to the line pursued in the case of quotation, we must accept indirect discourse as involving an irreducibly non-extensional occurrence of one sentence in another. If so, then indirect discourse resists the schematism lately put forward for scientific language.

It is the more interesting, then, to reflect that indirect discourse is in any event at variance with the characteristic objectivity of science. It is a subjective idiom. Whereas quotation reports an external event of speech or writing by an objective description of the observable written shape or spoken sound, on the other hand indirect discourse reports the event in terms rather of a subjective projection of oneself into the imagined state of mind of the speaker or writer in question. Indirect discourse is quotation minus objectivity and precision. To marshal the evidence for indirect discourse is to revert to quotation.

It is significant that the latitude of paraphrase allowable in indirect discourse has never been fixed; and it is more significant that the need of fixing it is so rarely felt. To fix it would be a scientific move, and a scientifically unmotivated one in that indirect discourse tends away from the very objectivity which science seeks.

Indirect discourse, in the standard form 'says that', is the head of a family which includes also 'believes that', 'doubts that', 'is surprised that', 'wishes that', 'strives that', and the like. The subjectivity noted in the case of 'says that' is shared by these other idioms twice over; for what these describe in terms of a subjective projection of oneself is not even the protagonist's speech behavior, but his subjective state in turn.

Further cases of non-extensional idiom, outside the immediate family enumerated above, are 'because' and the closely related phenomenon of the contrary-to-fact conditional. Now it is an ironical but familiar fact that though the business of science is describable in unscientific language as the discovery of causes, the notion of cause itself has no firm place in science. The disappearance of causal terminology from the jargon of one branch of science and another has seemed to mark the progress in understanding of the branches concerned.

Apart from actual quotation, therefore, which we have seen how to deal with, the various familiar non-extensional idioms tend away from what best typifies the scientific spirit. Not that they should or could be generally avoided in everyday discourse, or even in science broadly so-called; but their use dwindles in proportion as the statements of science are made more explicit and objective. We begin to see how it is that the language form schematized in §IV might well, despite its narrow limitations, suffice for science at its purest.

VI

Insofar as we adhere to that idealized schematism, we think of a science as comprising those truths which are expressible in terms of 'and', 'not', quantifiers, variables, and certain predicates appropriate to the science in question. In this enumeration of materials we may seem to have an approximation to a possible standard of what counts as "purely cognitive." But the standard, for all its seeming strictness, is still far too flexible. To specify a science, within the described mold, we still have to say what the predicates are to be, and what the domain of objects is to be over which the variables of quantification range. Not all ways of settling these details will be congenial to scientific ideals.

Looking at actual science as a going concern, we can fix in a general way on the domain of objects. Physical objects, to begin with—denizens of space-time—clearly belong. This category embraces indiscriminately what would anciently have been distinguished as substances and as modes or states of substances.

A man is a four-dimensional object, extending say eighty-three years in the time dimension. Each spatio-temporal part of the man counts as another and smaller four-dimensional object. A president-elect is one such, two months long. A fit of ague is another, if for ontological clarity we identify it, as we conveniently may, with its victim for the duration of the seizure.

Contrary to popular belief, such a physical ontology has a place also for states of mind. An inspiration or a hallucination can, like the fit of ague, be identified with its host for the duration. The feasibility of this artificial identification of any mental seizure, x, with the corresponding time slice x' of its physical host, may be seen by reflecting on the following simple maneuver. Where P is any predicate which we might want to apply to x, let us explain P' as true of x' if and only if P is true of x. Whatever may have been looked upon as evidence, cause, or consequence of P, as applied to x, counts now for P' as applied to x'. This parallelism, taken together with the extensionality of scientific language, enables us to drop the old P and x from our theory and get on with just P' and x', rechristened as P and x. Such, in effect, is the identification. It leaves our mentalistic idioms fairly intact, but reconciles them with a physical ontology.

This facile physicalization of states of mind rests in no way on a theory of parallelism between nerve impulses, say, or chemical concentrations, and the recurrence of predetermined species of mental state. It might be, now and forever, that the only way of guessing whether a man is inspired, or depressed, or deluded, or in pain, is by asking him or by observing his gross behavior; not by examining his nervous workings, albeit with instruments of undreamed-of subtlety. Discovery of the suggested parallelism would be a splendid scientific achievement, but the physicalization here talked of does not require it.

This physicalization does not, indeed, suffice to make 'inspiration', 'hallucination', 'pain', and other mentalistic terms acceptable to science. Though these become concrete general terms applicable to physical objects, viz., time slices of persons, still they may, some or others of them, remain too vague for scientific utility. Disposition terms, and other predicates which do not lend themselves to immediate verification, are by no means unallowable as such; but there are better and worse among them. When a time slice of a person is to be classified under the head of inspiration or hallucination, and when not, may have been left too unsettled for any useful purpose. But what is then at stake is the acceptability of certain predicates, and not the acceptability of certain objects, values of variables of quantification.

Let us not leave the latter topic quite yet: ontology, or the values available to variables. As seen, we can go far with physical objects. They are not, however, known to suffice. Certainly, as just now argued, we do not need to add mental objects. But we do need to add *abstract* objects, if we are to accommodate science as currently constituted. Certain things we want to say in science may compel us to admit into the range of values of the variables of quantification not only physical objects but also classes and relations of them; also numbers, functions, and other objects of pure mathematics. For, mathematics—not uninterpreted mathematics, but genuine set theory, logic, number theory, algebra of real and complex numbers, differential and integral calculus, and so on—is best looked upon as an integral part of science, on a par with the physics, economics, etc., in which mathematics is said to receive its applications.

Researches in the foundations of mathematics have made it clear that all of mathematics in the above sense can be got down to logic and set theory, and that the objects needed for mathematics in this sense can be got down to a single category, that of *classes*—including classes of classes, classes of classes of classes, and so on. Our tentative ontology for science, our tentative range of values for the variables of quantification, comes therefore to this: physical objects, classes of them, classes in turn of the elements of this combined domain, and so on up.

We have reached the present stage in our characterization of the scientific framework not by reasoning a priori from the nature of science qua science, but rather by seizing upon traits of the science of our day. Special traits thus exploited include the notion of physical object, the four-dimensional concept of space-time, the classial mold of modern classical mathematics, the true–false orientation of standard logic, and indeed extensionality itself. One or another of these traits might well change as science advances. Already the notion of a physical object, as an intrinsically determinate portion of the space-time continuum, squares dubiously with modern developments in quantum mechanics. Savants there are who even suggest that the findings of quantum mechanics might best be accommodated by a revision of the true–false dichotomy itself.

To the question, finally, of admissible predicates. In general we may be sure that a predicate will lend itself to the scientific enterprise only if it is relatively free from vagueness in certain crucial respects. If the predicate is one which is mainly to be used in application to the macroscopic objects of common sense, then there is obvious utility in there being a general tendency to agreement, among observers, concerning its application to those objects; for it is in such applications that the intersubjective verifiability of the data of science resides. In the case of a predicate which is mainly applicable to scientific objects remote from observation or common sense, on the other hand, what is required is that it be free merely from such vagueness as might blur its theoretical function. But to say these things is merely to say that the predicates appropriate to science are those which expedite the purposes of intersubjective confirmation and theoretical clarity and simplicity. These same purposes govern also the ontological decision—the determination of the range of quantification; for clearly the present tentative ontology of physical objects and classes will be abandoned forthwith when we find an alternative which serves those purposes better.

In science all is tentative, all admits of revision—right down, as we have noted, to the law of the excluded middle. But ontology is, pending revision, more clearly in hand than what may be called *ideology*—the question of admissible predicates. We have found a tentative ontology in physical objects and classes, but the lexicon of predicates remains decidedly open. That the ontology should be relatively definite, pending revision, is required by the mere presence of quantifiers in the language of science; for quantifiers may be said to have been interpreted and understood only insofar as we have settled the range of their variables. And that the fund of predicates should be forever subject to supplementation is implicit in a theorem of mathematics; for it is known that for any theory, however rich, there are classes which are not the extensions (cf. §V) of any of its sentences.

23

❧ *Posits and Reality*

I. SUBVISIBLE PARTICLES

According to physics my desk is, for all its seeming fixity and solidity, a swarm of vibrating molecules. The desk as we sense it is comparable to a distant haystack in which we cannot distinguish the individual stalks; comparable also to a wheel in which, because of its rapid rotation, we cannot distinguish the individual spokes. Comparable, but with a difference. By approaching the haystack we can distinguish the stalks, and by retarding the wheel we can distinguish the spokes. On the other hand no glimpse is to be had of the separate molecules of the desk; they are, we are told, too small.

Lacking such experience, what evidence can the physicist muster for his doctrine of molecules? His answer is that there is a convergence of indirect evidence, drawn from such varied phenomena as expansion, heat conduction, capillary attraction, and surface tension. The point is that these miscellaneous phenomena can, if we assume the molecular theory, be marshaled under the familiar laws of motion. The fancifulness of thus assuming a substructure of moving particles of imperceptible size is offset by a gain in naturalness and scope on the part of the aggregate laws

Written about 1955 for the beginning of *Word and Object,* but eventually superseded. First published along with a Japanese translation in S. Uyeda, ed., *Basis of the Contemporary Philosophy,* Vol. 5 (Tokyo: Waseda University Press, 1960). It has appeared also in Italian, *Rivista di Filosofia,* 1964.

of physics. The molecular theory is felt, moreover, to gain corroboration progressively as the physicist's predictions of future observations turn out to be fulfilled, and as the theory proves to invite extensions covering additional classes of phenomena.

The benefits thus credited to the molecular doctrine may be divided into five. One is simplicity: empirical laws concerning seemingly dissimilar phenomena are integrated into a compact and unitary theory. Another is familiarity of principle: the already familiar laws of motion are made to serve where independent laws would otherwise have been needed. A third is scope: the resulting unitary theory implies a wider array of testable consequences than any likely accumulation of separate laws would have implied. A fourth is fecundity: successful further extensions of theory are expedited. The fifth goes without saying: such testable consequences of the theory as have been tested have turned out well, aside from such sparse exceptions as may in good conscience be chalked up to unexplained interferences.

Simplicity, the first of the listed benefits, is a vague business. We may be fairly sure of this much: theories are more or less simple, more or less unitary, only relative to one or another given vocabulary or conceptual apparatus. Simplicity is, if not quite subjective, at any rate parochial. Yet simplicity contributes to scope, as follows. An empirical theory, typically, generalizes or extrapolates from sample data, and thus covers more phenomena than have been checked. Simplicity, by our lights, is what guides our extrapolation. Hence the simpler the theory, on the whole, the wider this unchecked coverage.

As for the fourth benefit, fecundity, obviously it is a consequence of the first two, simplicity and familiarity, for these two traits are the best conditions for effective thinking.

Not all the listed benefits are generally attributable to accepted scientific theories, though all are to be prized when available. Thus the benefit of familiarity of principle may, as in quantum theory and relativity theory, be renounced, its loss being regretted but outweighed.

But to get back. In its manifest content the molecular doctrine bears directly on unobservable reality, affirming a structure of minute swarming particles. On the other hand any defense of it has to do rather with its indirect bearing on observable reality. The doctrine has this indirect bearing by being the core of an integrated physical theory which implies truths about expansion, conduction, and so on. The benefits which we have been surveying are benefits which the molecular doctrine, as core, brings to the physics of these latter observable phenomena.

Suppose now we were to excise that core but retain the surrounding ring of derivative laws, thus not disturbing the observable consequences. The retained laws could be viewed thenceforward as autonomous empirical laws, innocent of any molecular commitment. Granted, this combination of empirical laws would never have been achieved without the unifying aid of a molecular doctrine at the center; note the recent remarks on scope. But we might still delete the molecular doctrine once it has thus served its heuristic purpose.

This reflection strengthens a natural suspicion: that the benefits conferred by the molecular doctrine give the physicist good reason to prize it, but afford no evidence of its truth. Though the doctrine succeed to perfection in its indirect bearing on observable reality, the question of its truth has to do rather with its direct claim on unobservable reality. Might the molecular doctrine not be ever so useful in organizing and extending our knowledge of the behavior of observable things, and yet be factually false?

One may question, on closer consideration, whether this is really an intelligible possibility. Let us reflect upon our words and how we learned them.

II. POSITS AND ANALOGIES

Words are human artifacts, meaningless save as our associating them with experience endows them with meaning. The word 'swarm' is initially meaningful to us through association with such experiences as that of a hovering swarm of gnats, or a swarm of dust motes in a shaft of sunlight. When we extend the word to desks and the like, we are engaged in drawing an analogy between swarms ordinarily so-called, on the one hand, and desks, etc., on the other. The word 'molecule' is then given meaning derivatively: having conceived of desks analogically as swarms, we imagine molecules as the things the desks are swarms of.

The purported question of fact, the question whether the familiar objects around us are really swarms of subvisible particles in vibration, now begins to waver and dissolve. If the words involved here make sense only by analogy, then the only question of fact is the question how good an analogy there is between the behavior of a desk or the like and the behavior, e.g., of a swarm of gnats. What had seemed a direct bearing of the molecular doctrine upon reality has now dwindled to an analogy.

Even this analogical content, moreover, is incidental, variable, and at length dispensable. In particular the analogy between the swarming of the molecules of a solid and the swarming of gnats is only moderately faithful; a supplementary aid to appreciating the dynamics of the molecules of a solid is found in the analogy of a stack of bedsprings. In another and more recondite part of physics, the theory of light, the tenuousness of analogy is notorious: the analogy of particles is useful up to a point and the analogy of waves is useful up to a point, but neither suffices to the exclusion of the other. Faithful analogies are an aid to the physicist's early progress in an unaccustomed medium, but, like water-wings, they are an aid which he learns to get along without.

In §I we contrasted a direct and an indirect bearing of the molecular doctrine upon reality. But the direct bearing has not withstood scrutiny. Where there had at first seemed to be an undecidable question of unobservable fact, we now find mere analogy at most and not necessarily that. So the only way in which we now find the molecular doctrine genuinely to bear upon reality is the indirect way, via implications in observable phenomena.

The effect of this conclusion upon the status of molecules is that they lose even the dignity of inferred or hypothetical entities which may or may not really be there. The very sentences which seem to propound them and treat of them are gibberish by themselves, and indirectly significant only as contributory clauses of an inclusive system which does also treat of the real. The molecular physicist is, like all of us, concerned with commonplace reality, and merely finds that he can simplify his laws by positing an esoteric supplement to the exoteric universe. He can devise simpler laws for this enriched universe, this "sesquiverse" of his own decree, than he has been able to devise for its real or original portion alone.

In §I we imagined deleting the molecular doctrine from the midst of the derivative body of physical theory. From our present vantage point, however, we see that operation as insignificant; there is no substantive doctrine of molecules to delete. The sentences which seem to propound molecules are just devices for organizing the significant sentences of physical theory. No matter if physics makes molecules or other insensible particles seem more fundamental than the objects of common sense; the particles are posited for the sake of a simple physics.

The tendency of our own reflections has been, conversely, to belittle molecules and their ilk, leaving common-sense bodies supreme. Still, it may now be protested, this invidious contrast is unwarranted. What are given in sensation are variformed and varicolored visual patches, varitextured and varitemperatured tactual feels, and an assortment of tones, tastes, smells, and other odds and ends; desks are no more to be found among these data than molecules. If we have evidence for the existence of the bodies of common sense, we have it only in the way in which we may be said to have evidence for the existence of molecules. The positing of either sort of body is good science insofar merely as it helps us formulate our laws—laws whose ultimate evidence lies in the sense data of the past, and whose ultimate vindication lies in anticipation of sense data of the future. The positing of molecules differs from the positing of the bodies of common sense mainly in degree of sophistication. In whatever sense the molecules in my desk are unreal and a figment of the imagination of the scientist, in that sense the desk itself is unreal and a figment of the imagination of the race.

This double verdict of unreality leaves us nothing, evidently, but the raw sense data themselves. It leaves each of us, indeed, nothing but his own sense data; for the assumption of there being other persons has no better support than has the assumption of there being any other sorts of external objects. It leaves each of us in the position of solipsism, according to which there is nobody else in the world, nor indeed any world but the pageant of one's own sense data.

III. RESTITUTION

Surely now we have been caught up in a wrong line of reasoning. Not only is the conclusion bizarre; it vitiates the very considerations that lead to it. We cannot properly represent man as inventing a myth of physical objects to fit past and present sense data, for past ones are lost except to memory; and memory, far from being a straightforward register of past sense data, usually depends on past posits of physical objects. The positing of physical objects must be seen not as an *ex post facto* systematization of data, but as a move prior to which no appreciable data would be available to systematize.

Something went wrong with our standard of reality. We became doubtful of the reality of molecules because the physicist's statement that there are molecules took on the aspect of a mere technical convenience in smoothing the laws of physics. Next we noted that common-sense bodies are epistemologically much on a par with the molecules, and inferred the unreality of the common-sense bodies themselves. Here our bemusement becomes visible. Unless we change meanings in midstream, the familiar bodies around us are as real as can be; and it smacks of a contradiction in terms to conclude otherwise. Having noted that man has no evidence for the existence of bodies beyond the fact that their assumption helps him organize experience, we should have done well, instead of disclaiming evidence for the existence of bodies, to conclude: such, then, at bottom, is what evidence is, both for ordinary bodies and for molecules.

This point about evidence does not upset the evidential priority of sense data. On the contrary, the point about evidence is precisely that the testimony of the senses *does* (contrary to Berkeley's notion) count as evidence for bodies, such being (as Samuel Johnson perceived) just the sort of thing that evidence is. We can continue to recognize, as in §II, that molecules and even the gross bodies of common sense are simply posited in the course of organizing our responses to stimulation; but a moral to draw from our reconsideration of the terms 'reality' and 'evidence' is that posits are not *ipso facto* unreal. The benefits of the molecular doctrine which so impressed us in §I, and the manifest benefits of the aboriginal posit of ordinary bodies, are the best

evidence of reality we can ask (pending, of course, evidence of
the same sort for some alternative ontology).

Sense data are posits too. They are posits of psychological
theory, but not, on that account, unreal. The sense datum may be
construed as a hypothetical component of subjective experience
standing in closest possible correspondence to the experimentally
measurable conditions of physical stimulation of the end organs.
In seeking to isolate sense data we engage in empirical psychology, associating physical stimuli with human resources. I shall
not guess how useful the positing of sense data may be for
psychological theory, or more specifically for a psychologically
grounded theory of evidence, nor what detailed traits may
profitably be postulated concerning them. In our flight from the
fictitious to the real, in any event, we have come full circle.

Sense data, if they are to be posited at all, are fundamental in
one respect; the small particles of physics are fundamental in a
second respect, and common-sense bodies in a third. Sense data
are *evidentially* fundamental: every man is beholden to his
senses for every hint of bodies. The physical particles are
naturally fundamental, in this kind of way: laws of behavior of
those particles afford, so far as we know, the simplest formulation
of a general theory of what happens. Common-sense bodies,
finally, are *conceptually* fundamental: it is by reference to them
that the very notions of reality and evidence are acquired, and
that the concepts which have to do with physical particles or
even with sense data tend to be framed and phrased. But these
three types of priority must not be viewed as somehow determining three competing, self-sufficient conceptual schemes. Our one
serious conceptual scheme is the inclusive, evolving one of
science, which we inherit and, in our several small ways, help to
improve.

IV. WORKING FROM WITHIN

It is by thinking within this unitary conceptual scheme itself,
thinking about the processes of the physical world, that we come
to appreciate that the world can be evidenced only through
stimulation of our senses. It is by thinking within the same
conceptual scheme that we come to appreciate that language,

being a social art, is learned primarily with reference to intersubjectively conspicuous objects, and hence that such objects are bound to be central conceptually. Both of these *aperçus* are part of the scientific understanding of the scientific enterprise; not prior to it. Insofar as they help the scientist to proceed more knowingly about his business, science is using its findings to improve its own techniques. Epistemology, on this view, is not logically prior somehow to common sense or to the refined common sense which is science; it is part rather of the overall scientific enterprise, an enterprise which Neurath has likened to that of rebuilding a ship while staying afloat in it.

Epistemology, so conceived, continues to probe the sensory evidence for discourse about the world; but it no longer seeks to relate such discourse somehow to an imaginary and impossible sense-datum language. Rather it faces the fact that society teaches us our physicalistic language by training us to associate various physicalistic sentences directly, in multifarious ways, with irritations of our sensory surfaces, and by training us also to associate various such sentences with one another.

The complex totality of such associations is a fluctuating field of force. Some sentences about bodies are, for one person or for many, firmly conditioned one by one to sensory stimulation of specifiable sorts. Roughly specifiable sequences of nerve hits can confirm us in statements about having had breakfast, or there being a brick house on Elm Street, beyond the power of secondary associations with other sentences to add or detract. But there is in this respect a grading-off from one example to another. Many sentences even about common-sense bodies rest wholly on indirect evidence; witness the statement that one of the pennies now in my pocket was in my pocket last week. Conversely, sentences even about electrons are sometimes directly conditioned to sensory stimulation, e.g., via the cloud chamber. The status of a given sentence, in point of direct or indirect connection with the senses, can change as one's experience accumulates; thus a man's first confrontation with a cloud chamber may forge a direct sensory link to some sentences which hitherto bore, for him, only the most indirect sensory relevance. Moreover the sensory relevance of sentences will differ widely from person to person; uniformity comes only where the pressure for communication comes.

Statements about bodies, common-sense or recondite, thus commonly make little or no empirical sense except as bits of a collectively significant containing system. Various statements can surely be supplanted by their negations, without conflict with any possible sensory contingency, provided that we revise other portions of our science in compensatory ways. Science is empirically underdetermined: there is slack. What can be said about the hypothetical particles of physics is underdetermined by what can be said about sensible bodies, and what can be said about these is underdetermined by the stimulation of our surfaces. An inkling of this circumstance has doubtless fostered the tendency to look upon the hypothetical particles of physics as more of a fiction than sensible bodies, and these as more of a fiction than sense data. But the tendency is a perverse one, for it ascribes full reality only to a domain of objects for which there is no autonomous system of discourse at all.

Better simply to explore, realistically, the less-than-rigid connections that obtain between sensory stimulus and physical doctrine, without viewing this want of rigidity as impugning the physical doctrine. Benefits of the sort recounted in §I are what count for the molecular doctrine or any, and we can hope for no surer touchstone of reality. We can hope to improve our physics by seeking the same sorts of benefits in fuller measure, and we may even facilitate such endeavors by better understanding the degrees of freedom that prevail between stimulatory evidence and physical doctrine. But as a medium for such epistemological inquiry we can choose no better than the selfsame world theory which we are trying to improve, this being the best available at the time.

24

ஃ *On Simple Theories of a Complex World*

It is not to be wondered that theory makers seek simplicity. When two theories are equally defensible on other counts, certainly the simpler of the two is to be preferred on the score of both beauty and convenience. But what is remarkable is that the simpler of two theories is generally regarded not only as the more desirable but also as the more probable. If two theories conform equally to past observations, the simpler of the two is seen as standing the better chance of confirmation in future observations. Such is the maxim of the simplicity of nature. It seems to be implicitly assumed in every extrapolation and interpolation, every drawing of a smooth curve through plotted points. And the maxim of the uniformity of nature is of a piece with it, uniformity being a species of simplicity.

Simplicity is not easy to define. But it may be expected, whatever it is, to be relative to the texture of a conceptual scheme. If the basic concepts of one conceptual schema are the derivative concepts of another, and vice versa, presumably one of two hypotheses could count as simpler for the one scheme and the other for the other. This being so, how can simplicity carry any peculiar presumption of objective truth? Such is the implausibility of the maxim of the simplicity of nature.

Written in 1960 for J. H. Woodger's seventieth birthday. In company with other such papers, it appeared in *Synthese* (Volume 15, 1963), and afterward in J. R. Gregg and F. T. C. Harris, eds., *Form and Strategy in Science* (Dordrecht, Holland: D. Reidel Publishing Co., 1964).

Corresponding remarks apply directly to the maxim of the uniformity of nature, according to which, vaguely speaking, things similar in some respects tend to prove similar in others. For again similarity, whatever it is, would seem to be relative to the structure of one's conceptual scheme or quality space. Any two things, after all, are shared as members by as many classes as any other two things; degrees of similarity depend on which of those classes we weight as the more basic or natural.

Belief in the simplicity of nature, and hence in the uniformity of nature, can be partially accounted for in obvious ways. One plausible factor is wishful thinking. Another and more compelling cause of the belief is to be found in our perceptual mechanism: there is a subjective selectivity that makes us tend to see the simple and miss the complex. Thus consider streamers, as printers call them: vertical or diagonal white paths formed by a fortuitous lining up of the spaces between words. They are always straight or gently curved. The fastidious typesetter makes them vanish just by making them crooked.

This subjective selectivity is not limited to the perceptual level. It can figure even in the most deliberate devising of experimental criteria. Thus suppose we try to map out the degrees of mutual affinity of stimuli for a dog, by a series of experiments in the conditioning and extinction of his responses. Suppose further that the resulting map is challenged: suppose someone protests that what the map reflects is not some original spacing of qualities in the dog's pre-experimental psyche or original fund of dispositions, but only a history of readjustments induced successively by the very experiments of the series. Now how would we rise to this challenge? Obviously, by repeating the experiments in a different order on another dog. If we get much the same map for the second dog despite the permutation, we have evidence that the map reflects a genuinely pre-experimental pattern of dispositions. And we then have evidence also of something more: that this pattern or quality space is the same for both dogs. But now I come to the point of my example: we cannot, by this method, get evidence of pre-experimental quality spaces unlike for the two dogs. By the very nature of our criterion, in this example, we get evidence either of uniformity or of nothing. An analysis of experimental criteria in other sciences would no doubt reveal many further examples of the same sort of experimentally imposed bias in favor of uniformity, or in favor of simplicity of other sorts.

This selective bias affords not only a partial explanation of belief in the maxim of the simplicity of nature but also, in an odd way, a partial justification. For, if our way of framing criteria is such as to preclude, frequently, any confirmation of the more complex of two rival hypotheses, then we may indeed fairly say that the simpler hypothesis stands the better chance of confirmation; and such, precisely, was the maxim of the simplicity of nature. We have, insofar, justified the maxim while still avoiding the paradox that seemed to be involved in trying to reconcile the relativity of simplicity with the absoluteness of truth.

This solution, however, is too partial to rest with. The selective bias in favor of simplicity, in our perceptual mechanism and in our deliberate experimental criteria, is significant but not overwhelming. Complex hypotheses do often stand as live options, just as susceptible to experimental confirmation as their simpler alternatives; and in such cases still the maxim of simplicity continues to be applied in scientific practice, with as much intuitive plausibility as in other cases. We fit the simplest possible curve to plotted points, thinking it the likeliest curve pending new points to the contrary; we encompass data with a hypothesis involving the fewest possible parameters, thinking this hypothesis the likeliest pending new data to the contrary; and we even record a measurement as the roundest near number, pending repeated measurements to the contrary.

Now this last case, the round number, throws further light on our problem. If a measured quantity is reported first as 5.21, say, and more accurately in the light of further measurement as 5.23, the new reading supersedes the old; but if it is reported first as 5.2 and later as 5.23, the new reading may well be looked upon as confirming the old one and merely supplying some further information regarding the detail of further decimal places. Thus the "simpler hypothesis," 5.2 as against 5.21, is quite genuinely ten times likelier to be confirmed, just because ten times as much deviation is tolerated under the head of confirmation.

True, we do not customarily say "simple hypothesis" in the round-number case. We invoke here no maxim of the simplicity of nature, but only a canon of eschewing insignificant digits. Yet the same underlying principle that operates here can be detected also in cases where one does talk of simplicity of hypotheses. If we encompass a set of data with a hypothesis involving the fewest possible parameters, and then are constrained by further experiment to add another parameter, we are likely to view the emendation not as a refutation of the first result but as a confirmation plus a refinement; but if we have an extra parameter in the first hypothesis and are constrained by further experiment to alter it, we view the emendation as a refutation and revision. Here again the simpler hypothesis, the one with fewer parameters, is initially the more probable simply because a wider range of possible subsequent findings is classified as favorable to it. The case of the simplest curve through plotted points is similar: an emendation prompted by subsequent findings is the likelier to be viewed as confirmation-cum-refinement, rather than as refutation and revision, the simpler the curve.[1]

We have noticed four causes for supposing that the simpler hypothesis stands the better chance of confirmation. There is wishful thinking. There is a perceptual bias that slants the data in favor of simple patterns. There is a bias in the experimental criteria of concepts, whereby the simpler of two hypotheses is sometimes opened to confirmation while its alternative is left inaccessible. And finally there is a preferential system of score-keeping, which tolerates wider deviations the simpler the hypothesis. These last two of the four causes operate far more widely, I suspect, than appears on the surface. Do they operate widely enough to account in full for the crucial role that simplicity plays in scientific method?

---

[1] I expect that Kemeny has had all this in mind. He remarks on the kinship of the rule of significant digits to that of simplicity on p. 399.

◢ð *On Multiplying Entities*

It would be satisfying to contrive a systematic account of the world while staying strictly within an ontology of physical objects, and indeed physical objects big enough to be perceived. I would not limit them to bodies; that notion is both too vague and too narrow. It is too vague in that we are not told how separate and cohesive and well rounded a thing has to be in order to qualify as a body. And it is too narrow, since for ontological purposes any consideration of separateness and cohesiveness and well-roundedness is beside the point. We may understand a physical object rather as the aggregate material content of any portion of space-time, however ragged and discontinuous.

Besides sparing us the pointless task of demarcating bodies, this liberal notion of physical object brings further benefits. It neatly accommodates mass terms such as 'sugar' and 'air' and 'water'. Such a term cannot be said to name a body, but it can be construed as naming a physical object. We can identify sugar with a single large and spatiotemporally scattered physical object consisting of all the sugar anywhere, ever.

This short piece is made up of bits of three publications. One of them, "Existence," was presented at a colloquium at the University of Denver in May 1966 and published in W. Yourgrau, ed., *Physics, Logic, and History* (New York: Plenum, 1969). Another, "Grades of theoreticity," was presented as a lecture at the University of Massachusetts in April 1969 and published in L. Foster and J. W. Swanson, eds., *Experience and Theory* (Amherst: University of Massachusetts Press, 1970). The third, "Whither physical objects?", is to appear in a volume of the Boston Studies in the Philosophy of Science in memory of Imre Lakatos.

With a little stretch of the imagination, this notion of physical object can even be made to accommodate physical processes or events, on a par with bodies. A ball game might be identified with the scattered sum of the appropriate temporal segments of the players, taking each player for the duration of his play.

Such an account of events does not distinguish between events that happen to take up just the same portion of space-time. If a man whistled a song all the while he was walking to the bus stop and not a moment more, then presumably the event of his whistling the song and the event of his walking to the bus would both be identified with the same temporal segment of the man. This outcome will be unwelcome if one feels that the event of the whistling and the event of the walking should be distinguished. However, it is not clear to me that they need to be. We still have the general distinction between whistling the song and walking to the bus, because sometimes people do walk to the bus without whistling the song, and even vice versa. Thus we still convey information when we say that the man whistled the song all the way to the bus. We do not trivialize this statement in identifying the events.

In describing physical objects as the material contents of space-time regions, I do not mean to concede any ontological standing to the regions themselves. It is just my way of showing how broad a scope I intend for my notion of physical object. We may take the material content and let the regions go.

I proposed further that the physical objects accepted be big enough to be perceived. This is vague, but at any rate I mean it to exclude things that can be detected only by such devices as microscopes and cloud chambers. What I am counting as perceived in such cases is just the image on the plate or the bubble in the chamber.

This frugal ontology would seem to be adequate to common sense and historiography and natural history. It recognizes no numbers or sets or other abstract objects. Still, at this level you can simulate about enough set theory to cover what is useful in the common man's references to classes or properties. You can do this by what I call the virtual theory of classes; seeming references to classes are explained away by contextual definition.[1]

---

[1] See my *Set Theory and Its Logic*, pp. 16–27.

Moreover, while not recognizing numbers as objects you can still make sense of practical arithmetic at the elementary level, again exploiting tricks of contextual definition.[2] The mathematical equipment thus available is meager, but the mathematical requirements of historiography and natural history are modest.

A systematic account of the world in such terms would be welcome if it could be managed. However, we keep finding that our account can be made simpler and more systematic by positing supplementary entities. Thus consider how the positing of classes can contribute to systematic theory. To begin with the old standby, consider two two-place predicates, 'P' for parent and 'A' for ancestor. 'Pxy' means that x is parent of y, and 'Azy' means that z is ancestor of y. Particulars, people, are values of these variables. Universals, parenthood or ancestorhood, are not here assumed as values of variables. But if we do assume certain universals as values of our variables, namely classes, then we can define 'A' in terms of 'P' and the two-place predicate 'ϵ' of class membership. As has been known since Frege and well known since Dedekind, we can explain 'Azy' as meaning that z is a member of every class that contains as members all parents of its own members and also y.

It would be a poor bargain, of course, to posit classes as new objects in our universe simply in order to reduce one pair of two-place predicates, 'P' and 'A', to another pair of two-place predicates, 'P' and 'ϵ'. The gain is seen rather in the fact that for every two-place predicate there is another two-place predicate, its *closed iterate* we might call it, that stands to it as ancestor stands to parent. Now the assumption of classes and 'ϵ' enables us to express, without further apparatus, the closed iterate of every available two-place predicate. This could not, presumably, have been accomplished by adding any one or several predicates of particulars to our vocabulary, but it is accomplished by adding the predicate 'ϵ' and assuming classes for it to apply to.

Another of the many systematic benefits of assuming classes can be seen in the avoidance of modality at certain points. Thus compare 'All crows are black' and 'All black crows are black':

$$(x)(Cx \supset Bx), \qquad (x)(Bx \,.\, Cx \,.\supset Bx).$$

[2]Partial suggestions may be found in my *Roots of Reference*, pp. 116f, and in Goodman and Quine.

We might like to regard the first of these two statements as holding merely as a matter of fact and not by logical necessity. But the other patently holds by necessity, and we might like to record this trait by changing its material conditional to a strict one:

$$(x)(Bx \cdot Cx \cdot \prec Bx).$$

On the other hand there are various reasons for preferring to avoid modal connectives.[3] Now generality is often a satisfactory substitute for necessity. The need we felt to add a note of necessity to 'All black crows are black' can perhaps be met well enough by just abstracting from the specificity of 'black' and 'crow' and saying that the rule holds generally: for any classes y and z, whatever belongs to both y and z belongs to y. Thus it is that the admission of classes as values of variables, and the adoption again of 'ϵ', can enable us to avoid modal logic.[4] The need felt for modal logic cannot always be met thus by generality, but it often can.

There are also other ontological posits, besides that of classes, that can have the effect of resolving modality. Thus suppose, to return to 'All black crows are black', that someone is not satisfied with the generalization over classes which was our substitute for necessity. An alternative line would be to keep the specific predicates 'black' and 'crow' and then get the force of necessity by quantifying over not just actual particulars but possible particulars: 'All possible black crows are black'. Here we see another example of resolving modality by enlarging the universe. This expedient does not really recommend itself, though, for unactualized particulars are in various ways an obscure and troublesome lot.

It is the quest of system and simplicity that has kept driving the scientist to posit further entities as values of his variables. The classical example is the kinetic theory of gases. Viewed in terms of gross bodies, Boyle's law of gases was a quantitative description of the behavior of pressurized chambers. By positing molecules, the law could be assimilated into a general theory of bodies in motion. Subsequent advances in physics have kept prompting the positing of further and further, smaller and smaller

[3]See "Three grades of modal involvement," Essay 15 above.
[4]See Putnam on the use of necessity, conversely, to reduce ontology.

particles—sometimes as a means of actually simplifying previous theory, as in the kinetic theory of gases, and sometimes only as a means of accommodating new observations without too much loss of simplicity.

Increasingly serious use of mathematics has been called for by these developments, and meanwhile the mathematicians have also been doing, on their own, the same trick as the physicists: multiplying entities, positing ever weirder species in order to simplify theory. Classical examples were the positing of ratios to make division generally applicable, the positing of negative numbers to make subtraction generally applicable, and the positing of irrationals and finally imaginaries to make exponentiation generally applicable. Less classical examples are burgeoning in the theory of infinite sets. Man's drive for system and simplicity leads, it seems, to ever new complexities.

I turn finally to a general question regarding the benefits that the positing of supplementary objects can confer. Might all supplementation of the range of values of variables be in principle dispensable early and late if not wanted in the end? Thus consider a statement whose variables range over some broad universe, and suppose that the only consequences of this statement that interest us in the end are statements whose variables are restricted to some narrower subuniverse. The question is whether, in general, a restricted statement can be constructed that has the same restricted consequences as the original unrestricted statement.

The answer is negative. This can perhaps be shown elegantly; I can show it with the help of heavy artillery, as follows. The set theory of von Neumann and Bernays has a finite list of axioms, or, since we may conjoin them, a single axiom. Now we consider in particular, from among the theorems of this set theory, the ones that have all their variables restricted to a certain subuniverse. These are known to be precisely the theorems of another set theory, Zermelo's. So, if the answer to our question were affirmative, there would be a formula, with its variables restricted to the subuniverse, that would encompass precisely Zermelo's set theory. But it is known from work of Wang and McNaughton that Zermelo's set theory is irreducible to a single axiom.[5]

[5]See my *Set Theory and Its Logic*, pp. 320f.

We have to conclude that multiplication of entities can make a substantive contribution to theory. It does not always contribute. Of itself multiplication of entities should be seen as undesirable, comformably with Occam's razor, and should be required to pay its way. Pad the universe with classes or other supplements if that will get you a simpler, smoother overall theory; otherwise don't. Simplicity is the thing, and ontological economy is one aspect of it, to be averaged in with others. We may fairly expect that some padding of the universe is in the interest of the overall net simplicity of our system of the world.

&r *Ontological Remarks on the Propositional Calculus*

Whereas there is fairly general agreement relatively to such principles and methods as are involved in the technical development of the so-called theory of deduction or calculus of propositions, on the other hand there is no such uniformity of attitude regarding the nature of the entities to which that calculus is supposedly applied.

Wittgenstein[1] construes the proposition as a sign, namely the *sentence;* but it is the proposition as the denotation of the sentence, i.e., as the entity, if any, whereof the sentence is a symbol, that is the present concern. It is these elusive entities, presumably, that are the elements of the propositional calculus and are denoted therein by the variables 'p', 'q', etc., and their combinations. But what manner of things are these, whose names are sentences? Not facts, for that would leave no place for false propositions. Are they then judgments? Or abstract possibilities, Platonic ideas? Or are they merely, as with Frege,[2] the two truth values, truth and falsity?

Closely related to the question "What is a proposition?" is the question "When are propositions identical?" or better "When do two sentences denote the same proposition?" The notion of

---

First published in *Mind* (Volume 43, 1934). Reprinted by permission of the editor of *Mind*.

[1] *Tractatus Logico-Philosophicus,* 3.12, 3.31.
[2] *Grundgesetze der Arithmetik,* Band I, S. 50.

propositions as truth values occupies an extreme in this respect; under this doctrine the material equivalence of propositions, i.e., their agreement in point of truth or falsity, is tantamount to their identity. The opposite extreme would be to demand that no two sentences express the same proposition, i.e., that the expressibility of propositions by physically unlike sentences is tantamount to their diversity. An unlimited variety of intermediate views are possible, e.g., that propositions are identical if and only if they are mutually derivable by the principles of logic. Whereas in the logistical development of the theory of deduction logicians examine the various truth-value connections of propositions, e.g., material equivalence, conjunction, etc., and whereas they examine also the various heuristic relationships of propositions, e.g., consistency, relative deducibility, etc., on the other hand such considerations of propositions as would relate to propositional identity or diversity are customarily omitted from the formal developments. Yet logicians frequently entertain the notions of propositional identity and diversity in an informal way, e.g., when they claim that 'p' and 'p is true' (or 'not p' and 'p is false') do not represent the same proposition.

Outside discussions of logic we never bestow consideration upon propositions, in the sense of non-sentences whereof sentences are symbols, but engage only in the manipulation of the sentences themselves. We do not, e.g., have occasion to observe that 'Boston is east of Chicago' and 'Chicago is west of Boston' are (or are not) two names for the same proposition; indeed, whereas we may have occasion to reflect that 'Boston' is the name of a city, we do not have occasion to regard 'Boston is east of Chicago' as a name of anything whatever. Thus it is that in the theory of deduction, as a formal systematization of certain aspects of the ordinary use of language and exercise of reason, there is no call to consider what manner of entity a proposition may be or to formulate the conditions under which propositions are identical. Propositions are hypostatized entities, inferred denotations of given signs.

Once we postulate entities whereof sentences are symbols, the logical principles for manipulating sentences become principles *concerning* the entities—propositions—which the sentences denote. Insofar the theory of deduction becomes a calculus of propositions; but it remains a very partial calculus in that respect, since its only principles are those which governed the manipulation of sentences antecedently to the notion that sentences were names of anything. Hence, while we are apprised of a wide array of logical properties of propositions, concerning which there is little essential disagreement, on the other hand as to the residual character of propositions we have that full latitude of choice which attends the development of gratuitous fictions.

When the theory of deduction is woven into a broad and unified logistical system treating of other topics as well, the structure and primitive machinery of the total system might happen to be improved in point of simplicity and economy by thus construing sentences as denotative of certain entities, "propositions," and then identifying these entities with some manner of definite technical entities which figure also in other aspects of the total logistical system.[3] But such considerations will depend upon the structure of the broader system in question. When, as is ordinarily the case, the theory of deduction is developed and considered in isolation from other parts of logistic, the whole notion of sentences as names is superfluous and figures only as a source of illusory problems.

Without altering the theory of deduction internally, we can so reconstrue it as to sweep away such fictive considerations; we have merely to interpret the theory as a formal grammar for the manipulation of sentences, and to abandon the view that sentences are names. Words occurring in a sentence may be regarded severally as denoting things, but the sentence as a whole is to be taken as a verbal combination which, though presumably conveying some manner of intelligence (I write with deliberate vagueness at this point), yet does not have that particular kind of meaning which consists in denoting or being a name of something.

In the theory of deduction the signs 'p', 'q', etc., are customarily construed as proposition variables, i.e., as signs ambiguously denotative of propositions, i.e., as signs ambiguously denotative of the things which sentences denote. We now cancel this circuit through denoted entities, and explain the signs 'p', 'q', etc., directly as ambiguously abbreviated sentences—which comes to

[3] Such has been my procedure in *A System of Logistic*, Chap. 3.

the same thing as before except that the existence of denoted entities, propositions, is no longer presupposed.

The expression '$\sim p$' is construed in the propositional calculus as denoting the contradictory of the proposition p; here again we may short-cut the passage through propositions, by construing the sign '$\sim$' as shorthand for the word 'not' or for the words 'It is false that'. Thus, where 'p' is an abbreviation for a sentence '———' the sign '$\sim p$' becomes an abbreviation for the sentence 'It is false that ———'. Similarly '$p \vee q$', ordinarily explained as denoting the alternation of the propositions p and q, comes now to be explained by construing '$\vee$' as a new spelling of the word 'or'; '$\vee$' is a connective enabling us to build new sentences from old, without question of denotation. In the same way the dot in '$p \cdot q$' comes to be explained as shorthand for 'and', and the sign '$\supset$' is so explained that '. . . $\supset$ ———' is 'If . . . then ———'.

Thus reconstrued the theory of deduction remains unchanged in structure, but ceases to be a system in the usual sense. The usual sort of system treats of some manner of elements, say cardinal numbers or geometrical points, which are denoted ambiguously by variables; operative upon these elements are certain operations or relations, appropriately expressed within the language of the system. The theory of deduction, when construed as a calculus of propositions, is a system of this kind; its elements are propositions denoted by the variables 'p', 'q', etc., and its operations are the propositional operations of denial, alternation, material implication, etc., denoted by prefixture or interfixture of the signs '$\sim$', '$\vee$', '$\supset$', etc. When, on the other hand, the theory of deduction is reconstrued in the foregoing manner as a mere organon of sentences, it ceases to be concerned with elements subject to operations; the former proposition variables 'p', 'q', etc., become ambiguous sentences, symbols *of* nothing, and the signs '$\sim$', '$\vee$', '$\supset$', etc., become connectives of sentences, innocent of operational correlates in the realm of denotations.

Consider, e.g., the theorem '$p \supset (p \vee q)$' of the theory of deduction. According to the usual interpretation this expression represents an element of the system, i.e. a proposition, built up in the indicated manner from any propositions p and q by the operations of alternation and material implication; the occurrence of the expression as a theorem is as much as to say that any proposition thus constructed is true. When, on the other hand, we reconstrue the theory of deduction so as to eliminate the notion of denotations of sentences, '$p \supset (p \lor q)$' ceases to denote an element of the system: for the whole notion of the systematization of elements has dropped out. Instead the expression becomes merely an abbreviation of any sentence of the form 'If so-and-so then so-and-so or such-and-such'. In enunciating '$p \supset (p \lor q)$' and the other theorems of the theory of deduction we are engaged merely in affirming sentences which, though ambiguous, are ambiguous in respects immaterial to truth.

From this point of view all speculation as to the nature of propositions drops out. The theory of deduction becomes a paradigm depicting the use of the connectives 'or', 'if–then', etc., with a view to the truthfulness of the sentences which they generate. There are no inferred entities, no flights of abstraction beyond the realm of everyday uses of words.

It was suggested above that in the ordinary calculus of propositions the theorems are expressions denoting certain of the elements of the system. This is an anomaly upon which mathematicians have looked askance. It is customary to consider systems in abstraction from the nature of their elements; the theorems of a system, thus viewed, become sentences telling us various properties of unidentified elements. But to abstract from the fact that the elements of the propositional calculus are propositions is to deprive the theorems *themselves* of their character as sentences, since in that calculus the theorems are symbols of elements of the system. The student of systems in the abstract thus comes to an *impasse* when he takes up the calculus of propositions. Hence the mathematician may not be displeased to see the calculus of propositions eliminated, and to find in its stead a theory of deduction proceeding merely on the basis of abbreviations of sentences and making no pretense to being a system in the ordinary sense. Besides the previously noted advantage of eliminating useless lumber and diverting all speculation regarding elusive entities called propositions, the procedure has this further advantage of extruding an anomalous case from the theory of systems.

But there is a way of gaining these advantages without persisting in the exclusion of the theory of deduction from the orthodox realm of systems. The theory can be reinterpreted in such a way that the signs 'p', 'q', etc., resume their status of variables denoting elements of the system, without return to the fiction of propositions as denotations of sentences. We can reconstrue the theory of deduction as a branch of semantic, a system whose *elements* are shapes, signs, specifically sentences. The signs 'p', 'q', etc., thus become sentence variables; neither signs ambiguously denotative of propositions nor signs ambiguously abbreviative of sentences, but signs ambiguously denotative of sentences. The sign '$\sim$' of denial comes to indicate a semantic operation, the operation of introducing 'not', 'does not', etc., properly into the interior of a sentence p. The sign '$\vee$' comes to indicate the semantic operation of stringing out two sentences and interposing the word 'or'. Similarly for the rest. The signs '$\sim$', '$\vee$', '$\supset$', etc., are thus no longer condensed spellings for certain adverbs and conjunctions, but are signs of the operations of properly inserting such adverbs and conjunctions.

The expression '$p \supset (p \vee q)$' is no longer an ambiguous sentence, but a symbol ambiguously *denoting* sentences; it denotes any sentence of the form 'If so-and-so then so-and-so or such-and-such'. So long therefore as the theorems of a system are to be sentences, rather than names of sentences, '$p \supset (p \vee q)$' is inadmissible as a theorem; it requires a prefix, say '$\vdash$', which may be read as a predicate to the effect that the element denoted in its wake is a true (i.e., truthful, truth-telling) sentence. Thus the so-called assertion sign '$\vdash$', customarily used in the theory of deduction as a convenient but formally extraneous tag marking off theorems and postulates, comes now to assume an essential role within the system as denotative of a property of sentences. Yet '$\vdash$' remains confined in the customary fashion to initial occurrence in theorems and postulates: for '$\sim$', '$\vee$', '$\supset$', etc., attach only to names of sentences, whereas '$\vdash p$' is itself a sentence (about a sentence) rather than a name of a sentence.

If now with Wittgenstein we take "proposition" as meaning simply "sentence," the calculus of sentences just now discussed becomes a calculus of propositions; common usage is thereby superficially restored, to the extent that the theory of deduction is once again a calculus of propositions. But such verbal maneuvers do not affect the real distinction: that, namely, between a system whose elements are sentences and a system whose elements are denoted by sentences. In a calculus of propositions in the former of these senses the propositional operations represented by '$\sim$', '$\vee$', '$\supset$', etc., become semantic operations upon sentences; the notion of entities denoted by sentences goes by the board, and the question of propositional identity comes to admit of one or another definite answer in terms of geometrical similarity or conventional correspondence of written marks. This calculus of sentences is, moreover, a system of the orthodox pattern: its theorems are not expressions of its elements, but statements about its elements, viz., statements that elements (sentences) of such and such form have the property ⊢.

27

~~ *The Variable*

The variable *qua* variable, the variable *an und für sich* and *par excellence*, is the bindable objectual variable. It is the essence of ontological idiom, the essence of the referential idiom. But it takes some distilling, for it has strong affinities with quite a variety of closely associated notions and devices.

It used to be necessary to warn against the notion of variable numbers, variable quantities, variable objects, and to explain that the variable is purely a notation, admitting only fixed numbers or other fixed objects as its values. This dissociation now seems to be generally understood, so I turn to others.

There is the schematic letter. As late as 1945, and in as sophisticated a medium as the *Journal of Symbolic Logic*, I still felt I had to devote three pages to explaining the status of the schematic sentence letters and predicate letters as used in the logic of truth functions and quantification. These letters refer to no objects as values. The sentence letters refer neither to propositions nor to truth values as their values, much less to sentences, and the predicate letters refer neither to properties nor to classes as values, much less to predicates. They are not bindable, they are not objectual, and they do not occur in sentences. They occur in schemata. I devoted three pages to the matter, not with any sense of creativity, but still with a lively sense of warding off basic misunderstandings on the part of most readers. Just five

This was the inaugural lecture of the Boston Logic Colloquium, October 12, 1972. It is to appear in Rohit Parikh, ed., *Logic Colloquium*, Springer Lecture Notes in Mathematics, vol. 453. Portions are omitted here in favor of cross-references to other essays in the present book.

years earlier, in *Mathematical Logic*, I had even thought it unwise to court such misunderstandings by using schematic letters at all. In that book I presented the logic of truth functions and quantification wholly in a metalogical notation of Greek letters and corners. The schematic sentence letters and predicate letters had already been in general use, but the trouble was that their schematic status was seldom clearly appreciated. Now and again they would even get quantified.

A further device that we must take pains to dissociate from the objectual variable is the bindable substitutional variable. The schematic letter itself of course is already purely substitutional: it does not refer to any objects as values, but merely admits appropriate expressions as substitutes. But besides schematic letters, which are not bindable, there is the use by Ruth Marcus and others of substitutional variables that can be bound by quantifiers and embedded in sentences.[1]

Our quantification over individuals is seen most naturally as objectual. To take it as substitutional would require assuming in our language a name, or some uniquely designating expression, for every individual, every creature or particle, however obscure and remote; and this would be artificial at best. When we come to quantify over classes, the substitutional version does look tempting; however, a problem arises.[2] Consider the law:

$$(W)(W \text{ has members}$$
$$. \supset (\exists Z)(Z \text{ has a member of } W \text{ as sole member})).$$

This is gospel for classical set theory. It may be called the law of unit subclasses. But what does it come to when 'W' and 'Z' are substitutional? It then requires, of every closed class term that we can write in our language, that if its membership condition happens to be true of any individuals, however obscure and remote, we must be able to write another condition that singles out one of those individuals uniquely. This is as unwelcome as assuming outright in our language a uniquely designating expression for every individual; and if that were welcome, our individual variables could go substitutional too.

---

[1]See "Reply to Professor Marcus," Essay 16 above.
[2]I am indebted to Oswaldo Chateaubriand and Gilbert Harman for starting me on the following line of thought.

Parsons has proposed a modified truth condition for substitutional quantification that averts this effect. For him an existential quantification still counts as true as long as it has a substitution instance that contains free objectual variables and comes out true for some values of them. By this standard the law of unit subclasses is true.

I said that the bindable objectual variable has close associations with quite a variety of notions and devices. I have now dissociated it from variable numbers and other variable objects, there being for these no place in the universe. I have dissociated it also from the schematic letter, fond though I am of both the variable and the schematic letter. And I have dissociated it now from the bindable substitutional variable, though recognizing this variable as clear and legitimate as far as it goes.

I have thus been dissociating the bindable objectual variable from associates with which it was apt to be confused. I want next to dissociate it even from quantification, so as to reveal its nature uncolored by those two familiar contexts, the quantifiers.

We tend to think of bound variables primarily in quantification. This is because we know how to paraphrase other uses of bound variables into the quantificational use, and because, moreover, there are algorithmic benefits to be gained by doing so. The 'x' of the description '$(\imath x)Fx$' goes over into an 'x' of quantification under Russell's contextual definition of description. The 'x' of the class abstract '$\{x: Fx\}$' goes over into an 'x' of quantification when '$\{x: Fx\}$' is defined as a description '$(\imath y)(x)(x \,\epsilon\, y \,.\!\equiv Fx)$'. The '$x$' of the functional abstract '$\lambda_x fx$' fares similarly.[3] So does the bound variable of the differential and integral calculus, for it is ultimately a variable of functional abstraction.

Reductions can be made in alternative directions too. Functional abstraction or class abstraction can be taken as basic, and quantification can be defined in terms of either of them. Church took the one line in his lambda calculus, and I the other in my logic based on inclusion and abstraction. Even Peano had a full-blown class abstraction on which he based his existential quantification, though his universal quantification took another line. However, reduction to quantification is generally to be preferred to these alternative reductions, because quantification is wanted not only

[3]See next essay.

in set theory but also in elementary theories where there is no call for classes or functions; and moreover the logic of quantification, unlike set theory, is complete, compact, and convenient.

Such, then, is a *standard theory*, in Tarski's phrase; it is simply quantification logic, or the predicate calculus, with one or another fixed lexicon of predicates appropriate to one or another particular subject matter. The ontology of a theory, thus standardized, is the range of values of the variables of quantification; for the variables *are* the variables of quantification. And of course it is clear from the readings of objectual quantification in ordinary language that the ontology consists of those values; for the quantifiers mean 'everything is such that' and 'something is such that'.

Very well, then; where does the dissociation come in? The point I want to make is that the quantitative force of the quantifier, the 'all' and 'some', is irrelevant to the distinctive work of the bound variable and irrelevant to its referential function. The quantitative component needs no variable; it is fully present in the traditional categoricals 'All men are mortal', 'Some Greeks are wise'. Conversely the bound variable is fully taken up with its distinctive work when used in description, class abstraction, functional abstraction, integration, no less than when used in quantification; and yet these other uses connote nothing of 'all' and 'some', except of course as we impose reductive definitions in the direction of quantification.

Minutes ago I extolled that direction of reduction, as in a sense more basic than reduction to class abstraction or functional abstraction. There is, however, a use of the bound variable that is more basic still than its use in quantification. It carries no connotation of 'all' or 'some' or class or function, but shows rather the distinctive work of the bound variable without admixture. This basic and neglected idiom is the relative clause, mathematically regimented as the 'such that' idiom: 'x such that Fx'. It is not a singular term, neither a singular description nor a class abstract; it is a general term, a predicate. It has its use where we have a complex sentence that mentions some object a perhaps midway, perhaps repeatedly, and we want to segregate a complex adjective or common noun that may be simply predicated of the object a with the same effect as the original sentence. Where the original sentence is thought of schematically as 'Fa', the relative clause is the explicit segregation of the 'F'. The 'such that' construction is the relative clause simplified in respect of word order and fitted with a bound variable to avert ambiguities of cross-reference.

Other uses of the bound variable are readily represented as parasitic upon this use. The quantifiers are 'there is something x *such that*' and 'everything is (a thing) x *such that*'; the description operator is 'the (thing) x *such that*'; the operator of class abstraction is 'the class of (the things) x *such that*'. Quantification can be thought of as application of a functor '∃' or '∀' to a predicate; and this functor is what carries the pure quantitative import, with no intrusion of variables. Similarly description can be thought of as application of a functor 'ɿ' to a predicate; and class abstraction can be thought of correspondingly. What brings the variable, if any, is the predicate itself, in case it is a relative clause rather than a simple adjective or perhaps some Boolean compound.

Peano saw this, but then slipped into a confusion. He introduced the inverted epsilon for the words 'such that', or for the equivalent words in his three romance languages, and he introduced the functors '∃' and 'ɿ' just as I have described them. But he introduced no functor for class abstraction. He saw his inverted epsilon as already class abstraction; here was his confusion. He did not distinguish between the general term, or predicate, and the class name, a singular term.

The same conflation may be seen in Peano's upright epsilon. For the epsilon that is now standard in set theory comes from Peano; and he adopted it as his copula of predication, the initial of the Greek ἐστί. He inverted it for his 'such that' because this is the inverse of predication; the two cancel. Peano was thus sensitive to the relation between predication and relative clauses: 'a is a thing x such that Fx' reduces to 'Fa'. He was indeed sensitive to the role of the variable as relative pronoun; he was explicit on this. But he must be convicted of the conflation, on two counts. He provides explicitly that his 'such that' expressions designate classes; '$(x \ni p) \, \epsilon \, \text{Cls}$'. And, what is more to the point, he quantifies over them with bound variables; whereas a relative clause or 'such that' clause properly conceived is rather a predicate, susceptible at best of substitution for an unbindable schematic predicate letter. (In this historical context we may pass over the further alternative of a bindable substitutional predicate variable.) With all his sensitivity to grammar he was insensitive to the distinction between general and abstract singular; insensitive to the ontological import of values of variables.

Happily Peano's inverted epsilon has caught on, in informal mathematical contexts, as a sign purely for 'such that'; and I shall so use it.

Russell carried Peano's 'such that' over into *Principles of Mathematics* without improving matters. The so-called propositional function that ended up in *Principia Mathematica* is largely more of the same, but muddled now by triple confusion: property, open sentence, predicate. The term 'propositional function' was adapted from Frege, whose functions might indeed be seen as fictitious designata of relative or 'such that' clauses. I say 'fictitious' because a general term does not designate; and this accords with Frege's characterization of his so-called functions as *ungesättigt*, meaning in a way that there were not really any such things.

One senses in the modern history of logic a distaste for the general term, or predicate. It is partly the effect and partly the cause, I expect, of our slowness to appreciate the schematic status of predicate letters. One tends to conflate such letters with objectual variables, and so reconstrue general terms as abstract singular terms designating properties or classes. Thereby the relative clause, or 'such that' clause, becomes class abstraction; and here we have Peano. Or, fleeing this abstract ontology, one presses the bound variables into purely quantificational duty and thus can operate in sentences. Predicates have been an uneasy intermediate between abstract singular terms on the one hand and out-and-out sentences on the other.

We have to appreciate and exploit schematic letters in order to isolate and appreciate the work of the bound variable itself. It is in representing the 'such that' clauses by steadfastly schematic predicate letters, and not letting these letters into quantifiers, that we can witness the work of the bound variable as a relative pronoun unencumbered by class abstraction.

When logicians became interested in distinguishing between elementary or first-order theories and higher-order theories, schematic use of predicate letters became virtually indispensible. It had become common among Continental logicians by 1930, though generally subject to no clear appreciation of its semantic status. The predicate letter tended to be seen rather as a free variable for properties or classes, bindable in wider contexts and free merely throughout the subcalculus under investigation. Still it is as a schematic predicate letter that we may most clearly view it in retrospect.

But it did not have the effect of freeing logicians to introduce 'such that' clauses into their first-order theories as ontologically innocent predicates; they avoided them as if they were class names. They treated the schematic letter '*F*' as subject to substitution only indirectly, therefore, through substitution of whole open sentences for '*Fx*' or '*Fxy*'. The rules for such substitution are complex, for they must coordinate the sentences substituted for '*Fx*' and '*Fz*', or for '*Fxy*' and '*Fzw*'. When such rules were at length devised, they invoked auxiliary open sentences that served much the purpose of 'such that' clauses after all, though behind the scenes. Hilbert and Bernays, 1934, called them *Nennformen*. Two sentences may be substituted respectively for '*Fxy*' and '*Fzw*' if they can both be got from some *Nennform* by substituting '*x*' and '*y*' on the one hand and '*z*' and '*w*' on the other. By coincidence I proceeded similarly in the same year, 1934, in my first book. In later books I made the *Nennformen* more graphic by use of circled numerals. I called these formulas *stencils* in *Elementary Logic*, 1941. They were sentences with indexed blanks. Expressions to much the same effect had been called *rhemes* by C. S. Peirce in 1892, though not in explicit connection with a problem of substitution. Also they could vaguely be called propositional functions, in one sense of that resilient term. It was not until my 1945 paper that it dawned on me to call them predicates, thus recognizing at last that they were playing the role of the relative clause, the 'such that' clause. And still I kept them behind the scenes. They were devices for calculating substitution, and formed no part of the resulting sentences or schemata.

But in fact they can contribute much to the explicit formalism, quite apart from substitution. They can contribute even to set theory, where genuine abstraction is already available too. Thus consider the axiom schema of *replacement* in the Zermelo-Fraenkel system.

$$(x)(y)(z)(Fxz \, . \, Fyz \, . \supset . \, x = y) \supset$$
$$(u)(\exists w)(x)(x \in w \, . \equiv (\exists z)(Fxz \, . \, z \in u)).$$

It remains thus turgid as long as we confine predicate letters thus to positions of predication—'Fxz', 'Fyz'. The effect of 'such that', however, is to free the complex predicate from such embedding. We can then define and apply certain functors to complex predicates as follows, paralleling definitions that are already familiar for classes.

$$F``u = {}_{\mathrm{df}}\ x \ni (\exists z)(Fxz \ . \ z \in u).$$

$$\text{Func } F = {}_{\mathrm{df}}\ (x)(y)(z)(Fxz \ . \ Fyz \supset . \ x = y).$$

The axiom schema of replacement is then easily grasped:

$$\text{Func } F \supset (u)(\exists w)(x)(x \in w \ . \equiv (F``u)x).$$

Under the conventions of my *Set Theory and Its Logic* it boils down yet further, but I shall not pause over them.

The notation of predicates and predicate functors serves some purposes of the class name while not requiring the class to exist. Such was the above case; for the purpose of the axiom schema would be defeated by assuming existence of the class $\{xy: Fxy\}$.

Gödel in his 1940 monograph availed himself of this convenience, though not calling them relative clauses or general terms. He introduced the expressions as eliminable quasi-names of imaginary classes which he called *notions*. At a more elementary level but in a more explicit way I did much the same under the head of *virtual classes* in my Portuguese lectures of 1942, which came out in 1944. In *Set Theory and Its Logic* twenty years later I worked up a streamlined general formalism for virtual classes, closely integrated with the formalism for real classes. There is a note of pathos in presenting the notation for notions or virtual classes thus as a simulation of class names when it is really a matter of relative clauses, general terms, and should be seen as prior to any thought of classes. Still it should be said that in *Set Theory and Its Logic* some simplicity is gained from the close integration of virtual and real classes.

Care must be taken not to confuse notions or virtual classes with ultimate or so-called "proper" classes. These latter are real classes, values of bound variables, and differ from sets only in not being members of further classes. The notions or virtual classes, on the other hand, are only a manner of speaking and not really there at all, not being values of bound variables. Their seeming names are really predicates, and their seeming variables are schematic predicate letters. What are represented as ultimate or "proper" classes in Bernays's system of 1958 are mere notions or virtual classes, for they are not values of bound variables; but the ultimate or "proper" classes in his system of 1937–1954 are the real thing. It is an open question whether Cantor and König were anticipating the one or the other in some brief passages around the turn of the century.[4]

We are noting how unready logicians have been to think directly in terms of a calculus of complex predicates. They gravitate toward sentences on the one hand or toward class names on the other, even to the point of simulating names of imaginary classes. This bias has long been visible at the most elementary level, indeed, in the attitude toward the perversely so-called Boolean calculus of classes. There is no call for classes there. This bit of logic has its whole utility as an algebra of predicates, represented by schematic letters subject to functors of union, intersection, complement, inclusion, coextensiveness, and Peano's '∃' of non-emptiness and its dual '∀'. Three of these functors form predicates from predicates, and four form sentences from predicates. Then we add truth functions for compounding these sentences into further ones.

This Boolean calculus of predicates and predicate functors is the easy version of monadic quantification theory; and there are no quantifiers and no variables, but only the schematic letters. It is only in the new third edition of *Methods of Logic* that I have switched to this calculus for the basic presentation of monadic logic. I avoid the identity notation '$F = G$' in order not to encourage at this level any thought of classes; for 'F' and 'G' are still the schematic predicate letters of the logic of quantification. The convenience of Boolean notation has often been forgone because of the mistaken belief that it calls for classes. And conversely there is the new irony in elementary schools of a so-called set theory that is just this Boolean bit of monadic logic and should not be seen as set theory at all.

Behmann should be mentioned as one who, in 1927, treated the Boolean functors in very much the style of predicate functors. However, he then promptly spoiled matters by quantifying and

[4]See my *Set Theory and Its Logic*, p. 212n.

thus effectively according his predicates the status of class names after all. It is the familiar pitfall.

My theme was the variable. We may do well now to retrace it. I am persuaded that the embryo of the bindable variable, psychogenetically, is the relative pronoun.[5] Its status as bindable variable stands forth explicitly when we regiment the relative clause using 'such that'. Relative clauses are adjectives, general terms, that is, predicates. How is a logician to frame a formal calculus of such expressions, a calculus of predicates? He will need to represent the predicates by letters as dummies. He is dim on schematic letters, so he thinks these letters must be variables with some sort of abstract objects as values; and so his relative clauses become abstract singular terms and his 'such that' becomes class abstraction. A later logician, alive to schematic letters, reacts with a true calculus of predicates; and it is the familiar quantification logic in its usual modern style of exposition. But he overreacts: he insists on keeping his predicate letters embedded with their arguments, fearing that a predicate floating free and *ungesättigt* would be a class name again. He has failed to appreciate 'such that' as an ontologically innocent operator for isolating pure complex predicates, representable by free-floating schematic letters. And so, incidentally, he has needlessly surrendered his little old Boolean logic to his unregenerate predecessor the set theorist.

Its restoration involves curious ironies. Its restoration depends, we saw, on a better appreciation of the bindable variable as an appurtenance of the relative clause, not of the class abstract. But the schematic predicate letters then become detachable from their variable arguments, and so the variables themselves disappear.

Bound variables vanish thus from the scene, in our Boolean calculus of predicates, but they lurk in the wings. They figure in the programming, to switch to a computer metaphor. For when we apply this calculus to verbal examples, we shall want usually to interpret 'F', 'G', etc., not just by substitution of pat words or phrases such as 'man' or 'Greek' or 'white whale' but by substitution of such relative clauses as '$x \ni (\exists y)(y$ is son of $x)$' or '$x \ni (3x^2 > 2x)$'; and here we have the bound variable at its proper work. Also we might still use this variable in hidden foundations of our Boolean calculus of predicates, thus:

[5]See my *The Roots of Reference*, pp. 93–101.

$$\bar{F} =_{df} x \ni \sim Fx,$$
$$F \cap G =_{df} x \ni (Fx \ . \ Gx),$$
$$F \cup G =_{df} x \ni (Fx \vee Gx),$$
$$F \subseteq G =_{df} \forall(x \ni (Fx \supset Gx)).$$

We well know that quantification theory, which is so much more complex than the Boolean predicate calculus, has its serious motivation in polyadic predicates. When we move to polyadic logic, the bound variable quits the wings and gets into the act. The basic job of the bound variable is cross-reference to various places in a sentence where objective reference occurs; and whereas monadic logic calls for this service only in the preparations, polyadic logic calls for it also within the ongoing algorithm, in order to keep track of permutations and identifications of arguments of polyadic predicates. It is in such permutations and identifications that the bound variable enters essentially into the algorithm, and here it is, by the way, that decision procedures cease to be generally available.

There is evidence of a connection. Polyadic logic remains decidable, like monadic logic, as long as there is no crossing up of argument places. There is a decision procedure covering every quantificational schema that is *fluted*, as we might say, in the following sense. Every predicate letter has the same variable 'x' as its first argument, though this repeated letter may in its different occurrences be bound by different occurrences of '(x)' or '$(\exists x)$'. Every predicate letter has one and the same letter 'y' as its second argument, if any; and so on. And, a final requirement, each occurrence of a 'y' quantifier stands in the scope of some 'x' quantifier; each occurrence of a 'z' quantifier stands in the scope of some 'y' quantifier; and so on. I gave a decision procedure for such formulas at the Congress of Vienna. (A further proviso was that all the predicate letters have the same number of argument places; but this appears superfluous.)

The variable, then, it seems, is the focus of indecision. It does not, however, set bounds to algebrization. By supplementing the Boolean predicate functors with a few more predicate functors we can, if we wish, still banish the bound variable for good. For there are predicate functors that will do all necessary linking and permuting of argument places. See below.

ᴁ *Algebraic Logic and Predicate Functors*

I. ALGEBRA AND ANALYSIS

Try to think back over the years to the time, in school or in college, when you finished algebra and started the differential calculus. Algebra had been neat and clear. It was put together of clean-cut blocks. You substituted blocklike expressions for variables. Also, on the strength of previous equations, you substituted them for one another. The calculus, in contrast, was enveloped in fog. There were variables and there were constants, so-called. You had $dc/dx = 0$, where 'c' was a constant and 'x' a variable. But could you substitute? For the variables, no. For the constants, yes: $d9/dx = 0$. For the variables you could not even substitute on the strength of previous equations. You had $dx^2/dx = 2x$; still, given further that $x = 3$, you could not substitute and conclude that $d9/dx = 6$. You had $d9/dx = 0$.

Maybe some of you were given a better introduction to the calculus than I was. The thing can of course be made straightforward. We should view 'dx^2/dx' as expressing the application of an operator not to a number x^2 but to a function, square-of, to yield not a number $2x$ but a function, double-of. Using Frege's functional abstraction (in Church's lambda notation), we can put the matter clearly:

Published in 1971 by Bobbs-Merrill in two forms, first as a pamphlet and then as a chapter in Richard Rudner and Israel Scheffler, eds., *Logic and Art: Essays in Honor of Nelson Goodman*. I have now revised §§ VII through X to accommodate an improved permutation functor due to George Myro.

$$D \; \lambda_x(x^2) \; = \; \lambda_x(2x).$$

Even the identity '$d9/dx = 0$' should be seen as treating not of numbers but of constant functions: $D \; \lambda_x 9 = \lambda_x 0$. But even when it is thus clarified the calculus lacks the neat and blocklike character of algebra. We can put a name to the contrast now: it is that the calculus binds variables. The variable of functional abstraction is bound. This has long struck me as the great contrast between the spirit of algebra and the spirit of analysis: analysis binds variables.

We know how to reduce all use of bound variables to quantification. For instance '$\lambda_x(x^2)$' can be eliminated from any sentential context, say '$\phi \; \lambda_x(x^2)$', by explaining this whole as:

$$(\exists f)(\phi f \; . \; (x)(f'x \; = \; x^2))$$

or, in terms more purely of set theory:

$$(\exists z)(\phi z \; . \; (y)(x)(\langle y, x \rangle \; \epsilon \; z \; .\!\equiv\!. \; y \; = \; x^2)).$$

We can reduce all use of free variables to quantification too, if we like, since an open sentence has its uses ultimately only as a clause of various closed sentences in which its variables have become bound.

But in a way the opposite reduction is much more attractive, if it can be done: the elimination of bound variables in favor of just free ones. This would be a reduction of the analytic style to the algebraic style. Since all use of bound variables can be limited to quantification, the problem is that of algebrizing quantification. Whether or not this result would be practically useful, it should be theoretically significant as an analysis of the idea of the bound variable: an explanation of it with all the clarity of the discrete and blocklike terms and simple substitutions characteristic of algebra. It should, in addition, yield a deeper understanding of variables as such, bound or free; for, as I just remarked, free variables themselves are for binding in broader contexts. Thus the algebrization of quantification could prove illuminating in two ways: in analyzing away bound variables and in enhancing our understanding even of the free variables surviving in the algebra itself.

In part the algebrization of quantification is a step backward; for part of what quantification does was previously done algebraically by talking of classes in the manner of Boole and of relations in the manner of Peirce and Schröder. Instead of '$(x)(Fx \supset Gx)$' and '$(\exists x)(Fx \cdot Gx)$', one would treat the predicate letters as class names and write '$F \subseteq G$' and '$F \cap G \neq \Lambda$'. Instead of:

$$(x) \sim Fxx, \qquad (x)(y)(Fxy \supset Fyx), \qquad (x)(y)(z)(Fxy \cdot Fyz \cdot \supset Fxz),$$

one would treat the predicate letter as a relation name and write '$F \cap I = \Lambda$', '$\breve{F} \subseteq F$', and '$F \mid F \subseteq F$'. Here, then, we have some of the algebraic notations that help us get rid of quantifiers and their variables: '$\cap$', '$\subseteq$', '$=$', 'Λ', 'I', '$\breve{}$', '$\mid$'. The problem is to pick an assortment of such devices adequate to the general case.

II. FUNCTIONAL ABSTRACTION

Schönfinkel succeeded in eliminating bound variables in 1924,[1] and his work took an interestingly different line. The best approach to his idea is through functional abstraction rather than quantification. We saw how the use of bound variables in functional abstraction could be reduced to their use in quantification; but the opposite reduction is possible as well. In fact the only devices we need besides functional abstraction are functional application, as in '$f'x$', and the identity sign '$=$'. These can be made to suffice if we follow Frege in taking true sentences as names of a certain thing T, and false sentences as names of a certain thing ⊥. A class then can be seen as a function that gives the value T when applied to the members and the value ⊥ otherwise. Thus take the class of prime numbers. It becomes identified with the function f such that $f'x = $ T for prime x and $f'x = $ ⊥ for other x. But wait: we can say also that (x is prime) = T for prime x and (x is prime) = ⊥ for other x. So $f'x = $ (x is prime) for each x. So the function f is $\lambda_x(x$ is prime). We see from this example that functional abstraction does the work, in particular, of class abstraction; $\{x: x$ is prime$\}$ becomes $\lambda_x(x$ is prime).

That much was already in Frege. Now I shall go on from there and show how functional abstraction, functional application, and

---

[1] Schönfinkel's line is developed in an extensive literature, largely by Curry.

identity can yield quantification. In view of what we just saw, the universal class V or $\{x: x = x\}$ can be defined as $\lambda_x(x = x)$; and thereupon the universal quantification '$(x)Fx$', with any open sentence in place of 'Fx', can be defined as $\lambda_x(Fx) = V$. The existential quantifier '$(\exists x)$' can then be explained in turn in the usual manner as '$\sim(x)\sim$', provided that we can define negation. To do this we first pick some arbitrary falsehood expressible in our notation; say '$(x)(x = V)$'. Then we define '$\sim y$' in general as '$y = (x)(x = V)$', taking advantage again of the fact that sentences are names and false sentences are names of the one object $\bot$.

In explaining how to define the two kinds of quantification in terms of functional abstraction, application, and identity, I have talked of the objects $\top$ and $\bot$, the two truth values. I have not used these symbols in the definitions, and I have not defined them. We can formally define them, though, if we like. We can choose again our arbitrary falsehood '$(x)(x = V)$' and define '$\bot$' as short for it, and '$\top$' as '$\sim\bot$'.

We can get all the truth functions. The trick is to get conjunction; everyone knows how to get the others from it and negation. The trick for defining conjunction is one that I have adapted from a 1923 paper of Tarski's: define the conjunction '$x \cdot y$' as '$(z)(x = (z'x = z'y))$'. My use of variables in conjunction here, and under negation earlier, looks odd; we have to remind ourselves that sentences now count as names. To see how conjunction as thus defined compels x and y to be $\top$, try taking z first as $\lambda_w x$ and then as $\lambda_w w$. We get $x = (x = x)$ and $x = (x = y)$ and so $x = \top = y$.

We have now seen that functional abstraction, application, and identity are enough for elementary logic—that is, enough for the truth functions, quantification, and identity. But they are enough also for much more. We have seen that class abstraction is at hand, as the special case of functional abstraction where the function's values are truth values. Equally, class membership is at hand; it is the special case of functional application where the function's values are truth values. For, recall the class f of all primes. We saw that $f'x$ was $\top$ for prime x and $\bot$ for other x; and this is precisely what we want $x \in f$ to be.

We have overreached ourselves. We wanted to see how the bound variables of quantification could be got down to the bound variable of functional abstraction. What we have found is that functional abstraction, along with the seemingly minimal auxiliary notations of application and identity, are enough for logic and set theory and hence mathematics generally.[2]

III. COMBINATORS

What I want to trace next, proceeding from this notation, is Schönfinkel's elimination of bound variables. We define two specific functions:

$$(1) \qquad\qquad C = \lambda_x\lambda_y x.$$
$$(2) \qquad\qquad S = \lambda_x\lambda_y\lambda_z((x'z)'(y'z)).$$

Conversely, as we shall find, all use of functional abstraction is eliminable in favor of C and S.

C is the function that carries any object into the corresponding constant function. $C'9$ is the constant function $\lambda_y 9$ whose value is always 9. And what is S? Words fail one. It is the functional which, applied to any function x, yields the functional which, applied to any function y, yields the function which, applied to anything z, yields what the function $x'z$ would yield when applied to $y'z$.

The content of equations like (1) and (2) can be put into a more convenient form by applying both sides. Thus (1) tells us that $C'x = \lambda_y x$, and hence that $(C'x)'y = x$. Similarly (2) tells us, after three such steps, that

$$((S'x)'y)'z = (x'z)'(y'z).$$

Further let us adopt a convention of Schönfinkel's for economy of parentheses in iterated functional application:

$$(3) \qquad\qquad a'b'c = (a'b)'c.$$

So our two results now run thus:

$$(4) \qquad\qquad C'x'y = x.$$
$$(5) \qquad\qquad S'x'y'z = x'z'(y'z).$$

C and S, and all the functions compounded of them by functional

---

[2]The adequacy of this combination was noted at the end of my "Unification of universes in set theory."

application, have come to be called *combinators*. Example: $S'C$. What is it? By (5), $S'C'y'z$ is $C'z'(y'z)$. So, by (4),

(6) $$S'C'y'z = z.$$

Another example: $S'C'C$. By (6), $S'C'C'z = z$. Thus $S'C'C$ is the identity function. Abbreviating it as 'I', we have:

(7) $$I'z = z.$$

Another example: $S'(C'S)'C$. By (5),

$$
\begin{aligned}
S'(C'S)'C'w &= (C'S)'w'(C'w) \\
\text{(by (3))} &= (C'S'w)'(C'w) \\
\text{(by (4))} &= S'(C'w).
\end{aligned}
$$

Following Schönfinkel, let us refer to $S'(C'S)'C$ briefly as Z. So $Z'w$ is $S'(C'w)$. So

$$
\begin{aligned}
Z'w'y'x &= S'(C'w)'y'x \\
\text{(by (5))} &= (C'w)'x'(y'x) \\
\text{(by (3))} &= (C'w'x)'(y'x).
\end{aligned}
$$

So, by (4),

(8) $$Z'w'y'x = w'(y'x).$$

You see how mechanically the evaluation of combinators proceeds. You will find by further computation of the same sort that, where 'R' stands for '$S'(Z'Z'S)'(C'C)$',

(9) $$R'x'y'z = x'z'y.$$

Also, where 'W' stands for '$R'S'I$', that

(10) $$W'x'y = x'y'y.$$

As a convenient adjustment of detail, next, let us dispense with '$=$' in favor of the unit-class function ι. The two are interdefinable, since

$$\iota = \lambda_x\lambda_y(x = y), \qquad \iota'x'y = (x = y).$$

The advantage of this shift is a simplification of grammatical categories. There are now just variables and the letters for specific functions ('S', 'C', 'ι') and the 'λ' of abstraction and the inverted comma and parentheses of functional application. What we want to show is that the 'λ' can be eliminated.

IV. ELIMINATION OF VARIABLES

I shall prepare the way by first proving some things about terms that lack 'λ'. By the *superficial* components of such a term I shall mean the terms that occur in it unenclosed in any parentheses when parentheses have been suppressed to the extent that convention (3) allows. Thus a formula has the form $\ulcorner\phi_1{}^\backprime\phi_2{}^\backprime \ldots {}^\backprime\phi_n\urcorner$ where ϕ_1, ϕ_2, ..., and ϕ_n are its superficial components. Now consider a superficial occurrence of some variable, say 'x', in a term ζ. We can assure that this occurrence is not initial to ζ, since by (7) we can change 'x' to '$I'x$'. So ζ has the form $\ulcorner\phi{}^\backprime x{}^\backprime\psi_1$ $^\backprime \ldots {}^\backprime\psi_n\urcorner$, where $\phi, \psi_1, \ldots, \psi_n$ can be complex. Now either $n = 0$, so that this occurrence of 'x' is already terminal to ζ, or else the occurrence can be maneuvered into terminal position as follows. By (9), the beginning $\ulcorner\phi{}^\backprime x{}^\backprime\psi_1\urcorner$ of ζ can be rendered $\ulcorner R{}^\backprime\phi{}^\backprime\psi_1{}^\backprime x\urcorner$, so that ζ becomes

$$\ulcorner R{}^\backprime\phi{}^\backprime\psi_1{}^\backprime x{}^\backprime\psi_2{}^\backprime\psi_3{}^\backprime \ldots {}^\backprime\psi_n\urcorner.$$

By (9) again, the beginning $\ulcorner R{}^\backprime\phi{}^\backprime\psi_1{}^\backprime x{}^\backprime\psi_2\urcorner$ of this can be rendered $\ulcorner R{}^\backprime(R{}^\backprime\phi{}^\backprime\psi_1){}^\backprime\psi_2{}^\backprime x\urcorner$. So ζ as a whole has now become:

$$\ulcorner R{}^\backprime(R{}^\backprime\phi{}^\backprime\psi_1){}^\backprime\psi_2{}^\backprime x{}^\backprime\psi_3{}^\backprime\psi_4{}^\backprime \ldots {}^\backprime\psi_n\urcorner.$$

Continuing thus, we push the occurrence of 'x' until it terminates the whole formula.

Such is the proof of

LEMMA 1. *If ζ lacks 'λ' and has a superficial occurrence of 'x', then*, roughly speaking, *that occurrence can be worked around to the end;* accurately speaking, ζ is equivalent to a term of the form $\ulcorner\eta{}^\backprime x\urcorner$ lacking 'λ' and lacking any added occurrences of variables.

This lemma was a matter of using the combinator R to push a superficial occurrence of 'x'. The next is a matter of using Z to surface an occurrence of 'x'.

LEMMA 2. *If ζ lacks 'λ' and contains 'x', then some occurrence of 'x' is superficial or*, roughly speaking, *can be rendered superficial;* accurately speaking, ζ is equivalent to a term containing a superficial occurrence of 'x' and no 'λ' nor any added occurrences of variables.

Proof. An occurrence of 'x' in ζ is enclosed by, say, k pairs of parentheses. Say the term occupying the innermost pair is θ. The occurrence of 'x' is superficial in θ; so, by Lemma 1, θ becomes $\ulcorner\eta{}^\backprime x\urcorner$. This parenthetical expression $\ulcorner(\eta{}^\backprime x)\urcorner$ is situated subject to some functional application, $\ulcorner\phi\dot{}(\eta\dot{}x)\urcorner$; and this latter can, by (8), be rendered $\ulcorner Z\dot{}\phi\dot{}\eta\dot{}x\urcorner$, thus extricating the '$x$' from one of the k pairs of parentheses. By k such steps we bring 'x' to the surface.

Observe now how the two lemmas combine. If a term ζ contains occurrences of 'x' and none of 'λ', we can assure by Lemma 2 that an occurrence of 'x' is superficial; and then by Lemma 1 we can render it terminal, so that ζ reduces to the form $\ulcorner\eta\dot{}x\urcorner$. Then we reduce η similarly to the form $\ulcorner\theta\dot{}x\urcorner$, so that ζ becomes $\ulcorner\theta\dot{}x\dot{}x\urcorner$ and so, by (10), $\ulcorner W\dot{}\theta\dot{}x\urcorner$. This last has fewer occurrences of 'x' than ζ had, and one of them is terminal. Iteration of this process assures

LEMMA 3. *Any term lacking 'λ' and containing 'x' is reducible to the form* $\ulcorner\eta\dot{}x\urcorner$ *where η lacks 'λ' and 'x'.*

Now we are ready to attend to 'λ'. Consider $\ulcorner\lambda_x\zeta\urcorner$, where ζ itself lacks 'λ'. By Lemma 3 we convert ζ to $\ulcorner\eta\dot{}x\urcorner$ where η lacks 'λ' and 'x'. But $\ulcorner\lambda_x(\eta\dot{}x)\urcorner$ is equivalent to η alone. In this way, given any term at all, we can eliminate each of its innermost 'λ's, and so, continuing outward, eliminate all its 'λ's. Such is our theorem.

Elimination of 'λ' means elimination of bound variables, since only 'λ' binds variables. Elimination of bound variables means also, in a way, elimination of free variables, since open expressions are wanted ultimately only for embedding in closed ones. So our vocabulary is down now to just the three constant terms 'S', 'C', and 'ι' and the inverted comma and parentheses of functional application. This, we see, is adequate for logic and set theory and hence for mathematics generally. This is Schönfinkel's result, except in detail. The detail is that he used something else instead of 'ι'.

Schönfinkel was the first to reduce analysis to algebra. He was the first to analyze the variable, by showing how to translate it contextually into constant terms. But his treatment is less pure than one could wish; it analyzes the variable only in combination with a function theory that is in effect general set theory.

V. TOWARD A CALCULUS OF CONCEPTS

In a paper of 1936 under the above title, I showed how quantification could be dealt with in algebraic terms less powerful than Schönfinkel's. In calling the envisaged algebra a calculus of concepts, I was using the unhappy term 'concept' generally to cover truth values, classes, and relations. The truth values, two in number, were concepts of degree 0. Classes of individuals of some supposedly preassigned domain were concepts of degree 1. Relations of those individuals were concepts of degree 2 and higher, according as the relations were dyadic, triadic, etc. The degrees were mutually exclusive even to their null elements; the null concept of degree 0 was the truth value $\bot$, the null concept of degree 1 was the null class, and so on up. The concepts were the elements of the envisaged algebra, the values of the free variables, which I shall now render 'X', 'Y', etc. Individuals figured only in the informal explanations.

I shall continue for a while to speak of X, Y, etc., as concepts, rather than as classes of sequences, for two weak reasons. One is that in this calculus the null concepts of different degrees are viewed as different. The other is that sequences of different lengths are not allowed under the same concept.

For any concepts X and Y of degrees m and n there was the *Cartesian product* $X \times Y$ of degree $m + n$, comprising all the sequences obtainable by concatenating sequences belonging to X with sequences belonging to Y. Further I assumed the Boolean complement, yielding, for each concept X of degree n, the complementary concept $-X$ of degree n. Further there was the *image*. Where the degrees of X and Y are 2 and 1, the image $X"Y$ has the familiar meaning: it is the class of all the things that bear the relation X to members of Y. Where X is of degree $m + n$ and Y is of degree n, more generally, $X"Y$ comprises all sequences $\langle x_1, \ldots, x_m \rangle$ such that $\langle x_1, \ldots, x_m, y_1, \ldots, y_n \rangle$ is in X for some sequence $\langle y_1, \ldots, y_n \rangle$ in Y.

A fourth and last operation was a duplicating operation, written 'I' but not to be confused with Schönfinkel's identity function.[3] Where X is of degree n, IX comprises all sequences $\langle x_1, \ldots, x_n, x_1, \ldots, x_n \rangle$ such that $\langle x_1, \ldots, x_n \rangle$ is in X.

My present expository use of the sequence notation and the lowercase variables 'x_1', 'x_2', 'y_1', etc., is foreign to the calculus of concepts itself. So are the symbols '$\top$' and '$\bot$' and the talk of degree.

---

[3] I presented these four operations explicitly as basis in "Concepts of negative degree." In "Toward a calculus of concepts" I compacted three of the four artificially and uninterestingly into a single two-place operation.

The notation of the calculus of concepts comprises only the capital letters for concept variables and the symbols for Cartesian product, complement, image, and duplication.

For a representatively devious example of the construction of other notions from these four, consider in its generalized form the notion of a *converse* of a relation. Where the degree of X is n, one of the $n - 1$ converses of X comprises the transposed sequences $\langle x_{i+1}, \ldots, x_n, x_1, \ldots, x_i \rangle$ such that $\langle x_1, \ldots, x_n \rangle$ is in X; and X has a different such converse for each $i < n$. But in fashioning the calculus of concepts I avoided numerals and appealed instead to concept variables themselves as measures of degree. So, instead of specifying this converse of X as the one that comes of breaking after the ith place, I specified it as the converse of X that comes of breaking after the degree of some other appropriately chosen concept Y. Nearly enough, the notation was 'Conv$_Y X$' and its definition was this:

(11) $((I - (I(X \times Y)" - (X \times Y)))"(I - (IY \times -Y)))"X.$

Let us see why. For simplicity let us suppose the degrees of X and Y to be 2 and 1, and let us then see why (11) gives the familiar converse of X.

It is evident that when Y and Z are of equal degree, the image $IY"Z$ reduces to the Boolean intersection $Y \cap Z$. So, in particular, $IY" - Y$ is the null concept in the degree of Y; hence the null class, since Y is of degree 1. So $-(IY" - Y)$ is the universal class; call it V^1. Similarly, since $X \times Y$ is of degree 3,

$$-(I(X \times Y)" - (X \times Y)) = V^3.$$

So (11) boils down to $(IV^3"IV^1)"X$. But IV^3 comprises all sequences of the form $\langle x, y, z, x, y, z \rangle$, and IV^1 comprises all pairs $\langle y, z \rangle$ such that $y = z$; so the image $IV^3"IV^1$ comprises all sequences of the form $\langle x, y, z, x \rangle$ such that $y = z$. In short, $IV^3"IV^1$ comprises all sequences of the form $\langle x, y, y, x \rangle$. But then the image $(IV^3"IV^1)"X$, in turn, comprises all pairs $\langle x, y \rangle$ such that $\langle y, x \rangle$ is in X; and this is just the familiar converse of X that we hoped (11) would give.

Let us next consider how to translate a schema of the ordinary logic of quantification, say:

(12) $(x)(Fx \supset (\exists y)(Fy . Gxy)),$

into the calculus of concepts. With the predicate letters 'F' and 'G' changed to concept variables 'X' and 'Y', this clearly amounts to '$X \subseteq Y"X$'. Moreover, it is evident from the general explanation of image that, when any concepts X and Z are alike in degree, $X"Z$ reduces to a mere truth value: to T if X and Z overlap, and to $\bot$ otherwise. In other words, '$X"Z$' becomes a statement to the effect that X overlaps Z. So '$X \subseteq Y"X$', which denies that X overlaps $-(Y"X)$, can be rendered:

$$(13) \qquad\qquad -(X" - (Y"X)).$$

Such, then, is a translation of (12) into the calculus of concepts.

However, the same (13) can be reached equally as a translation of any of the further logical schemata of the form:

$$(14) \quad (x_1) \ldots (x_n)(Fx_1 \ldots x_n \supset$$
$$(\exists y_1) \ldots (\exists y_n)(Fy_1 \ldots y_n \cdot Gx_1 \ldots x_n y_1 \ldots y_n)),$$

including even the case, '$p \supset pq$', where n is 0. (13) can even be reached as a translation of certain nonsentential terms for classes and relations, e.g.:

$$\{z: (x)(Fzx \supset (\exists y)(\exists w)(Fyw \cdot Gxyw))\}$$

and in fact all of this form:

$$(15) \quad \{x_1 \ldots x_m: \ (x_{m+1}) \ldots (x_n)(Fx_1 \ldots x_n \supset$$
$$(\exists y_1) \ldots (\exists y_n)(Fy_1 \ldots y_n \cdot Gx_{m+1} \ldots x_n y_1 \ldots y_n))\}.$$

The sentential cases (14) are merely the cases of (15) where $m = 0$.

Thus the calculus of concepts diverges from the ordinary logic of quantification in its aloofness from details of degree. Predicate letters in the schemata of quantification logic are of visible degree, shown by the number of appended variables, whereas degree in the calculus of concepts is left open. I proved in effect[4] that the logic of quantification and identity was translatable into the calculus of concepts to within this latitude of indeterminacy. It would have been natural and easy to add indices of degree to my concept variables and thus fix translation in full; but at the time I was more interested in the abstraction.

---

[4] In "Toward a calculus of concepts." Anyone consulting that paper should be warned that 'α', 'β', etc., there play the role of my present 'X', 'Y', etc., whereas 'X', 'Y', etc., there range over sequences.

I devised no definitive proof procedure for the calculus of concepts. If one were to be devised, it should be devised for proving as theorems not just the formulas that come out true for all values of their concept variables, but all the formulas that designate universal concepts V^n for all values of their variables. This policy is wanted because of what was illustrated by (15) in relation to (13): in omitting degree we suppress any general distinction between sentential formulas and others. Some forms are unequivocally sentential, notably 'X"X', but most are not.

A curious simplification of the calculus of concepts comes of admitting concepts of negative degree, as I showed in my paper of that title. Cartesian multiplication can thereupon be dropped as a primitive operation, for $X \times Y$ becomes definable as X"$((Y$"$Y)$"$Y)$; and the laws undergo a similarly gratifying reduction. But I never thought of a natural or interesting interpretation of negative degree.

The calculus of concepts contrasts with Schönfinkel's scheme in retaining free variables. These may indeed be reassessed as schematic letters (cf. § VIII below), but they are not eliminable in favor of constants; for besides them there are only the four operation signs, which cannot make formulas by themselves. 'C', 'S', and 'ι', in contrast, were terms, proper names of three abstract objects; they were complete formulas as they stood, and they gave rise to the rest of Schönfinkel's formulas through functional application to one another, unaided by variables or schematic letters.

A related and more profound contrast is that we are not faced in the calculus of concepts with a runaway ontology, as Schönfinkel was. A denumerable universe of concepts would suffice, finite for each degree and denumerable over all.

VI. CYLINDRICAL ALGEBRA

In 1951 and thereafter, Tarski and his pupils developed what they called *cylindrical algebra*.[5] Its elements are classes of infinite sequences of the individuals of some domain. Its universe is, so to

---

[5]Tarski and Thompson; also Henkin. A somewhat similar plan has been advanced by Halmos under the name of "polyadic algebra."

speak, the missing degree ω of the calculus of concepts and that only.

The algebra is presented as presupposing the usual Boolean algebra of classes along with the usual truth-function logic. It uses free variables for classes—let us say the letters 'X', 'Y', etc. In addition there are infinitely many constants 'd_{11}', 'd_{12}', etc., explained thus: d_{ij}, called a *diagonal element*, is the class of all infinite sequences whose ith and jth places match. Finally there are infinitely many operators 'C_1', 'C_2', etc., upon classes of sequences, and they are explained thus: C_iX, called a *cylindrification* of the class X, is the class that comprises all the sequences in X and, in addition, all the sequences obtainable from them by ringing changes on the ith place.

Toward seeing how this bears on quantification, think back on the concept of satisfaction in Tarski's *Wahrheitsbegriff*. Suppose a quantificational language of the familiar sort, with its infinite alphabet of quantifiable variables 'w', 'x', 'y', 'z', 'w'', etc. A sequence of objects satisfies an open sentence ϕ of this language if ϕ comes out true when the first object of the sequence is assigned as value of 'w', and the second as value of 'x', and so on through the alphabet. Let X be the class of all the infinite sequences that thus satisfy ϕ. Now quantify ϕ existentially, using say 'y', the third variable of the alphabet. What sequences will satisfy $\ulcorner(\exists y)\phi\urcorner$? All those in X and more: all those that can be got from sequences in X by ringing changes on the third place. Thus the class of sequences satisfying $\ulcorner(\exists y)\phi\urcorner$ will be C_3X.

Such is the link between cylindrification and existential quantification. A more extended argument would of course be needed to show that cylindrical algebra fully accommodates the usual quantification theory. Indeed there is a difficulty in the way of showing this; for cylindrical algebra, like the calculus of concepts, preserves a certain abstractness in relation to the number of places in predicates.

Bernays, however, in 1959, takes the further step of resolving this abstractness by attaching numerical indices to the class variables, thus: 'X^1', 'Y^2', 'Z^1', etc. True, the classes already all have the uniform degree ω, in the sense of being classes of sequences of that length. But what Bernays's indices indicate rather is *effective* degree, in this sense: a class is of degree n if only the first n places of sequences are relevant to it. That is, whenever two sequences are alike in their first n places, they are both in the class or both out. Bernays admits classes only of finite degree, in *this* sense, as values of variables. Note that, by this definition, degree is cumulative; classes of degree n are of all degrees $m > n$. Thus modified, cylindrical algebra is shown by Bernays to afford full translation of the ordinary logic of quantification and identity.

Limitation of the elements of cylindrical algebra to classes of finite degrees in this sense gives what Tarski and his pupils call *locally finite* cylindrical algebra. Once this limitation is adopted, no further power is lost by forgetting infinite sequences and simply viewing X^n as a class of sequences of length n. Degree ceases to be cumulative, and becomes substantially what it was in the calculus of concepts. There is the difference, though, that the null relations now all boil down to the null class. As for whether a class should now admit sequences of unlike lengths, this is really a question of style; but the negative decision seems more convenient. We can still get the benefits of any such mixed class by just thinking of its short members as prolonged in all possible ways to gain uniformity of length.

Bernays presents another algebra following this latter line. Its primitive ideas differ from those of cylindrical algebra. They are as follows. There is Boolean algebra as before, and there are the truth functions. Further there is the Cartesian product $X^m \times Y^n$. There is a class constant 'I' (that overworked letter), now designating the identity relation; that is, the class of degree 2 comprising all pairs $\langle x, x \rangle$. There is an infinite lot of *permutation functors* 'p_{11}', 'p_{12}', etc.; where $i, j \leq n$, $p_{ij}X^n$ is the class of all the sequences obtainable from those in X^n by switching their ith and jth places.

Finally there is a *cropping* functor which has the effect of decapitating all the sequences in a class X^{n+1}, leaving a class of degree n which I shall refer to as $\mathbf{)}X^{n+1}$. Its members are the sequences $\langle x_1, \ldots, x_n \rangle$ such that, for some x_0, $\langle x_0, \ldots, x_n \rangle$ belongs to X^{n+1}. My symbol is meant to connote excision of the left column of X^{n+1}. Later we shall see an inverse functor of *padding*, $\mathbf{(}X^n$, which adds a left column to produce a class of degree $n + 1$.

Bernays refers to the class $\mathbf{)}X^{n+1}$ rather as DX^{n+1} and calls the operation *Domainbildung*. One apparent reason is that $\mathbf{)}X^2$, or DX^2, is what Whitehead and Russell called the converse domain of the relation X^2. E.g., where X^2 is the love relation, $\mathbf{)}X^2$ is the class of the loved. Another reason is that, where the relation X^2 is a function, ιX^2 is its domain commonly so called: the class of its arguments. Tarski has called the operation *projection*, which is very much its geometrical force. Thus consider a class X^3 of triples $\langle x, y, z \rangle$. Each such triple can be viewed as the point having x, y, z as its coordinates in 3-space, and the class X^3 can be a solid composed of such points. The class ιX^3 then abstracts from the first of these dimensions—height, say. ιX^3 then is the two-dimensional shadow of X^3; it is the plane figure composed of those points $\langle y, z \rangle$ lying directly beneath points $\langle x, y, z \rangle$ of X^3.

VII. SOME ECONOMIES

Bernays notes that Cartesian multiplication becomes dispensable as soon as, with Tarski, we reconstrue each class X^n by prolonging its n-length sequences ad infinitum in all ways. For you can thereupon explain $X^1 \times Y^1$ as $X^1 \cap p_{12}Y^1$; and the trick is easily generalized to $X^m \times Y^n$, which becomes

$$(16) \qquad X^m \cap p_{1(m+1)}p_{2(m+2)} \ldots p_{n(m+n)}Y^n.$$

Observe, however, that we can use this same trick without confessing to infinite sequences and without turning back to cumulative degrees. We can get the same effect while continuing to think of X^n as strictly a class of n-length sequences, if we just embellish the interpretations of '$\cap$' and 'p_{ij}' a bit. Instead of recognizing $X^m \cap Y^n$ only where $m = n$, as Bernays had done, we can recognize it generally; we can take it as the class of all sequences in X^m that begin with sequences in Y^n, or vice versa, according as $m \geqq n$ or $m \leqq n$. Instead of recognizing $p_{ij}X^n$ only where $i, j \leqq n$, as Bernays had done, we can recognize it generally. When $i, n \leqq j$, we can take it as $p_{ij}X^j$ where X^j is the class of all the j-length sequences that begin with sequences in X^n. Correspondingly, of course, when $j, n \leqq i$. So now we are as free as Tarski to define $X^m \times Y^n$ away as (16).

Further economy can be gained by reviving Frege's idea of sentences as names of the truth values, and viewing the truth values as classes of degree 0. This enables us to treat existential quantifications more uniformly. The formula '$(\exists y)(\exists x)(\langle x, y \rangle \,\epsilon\, X^2)$' of ordinary notation would go over into Bernays's algebra in two dissimilar steps as follows: first to '$(\exists y)(y \,\epsilon\, \iota X^2)$' and then to

'$\jmath X^2 \neq \Lambda$'. Our new plan allows two uniform steps, issuing in '$\jmath\jmath X^2$', which counts as sentential because the degree is 0. Moreover, this new plan assimilates negation and conjunction to Boolean complementation and intersection. The two truth functions become merely the zero cases, $-X^0$ and $X^0 \cap Y^0$. The Boolean '$\subseteq$' and '$=$' are dispensable too, since '$X^n \subseteq Y^n$' comes down to '$\sim\jmath\jmath \ldots \jmath (X^n \cap -Y^n)$' and '$X^n = Y^n$' comes down to '$X^n \subseteq Y^n$. $Y^n \subseteq X^n$'. So the whole auxiliary apparatus of Boolean algebra and truth functions boils down now to '$-X^n$' and '$X^n \cap Y^n$' for the various $n \geqq 0$. This is not to say that the idea of individual identity drops out; it is with us in 'I'.

Further economy can be gained in the permutation functors. Far from needing Bernays's infinite lot, viz. 'p_{ij}' for each i and j, we can get all rearrangements of n things using just a single permutation functor together with the cropping functor '$\jmath$' and one more functor, the *padding* functor '$\mathfrak{t}$'. $\mathfrak{t}X^n$ is to be $V \times X^n$, hence the class of all sequences $\langle x_0, \ldots, x_n \rangle$ such that $\langle x_1, \ldots, x_n \rangle \in X^n$. The single permutation functor, 'p', is to be such as to drive the second element of each sequence to the end; thus pX^n is the class of all sequences $\langle x_1, x_3, \ldots, x_n, x_2 \rangle$ such that $\langle x_1, \ldots, x_n \rangle \in X^n$.

To show how to get all permutations, I first define

(17)   '$p_i X^n$, for '$p^{n-i-1}\jmath p^i \mathfrak{t} X^n$,

where 'p^i' stands for '$pp \ldots p$' to i occurrences. Let us analyze this. If $\langle x_1, \ldots, x_n \rangle \in X^n$, then $\langle x_0, \ldots, x_n \rangle \in \mathfrak{t}X^n$; then $\langle x_0, x_2, \ldots, x_n, x_1 \rangle \in p \, \mathfrak{t}X^n$; then $\langle x_0, x_3, \ldots, x_n, x_1, x_2 \rangle \in pp\mathfrak{t}X^n$; and so on. Thus $\langle x_0, x_{i+1}, \ldots, x^n, x_1, \ldots, x_i \rangle \in p^i\mathfrak{t}X^n$, and so $\langle x_{i+1}, \ldots, x_n, x_1, \ldots, x_i \rangle \in \jmath p^i\mathfrak{t}X^n$, and finally $\langle x_{i+1}, x_1, \ldots, x_i, x_{i+2}, \ldots, x^n \rangle \in p_i X^n$ as of (17). Thus $p_i X^n$ is the class of sequences resulting from those in X^n by bringing the $i + 1$st elements to the front. The reason I write 'p_i' for the transfer of the $i + 1$st element, rather than of the ith, is just not to waste 'p_1'. The subscript says how many places are leaped.

It is easy now to see how to get any desired permutation. Pick out, in the given sequence, the element that is destined for last place in the desired rearrangement, and bring it to the front, if it is not already there. Then do the same for the element that is destined for next-to-last place. At most n such applications of 'p_i', for the appropriate choices of i, suffice to build up the desired order from back to front.

Formerly I had had two permutation functors. The reduction to the single 'p' was shown me in 1971 by George Myro.

Let us ponder the relation of padding to cropping. Cropping is the inverse of padding; $\mathsf{J}\mathfrak{c}X^n = X^n$. Padding is an inverse of cropping; in general $X^n \subseteq \mathfrak{c}\mathsf{J}X^n$. Geometrically, just as $\mathsf{J}X^3$ may be seen as the projection of the solid X^3 upon a chosen plane, so $\mathfrak{c}X^2$ comprises all the points that would project onto the plane figure X^2. $\mathfrak{c}X^2$ is the infinite right cylinder whose plane cross-section is X^2. Yet $\mathfrak{c}X^2$ is not Tarski's cylindrification. The latter— if for the sake of comparison we descend from Tarski's $\aleph_0$ dimensions to three—is an operation that carries solids into solids rather than plane figures into solids; it cylindrifies around a preexisting protuberance. The operation expressed by '$\mathfrak{c}$' might be distinguished from Tarski's cylindrification by the name of *hypercylindrification*, in allusion to the adding of a dimension, just as we speak of hypercubes, hyperspheres, etc., in 4-space. But the terms 'cropping' and 'padding' are the ones that become graphic when, turning away from geometry, we think of a class X^n rather as an n-column stack of sequences.

We saw, awhile back, how Tarski's cylindrification corresponded to existential quantification. We saw later how cropping, 'J', corresponded to existential quantification. Yet the two seem opposed; cropping is the inverse of hypercylindrification. I mention this as a curiosity.

My modification of Bernays's modification of Tarski's cylindrical algebra, then, has just these primitive notations: the Boolean functors '$-$' and '$\cap$', the cropping and padding functors 'J' and '$\mathfrak{c}$', the permutation functor 'p', the class constant 'I', and the free class variables with their indices. It is easy to compute the degree of a class specified in these terms, and to see when it goes to 0. The degree of $-X^n$ and pX^n is n. The degree of $X^m \cap Y^n$ is max (m, n). The degree of $\mathsf{J}X^{n+1}$ is n and that of $\mathfrak{c}X^n$ is $n + 1$. The degree of I is 2.

Schönfinkel's convention of parentheses, (3) above, reflects an important formal difference between his scheme and the present one. My '$-$', 'p', 'J', and '$\mathfrak{c}$' offer scope for no such convention, for they are not names of functions. They are not terms at all, but functors, mere markers of operations. They attach to the ensuing term to produce a complex term which is accessible to further operations; they are not themselves operated upon. For them the association is unswervingly to the right, without benefit of convention or parentheses. What I am saying of this present algebra applies equally of course to Tarski's and Bernays's.

VIII. PREDICATE-FUNCTOR LOGIC

The universe of the algebra that we have been considering has only to contain I and be closed under the Boolean operations and permutation, cropping, and padding. A denumerable universe of classes, finite for each degree, is not too poor for these conditions. In fact there is no longer any need to view this algebra in set theoretic terms at all, however modest. This is not to say that it can be treated as an abstract algebra; that would be a trivial remark. My point is rather that we can treat these so-called free class variables simply as schematic predicate letters, on a par with those of the ordinary logic of quantification. We can rewrite 'X^n', 'Y^n', etc., as 'F^n', 'G^n', etc.: as schematic letters for n-place predicates or, where $n = 0$, for sentences. There is no thought any longer of reference to classes nor to truth values. The functors '$-$', '$\cap$', 'p', '$\mathfrak{z}$', and '$\mathfrak{t}$' become functors on predicates and sentences, yielding predicates and sentences. 'I' becomes a two-place identity predicate, tantamount to '$=$'. We come to be doing what we may call *predicate-functor logic*.

When we thus shift our attitude, we find that our notation of predicate-functor logic is *just* adequate to the ordinary logic of quantification and identity; it goes no farther. I will now show how the translation proceeds, forward and backward.

It will be convenient to adopt three conventions of abbreviation. One of them was already seen in (17), but should now be put thus:

$$\text{'p}_i F^n\text{' for 'p}^{n-i-1}\mathfrak{z}\text{p}^i\mathfrak{t}F^n\text{'}.$$

One of them restores the notation of the Cartesian product, thus:

$$\text{'}F^m \times G^n\text{' for '}F^m \cap \mathfrak{t}\mathfrak{t} \ldots \mathfrak{t}G^n\text{'}$$

to m occurrences of '$\mathfrak{t}$'. The remaining one introduces the self functor:

$$\text{'}SF^n\text{' for '}\mathfrak{z}(I \cap F^n)\text{'}.$$

To say that $SF^n x_2 x_3 \ldots x_n$ is to say that $F^n x_2 x_2 x_3 \ldots x_n$. I use the letter '$S$' because this functor is a generalization of the self functor so written by Peirce; there is no connection with Schönfinkel's S as of (2) above.

I propose to show that if a schema of the ordinary logic of quantification and identity is closed, that is, if it has no free variables of the quantifiable sort 'w', 'x', etc., then it can be translated into predicate-functor logic. Given any such schema, we begin by turning it into a certain normal form as follows. Translate all universal quantifiers into existential quantification and negation. Translate the scope of each innermost existential quantifier into alternational normal form and distribute the quantifier through the alternation. Thereupon each innermost quantifier comes to govern, at worst, a conjunction of atomic formulas with or without negation signs attached to them. Rewrite each identity using the predicate 'I'; '$x = y$' becomes 'Ixy'. Rewrite the negation sign '$\sim$' now as '$-$' each time, thus thinking of it as applying no longer to the atomic formulas but to the predicates, and as expressing the Boolean complement. Thus adjusted, the expression following each innermost quantifier is just a simple predication such as 'Ixy', '$-Iyz$', 'F^3zyz', '$-F^3xyz$', etc., or a conjunction of such. Next, if it is a conjunction, merge it into a single predication by forming the Cartesian product of the predicates and concatenating the strings of variables. For instance the conjunction:

$$-Iyz \, . \, F^3zyz \, . \, -F^3xyz$$

becomes:

$$(-I \times F^3 \times -F^3)yzzyzxyz.$$

So now each innermost quantifier governs just a single predication. Next we bring 'p_i' to bear upon this Cartesian product so as to permute the strings of variables. The permutation wanted is that which brings all recurrences of the variable of the quantifier leftward. If our quantification is '$(\exists y)$' followed by the above example, it becomes:

$$(\exists y)p_6 p_3(-I \times F^3 \times -F^3)yyyzzzxz.$$

Next we delete any repetitions of that variable by applying 'S' that many times to the complex predicate. Our example becomes:

$$(\exists y)SSp_6 p_3(-I \times F^3 \times -F^3)yzzzxz.$$

Finally, prefixing '$\mathfrak{z}$' to the complex predicate, we can drop the quantifier and its variable. Our example becomes:

$$\mathfrak{z}SSp_6p_3(-I \times F^3 \times -F^3)zzzxz,$$

having once been '$(\exists y)(y \neq z \,.\, F^3zyz \,.\, \sim F^3xyz)$'.

We have now seen how to eliminate each innermost quantifier. Applying this method then to each surviving quantifier as it becomes innermost, we eliminate all quantifiers and hence all bound variables. In particular a closed schema goes over into a formula purely of predicate-functor logic.

Note that this way of translating innermost quantifications uses just these six devices of predicate-functor logic: '$-$', '$\mathfrak{z}$', 'I', and the defined '$\times$', 'S', and 'p_i'. Nor is any additional provision needed for the truth functions, ultimately negation and conjunction, in which the quantifications may be embedded. For negation, as remarked, is covered by '$-$' in application to formulas of degree 0. Conjunction is similarly covered by '$\cap$', as remarked, but actually '$\cap$' is not needed for the purpose when we have '$\times$'. Applied to formulas of degree 0, '$\cap$' and '$\times$' both collapse to conjunction.

For translating from ordinary logic, therefore, the above six are a more directly useful stock of primitive notations than the ones we adopted; '$\times$', 'S', and 'p_i' are more directly suited to the purpose than '$\mathfrak{r}$', 'p', and '$\cap$'. But I would rather be guided by considerations of intrinsic simplicity than by those of ease of translation. I would seek maximum benefit from the shift of system rather than cling to vestiges of the old. The hope of gaining new insights from the shift of viewpoint is thereby increased.[6]

IX. REVERSE TRANSLATION

Translation in the opposite direction, from predicate-functor logic into the ordinary logical notation, is implemented by the following equivalences.

---

[6]Predicate-functor logic was the burden of my abstract in the *Journal of Symbolic Logic* 24 (1959), 324f, and of my paper "Variables explained away." In that version I took the Cartesian product and the self functor as primitive, instead of intersection, padding, and 'I'. Also there were two permutation functors instead of just 'p'; and cropping operated on the ends of sequences rather than the beginnings. Also the nomenclature and notation were different.

(18) $$-F^n x_1 \ldots x_n \equiv\ \sim F^n x_1 \ldots x_n.$$

(19) $$(F^m \cap G^n) x_1 \ldots x_{\max(m,n)} \equiv_. F^m x_1 \ldots x_m . G^n x \ldots x_n.$$

(20) $$\mathrm{p} F^n x_1 x_3 \ldots x_n x_2 \equiv F_n x_1 \ldots x_n.$$

(21) $$\mathrm{t} F^n x_0 \ldots x_n \equiv F^n x_1 \ldots x_n.$$

(22) $$\mathrm{J} F^n x_2 \ldots x_n \equiv (\exists x_1) F^n x_1 \ldots x_n.$$

(23) $$I x y \equiv_. x = y.$$

Since the predicate-functor logic has no variables 'x_1', 'x_2', etc., any sentential formula of that logic will be of one of the forms (18)–(19) with $m = n = 0$ or else (22) with $n = 1$. As we translate it inward by (18)–(23), structure by structure, variables creep in through the 'x_1' position in (22). Example:

$$\mathrm{J}(G^1 \cap \mathrm{JJ}-\mathrm{pt}(H^2 \cap \mathrm{J}K^2)).$$

This is a case of (22) with $n = 1$. It becomes:

$$(\exists x)(G^1 \cap \mathrm{JJ}-\mathrm{pt}(H^2 \cap \mathrm{J}K^2))x.$$

Here we see, after '$(\exists x)$', a case of (19) with $m = n = 1$. It becomes, with '$(\exists x)$' reattached afterward, this:

$$(\exists x)(G^1 x . \mathrm{JJ}-\mathrm{pt}(H^2 \cap \mathrm{J}K^2)x).$$

The part '$\mathrm{JJ}-\mathrm{pt}(H^2 \cap \mathrm{J}K^2)x$' here has the form (22), with $n = 2$. By (22) twice and (18) it becomes:

$$(\exists y)(\exists z) \sim \mathrm{pt}(H^2 \cap \mathrm{J}K^2)zyx$$

and so, by (20),

$$(\exists y)(\exists z) \sim \mathrm{t}(H^2 \cap \mathrm{J}K^2)zxy$$

and so, by (21),

$$(\exists y) \sim (H^2 \cap \mathrm{J}K^2)xy.$$

Thus the whole becomes:

$$(\exists x)(G^1 x . (\exists y) \sim (H^2 \cap \mathrm{J}K^2)xy).$$

The part '$(H^2 \cap \mathrm{J}K^2)xy$' here is a case of (19) with $m = 2$ and $n = 1$, and so becomes '$H^2 xy . \mathrm{J}K^2 x$'. Its part '$\mathrm{J}K^2 x$', finally, becomes '$(\exists z)K^2 zx$' by (22). So the translation of the whole is:

$$(\exists x)(G^1 x . (\exists y) \sim (H^2 xy . (\exists z)K^2 zx)).$$

Since the predicate-functor logic is just intertranslatable with the ordinary logic of quantification and identity, its elimination of variables may be seen as a purer analysis of the variable than Schönfinkel's. Actually both analyses bring out that the essential services of the variable are the permutation of predicate places and the linking of predicate places by identity. The permutation job is discharged in our predicate-functor logic by the functors 'p_i', and the linking job by the self functor 'S'. In Schönfinkel's approach the permutation job was discharged mainly by his combinator S (unrelated to the self functor) and the linking job by the combinator W. But the burden of the variable is less clearly divided and apportioned in Schönfinkel's scheme because his scheme bears so much further burden.

X. EXISTENCE AND SINGULAR TERMS

The existential force of quantification, at any rate, is no essential or distinctive service of the variable; it is carried as well by the cropping functor '$\mathfrak{z}$' and, for that matter, by the Boolean '$\neq \Lambda$'.

Care must be taken here against a possible misunderstanding. When a theory is given the usual quantificational form, the things that the theory accepts as existing are indeed the things that it accepts as the values of its variables of quantification. If a theory is given another form, moreover, there is no sense in asking what the theory accepts as existing except as we are in a position to say how to translate the theory into the usual quantificational form. I have long urged these points, and I continue to. When we switch to predicate-functor logic, such a mode of translation is available; we have just seen it. In the light of it, we find that the things that a theory in predicate-functor form accepts as existing are the things that satisfy its predicates; the things that any of its one-place predicates (complements included!) are true of. But then we note also this special further circumstance: the things that a theory in the usual quantificational form accepts as existing could *also* be described as the things that satisfy its predicates (and their complements). These are the same as the values of the quantified variables, for a theory in the usual quantificational form. So the characterization in terms of satisfaction of predicates does have the advantage of applying equally and outright to theories in quantificational form and theories in predicate-functor form, without having to be funneled through a translation.

It is well known that theories in ordinary quantificational form can get along without any singular terms beyond the variables of quantification. A name, say 'a', can be dispensed with in favor of a predicate 'A' that is true uniquely of the object a; for we can then paraphrase 'Fa' as '$(\exists x)(Fx \cdot Ax)$'. Complex singular terms can be dispensed with in a somewhat similar fashion. Practically the move is a poor one, since it sacrifices the natural and convenient steps of inference that consist in direct substitution of names and complex terms for variables. Theoretically it is of interest, as simplifying certain systematic formulations.

The elimination of quantifiers and their variables which the predicate-functor logic achieves is not, it will be noted, an elimination by restoration of names or other singular terms. Schönfinkel's procedure depended indeed on constant abstract singular terms, which named functions; but predicate-functor logic does not. There are no singular terms any more—neither variables nor the constants that might have been substituted for them. So what becomes of a theory's names, one may ask, when the theory is put into predicate-functor form? First they are dropped in favor of predicates, as just explained; 'a' in favor of 'A'. Then these predicates survive under the predicate-functor plan. What had been *one* way of handling names, and a way having only theoretical interest, comes now to be *the* way. 'Fa' goes into the predicate-functor idiom as '$\mathbf{1}(F^1 \cap A^1)$', via the intermediate stage '$(\exists x)(Fx \cdot Ax)$'.

It is in keeping with the motivation of the present study that a way of handling names that was of purely theoretical value and practically inconvenient in the quantificational setting should become mandatory in the predicate-functor setting. For the purpose of predicate-functor logic is itself theoretical: a deeper understanding of the variable. There is no thought of forswearing the practical convenience of quantification and the convenience of substituting names and complex singular terms for quantified variables.

XI. PROOF PROCEDURE

Since the predicate-functor approach to logic differs so radically from the quantificational approach, and since it seems somehow more basic, one wonders how a simple and complete proof procedure for it might look, and what new light it might shed on logic.

Bernays presents axioms for one form of his algebra, and proves that they are complete. He presupposes a usual logic of truth functions, identity, and Boolean equations. To this basis he adds thirteen axioms or axiom schemata, mostly in the form of equations, governing cylindrification, degree, his permutation operators, and I.

Our predicate-functor logic calls rather for an autonomous proof procedure, presupposing no prior logic. Instead of undertaking to limit the theorems to schemata of degree 0 whose instances are true sentences, it is convenient to welcome as theorems all schemata of any degree whose instances are predicates satisfied by all sequences of that length.[7] As an infinite initial stock of axiom schemata, then, we may accept all tautologous Boolean functions; that is, all compounds built of '$-$' and '$\cap$' after the pattern of a truth-table tautology in '$\sim$' and '$.$'. A natural rule of inference to adopt is the analogue, in these Boolean terms, of *modus ponens*; viz.,

$$\text{If } \vdash \zeta \text{ and } \vdash \ulcorner \zeta \supset \eta \urcorner \text{ then } \vdash \eta$$

where the *implex* '$F^m \supset G^n$' is defined as '$-(F^m \cap -G^n)$'. Further there is this triple rule:

$$\text{If } \vdash \zeta \text{ then } \vdash \ulcorner p\zeta \urcorner, \ \vdash \ulcorner \mathfrak{c}\zeta \urcorner, \text{ and } \vdash \ulcorner -\mathfrak{z}-\zeta \urcorner.$$

Also a rule of substitution for predicate letters is wanted, allowing substitution of predicate expressions of any degree for predicate letters of that degree. This rule includes the subsidiary rule, explained earlier, for computing the degree of a complex expression.

Some of the axiom schemata that suggest themselves, in addition to the Boolean tautologies, are these:

$$\mathfrak{z}I, \quad (I \cap F^n) \supset \mathrm{p}^{n-2}\mathfrak{z}\mathrm{p}\mathfrak{c}F^n, \quad -\mathfrak{z}F^n \supset \mathfrak{z}-F^n, \quad F^n \supset \mathfrak{c}\mathfrak{z}F^n.$$

Before stating further ones, it will be convenient to adopt as an abbreviation one more Boolean functor along with '$\supset$'. The *concourse* or symmetric quotient $F^m \# G^n$ is defined as $(F^m \supset G^n) \cap (G^n \supset F^m)$; thus it is $(F^m \cap G^n) \cup (-F^m \cap -G^n)$.[8] Just as '$\supset$' as main connective in an axiom does the work of '$\supset$', so '$\#$' does the work of '$\equiv$' or '$=$'. Provision would be made for a

---

[7] This and other features of the system were anticipated by Nolin.

[8] The names and symbols of the implex and concourse are from my *System of Logistic*.

convenient metatheorem allowing replacement, anywhere, of one side of a proved concourse by the other.

Here, then, are two likely further axiom schemata.

$$F^n \mathrel{\#} \mathrm{p}^{n-1}F^n, \qquad\qquad F^n \mathrel{\#} \mathfrak{X}F^n.$$

Also there are these distribution laws.

$$\mathfrak{r} - F^n \mathrel{\#} -\mathfrak{r}F^n, \qquad \mathfrak{r}(F^m \cap G^n) \mathrel{\#} (\mathfrak{r}F^m \cap \mathfrak{r}G^n),$$
$$\mathrm{p} - F^n \mathrel{\#} -\mathrm{p}F^n, \qquad \mathrm{p}(F^m \cap G^n) \mathrel{\#} (\mathrm{p}F^m \cap \mathrm{p}G^n).$$

(For the last of the four we should require that $m, n > 2$.) A major agendum is a proof of the completeness of some such proof procedure, or, better, of some other and more instructively unified sort of proof procedure for predicate-functor logic.

29

🐦 *Truth and Disquotation*

I. INTRODUCTION

The reader is familiar, I shall assume, with Tarski's method of defining truth.[1] Let me nevertheless sum up, for later reference, some of its significant traits. The goal is a truth predicate, 'is true', that is defined for the general context 'x is true', but defined in such a way as to fulfill the following schema whenever applied to the quotation of an actual sentence:

(1) $\qquad$ ' . . . . . . ' is true $\equiv$ . . . .

Tarski shows how to achieve this for any formalized language whose logical form is the classical logic of quantification. Most of the construction is an inductive definition of satisfaction, conceived as a relation of sequences to open or closed sentences. This inductive definition consists of a finite lot of sentences couched in a metalanguage that is an extension of the object language. The metalanguage contains, in addition to the object language, a name of each sign of the object language; also a functor whereby to refer to arbitrary complex expressions of the object language as functions of their components. Also it contains apparatus for referring to sequences of objects and recovering the occupants of their successive places. Also it contains the

Talks with Donald Davidson prompted my renewed preoccupation with Tarski's theory of truth and did much to set the lines of the present study. In 1970 I submitted the paper as an advance contribution to the symposium that was held in honor of Tarski at Berkeley in June 1971. It is reprinted with permission of the American Mathematical Society from *Proceedings of Symposia in Pure Mathematics*, vol. 25, pp. 373–384, © 1974. Portions are omitted in favor of cross-references.

[1]For a quick account see Chap. 3 of my *Philosophy of Logic*.

definiendum itself, the two-place predicate of satisfaction; for the definition, being inductive, does not in general make for elimination of its definiendum in the presence of variable arguments. Or, as Tarski observes, we can render the satisfaction predicate eliminable by furnishing the metalanguage with as much of the machinery of set theory as is needed for turning the inductive definition into a direct one.

Tarski's project was directed upon deductive systems, and he required that each instance of his schema (1) be deducible from the truth definition. But I shall be concerned with interpreted languages without regard to axiomatization, so I require only that the truth definition make the instances of the schema (1) come out true.[2]

The sequences to which Tarski's definition appeals are infinite sequences. There is a way of making do with finite sequences, but still it appeals to those sequences in their infinite generality, without limit of length. Moreover, one among the clauses of Tarski's inductive definition stands forth as more devious and complex than the rest; namely, the clause that copes with quantification. Both of these complications in Tarski's definition are occasioned by the apparatus, in the object language, of quantification and variables. One's thoughts consequently turn to other styles of logic, in which the work of quantifiers and variables is managed by constants. Will such systems open a shorter avenue to the truth predicate? I propose to explore this question in connection with Schönfinkel's combinatory logic,[3] which is a language of full set-theoretic strength, and in connection also with what I call predicate-functor logic, which is no stronger than the ordinary logic of quantification and identity. For Schönfinkel's language we get something that may be called *disquotation*— and in a stronger sense of the word than what Tarski's schema (1) above requires. We shall observe, further, why a general inductive definition of disquotation for arbitrary notations does not go through similarly. Finally, reverting to quantification of

[2] I am indebted to John Wallace for prompting this caveat.

[3] See §§II–IV of the preceding essay. But I now depart from the notation there used for functional application, namely the inverted comma, in favor of the form of notation '*f(x)*'. I do so to avoid confusion with quotation marks, and also so as not to have to add rules for the use of parentheses in grouping. These considerations matter now because of a need to be explicit about metalogical maneuvers.

a sort, we shall consider what happens to the truth definition when quantification is construed in terms of substitution rather than objective reference.

II. TRUTH FOR SCHÖNFINKEL'S LANGUAGE

The inductive truth definition for this object language will be couched in a metalanguage that contains the object language and contains in addition only the definiens ('$\triangle$', below) and a notation for naming the expressions of the object language. The names of the letters 'S', 'C', and 'ι' will be formed, as just here, by direct quotation. The form of expression 'ap(x, y)' will be used in the metalanguage to refer to the complex name that is formed by functional application from the respective names x and y in the object language. In other words, ap(x, y) consists of x followed by y in parentheses. Thus

$$\text{ap('}S\text{', '}C\text{')} = \text{'}S(C)\text{'.}$$

Tarski defined the truth of a closed sentence as a special or limiting case of satisfaction. A comparable indirectness is called for here, but now the intermediate concept to be inductively defined is that of the *designatum* rather than satisfaction. I shall write '$\triangle(x)$' for the designatum of x, the thing named by the formula x. The aim of the definition is to assure that every equation of the form

$$(2) \qquad\qquad \triangle(\text{' } \ldots \ldots \text{'}) = \ldots \ldots ,$$

with any one name in the blanks, come out true. This is achieved by an inductive definition which, in a preliminary rendering, runs simply thus:

$$(3) \qquad \triangle(\text{'}S\text{'}) = S, \qquad \triangle(\text{'}C\text{'}) = C, \qquad \triangle(\text{'}\iota\text{'}) = \iota,$$

$$(4) \qquad\qquad \triangle(\text{ap}(x, y)) = \triangle(x)(\triangle(y)).$$

This already defines truth. For, truth is the special case of $\triangle$ where the argument is a sentence. Where x is a sentence, '$\triangle(x)$' amounts to 'x is true'. This is evident from the schemata (1) and (2) when we keep in mind that sentences now are names, names of ⊤ and ⊥.

I called (3)–(4) a preliminary rendering because it is couched in an excessive idiom. We see these further symbols that are foreign to the announced metalanguage: '=', 'x', 'y', and the comma of 'x, y'. I shall dispose of the comma first. Schönfinkel explained two-place functions in Frege's way: he explained a two-place function f as the one-place function which, applied to anything x, yields as value $f(x)$ a one-place function which, applied to anything y, yields as value the desired $f(x, y)$. In short, $f(x, y)$ is $f(x)(y)$. We may render 'ap(x, y)' accordingly. (4) becomes

(5) $$\triangle(\mathrm{ap}(x)(y)) = \triangle(x)(\triangle(y)).$$

The variables 'x' and 'y' will next be disposed of. It is known that Schönfinkel's S and C are *combinatorially complete*, in this sense: any desired permutation and regrouping of any of the terms in a formula beyond the first, and any fusing of recurrences, can be achieved by applying to the first term some function compounded purely of S and C. In particular we can express, purely in terms of S, C, and functional application, two functions Φ and Ψ that have the following effects:

$$\Phi(\triangle)(\mathrm{ap})(x)(y) = \triangle(\mathrm{ap}(x)(y)).$$

$$\Psi(\triangle)(x)(y) = \triangle(x)(\triangle(y)).$$

Accordingly (5) becomes

$$\Phi(\triangle)(\mathrm{ap})(x)(y) = \Psi(\triangle)(x)(y).$$

But to affirm this for all x and y is simply to identify the functions thus:

$$\Phi(\triangle)(\mathrm{ap}) = \Psi(\triangle).$$

Finally, we know how to translate '=' into terms of ι; '$x = y$' becomes '$\iota(x)(y)$'. So the above equation and those in (3) go over into full Schöfinkel style thus:

(6) $\iota(\triangle('S'))(S)$, $\iota(\triangle('C'))(C)$, $\iota(\triangle('\iota'))(\iota)$, $\iota(\Phi(\triangle)(\mathrm{ap}))(\Psi(\triangle))$.

For readers conversant with Schönfinkel it would be a routine exercise to expand 'Φ' and 'Ψ' appropriately into terms of S and C. So now the four clauses of the inductive definition of designatum are couched completely in the signs of the object language plus their quotations and 'ap' (and of course the definiendum itself). The version (3)–(4), however, is the one to turn to whenever perspicuity is in point.

III. CONTRAST WITH TARSKI'S CONSTRUCTION

A certain similarity was noted between the role of designatum in the above definition of truth and the role of satisfaction in Tarski's. Both are defined inductively, as a means of defining truth. In both constructions, truth falls out at the end as a special case. But there are notable differences. One difference is that truth is a special case more directly of designatum than of satisfaction.

A more conspicuous contrast between the two constructions is seen in Tarski's dependence on an apparatus of sequences, and in the complexity of his recursion clause regarding quantifiers (see §I above). The striking simplicity of the present inductive definition of designatum and truth for combinatory logic is due to the freedom of this object language from variables and quantifiers.

Expressions that are built up in the metalanguage by applying 'ap' to quoted letters may in a broad sense be called *quotations*. They are, in Tarski's phrase, structural-descriptive equivalents of quotations. E.g.,

$$\text{ap}(\text{ap}(`\iota', `S'), `S') = `\iota(S)(S)'.$$

(For perspicuity I revert to the style of 'ap(x, y)' now that (6) is finished.) Now an interesting third point of contrast between the designatum approach to truth and Tarski's approach is that the designatum approach renders truth as a direct *disquotation*. That is, if you attribute truth to a sentence by attaching the truth predicate (or '$\triangle$') to a quotation of the sentence, and then you eliminate '$\triangle$' step by step according to the inductive definition (6) (or, more intuitively, (3)–(4)), you come out with the very sentence that had been quoted and not just some equivalent.

Thus take the above example. We want to say that '$\iota(S)(S)$' is true. That is,

$$(7) \qquad\qquad \triangle(\text{ap}(\text{ap}(`\iota', `S'), `S')).$$

Now let us unwind this according to the definition (3)–(4). By (4) we reduce (7) successively thus:

$$\triangle(\text{ap}(`\iota', `S'))(\triangle(`S')), \qquad \triangle(`\iota')(\triangle(`S'))(\triangle(`S')),$$

and this reduces by (3) to:

$$\iota(S)(S).$$

If we work not with the inductive definition (3)–(4) but with its equivalent (6) in Schönfinkel style, the unwinding of (7) will depend in part upon laws governing the Φ and Ψ that were used in (6). Those laws would come down ultimately to the logical laws governing S and C. So, when I say that the inductive definition (6) renders truth as direct disquotation, I do not deny the need of logical transformations in the unwinding. My point is rather this: as soon as the unwinding has done its job of eliminating the last metalinguistic sign so that only a formula of the object language remains, that formula will be literally the formula that was quoted in the first place and not just an equivalent.

This disquotational property is stronger than what is called for by Tarski's classical schema (1), and it is not preserved under Tarski's inductive definition of satisfaction. What we usually come out with under Tarski's truth definition is not literally the sentence to whose quotation the truth predicate had been attached, but another sentence that is equivalent to it under the logical laws of quantification and identity.

The direct disquotational character that we have observed in our truth construction holds, of course, for our designatum construction generally. It matters none whether the formula whose quotation is appended to '$\triangle$' is a sentence or is a name of a function; the effect is just to disquote the quoted formula, whatever it is. Take, say, '$S(C(\iota)(S))$'; that is,

$$\text{ap}('S', \text{ap}(\text{ap}('C', '\iota'), 'S')).$$

Apply $\triangle$:

(8) $$\triangle(\text{ap}('S', \text{ap}(\text{ap}('C', '\iota'), 'S'))).$$

Proceeding then to unwind by (3) and (4), we recover precisely the formula originally quoted:

(9) $$S(C(\iota)(S)).$$

This is obvious from (3) and (4). But it is not obvious in the way one imagines who might say, "Of course, that is what 'designatum' means: the very formula that was named." That would be a confusion. Any version of designatum would be worthy of the name as long as it fulfilled the schema (2); and it could fulfill (2) even though its definition were to unwind (8) not into (9)

but into the different expression '$S(\iota)$'. For it happens that $S(\iota)$
and $S(C(\iota)(S))$ are the same object, the same function, since
$C(x)(y) = x$. This thing $S(\iota)$ *is* the designatum of

$$\text{ap}(\text{'}S\text{'}, \text{ap}(\text{ap}(\text{'}C\text{'}, \text{'}\iota\text{'}), \text{'}S\text{'})),$$

that is, of '$S(C(\iota)(S))$', just as genuinely as is $S(C(\iota)(S))$; for
$S(\iota)$ is $S(C(\iota)(S))$. But the special point about the definition
(3)–(4) of designatum is that it unwinds (8) directly and literally
into (9) rather than into '$S(\iota)$', and that it unwinds '$\triangle(\text{ap}(\text{'}S\text{'},$
'ι'))' directly and literally into '$S(\iota)$' rather than into (9).

IV. DISQUOTATION IN THE GENERAL CASE

Thus '$\triangle$' emerges as a disquotation operator. To this trait we
are indebted for two advantages that the designatum approach
has been seen to have over the satisfaction approach: the avoidance of sequence theory, and the avoidance of the complex recursion condition regarding quantification. To what extent are
these benefits tied to the Schönfinkel style of language? Can we
define disquotation for languages more generally?

At first it seems so. Consider an arbitrary language. Suppose
its signs are the Greek letters. To define a general disquotation
operator 'disq' for this language inductively, we begin with twenty-
four definitions explaining the notations:

disq alpha, disq beta, . . . , disq omega

respectively as:

$$\alpha, \beta, \ldots, \omega,$$

and then, using Tarski's arch symbol of concatenation, we provide
for recursion by explaining 'disq $x^\frown y$' in general as 'disq x disq y'.

Disquotation for Schönfinkel's formulas took the form of a
designatum function $\triangle$, since all his formulas are names—whether
of functions or of truth values. I have had now to write 'disq'
instead of '$\triangle$', because the expressions of our unspecified Greek-
letter language are not known to be names. For the same reason,
I am unable to render the inductive definition of 'disq' by the
equations:

disq alpha = α, . . . , disq omega = ω,

$$\text{disq } x \,^\frown y = \text{disq } x \text{ disq } y$$

since, failing some special convention, it is incoherent to put '=' between expressions other than singular terms. For the same reason we can write no analogue of the schema (1) or (2) for disquotation generally; '=' is not available, nor '≡'.

Note that 'alpha', 'beta', 'alpha⁀beta', etc., are indeed names or singular terms in good standing in the metalanguage; and 'disq' is an operator on such terms. But it is an odd one, yielding in general neither a term nor a sentence as output. Some of the expressions 'α', 'β', '$\alpha\beta$', etc., that are named by 'alpha', 'beta', 'alpha⁀beta', etc., can be gibberish.

We begin to see the obstacle to such a general inductive definition of disquotation. We may see the obstacle more clearly if, to begin with, we consider how far we can proceed unobstructed. For definitions in the narrow sense, the genuinely eliminative definitions, any medium of presentation is of course welcome as long as it gives an effective procedure for transforming the defined sign or its contexts into previous notation. Thus the account of 'disq' three paragraphs back satisfactorily defines 'disq' in application to all singular cases, however long; all constant spellings. For it gives an effective procedure for eliminating 'disq' from any such context. It explains 'disq alpha⁀kappa⁀rho⁀omicron⁀nu' as '$\alpha\kappa\rho\sigma\nu$', and no matter whether this string of signs is a name or a sentence or an incoherency in the imagined language.

But that account of 'disq' is no good as an inductive definition of 'disq x' for variable 'x'. For consider what is wanted of such a definition. One way in which its clauses may be used is as axioms governing 'disq' but not eliminating it. For such axiomatic use the clauses must have the explicit form of sentences in the metalanguage. Or perhaps the inductive definition is destined to be turned into a direct and eliminative definition of 'disq x', by recourse to a sufficiently strong set theory. But a direct definition so obtained incorporates those clauses as component sentences. Thus for either purpose the inductive definition would have to use 'disq' in some grammatical position in sentences. But in the general case this is impossible. In general 'disq' attaches to a singular term uniformly enough, but the trouble is that the grammatical category of the resulting compound may be any or none, depending as it does on the reference of that singular term.

V. PREDICATE FUNCTORS

Schönfinkel's language lent itself to an inductively well-defined and generally applicable disquotation operator '$\triangle$'. One conspicuous trait of that language is the absence of variables. Another trait, which contributed to the success of the definition, is that each formula of Schönfinkel's language is a name of something. One is disinclined, however, to rest with Schönfinkel's language. One is put off by its excessive power. It is adequate for general set theory, and is heir to all the problems raised by the antinomies of set theory.

Tarski's inductive definition of satisfaction, and therewith of truth, is geared to any system couched in the framework of the classical logic of quantification; it is not reserved to strong object languages. So a natural next thought is to see how disquotation might fare in what I call *predicate-functor* logic.[4] For this is no stronger than the classical logic of quantification and identity; indeed it is intertranslatable with that. And at the same time it resembles Schönfinkel's logic in dispensing with variables. Its way of dispensing with them even resembles Schönfinkel's, up to a point.

In Schönfinkel's language the well-formed formulas were names. They named functions or, at the extreme, truth values. Hence the disquotation functor took the form there of the name of a designatum function. In the predicate-functor language, on the other hand, the well-formed formulas are n-place predicates or, at the extreme ($n = 0$), sentences. Here, consequently, disquotation will take the form of a functor 'sat' of satisfaction. It differs in category from Tarski's satisfaction, which is a relation. The functor 'sat' attaches to a name, or singular term, to form a predicate. In interesting cases, that singular term names a predicate.

EXAMPLE.

sat 'is human'.

The complex predicate thus formed may be read:

satisfies 'is human'

---

[4]See preceding essay, last four sections.

and is hence meant to be coextensive with the originally named predicate itself:

is human.

Since singular terms are foreign to predicate-functor logic, the functor 'sat' will require some adapting if it is to fit into a metalanguage that is a direct extension of this object language. In predicate-functor logic the role of singular terms is played by predicates. Instead of having a singular term that names an object x, we make do with a predicate that is true solely of x. Adapted accordingly, 'sat' becomes a predicate functor; where 'F^1' is a predicate that is true solely of a predicate 'G^n', 'sat F^1' becomes an n-place predicate coextensive with 'G^n'.

As George Myro has pointed out to me, however, trouble remains. We cannot determine the degree of 'sat F^1' without some prior knowledge as to what 'F^1' is true of. Consequently we cannot subject 'sat F^1' to predicate-functor logic; for it is evident from the explanation of the permutation functor, in particular, that the logical transformations can hinge upon the degree of a predicate.

Nor is the difficulty resolved by retreating to a metalanguage of ordinary quantificational form. Here 'sat' would revert to the status of a predicate-yielding functor upon singular terms; 'sat x' would become, for each predicate x, a predicate coextensive with x. Its degree would depend on that of x and would thus be indeterminate for variable 'x'. The ordinary logic of quantification has no place for a predicate symbol 'sat x' of variable degree.

Truth *can* be defined for a predicate-functor style of language in a predicate-functor style of metalanguage, or again in a quantificational style of metalanguage. This is assured by the fact that predicate-functor logic and the classical logic of quantification and identity are intertranslatable. We can use Tarski's truth definition in double translation: first we transform it to match the translation of the object language from quantificational style to predicate-functor style, and then we translate the resulting truth definition from its quantificational style of metalanguage into predicate-functor style. This is a routine exercise. A few corners can be cut, but not enough, so far as I have seen, to be interesting.

VI. SUBSTITUTIONAL QUANTIFICATION

Tarski's satisfaction relation has to do with objective reference, relating open sentences as it does to sequences of objects that are values of the variables. Disquotation as such is indifferent to objective reference; but in §IV our attempt at an inductive definition of disquotation broke down in the general case. An inductive definition of disquotation did go through nicely for Schönfinkel's combinatory logic, and this was because a suitable connective was available that was not available for the general case of disquotation. It was the connective '$=$' of identity (or its equivalent in terms of ι); and disquotation was the designatum function $\triangle$, a matter of objective reference after all. Are objective reference and the definition of truth then inseparable?

For further light on this question let us try defining truth for a quantificational form of language whose quantifiers are explained in terms not of objective values of variables but of notational substitutions for variables.[5]

Again our metalanguage is to contain qu tations of the signs of the object language and again the arch of concatenation and, as usual, the logic of quantification and identity (and hence singular description). In short, it is to contain what I have called protosyntax.[6] Its quantifiers may even be read substitutionally, since the relevant values of the variables are quotable expressions. Now it is well known that in protosyntax we can define notations to the following effect, if the object language follows usual and reasonable lines.

Sen x: x is a sentence (of the object language).
Var x: x is a variable (of the object language).
Term x: x is a singular term (of the object language).
$\text{subst}_y^z x$:   the result of substituting z for y in x.
$\text{qfn}_y x$:   the universal quantification of x on the variable y.

Let us now look to what one thinks of as the hard part of a truth definition: the recursion dealing with quantifiers. This goes through lucidly in terms of the truth predicate itself.

(10) $(x)(y)(\text{Sen } x \, . \, \text{Var } y \, . \supset .$
$$\text{True}(\text{qfn}_y x) \equiv (z)(\text{Term } z \supset \text{True}(\text{subst}_y^z x))).$$

[5]For more on substitutional quantification see Essays 16 and 27 above, "Reply to Professor Marcus" and "The variable."
[6]*Mathematical Logic*, last chapter.

There is no talk here of satisfaction or of sequences or, indeed, of objective reference at all.[7] Even the metalinguistic quantifiers '(x)', '(y)', and '(z)' in (10) can be read substitutionally, as remarked.

In the inductive definitions hitherto considered, the work has come in the recursion clauses. The initial clauses were effortless; witness (3). But now the tables turn. The recursion clause (10) is straightforward. The recursion clauses for truth functions are transparent.

(11) $\text{True}(\text{neg } x) \equiv {\sim}\text{True } x, \quad \text{True}(\text{conj } xy) \equiv . \text{True } x . \text{True } y.$

The initial clauses are now the serious part: the definition of truth for atomic sentences devoid of variables.

If substitutional quantification is not to resolve to mere finite conjunction without quantifiers, the supply of substitutible terms must be infinite or indefinite. Singular descriptions, moreover, are not in point; they are contextually definable as usual, and the definition uses quantification. They should be supposed eliminated by contextual definition at the start. But there will be, we may suppose, an infinite stock of constant terms, built from a finite lot of simple terms by iteration of a finite lot of grammatical constructions. The atomic sentences will consist each of a primitive predicate followed by one or more of these perhaps quite long terms as arguments. The sentences are atomic in the sense of containing no further sentences; they may contain complex terms.

EXAMPLE. '0' might be the sole simple term, and the grammatical construction might be application of the successor accent. Then the terms are the numerals '0', '0′', '0″', etc. The primitive predicates might be the triadic predicates 'Σ' and 'Π' of sum and product:

$$\Sigma xyz \equiv . x = y + z, \qquad \Pi xyz \equiv . x = yz.$$

Each atomic sentence consists of 'Σ' or 'Π' followed by three numerals. Truth functions and substitutional quantification complete the language—a redundant language of elementary number theory.

We can define truth directly for the atomic sentences of this language. Truth for them is decidable, and any decidable predicate of expressions is translatable into protosyntax. Since the re-

[7]This point is remarked by Parsons.

cursions (10) and (11) also can be rendered in that medium, we see that truth for this language of elementary number theory is inductively definable in protosyntax. Or, what is equivalent, it is inductively definable in elementary number theory via Gödel numbering. And indeed it was so defined, along just these lines, by Hilbert and Bernays.[8]

There is a striking contrast between this sort of truth definition and the others. No longer do we build up some preliminary and more general notion of satisfaction or designatum or disquotation, from which to draw truth as a special case. No longer does the disquotational pattern show itself at all, except slightly in the recursion clauses (11). No longer is there any appeal to sequences of objects, of course, nor to objective reference at all; for quantification here is reconstrued in terms of substitution of expressions that need not name anything.

And yet, curiously, the special subject matter of the object language plays a more distinctive role in this truth definition than in Tarski's. Tarski's definition could be fitted to any specific theory, of the classical quantificational pattern, by just filling in the predicates and names and functors specific to that theory. In defining truth for a theory built on substitutional quantification, on the other hand, the main job comes in the atomic sentences; and the lines that this job takes will vary utterly with the structure of the particular theory at hand. The lines that the job takes in our present example of number theory are those of the computation of sums and products.

In this particular example, the adequacy of protosyntax for an inductive definition of truth was assured by the direct protosyntactical definability of decidable predicates. But protosyntax is adequate likewise to an inductive definition of truth for theories in which the atomic sentences are not decidable. What is required, obviously, is just the direct protosyntactical definability of truth for the atomic sentences. This is a very liberal requirement. It does not even require that the atomic sentences admit of a complete proof procedure, let alone a decision procedure. The class of atomic truths can stand at any level of Kleene's arithmetical hierarchy; (10) and (11) will still round out the truth definition for atomic sentences into a full inductive truth definition, with protosyntax as metalanguage. If on the other hand a theory built on substitutional quantification has atomic sentences whose truth is stubborn to a hyperarithmetical degree, or is to be left open indefinitely for empirical determination, then there is in protosyntax no hope of an inductive truth definition for the theory. A truth definition in Tarski's style, not in protosyntax, could of course still be available.

References

Bar-Hillel, Yehoshua. "Bolzano's definition of analytic propositions," *Methodos* 2 (1950), 32–55 [= *Theoria* 16 (1950), 91–117].

Behmann, Heinrich. *Mathematik und Logik.* Leipzig, 1927.

———. "Sind die mathematischen Urteile analytisch oder synthetisch?" *Erkenntnis* 4 (1934), 1–27.

Bernays, Paul. "Axiomatische Untersuchungen des Aussagen-Kalkuls der 'Principia Mathematica,' "*Mathematische Zeitschrift* 25 (1926), 305–320.

———. "A system of axiomatic set theory," *Journal of Symbolic Logic* 2, 6–8, 13, 19 (1937, 1941–1943, 1948, 1954).

———. "Ueber eine natürliche Erweiterung des Relationenkalküls," in A. Heyting, ed., *Constructivity in Mathematics* (Amsterdam: North Holland, 1959), 1–14.

———, and A. A. Fraenkel. *Axiomatic Set Theory.* Amsterdam: North Holland, 1958.

Berry, G. D. W. "On the ontological significance of the Löwenheim-Skolem theorem," in *Academic Freedom, Logic, and Religion* (Philadelphia: University of Pennsylvania Press, for American Philosophical Association, 1953), 39–55.

Bridgman, P. W. "A physicist's second reaction to Mengenlehre," *Scripta Mathematica* 2 (1933–1934), 101–117, 224–234.

Cantor, Georg. *Gesammelte Abhandlungen mathematischen und philosophischen Inhalts.* Berlin, 1932.

Carnap, Rudolf. *Physikalische Begriffsbildung.* Karlsruhe, 1926.

———. *Der logische Aufbau der Welt.* Berlin, 1928.

———. *Logische Syntax der Sprache.* Vienna, 1934. Translation with additions: *The Logical Syntax of Language*, New York and London, 1937.

———. *Philosophy and Logical Syntax.* London, 1935.

———. *Meaning and Necessity.* Chicago: University of Chicago Press, 1947. 2d ed., with supplements, 1956.

———. *Logical Foundations of Probability.* Vol. 1, *Probability and Induction.* Chicago: University of Chicago Press, 1950.

———. "Die Antinomien und die Vollständigkeit der Mathematik," *Monatshefte für Mathematik und Physik* 41 (1934), 263–284.

———. "Ein Gültigkeitskriterium für die Sätze der klassischen Mathematik," ibid. 42 (1935), 163–190.

———. "Empiricism, semantics, and ontology," *Revue internationale de philosophie* 11 (1950), 20–40. Reprinted in *Meaning and Necessity*, 2d ed., and in Linsky.

——. "Meaning postulates," *Philosophical Studies* 3 (1952), 65–73. Reprinted in *Meaning and Necessity*, 2d ed.

Carroll, Lewis. "What the tortoise said to Achilles," *Mind* 4 (1895), 278–280.

Chomsky, Noam. "Linguistics and philosophy," in S. Hook, ed., *Language and Philosophy* (New York: New York University Press, 1969), 51–94.

Church, Alonzo. *A Bibliography of Symbolic Logic.* Providence, 1938. Reprinted from *Journal of Symbolic Logic* 1 (1936), 3 (1938).

——. *The Calculi of Lambda Conversion.* Princeton: Princeton University Press, 1941.

——. "An unsolvable problem of number theory," *American Journal of Mathematics* 58 (1936), 345–363.

——. "A note on the Entscheidungsproblem," *Journal of Symbolic Logic* 1 (1936), 40f, 101f.

——. Review of Quine, ibid. 8 (1943), 45–47.

——. "On Carnap's analysis of statements of assertion and belief," *Analysis* 10 (1950), 97–99.

Craig, William. "Replacement of auxiliary expressions," *Philosophical Review* 65 (1956), 38–55.

Curry, H. B. "Grundlagen der kombinatorischen Logik," *American Journal of Mathematics* 52 (1930), 509–536, 789–834.

——, and Robert Feys. *Combinatory Logic.* Amsterdam: North-Holland, 1958.

De Morgan, Augustus. *A Budget of Paradoxes.* London, 1872.

Dubislav, Walter. "Über das Verhältnis der Logik zur Mathematik," *Annalen der Philosophie* 5 (1925), 193–208.

Duhem, Pierre. *La théorie physique: Son objet et sa structure.* Paris, 1906.

Frege, Gottlob. *Grundlagen der Arithmetik.* Breslau, 1884. Reprint with English translation as *The Foundations of Arithmetic*, New York: Philosophical Library; Oxford: Blackwell's, 1950.

——. *Grundgesetze der Arithmetik.* Vol. 1, 1893; vol. 2, 1903. Jena.

——. Über Sinn und Bedeutung." *Zeitschrift für Philosophie und philosophische Kritik* 100 (1892), 22–50. Translated in *Translations from the Philosophical Writings of Gottlob Frege* (Oxford: Blackwell's, 1952).

Geach, P. T. "Subject and predicate," *Mind* 59 (1950), 461–482.

Gergonne, J. D. "Essai sur la théorie des définitions," *Annales de mathématique pure et appliquée* 9 (1818–1819), 1–35.

Gödel, Kurt. *The Consistency of the Continuum Hypothesis.* Princeton: Princeton University Press, 1940.

——. "Ueber formal unentscheidbare Sätze der Principia Mathematica und verwandter Systeme," *Monatshefte für Mathematik und Physik* 38 (1931), 173–198. Translated in van Heijenoort.

Goodman, Nelson. *The Structure of Appearance.* Cambridge, Mass.: Harvard University Press, 1951.

——, and W. V. Quine. "Steps toward a constructive nominalism," *Journal of Symbolic Logic* 12 (1947), 97–122.

Grelling, Kurt, and Leonhard Nelson. "Bemerkungen zu den Paradoxien von Russell und Burali-Forti," *Abhandlungen der Fries'schen Schule* 2 (1907–1908), 300–334.

Halmos, P. R. "Algebraic logic (II)," *Fundamenta Mathematicae* 43 (1956), 255–325.

Henkin, Leon, "The representation theorem for cylindrical algebras," in T. Skolem et al., *Mathematical Interpretations of Formal Systems* (Amsterdam: North Holland, 1953), 85–97.

Hilbert, David. "Die Grundlagen der Mathematik," *Abhandlungen aus dem mathematischen Seminar der Hamburgischen Universität* 6 (1928), 65–85.

———, and Wilhelm Ackermann. *Grundzüge der theoretischen Logik.* 2d ed., Berlin, 1938. Translation: *Principles of Mathematical Logic*, New York: Chelsea, 1950.

———, and Paul Bernays. *Grundlagen der Mathematik.* Vol. 1, 1934; vol. 2, 1939. Berlin.

Huntington, E. V. "A set of postulates for abstract geometry," *Mathematische Annalen* 73 (1913), 522–559.

Kemeny, J. G. "The use of simplicity in induction," *Philosophical Review* 62 (1953), 391–408.

Kleene, S. C. *Introduction to Metamathematics.* New York: Van Nostrand, 1952.

Kuratowski, Casimir. "Sur la notion de l'ordre dans la théorie des ensembles," *Fundamenta Mathematicae* 2 (1921), 161–171.

Lewis, C. I. *A Survey of Symbolic Logic.* Berkeley, Calif., 1918.

———, and C. H. Langford. *Symbolic Logic.* New York, 1932.

Linsky, Leonard, ed. *Semantics and the Philosophy of Language.* Urbana: University of Illinois Press, 1952.

Łukasiewicz, Jan. *Elementy logiki matematycznej.* Warsaw, 1929. Translation: *Elements of Mathematical Logic*, New York: Macmillan, 1964.

Marcus, Ruth B. "Modalities and intensional languages," *Synthese* 13 (1961), 303–322.

McNaughton, Robert. "A non-standard truth definition," *Proceedings of the American Mathematical Society* 5 (1954), 505–509.

Myhill, J. R. "A complete theory of natural, rational, and real numbers," *Journal of Symbolic Logic* 15 (1950), 185–196.

Neurath, Otto. "Protokollsätze," *Erkenntnis* 3 (1932), 204–214.

Nolin, L. "Sur l'algèbre des prédicats," in the colloquium volume *Le raisonnement en mathématiques et en sciences expérimentales* (Paris: Centre National de la Recherche Scientifique, 1958), pp. 33–37.

Parsons, Charles. "A plea for substitutional quantification," *Journal of Philosophy* 68 (1971), 231–237.

Peano, Giuseppe. *Formulaire de mathematiques*, Turin, 1894–1899; Paris, 1901.

Peirce, C. S. *Collected Papers*, vols. 2–4. Cambridge: Harvard University Press, 1932–1933.

Poincaré, Henri. *Science et méthode.* Paris, 1908.

Post, E. L. "Introduction to a general theory of elementary propositions," *American Journal of Mathematics* 43 (1921), 163–185.

———. "Finite combinatory processes," *Journal of Symbolic Logic* 1 (1936), 103–105.

Putnam, Hilary. "Mathematics without foundations," *Journal of Philosophy* 64 (1967), 5–22.

Quine, W. V. *A System of Logistic.* Cambridge, Mass., 1934.

———. *Mathematical Logic.* New York, 1940. Rev. ed., Cambridge, Mass.: Harvard University Press, 1951.

———. *Elementary Logic.* Boston, 1941. Rev. ed., Cambridge, Mass.: Harvard University Press, 1966.

———. *O sentido da nova lógica.* São Paulo: Martins, 1944.

———. *Methods of Logic.* New York: Holt, 1950. Rev. eds., 1959, 1972.

———. *From a Logical Point of View.* Cambridge, Mass.: Harvard University Press, 1953. 2d ed., 1961.

———. *Word and Object.* Cambridge, Mass.: MIT Press, 1960.

———. *Set Theory and Its Logic.* Cambridge, Mass.: Harvard University Press, 1963. Rev. ed., 1969.

———. *Selected Logic Papers.* New York: Random House, 1966.

———. *Philosophy of Logic.* Englewood Cliffs: Prentice-Hall, 1970.

———. *The Roots of Reference.* LaSalle, Ill.: Open Court, 1974.

———. "Concepts of negative degree," *Proceedings of the National Academy of Sciences* 22 (1936), 40–45.

———. "Toward a calculus of concepts," *Journal of Symbolic Logic* 1 (1936), 2–25.

———. "Set-theoretic foundations for logic," ibid., pp. 45–57. Reprinted in *Selected Logic Papers.*

———. "On Cantor's theorem," ibid. 2 (1937), 120–124.

———. "Logic based on inclusion and abstraction," ibid., pp. 145–152. Reprinted in *Selected Logic Papers.*

———. "New foundations for mathematical logic," *American Mathematical Monthly* 44 (1937), 70–80. Reprinted in *From a Logical Point of View.*

———. "Notes on existence and necessity," *Journal of Philosophy* 40 (1943), 113–127. Reprinted in Linsky.

———. "On the logic of quantification," *Journal of Symbolic Logic* 10 (1945), 1–12. Reprinted in *Selected Logic Papers.*

———. "Two dogmas of empiricism," *Philosophical Review* 60 (1951), 20–43. Reprinted in *From a Logical Point of View.*

———. "Interpretations of sets of conditions," *Journal of Symbolic Logic* 19 (1954), 97–102. Reprinted in *Selected Logic Papers.*

———. "Unification of universes in set theory," ibid. 21 (1956), 267–279.

———. "Variables explained away," *Proceedings of the American Philosophical Society* 104 (1960), 343–347. Reprinted in *Selected Logic Papers.*

———. "On the limits of decision," *Akten des XIV. Internationalen Kongresses für Philosophie* (Vienna, 1968), vol. 3, pp. 57–62.

———, and Nelson Goodman. "Elimination of extra-logical postulates," *Journal of Symbolic Logic* 5 (1940), 104–109.

Russell, Bertrand. *The Principles of Mathematics.* Cambridge, England, 1903.

———. *Our Knowledge of the External World.* London, 1914.

———. *Introduction to Mathematical Philosophy.* New York and London, 1919.

———. *An Inquiry into Meaning and Truth.* New York. 1940.

———. "Mathematical logic as based on the theory of types," *American Journal of Mathematics* 30 (1908), 222–262.

———. "The philosophy of logical atomism," *Monist* 28 (1918), 495–527; 29 (1919), 32–63, 190–222, 345–380.

Schlick, Moritz. *Allgemeine Erkenntnislehre.* Berlin, 1925.

Schönfinkel, Moses. "Über die Bausteine der mathematischen Logik," *Mathematische Annalen* 92 (1924), 305–316. Translated in van Heijenoort.

Shannon, C. E. "A symbolic analysis of relay and switching circuits," *Transactions of the American Institute of Electrical Engineers* 57 (1938), 713–723.

Sheffer, H. M. "A set of five independent postulates for Boolean algebras," *Transactions of the American Mathematical Society* 14 (1913), 481–488.

Sleigh, R. C. "On a proposed system of epistemic logic," *Noûs* 2 (1968), 391–398.

Smullyan, A. F. "Modality and description," *Journal of Symbolic Logic* 13 (1948), 31–37.

Strawson, P. F. *Introduction to Logical Theory.* London: Methuen; New York: Wiley, 1952.

———. "On referring," *Mind* 59 (1950), 320–344.

Study, Eduard. *Die realistische Weltansicht und die Lehre vom Raume.* Brunswick, 1914.

Tarski, Alfred. *Logic, Semantics, Metamathematics.* Oxford: Clarendon, 1956.

———. "Sur le terme primitif dans la logistique," *Fundamenta Mathematicae* 4 (1923), 196–200. Translated in *Logic, Semantics, Metamathematics.*

———. "Sur les truth-functions au sens de MM. Whitehead et Russell," ibid. 5 (1924), 59–74. Translated in *Logic, Semantics, Metamathematics.*

———. "Einige methodologische Untersuchungen über die Definierbarkeit der Begriffe," *Erkenntnis* 5 (1934), 80–100. Translated in *Logic, Semantics, Metamathematics.*

———. "Der Wahrheitsbegriff in den formalisierten Sprachen," *Studia Philosophica* 1 (1936), 261–405. Translated in *Logic, Semantics, Metamathematics.*

———, and F. B. Thompson. Abstracts in *Bulletin of the American Mathematical Society* 58 (1952), 65f.

Turing, A. M. "On computable numbers," *Proceedings of the London Mathematical Society,* ser. 2, vol. 42 (1937), 230–266; vol. 43 (1938), 544–545.

van Heijenoort, Jean, ed. *From Frege to Gödel: A Source Book in Mathematical Logic, 1879–1931.* Cambridge, Mass.: Harvard University Press, 1966.

von Neumann, John. "Zur Einführung der transfiniten Zahlen," *Acta Litterarum ac Scientiarum Regiae Universitatis Hungaricae Francisco-Josephinae* (Szeged), *Sectio scientiarum mathematicarum* 1 (1923), 199–208.

———. "Eine Axiomatisierung der Mengenlehre," *Journal für reine und angewandte Mathematik* 154 (1925), 219–240. Translated in van Heijenoort.

Wang, Hao. "Arithmetic models for formal systems," *Methodos* 3 (1951), 217–232.

———. "Truth definitions and consistency proofs," *Transactions of the American Mathematical Society* 73 (1952), 243–275.

Whitehead, A. N., and Bertrand Russell. *Principia Mathematica.* Vol. 1, 1910; vol. 2, 1912, vol. 3, 1913. 2d ed., Cambridge, England, 1925–1927.

Wiener, Norbert. "A simplification of the logic of relations," *Proceedings of the Cambridge Philosophical Society* 17 (1912–1914), 387–390. Reprinted in van Heijenoort.

Wittgenstein, Ludwig. *Tractatus Logico-Philosophicus.* London, 1922.

Woodger, J. H. *The Axiomatic Method in Biology.* Cambridge, England, 1937.
———. *Biology and Language.* Cambridge, England: Cambridge University Press, 1952.
Zermelo, Ernst. "Untersuchungen über die Grundlagen der Mengenlehre," *Mathematische Annalen* 65 (1908), 261–281. Translated in van Heijenoort.

Index

M

I